Italian Women's Writing 1860–1994

Women in Context

Women's Writing 1850–1990s

Series Editor: Janet Garton (University of East Anglia)

This new series provides a survey, country by country, of women's writing from the beginnings of the major struggle for emancipation until the present day. While the main emphasis is on literature, the social, political and cultural development of each country provides a context for understanding the position and preoccupations of women writers. Modern critical currents are also taken into account in relating feminist criticism to recent critical theory.

Already published
Norwegian Women's Writing 1850–1990
Janet Garton
0 485 91001 2   hb
0 485 92001 8   pb

Forthcoming
French Women's Writing 1850–1994
Diana Holmes
0 485 91004 7   hb
0 485 92004 2   pb
Swedish Women's Writing 1850–1995
Helena Forsås-Scott
0 485 91003 9   hb
0 485 92003 4   pb

In preparation
German Women's Writing

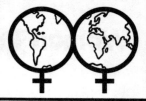

Women in Context

ITALIAN WOMEN'S WRITING 1860–1994

Sharon Wood

ATHLONE
LONDON & ATLANTIC HIGHLANDS, NJ

First published 1995 by
THE ATHLONE PRESS
1 Park Drive, London NW11 7SG
and 165 First Avenue,
Atlantic Highlands, NJ 07716

British Library Cataloguing in Publication Data
*A catalogue record for this book is available
from the British Library*

ISBN 0 485 91002 0 hb
0 485 92002 6 pb

Library of Congress Cataloging-in-Publication Data
Wood, Sharon, 1957–
    Italian women's writing, 1860–1994 / Sharon Wood.
        p.   cm. -- (Women in context series ; 2)
    Includes bibliographical references and index.
    ISBN 0-485-91002-0 (hb). -- ISBN 0-485-92002-6 (pb)
    1. Italian literature--Women authors--History and criticism.
    2. Italian literature--20th century--History and criticism.
    3. Literature and society--Italy.   4. Women--Italy--Social
conditions.   I. Title.   II. Series: Women in context (London,
England) ; 2.
    PQ4055.W6W66   1995
    850.9'9287--dc20   95-38296
                                                                 CIP

Typeset by
BIBLOSET

Printed and bound in Great Britain by
Bookcraft (Bath) Ltd

For my daughter, Lucy

Contents

Acknowledgements

I wish to thank the British Academy and the Carnegie Institute for the Universities of Scotland for grants and awards which have enabled me to carry out the research necessary for this book, and to the University of Strathclyde for sabbatical leave in which to complete the writing. I am grateful to the many colleagues who have read various parts of the manuscript for me, and especially to Joe Farrell for his enormous help and support.

Series Foreword

The aim of the *Women in Context* series is to present a country-by-country survey of women's writing from the beginnings of the struggle for emancipation until the present day. It will include not just feminist writers but women's writing in a more general sense, incorporating a study of those working independently of or even in direct opposition to the feminist aim of greater autonomy for women.

While the principal emphasis is on literature and literary figures, they are placed in the context of the social, political and cultural development without which their position cannot be properly understood, and which helps to explain the differing rates of progress in different areas. The volumes therefore combine survey chapters, dealing with women's place in the public and private life of a given period, with more in-depth studies of key figures, in which attention will be focused on the texts. There is no attempt at encyclopaedic completeness, rather a highlighting of issues perceived as specifically relevant by women, and of writers who have influenced the course of events or made a significant contribution to the literature of their day. Wherever possible, parallels with other countries are drawn so that the works can be placed in an international perspective. Modern critical currents are also taken into account in relating feminist criticism to recent critical theory.

Until quite recently women's writing has been virtually excluded from the literary canon in many countries; as a result there is often a dearth of information available in English, and an absence of good translations. *Women in Context* represents a move to remedy this situation by providing information in a way which does not assume previous knowledge of the language or the politics of the country concerned; all quotations are in English, and summaries of central texts are provided. The general reader or student of literature or women's studies will find the volumes a useful introduction to the field. For those interested in further research, there is a substantial bibliography of studies of women's writing in the country concerned and of individual authors, and of English translations available in modern editions.

Janet Garton

Introduction

When most people in English-speaking countries think of contemporary writing in Italy, the names of Umberto Eco and Italo Calvino are usually the first to come to mind; with novels such as *If on a winter's night a traveller* (1979) and *The Name of the Rose* (1981) the massive achievement of recent Italian writers was brought to the attention of an international public, fuelling a demand both in Italy and abroad for radically new work. Italian literature was suddenly perceived to be innovative, exciting, provocative, no longer bowed down by an overriding engagement with the turmoil of social and political history, no longer playing second fiddle to past and greater glories. In the last years women writers, too, have emerged in substantial numbers to great acclaim, to the surprise of not a few, both in Italy and abroad. For the first time, women writers are attracting as much public and critical attention as their male colleagues, and are finally resisting being ghettoized, sidelined, respected but ignored, read but then forgotten.

The new confidence of women writers in Italy reflects the changes in women's social and political status, and this volume attempts to trace the links between Italian society and politics and women's cultural response. It would be difficult – and dangerous – to make the connections too binding, just as it would be foolish to turn all women writers into unorthodox rebels or militant dissidents by virtue of their gender, ever and heroically contesting the patriarchal hegemony. More absorbing are the subtle interplays of text and ideology, or style and politics, the history of cultural forms as shaped by the collision of the public and the private which occurs on the blank page. Women have always been the object of specific ideological discourses in Italy – whether of the Church, Fascism, Futurism or simply conservative (and sometimes non-conservative) party politics. This book considers how women in Italy have fared with being both subject and object of discourse, as writers in a society with very particular views about the nature of femininity and the female role.

In a recent book on the lives of Italian women since Unification, Michela di Giorgio indicates the way in which the idea of 'woman' has consistently been pegged to the idea of the nation-state by a sequence of images, or myths:

> In the years from Unification up to now a whole series of representations of the *female* has, in chronological order, marked out the history of Italian women: the 'Italian woman' of the Risorgimento, the 'new woman' at the turn of the century, the 'new woman of the new Italy' immediately after the First World War, the 'new Italian' of Fascism' (*Le italiane dall'unità ad oggi* (Laterza, Bari 1992), pp. 4–5).

As Italy painfully struggled into existence, the role women were to play in the new state was much discussed. The democratic ideals of the Risorgimento suggested women should be accorded respect and honour as 'mothers of the nation', morally and intellectually suited to participate in this new political enterprise. Almost one hundred years were to pass before the role of women could be conceived outside their biological and reproductive function, while regressive laws left them with little economic autonomy and no independence from the family. Women's response was mixed, as in increasingly assertive tones they demanded their liberty. The paradoxical Neera confounded her own dogmatic hostility to feminism and Socialism by producing narratives which, with both compassion and humour, ruthlessly exposed the gulf between ideology and marital experience. Matilde Serao and Grazia Deledda were also ambivalent towards feminism, but fashioned texts which gave an astonishing picture of a nation emerging from centuries of historical and cultural inertia. Writing respectively about Naples and Sardinia, Serao and Deledda give an oblique view of life on the sidelines, of the conflict between old and new ideas, of age-old tradition and new political realities. It was for Sibilla Aleramo to articulate most lucidly the untenable nature of so many bourgeois marriages, to state a claim for independence, and to argue for a reform of writing by women to allow them to recover – or to invent – their own separate voice.

With the arrival of Fascism in 1922, the nascent *fin-de-siècle* women's movement at the turn of the century all but disappeared, most of its goals of emancipation still unachieved. Fascist expansionist policy required women to contribute to the new imperialist nationalism by willingly embracing maternity. Woman as mother was to stand side by side with man as soldier: the hand that rocked the cradle was to nurture the man who wielded the gun. Futurism, perhaps more significant as the initial seed-bed of all European avant-gardes than for any lasting impact on the majority of Italians, opened up new debates on social organization and gender roles, but failed to produce a body of work that would detach women from their conventional roles.

However, powerful voices were beginning to make themselves heard, and with the Resistance and Liberation new impetus was given to the drive to create Italy afresh, to establish a credible democracy and to develop cultural forms which would reflect a state finally modernized. While some women writers of the time adopted the new attitude to literature and culture as socially engaged, many more did not, keeping their distance from a movement, or a mood, which would sweep up all writers under the banner of politics. Of the post-war writers discussed in the second part of this book, the spare, suggestive work of Natalia Ginzburg most closely mirrors a society now in headlong change. Elsa Morante engages with the century's traumas in controversial work which rejects the orthodoxies of left-wing politics; her sympathy, and her political commitment, lie with those who are lost in the wheels and cogs of history. Anna Banti's work is, likewise, a profound meditation on history, on women's art and women as artists. Anna Maria Ortese's disillusion with Marxist ideology is reflected in a growing polemic with Neorealism, its literary outpost, in idiosyncratic texts, unique in the Italian tradition, which combine fantasy and metaphysics.

An economic boom in the post-war period was followed by the intimations of revolution and rebellion familiar elsewhere in 1960s Europe and America. Concluding that old-style Socialism and Communism were inimical to the aspirations of a new generation, women set up their own consciousness-raising groups, and feminism was reborn in Italy. The repressed anger and frustration of generations spilled out in a dynamic, wide-ranging and sometimes violent movement, which none the less achieved an enormous amount both in legislation and in terms of women's role in society.

Women set up their own cultural spaces and began to debate the vexed links between sexuality and textuality, establishing their own publishing houses, but they also succeeded in placing more material and immediately pressing issues such as abortion, childcare, women's health and legal reform firmly on the agenda. In writing consistently and consciously from the woman's point of view, writers such as Alba De Céspedes and Dacia Maraini took up the task begun by Aleramo: challenging women to change.

As a whole generation of younger writers began to emerge in the 1980s, women, too, began to achieve recognition – and sales – beyond the dreams of their forebears. If the feminist movement has waned, lacking the precise objectives which mobilized so many in the 1970s, women's writing flourishes as never before. Some continue to explore the dimension of gender and sexual difference, however obliquely. The relationship between mothers and daughters, much discussed in feminist theory, informs the work of Francesca Sanvitale and Fabrizia Ramondino. Other writers, perhaps taking the real struggles and achievements of feminism for granted, have gone on with increasing ambition to explore new subject matter and new forms for women's writing – fantasy and post-modernism as well as the more traditional realism. The last chapter of this book considers the interweaving of feminism and post-modernism in the work of Francesca Duranti, Sandra Petrignani and Paola Capriolo. The female writer in Italy is now as likely to be heading for her desk or for the airport as for the nursery. Whether a specifically female dimension or sensibility is being lost in this literary emancipation is something only time will tell.

In writing this book, choices have inevitably had to be made, and many writers merit more space than is allowed here. Some are included as representative of a mood or a moment; others have made a more lasting impact; some are a matter of personal taste. In some cases – Deledda, Serao, Ginzburg – I have attempted an overview of the writer's work, placing it within a shifting literary culture. In others – the last two chapters, on renegotiating motherhood and post-modernism – it seemed to me more valuable to discuss in greater detail works which deal with a similar theme, which address themselves to a female *Zeitgeist*.

Some of these writers are feminist, many are not. I have not attempted to limit them to specifically 'feminine' themes, content or forms, or to read them exclusively as messages from the battlefield about a specifically female condition. Rather, I have tried to outline what these writers have to say about culture, about humanity, about our common history; many of them just happen to do this from a female point of view.

PART I
1860–1922

1
Unification:
Making and Unmaking the Nation

MAKING ITALY, MAKING ITALIANS

The Italians were as surprised as the rest of Europe by the sudden sweep of events which led in 1860 to the first stages of Italian Unification, and the fulfilment of what had been regarded up to just a few months before as a far-off dream of national liberation and sovereignty. Venice was regained from the Austrians in 1866, while Rome was pushed into ceding to the new State just four years later. With the victory of the Risorgimento, the newly born Italy was faced with the mammoth task of pushing her way into an increasingly competitive modern world abroad, and creating a stable social and political society at home. Italy had a great deal of catching up to do if she was to trade on equal terms with neighbouring powerful and advanced capitalist economies. She had railways, banks and factories (textiles in particular), but the greater part of the economy remained rural, agricultural and labour-intensive, rarely made more efficient by modern farm machinery or methods and little advanced since the discovery of hydraulic power and the mechanical loom. In any case, such railways as there were, together with the greater part of the country's limited technological and industrial development, were largely confined to the Northern regions, while much of the South was still struggling to emerge from the grip of feudalism. Illiteracy levels were staggeringly high – almost total in some areas, and far above those of more advanced countries such as France, Britain or Germany. Problems of communications, already difficult in a country with little infrastructure, were compounded by the lack of a common national language, as the vast majority of the population still spoke dialect only.

Italian allegiance lay locally rather nationally, but in the government's haste to present Italy to Europe as a united, modern country, projects for regional autonomy were rapidly dropped in favour of increasing and massive centralization, and those who favoured a more federalist political structure worried that the fragile patriotism of Italians would lead to an increasingly authoritarian State in the attempt to cast the different regions of the country into a common mould. Centralization occurred rapidly as Piedmont imposed its own laws and political system on to newly annexed states, even while politicians in Turin remained blissfully ignorant about real conditions in the South: Cavour, architect of Unification, apparently believed that Sicilians spoke not Italian but Arabic.[1] Myths of the glorious Risorgimento were undermined by a consciousness of the divide between North and South and serious, if private, discussions between the Savoia and the Neapolitan Bourbons on a project for two Kingdoms of Italy.[2]

The goal behind the centralizing drive was the overriding imperative to modernize, in order to level the playing field with the rest of Europe. But a further wedge was driven between North and South, as agriculture was squeezed and money poured into nascent industries. Unpopular taxes, which increased the heavy burden already borne by the peasants, led to rioting and widespread unrest, viciously crushed by the new 'national' army – itself a thorny problem, as conscription was forcibly imposed on the South. Policies led to what one historian describes as 'a social fabric in which new and old were juxtaposed and interwoven, in which a capitalism with all the characteristics of imperialism in Lenin's analysis – a high degree of monopolistic concentration, a close interrelationship of banks and industry, state protection – co-existed with an agriculture which in some regions was still at a semi-feudal stage, and with omnipresent handicrafts at a cottage level'.[3]

The transformation of Italy into a modern capitalist economy in the last two decades of the nineteenth century was achieved largely through the notoriously low wage policy in operation and the lengthy working day imposed on male, female and child labour alike. Many of these workers were 'seasonal', moving into towns over the winter and back to the fields for the summer months, and the overlap between town and country, industrial and agricultural economies, was considerable. Silk, cotton and wool production were the major industries and accounted for the principal exports in the early days of Italy's industrial development, although the cheapening of long-distance transport led to fierce competition with China for the silk market. Women were involved in back-breaking and particularly unhealthy work such as rice planting and weeding.[4]

WOMEN IN THE NEW ITALY

Very little is known about the lives of ordinary working Italian women in the nineteenth century, while the few surveys carried out appeared to consider women's moral conduct and personal hygiene rather than their material living or working conditions. In the region of Foggia, it seems, according to one enquiry in the early 1870s:

> The women of the plain were cleaner than those in the hills, and less likely to be beaten. The Prefect of Bari reported that 'an ass, an ox, a sheep, are almost always worth more than a wife to the peasant, and the wife obeys her husband like a slave.' In Sardinia, on the other hand, 'the woman is loved and respected, and is considered an integral part of the family, in which ties of kinship are greatly esteemed'. But the Prefect of Agrigento was less impressed: 'superstitious, gossipy, quarrelsome and turbulent, the women pay little attention to their personal cleanliness and none whatsoever to that of their houses'.[5]

Italian industry at this stage employed a higher level of female labour than in any other country in Europe, concentrated in textile industries which already, in 1876, employed four times as many women as men.[6] By 1904 the overwhelming majority of women working in industry were employed in textiles, mainly in silk production, where they constituted well over half of the workforce. These figures have led some commentators to suggest that the take-off of early industrial capitalist development in Italy was paid for by exploited female labour, and indeed the statistics, while not always comprehensive or reliable, are astonishing. The 1881 Census found that 5.7 million out of 11 million females aged ten or over were 'active'. An 1876 survey of industry found 230,000 female industrial workers out of a total of 382,000. Women and girls thus formed approximately sixty per cent of *factory* labour, and the survey explicitly excludes other forms of labour such as housework and childcare. Wages were low and conditions appalling, while the 'sublime mission' of motherhood promulgated by political rhetoric meant in practice that women were habitually sacked at their first pregnancy; if they were lucky enough to remain in employment they returned to work within a few days of giving birth.

The Italian worker at the end of the last century was not only the worst paid in Europe, but also worked the longest hours. There was no legal limit to the length of the working day, which traditionally occupied the hours between sunup and sundown; daily hours could be as many as sixteen, and there was no legislation providing for breaks or weekly rest. Women and children were paid a half and a third respectively of a man's earnings. In 1886 a law was passed prohibiting employment of children younger than nine. Only in 1902 was this limit raised to twelve, but it was a law widely ignored.

With the Unification of Italy, a new national Civil Code was drawn up and published in 1865. Based largely on the Code granted by Carlo Alberto to Piedmont in 1848, it showed disappointingly little progress from the Napoleonic Code imposed during the period of French rule. Civil marriage was introduced, despite bitter opposition from the Church. Divorce was still unthinkable and, indeed, remained so for more than a century – until 1970. Most parties took a consistently anti-divorce stance in an attempt to appease the clerics infuriated by this new secular state, and to win their support in the fight against a rising swell of Socialist feeling in the country. According to the Code a wife was not permitted to administer her own property or even to have a bank account without her husband's permission, while the man could dispose at will of his wife's income and property. Authorization from the husband was required for almost all economic transactions – even inheritance, as Sibilla Aleramo was to find to her cost. The position of Italian women with regard to civil rights was substantially worse than that enjoyed in other parts of Europe.[7] In the eyes of the Law adultery could be committed only by the woman; the man was deemed guilty only if he brought his mistress into the conjugal home. Men were virtually immune from prosecution for 'crimes of passion' which avenged offended honour. Woman's guilt, on the other hand, knew no bounds; she was deemed capable of adultery 'even if [the man] lacked, through amputation, his male organ'.[8] While divorce was not countenanced, courts regularly annulled marriages where the wife turned out not to be a virgin. In some areas (Lombardy and parts of the Veneto, for example) women's position was actually worsened by the new Code, as political rights and private authority were removed from them. In almost all ways, patriarchal authority within the family was upheld, in a Code which largely remained the basis for Italian law through the Fascist period until after the Second World War.

WOMEN AND EDUCATION

One of the largest obstacles to progress for women was their lack of education. While lower-class boys received little enough education, which before Unification had never been compulsory, learning for middle-class women was considered positively harmful. The age-old arguments against extending education to women were rehearsed – the moral argument that ignorance equalled innocence, the transcendental social argument that the great mission of women was maternity, the physiological argument that to educate the head would be to wither the womb. Nor was philanthropic intervention by women such as Emiliana Fuà Fusinato (1834–76), who in the early days of the new Monarchy favoured women's education and did much valuable work in setting up women's schools, intended to remove the woman from domesticity. Rather, the aim was to equip her with the knowledge and skill the better to fulfil her role as Wife and Mother to the Nation. The means may have been radical, but the ends were archly conservative.

French thinking was more forceful than Italian on this point, with Voltaire, Diderot, Helvétius and Condorcet noting that women's inferiority was made by man and not by God. While a few enlightened women in Italy from the Renaisssance onwards, such as Veronica Gambara (1485–1550) and Modesta dal Pozzo (1551–92), had been calling for education for women, it was not until the mid-nineteenth century that even the most elementary education was a legal right for all children. A rapid national education programme was vital in a country where the majority were illiterate and several regions were mutually incomprehensible. Most Italians spoke some sort of dialect, while Italian was largely a written rather than a spoken language. Like medieval Latin, it was reserved for the intellectual elite and for literature – indeed, some writers even at the end of the twentieth century still describe a sense of alienation from the instrument of their trade. Again, the statistics present an extraordinary picture. At the time of Unification a mere 2.5 per cent of the population spoke Italian, and outside of Tuscany and Rome the numbers dwindle to zero.

The 1859 Casati Law stipulated two years' mandatory education for both sexes, and required local communities to provide free schools. In practice, however, if schools were built at all, they were provided for boys in preference to girls: women, who already suffered a higher illiteracy rate than men, could not keep pace with rising levels of male literacy. Education was vital for a knowledge of Italian rather than dialect, and a necessary passport to employment for middle-class women as teachers, telegraphists or government clerks. In the 1880s the chances of a secondary education increased dramatically as schools were officially opened to women. Access to the professions, however, was another matter. A number of teachers' colleges were opened to women, but conditions for these teachers were frequently appalling. Often sent to remote rural areas where residents had little desire or felt need for education, and traditional thinking equated paid work for women with prostitution, they were subject to almost pioneer circumstances. Even apart from exploitative pay, they faced the hostility of their male colleagues and the prejudice of a new community.

The progressive 'feminization' of education at elementary levels suggests that the male workforce was looking elsewhere for more remunerative employment. It is also highly likely that successive post-Unification governments regarded the employment of women on a massive scale in education as a way of achieving the long-promised levels of national literacy as cheaply as possible.[9] Many worked in the fields to supplement their meagre income; some of the less fortunate were even driven to suicide to escape the shame of harassment or the prospect of starvation. Women slowly gained access to all levels of education, and in 1874 the universities were opened to them, but many years were to pass before women graduated in more than negligible numbers; between 1877 and 1900, just over two hundred gained a university degree.[10] While women were allowed to practise medicine, they were not granted entry to the legal profession until 1919. Teresa

Labriola, Professor of Law at Rome University, was turned down by the Bar in 1913.

THE BEGINNINGS OF ITALIAN FEMINISM

Italian women's organized struggle for emancipation clearly began much later than parallel struggles in France, Britain or America, where rapid industrialization, urbanization and immigration had all affected the outcome of calls for female emancipation, education and admission to the male-dominated professions. In France, the eighteenth-century cult of Reason had led men and women to reconsider the role of women: for thinkers such as Diderot and Condorcet a woman's function as mother did not obviate her role as citizen, and the examples of Olympe de Gouges, Flora Tristan and Louise Michel constituted a powerful argument in favour of full social and political integration for women – as indeed did that of Eleonora Fonseca Pimentel in Naples. In Britain Mary Wollstonecraft had by 1791 already published her *Vindication of the Rights of Woman* in response to Edmund Burke's opposition to the French Revolution; John Stuart Mill published *The Subjection of Women* in 1869, while in America the anti-slavery movement had been accompanied by a heightened awareness of the condition of women. In Britain the women's movement was closely connected, in its early stages at least, with the labour movement – the 'Women's Social and Political Union' established by Emmeline Pankhurst in 1903 originally operated within the ambit of the Labour Party before becoming independent – and concentrated its attention on working-class women, prostitution, and exploitation in the factories as well as the fight for reform on maternity, divorce and the vote.

Feminist ideas and activity first took on a coherent shape in Italy in the mid-nineteenth century, a result of the frustrations of women who found themselves doing the same work as men at half the pay, combined with the experience of political organization and action gained by women over the years of the Risorgimento wars. The linkage between early feminism and the Risorgimento was typified by Cristina Belgioioso (1808–71), a romantic figure who would have graced any Renaissance court. Married at sixteen to a prince whom she then left, Cristina used her wealth for political purposes, financing Mazzini's expedition to Savoy and, in Paris, becoming the focal point for Italian exiles. The Austrians accused her of high treason, but in Paris she was a friend of such as Liszt, Chopin, Rossini and George Sand, and it was while she was in Paris that she translated the work of the Italian philosopher Giambattista Vico (1668–1735) into French.

Cristina founded journals hostile to the Austrian regime; when news of the 1848 insurrection reached her in Naples she put together a small army and headed for Milan to lend her support. She was well aware of the power of the press to form opinion, and articles such as 'Della presente condizione della donna e del loro avvenire' ('On the Present Condition of Women and their Future', *Nuova Antologia*, 1866) she argued persuasively for a widening of social and educational opportunities for women.

By 1906 Committees for Female Suffrage existed in all major cities in Italy as far south as Naples, although many women as well as men were strongly resistant to any move which appeared to threaten the constitution of the family. The year 1908 saw the First Congress of Italian Women, and 1910 the National Committee for Women's Suffrage. Most women's organizations concerned themselves with charitable works – running hostels for young working girls, founding schools in an attempt to combat illiteracy, providing school meals – but they also offered a forum in which to debate social and political issues. Radical, Socialist and Catholic feminists all agreed on the need to open up professions and win the vote, speaking out in favour of maternity leave, demanding a body of factory inspectors to regulate working conditions and the closure of brothels. These groups were, however, split on other family and educational issues, such as divorce.

Many of these groups had their intellectual and ideological roots in the Risorgimento struggles leading to Italian Unification. The Risorgimento was not a mass movement, but women, too, had taken part in the armed struggle, been imprisoned or exiled. However, the dramatic contribution made by women such as Anita Garibaldi (1821–49), Teresa Confalonieri (1787–1830) and Adelaide Cairoli (1806–71) did little immediately to impinge on the traditional image and, more especially, the legal and civic status of women as wives and mothers. Women gained little from the new national Constitution; it was not until after the Second World War that they gained the vote. Simone de Beauvoir's wry point that women are allowed to participate in revolution, but not in reconstruction,[11] held good after the Risorgimento, as it had for those who participated in the French Revolution. This being said, the experience of the Risorgimento was to provide the impetus for a fledgling feminist consciousness in Italy, a growing demand for equality and improved rights for women.

The call in Italy for women's emancipation was strongly influenced by the republican, secular theory of Giuseppe Mazzini (1805–72), the apostle of Italian unity. Mazzini was a firm believer in the unity of humanity and the equality of all races, and in a nationalism rooted in the Enlightenment of the eighteenth century. In his later years, he began to move from heroic nationalism to take an interest in the emancipation both of the working classes and of women. He was a progressive, but in his revaluation of woman's role he reiterated the Catholic position which would cast woman as 'patriot mother' fulfilling her 'natural' function as wife and mother, inhabiting the private rather than the public realm. Mazzini was in effect broadening a nationalist revolution into a moral crusade, politicizing the 'angel of the hearth', transforming the passive, domestic paragon of traditional religion and morality into a maternal, anticlerical revolutionary in her own right, companion and mother to men and women who shared her ideals.[12]

Women's participation in the Risorgimento had politicized their view of their roles as wife and mother; now they were to press the contacts and experience gained in the course of the Italian revolution into the service of raising their public and private status.

FEMINISM AND SOCIALISM: ANNA KULISCIOFF (1854–1925)

By the end of the nineteenth century, women were entering massively into public life and the workplace. Changing patterns of work and increasing female employment, especially among the middle classes, coincided with the rise of left-wing forces: first Anarchism (Bakunin spent a number of years in Naples, the first centre of anarchism in Italy), then Socialism and Communism. Andrea Costa (1851–1910), initially an anarchist, became the first Socialist deputy in 1882. With the expansion of the industrial infrastructure and the country's first uncertain moves towards modern capitalism, there was a simultaneous emergence

of the female masses on to the social and political scene: the
'woman question' grew in urgency as Italy's modest industrial
revolution, taking place almost one hundred years after that of
her major European competitors, led to substantial economic
and social change: 'women's widespread penetration into the
"male" world of work leads for the first time to the dramatic
explosion of the crisis which begins to attack the roots of
the traditional female role' (Puccini, p.35). Women were at
the forefront of strikes and protests over appalling working
conditions. During the First World War enormous numbers
of women moved into factory work, into heavy industry and
armaments, and by 1917 they constituted seventy per cent of
the workforce in munitions factories: 'male labour was substi-
tuted by female labour. Tens of thousands of women were
employed in factories, in offices, in the fields, on trains, rewarded
with salaries that were very low for work which lasted many
hours, day and night, and where conditions were in fact against
the law.'[13]

The 'woman question' for the orthodox Left was effectively
tied to the progress and development of Socialism by Augusto
Babel's highly successful and much-translated book *La donna e il
socialismo* (Women and Socialism, 1896). Babel followed Engels's
belief in the transition of society from matriarchy to patriarchy; in
connecting women's oppression to the spread of private property,
he looked forward to a time when all means of production
would be in the hands of the state, with perfect legal equality
between the sexes. This position was clearly not new in itself,
and was a familiar enough thesis in Britain and America, but
Babel's argument found much support among Italian Socialists.
In considering this conflation between the oppression of women
and the oppression of the working classes, the conviction that
liberation of the latter would bring in its wake freedom for
the former, some historians have been led to conclude that the
foundation of the Italian Socialist Party in 1892 effectively marked
the end of the autonomous campaign for women's emancipation
in Italy.[14]

The writer and militant activist Anna Kuliscioff kept alive
the question of women's oppression within the Socialist movement, polemically defining women in their current semi-slavery

as 'men's first domestic animals'.[15] Kuliscioff fostered a wide-ranging debate on the relationship of women's issues to the Socialist agenda which was to resurface only half a century later. She insisted on practical reforms such as equal pay for equal work, rejecting out of hand the argument that women's work was subsidiary, intended to supplement the family budget and hence of lesser importance. She exposed the wretched plight of women working outside the home while still carrying the full burden of domestic labour, and regarded women's lack of education as intellectually disabling. As a doctor, Kuliscioff was well placed to refute the aberrations of Cesare Lombroso's pseudo-positivist psychology, which regarded the working classes, and especially women, as an inferior species, whose dull, criminal and lascivious tendencies could be corroborated by measuring the weight of their brain and the length of their teeth.[16]

THE POLITICAL THEORIES OF ANNA MARIA MOZZONI

Despite the best efforts of Anna Kuliscioff, however, the question of women remained, for the Socialists, subservient to a Marxist analysis predicated on class struggle, and the issue of votes for women played second fiddle to the expediencies of party politics. Socialist influence may have blunted the edge of the exploitation of women, but it was unprepared to offer a serious challenge to the family and legal structures which upheld it.

Other feminists, such as Emilia Mariani (1843–1917) and Anna Maria Mozzoni (1840–1920), adopted a different political and strategic position to that of Kuliscioff. Mozzoni consistently argued for the question of women's emancipation and suffrage to be disengaged from trade-union and class debates. Anna Maria Mozzoni's pioneering theoretical and active engagement on behalf of women stretched from the beginnings of the new State up to 1920, just two years before the advent of Mussolini's Fascism. Mozzoni spoke with clarity and conviction of the need to complete the Risorgimento with the redemption of women, inserted into the unified State. Women had participated in those struggles, and it could no longer be claimed that they would be unable to make rational use of their liberty:

To deny woman complete educational reform, to deny her access to higher levels of instruction, to deny her work, to deny her a living in the city, to deny her a life in the nation, to deny her a public voice, is no longer possible. Those interests hostile to the 'risorgimento' of women can delay it with an unworthy battle, but they will never be able to prevent it.[17]

Mozzoni spoke out on moral issues such as prostitution and divorce, and analysed the role of the Church in maintaining traditional and oppressive family structures. She argued for parity of rights in work, education and property ownership, and was one of the very few to speak of a connection between women's social and political development and the problem of democracy. She was much influenced by the ideas of Fourier and his rebuttal of the supposedly 'natural' inferiority of women. A Mazzinian rooted intellectually in the French Enlightenment, later a radical Socialist, Mozzoni never completely identified with one political party, nor was there widespread consensus for her radical and revolutionary position within any one political grouping. Mozzoni's ambition was to unite women across political parties and classes, on the grounds that all women were oppressed by all institutions.

Mozzoni argued against viewing women in terms of their sacrificial mission on earth as wives and mothers; rather, she sought to consider women in terms of their social relations, not only within the family but also with religion, science and public opinion (*La liberazione*, p. 64). She rejected as misogynistic and repressive the conventional Simonist theory which viewed the two sexes as complementary, stressing that the institution of the family was a historical rather than a divine creation and, as such, was open to change. Women were, she declared, morally and intellectually individual and independent, and she refused to idealize the relationship between women and proletarian men, as Engels was to do in *The Origins of the Family, the State and Private Property* (1884). Oppressed by all social institutions, women, thought Mozzoni, would find liberation only through education and work, through participation in public life at all levels. In 1870 she translated John Stuart Mill's *On the Subjection of Women*, and was a leading contributor to the journal *La donna* (Woman), founded in Venice in 1868, which brought together those women whose demands for emancipation were based largely on the Mazzinian ideals of progress, humanity and equality. This journal also followed closely, and perhaps a touch ruefully, the progress of emancipation campaigns in other European countries.

The difference of approach between Mozzoni and Kuliscioff was starkly highlighted in 1898 by the projected protectionist laws which would make separate provision for women at work. Mozzoni was set firm against such a change, claiming that woman would swiftly be rushed back into the home, like a hen into the coop, 'to brood over her eggs in solitude and silence'. If women's work is protected, they will be 'condemned to die of hunger, but healthy, to stop them becoming ill through work'.[18] For Kuliscioff, on the other hand, these laws – eventually passed – regulating working conditions and hours for women were a real and tangible gain.

The disagreements between Mozzoni and Kuliscioff rehearse the arguments of neo-feminism almost one hundred years later. Mozzoni argued that the 'woman question' was not accessible to a purely economic solution, and that even with a Socialist revolution the position of women would remain fundamentally unchanged; women had to fight for their own rights, which could not be absorbed by the class struggle. Kuliscioff, on the other hand, in a move echoed in France several decades later in the 1970s, saw 'feminism' as a middle-class affliction, claiming that the position of women workers, who were economically more powerful, was actually better than that of unoccupied or underoccupied middle-class women. Women should fight not against men, but against a class system which oppressed men and women alike. Kuliscioff emphasized class solidarity rather than what she dismissively termed 'bourgeois interclassism'.[19]

THE FAILURE OF SUFFRAGE AND THE RETREAT INTO SILENCE

The climate of the post-Unification period, however, was largely hostile to women's issues. Parliamentary opposition was complemented by the indifference or ignorance of the great mass of women, divided by an abyss from official politics. The 'woman question' was virtually ignored by both Parliament and public opinion. The relationship between women and politics, despite Mozzoni's efforts, remained tentative at best. The demands of women such as Mozzoni foundered on the reality of feudal and archaic family structures in Italy: it was 'as if these women with their Enlightenment, their Rationalist discourse on democratic development, were speaking a completely different language' (Chiancse, p. 143).

The struggle for emancipation, whether on a Republican or a Socialist platform, failed. Almost all politicians and political activists, including those of the Left, still opposed female suffrage. According to the Right, women's ignorance of political and civic responsibilities would lead to a redundant doubling or shadowing of the male vote, while for the Left it would simply shore up conservatism. Italian Socialism tended to follow the anti-feminist line of Proudhon, which restricted female participation to the domestic sphere. Prime Minister Giolitti's electoral reform of 1912 extended 'universal' suffrage to illiterate men, but not to women: to grant them the vote would be, in his view, 'a leap in the dark'. This was a serious defeat, and the movement for emancipation died away with the onset of war, which was soon to be followed by the conservative and repressive policies of Fascism.

Some women continued to follow events abroad with keen interest, and the Russian experience – with suffrage immediately granted to women after the Revolution, and the legalization of divorce and abortion – made a great impact on women Communists in Italy. Camilla Ravera directed an influential column in Gramsci's journal, *L'Ordine Nuovo,* called 'Tribuna della donna' which attempted to go beyond the reductive view of women as simply workers, fostering a wider discourse on the female condition to take account of other activities such as housework. Alessandra Kollontai and Clara Zetkin encouraged new national Communist parties to attend to the 'woman question', but the discussion of contraception, abortion and divorce, by now familiar in Britain and Russia, was still far removed from the Italian political agenda.

Women's roles were changing, but extremely slowly, particularly in rural areas. With the crisis of agriculture, the failure of agrarian reform and heavy competition from both France and America, the South was unable to support its growing population. With no alternative employment available, men from the South began to emigrate on a massive scale. While some of this emigration was seasonal, or at least temporary, several hundred thousand men left each year for the United States, South America or other parts of Europe. Women were left to take over the tasks and responsibilities of their departed menfolk, thus breaking the pattern of a subordinate role or an exclusively private and domestic existence. The First World War had a contradictory effect on relations between the sexes, opening up spaces for a less restricted and more unorthodox sexuality. During the War women entered massively into heavy industry, their services required to fill the places vacated by men at the front; by 1917 seventy per cent of the arms manufacturing workforce was female. Despite the sudden and dramatic widening of women's image of their own potential, however, any long-term gain was minimal, and it has been argued that power relationships, in a society where women were 'sexual objects to be used as freely and brutally as the weakness of their social and personal position permitted', remained fundamentally unaltered by the war: 'Within the community, old roles were resumed, and the women forced back into traditional peasant silence, leaving the men to monopolize the claim to war honours.[20]

Radical feminism was born among working, middle-class women, but these women were few. Anna Kuliscioff, among others, emphasized the part middle-class women could play as they moved out of their traditional roles and into an increasingly industrial and competitive world. Girls of the middle classes, with no dowry and little hope of even a modest marriage, emerged into the professional arena as teachers, postal workers, doctors and lawyers:

> who find themselves rejected, held to ransom, mocked, and who must appeal to all the saints in a modern heaven, called equality and liberty, in order to live modestly and to provide for themselves.
>
> But habits, customs and laws are against them. And so we see the working woman of the middle classes too begin to feel the need to move into that great kitchen where laws are cooked up.[21]

But with the failure of Socialism to draw in middle-class women, subject to sharper ideological and cultural pressures than their proletarian counterparts, it is perhaps not surprising that they warmed to Fascism – that 'those women whom Italian socialists had hoped to see on the side of the workers, marching united in their demands and in their struggles, were to be captivated within a few short years by the empty rhetoric of Fascism and the "mystique" of femininity' (Puccini, p. 31). The working woman of the middle classes turned to Mussolini rather than to Mozzoni, and the only kitchen she inhabited was her own domestic hearth.

WOMEN AND LITERATURE 1861–1922

Italian writers in the post-Unification period reflected and examined the achievements of the Risorgimento, and began to come to terms with the new nation-state. The classicist Giosuè Carducci (1835–1907), for example, reacted eloquently and fiercely against the Romantic movement in poetry, which began with Lamartine. Carducci was firmly Mazzinian and patriotically Republican, and his professed desire was to be Bard to the new united State, poet to the new Italy.

Just a few short years after Unification, such an aim was already revealing itself to be utopian, representing an ideal of Italy which bore little resemblance to a reality of acute diversity, chronic poverty and endemic distrust of the new order. The *veristi*, the Italian adherents to an aesthetic of realism, set themselves the task of presenting Italy to the Italians; the leading exponents of *verismo*, Luigi Capuana (1839–1915) and Giovanni Verga (1840–1922), were both Sicilians, well aware of rural backwardness and familiar with Sicily's intellectual, emotional and psychological distance from Rome. Verga's tales, and his masterpiece *I Malavoglia* (*The House by the Medlar Tree*, 1881), describe the unromantic brutality of peasant life, the elemental world which lies below the level where ideals can exist. Despite Verga's political conservatism, his narratives effectively shatter the illusion of national unity once and for all; they are 'a reminder that the new Italy of the Risorgimento was the heir to the misrule of the Bourbons and the old Papal State, with that *problema del mezzogiorno* (Southern problem), more than the culture of the Renaissance'.[22]

The influence of Gabriele D'Annunzio's poetry and novels on literary aesthetics – as well as the influence of his daring, exhibitionist exploits on the public imagination – is difficult to overestimate, if almost equally difficult to come to terms with today. Anticipating the violent, anti-democratic methods of the Fascists, D'Annunzio (1863–1938) was fiercely nationalist in his politics, demanding that Fiume (modern-day Rijeka) be ceded to Italy after World War I and occupying the city by force with his own followers. In D'Annunzio's writing, the careful, patient analysis of realism gives way to a riotous aestheticizing of sensuality. His is not the compassionate searching out of social injustice but the decadent celebration of a superior ego which seeks its own refined pleasures. D'Annunzio's novels, such as *Il piacere* (Pleasure, 1889) and *L'innocente* (The Innocent, 1892), assert the triumph of the elect spirit, and the duty of submission of the mediocre, in an art which unashamedly embraces the concept of the *Übermensch* and largely relegates women to a position of inferiority, as providers of erotic satisfaction to the adventurous male.

Italy had her female poets and writers, too, but there was little, if any, sense of a tradition. While some critics were struck by the sheer number of women writers in the new Italy, most remained unpersuaded that men had anything to fear from the competition. Work by women was deemed merely derivative, and destined to remain so. Luigi Capuana quotes De Meis's view that the imaginative intellect is strictly masculine: that while female 'creativity' is derivative and mimetic, no matter how far women progress artistically, men will always be ahead of the game. In the distant future, perhaps, 'men will leave entirely to women the business of writing novels, lyrics, tragedies, plays, and, if they have acquired a taste for it, poetry; but these women will create nothing new. It will be an eternal repetition'.[23]

Even Capuana, who claims to distance himself from this view in his discussion of Deledda and Serao as well as some of the French writers, can go no further than praising compassion, tender emotion, sincerity and simplicity as the marks of female intelligence. Small wonder, then, that, as in Britain and France, women resorted to pseudonyms (Bruno Sperani, Luigi di San Giusto).

In Britain and France emancipationist movements were echoed, and in some cases heralded, by writers such as George Sand, Madame de Sévigné, the Brontë sisters and George Eliot.[24] In Italy the work of Renaissance poets such as Moderata Fonte (pseudonym for Modesta dal Pozzo, 1552–92), Veronica Franco

(1546–91) and Gaspara Stampa (*c.*1523–54) was hardly known; nor was there an Italian Aphra Behn or Elizabeth Barrett Browning. Women writers of this period, with some notable exceptions, tended to be much more limited in their ambitions, even if they occasionally enjoyed a vast readership. Writers such as Carolina Invernizio (1858–1916) had an enormous popular following with Gothic novels such as *Il bacio d'una morta* (*Dead Woman's Kiss*, 1889) and *La sepolta viva* (*Buried Alive*, 1896). Antonio Gramsci was later to regret the demise of 'this old trooper' who knew, unlike the aloof intellectuals who were to follow her, how to engage and move her audience – unlike the presumptuous male intellectual who 'considers himself like the bird made for the golden cage, who must be served mash and millet seed'.[25]

Women's writing underwent considerable changes over the last decades of the nineteenth century, stimulated by the new political and economic realities and movements for social reform as well as influence from abroad, above all from France. Memories of the Risorgimento provided material for the autobiographical work of Antonietta Giacomelli (1851–1938) and a dramatic backcloth to the intricate amorous adventures depicted in the prose and drama of the Sicilian sisters Caterina and Concetta Stazzone. Over the early years of the new Italian State the moral and religious poetry of writers such as Caterina Bon Brenzoni (1813–56) and Maria Alinda Bonacci Brunamonti (1841–1903) gave way to novels and stories depicting rural peasant life, much influenced by the work of George Sand and the Goncourt brothers. While it is difficult to be sure of numbers, many more women now appeared to be writing in between carrying out their domestic duties; the woman 'writes to escape the burden of her own self: once upon a time she used to weave, now she spins a novel or a tale'.[26] Luigia Codemo Gesternbrand's (1828–98) tales were an expression of genuine interest in and compassion for the lives of the poor, and she had great success with *Memorie di un contadino* (Memoirs of a Peasant, 1856), *Miserie e splendori della povera gente* (Miseries and Splendours of the Poor, 1865) and *La rivoluzione in casa* (Revolution at Home, 1889), which documented the passions of the Risorgimento in Lombard Veneto. Like Codemo, Caterina Percoto (1812–87) wrote, frequently in dialect, of her native land, Friuli, of its people and their struggle to free themselves from the

Austrian yoke. Percoto's tales of working life have been seen as a precursor to the work of Verga and the *veristi*, and were republished when writers and intellectuals of the post-Fascist period returned to a rural, realist aesthetic.

It was over the course of this period that women writers moved from being purveyors of 'an exquisite analysis of feeling, a delicate and refined understanding of the human heart, a love of truth which overcomes and surpasses all illusion',[27] to an engagement with the social issues foregrounded by Unification and the first contacts of the new Italian society with other more progressive and advanced nations. Women began to take stock of their condition, to subject it to a more rigorous intellectual analysis than many sentimental, rural novels had so far permitted. Jesse White Mario, an Englishwoman married to an Italian, who had actively participated in the Risorgimento, anticipates Matilde Serao and Anna Maria Ortese in her depiction of a Naples whose material squalor was matched only by the greed of those out to exploit the poor. In her report on the Veneto, White Mario cuts through the dominant ideology of the 'angel of the hearth' to reveal the patriarchal social mechanism which exploits women's labour both inside and outside the home as one which drives women literally insane.

Ideas of social change were beginning to ferment in the public mind. The D'Annunzian mystifications and fetishistic ideologies of eroticism of a novelist and poet such as Amalia Guglielminetti (1881–1941), whose aestheticizing evocations of adulterous passion functioned as a consolatory fantasy to a principally female readership, were gradually supplanted by a closer look at the uncomfortable realities of daily life. *Una fra tante* (One Among Many, 1878) by Emilia Ferretti Viola (1844–1929) was something of a *cause célèbre* in its denunciation of prostitution, which tended to be accepted as a fact of life by a complacent government; Serao and Aleramo were to be similarly outraged by the failure of politicians to deal with this running sore, while *One Among Many* marked a step forward in that it dealt not with the romantic figure of the 'fallen woman' or the '*femme fatale*' but with prostitution as a dramatic consequence of archaic, semi-feudal social structures in a self-proclaimed liberal society. The novel *In risaia* (*In the Ricefields*, 1878) by Marchesa Colombi (1846–1920) depicted the exploitation and despair faced by women workers in the Northern ricefields, and was considerably more authentic than Giuseppe De Santis's neorealist film of 1948, *Riso amaro* (Bitter Rice), where physical hardship is belied by the erotic presence of Silvana Mangano.

Other work, too, dealt with the hardships and injustices of women's lives. In 1864, Elisabetta Caracciolo Forino (1817 – ?) gave a devastating and personalized account of life in the cloisters which shook Italian public opinion; placed in an enclosed order in Naples against her will, Elisabetta remained behind the convent walls until she was released by the arrival of Garibaldi; she later became inspector of the city schools. Elisabetta's account of the brutalities of convent life and of the women driven to madness and suicide in the face of an indifferent clerical hierarchy, together with a fierce analysis of power maintained by an understanding between the clergy and the Bourbon powers, made for a lucid denunciation of a system utterly destructive to the lives and sanity of women.

Yet those women who remained in society frequently found marriage as rigidly tyrannical and unbending as the convent. Anna Franchi's (1866–1954) openly autobiographical novel *Avanti il divorzio!* (On with Divorce!, 1902) describes the hell of bourgeois marriage – the brutal shattering of her girlish dreams on her wedding night, repeated conjugal rape and sexual perversion, her husband's infidelity, profligacy and cruelty. Anna Franchi's experience prefigures that of Sibilla Aleramo; in deciding to abandon her home and start a new life with the man she loves, she discovers that in the eyes of the law it is she who is the guilty party, the adulterer, responsible for breaking up the family, unfit to take care of her children, not allowed to administer her own finances or have returned to her the money appropriated by her husband. While Franchi's work lacks Aleramo's biting analysis, it is a shocking denunciation of marriage as sexual and economic slavery.

Other aspects of women's changing lives were reflected in fiction, too. Clarice Tartufari (1868–1933) was one of a number of writers who bore witness to the trials and difficulties faced by a new generation of female teachers. The poet and novelist Ada Negri (1870–1945), a writer not from the upper but from the lower classes, had first-hand experience as a teacher in a village school. Her first collection of poems, *Fatalità* (Fatality, 1892), reveals a passionate sense of social justice matched only by her contempt for the parasitical world of the Italian bourgeoisie:

Oh fat world of crafty bourgeois
fed with calculations and croquettes,
world of well-fattened millionaires
   and young coquettes;

oh world of tiny anemic women
who go to Mass to see their lovers,
oh world of adulteries and plunder
   and hopes in tatters. . . .[28]

The last lines of this poem ('I, with whip of seething verse / shall strike you in the face'), were too much for the philosopher and critic Benedetto Croce, who took Negri to task for subordinating the aesthetic to the ideological,[29] for making her art slave to her ideas (and to her politics).

Inspired by the nascent Italian Socialist movement, Ada Negri, together with other writers such as Adele Beccari (who in 1869 set up the journal *La Donna*), produced poetry and narrative describing the conditions of the newly industrialized classes, and recognizing the double bind for women in their productive and reproductive roles. Yet the issue of maternity, central to Sibilla Aleramo's analysis of women's subjection and crucial to later feminist movments in the twentieth century, was largely deemed a matter of emotions and ethics rather than politics. While works such as Marchesa Colombi's *Un matrimonio in provincia* (A Provincial Marriage, 1885) gradually encroached upon the terrain of marriage, revealing it to be a one-sided bargain, the ideology of motherhood, the psychic myths which split women into good mother/bad whore, proved far more resilient in Italian culture. While she exposed marriage as a delusion, Neera extolled maternity; Ada Negri denounced the double burden of labour carried by women workers, but still wrote verses which idealized the relationship between mother and child as women's *raison d'être*. The work of Annie Vivanti (1868–1942), born in England of an Italian father and a German mother, young lover of the revered poet Giosuè Carducci and one of the most popular and successful writers in Italy around the turn of the century, is shot through with the idealization of maternity as the most profound expression of femininity. In *I divoratori* (The Devourers, 1911) the protagonists' willing sacrifice of their creative and artistic talents only underlines the message that maternity is women's greatest – indeed, only – route to self-fulfilment. *Vae victis!* (1918) foregrounds women raped by an invading army and made pregnant. While pregnancy is the result of male violence, maternity as mission cancels out crime and becomes an end in itself:

> Chérie, her hands crossed over her breast, did not listen, did not hear. In a concentrated pose of virginal ecstasy and humility she was listening to another voice: the voice of the unborn creature, who was asking her for the gift of life. And her blood answered that voice, her soul answered it, the sublime and triumphant instinct of Maternity.[30]

The history of women in post-Unification theatre has yet to be written or even studied systematically. The new Italy was united politically and geographically, but the bourgeois theatre attempted to portray a unitary ethical and social culture which held out the family as the primary patrimony of society. Carlo Goldoni became the model for a theatre which set itself the task of constructing a social ideology for the ruling class.

Clearly, the dramatic differences between regions and classes soon led theatre practitioners to explore the fractures in Italian society, and novelists such as Giovanni Verga, Luigi Capuana and De Roberto, while they shared Emile Zola's belief that real formal innovation took place in the novel, began to experiment with new dramatic languages, producing, among other works, Verga's *Cavalleria rusticana* (1884). Luigi Capuana's call for a national theatre was diverted into a celebration of dialect theatre, and it is here that the slender information about women as writers for the theatre is to be gleaned. Like male writers, women novelists also turned their hand to the stage; they included Clara Tartufari in Rome, Luigia Codema Gesternbrand in Treviso and Maria Alinda Bonacci Brunamonti (1841–1903), friend of the influential critic Francesco De Sanctis, in Perugia. Also successful in their day, but since forgotten, were the Sicilian Stazzone sisters, Cecilia and Concetta, who had plays performed in Catania.

Women were better known, or are better remembered, as performers. Emma and Irma Gramatica, Teresa Mariani and Bella Starace were admired, as Lydia Borelli was to be adored by spectators of silent cinema. Eleonora Duse (1858–1924) was, however, more than an actress. The refinement of her cultural choices, promoting the work of Ibsen (*A Doll's House*), Dumas *fils* (*Lady of the Camellias*) and Gabriele D'Annunzio, contributed to a marked renewal of public taste.

The four writers discussed in this Part encompass some of the most significant achievements – as well as dilemmas – of this post-Unification period. Neera was much admired by Croce for her firm anti-feminist stance, yet her exposure of the fallacy of romantic love and her depiction of the emotional desert of most bourgeois marriages is perhaps the stronger and the more striking for emerging from observation and experience rather than any *parti pris* or political ideology. Matilde Serao was inspired principally by the *petite bourgeoisie* of Naples, and her most powerful Realist works locate the small dramas of their protagonists (she pays especial attention to her female characters) within a clearly depicted and instantly recognizable social environment. Grazia Deledda, writing of her native Sardinia while living in Rome, exposes the vast gulf between the outposts of the new nation and the centralizing rhetoric of the new State: in her dark tales of guilty passion she dramatizes the clash between traditional and modern ethical codes. Finally, Sibilla Aleramo, the first major feminist writer in Italy, whose own turbulent experience prompts her not only to demand emancipation and equality before the law and to problematize maternity as an issue which is complex and social rather than private and ethical, but also to anticipate a new feminine aesthetic.

2
Confessions of a Woman Writer: Neera (1846–1918)

> 'I think all women are crosser than men,' said Maggie. 'Aunt Clegg's a great deal crosser than uncle Clegg, and mother scolds me more than father does.'
>
> 'Well, *you'll* be a woman some day,' said Tom, 'so *you* needn't talk.'
>
> 'But I shall be a *clever* woman,' said Maggie, with a toss.
>
> 'Oh, I daresay, and a nasty, conceited thing. Everybody'll hate you.'
>
> (George Eliot, *The Mill on the Floss*)

In March 1848 a spirit of revolt swept through the city of Milan as the civilian population rose against their Austrian rulers. The rising originated in a boycott of tobacco: the revenue of the Habsburg government would be reduced if the population of Milan denied itself the pleasure of smoking. The scuffles which broke out as troops continued to smoke cigars on the street swiftly turned into full-scale riots, and the subsequent upheavals and bitter fighting of the legendary 'cinque giornate', or five days, were to lead to the dramatic withdrawal from the city of the Austrian army, defeated by both the courage of the civilian population and the mass desertion of Italian troops from its ranks.

Opposite the military barracks in via Monte di Pietà, under heavy attack by the citizens of Milan, a two-year-old child was bundled across the gardens under her uncle's cloak to safety and away from the shooting. The child was Anna Zuccari, in later years known by the pseudonym Neera. Seventy years later, and in the midst of another war, Neera was to recall the drama which accompanied her earliest, haziest memories, underlining the heroic fervour and glory of the Risorgimento and Italian liberation which led to the rapid unification of the nation. The area of the city around via Monte di Pietà where Neera spent her early years is a 'precious document for the history of our Risorgimento'[1] which still bears traces of the passing of Federico Confalonieri, Silvio Pellico, Clara Maffei, heroes for the people of Milan; and above all of Giuseppe Verdi who, in his dramatic and nationalistic operas, gave life to the aspirations of the Italian people.

The life of Anna Zuccari spanned some of the most turbulent years in modern Italian history. She saw the troubled birth of the Italian nation, the rise of Socialist and feminist movements, the civic discontent of the late years of the nineteenth century, and the social and political disintegration of the First World War which was to clear the ground for the twenty years of Mussolini's Fascist dictatorship; she is 'sole survivor of a small world that has disappeared! Thinking back on it I seem to have lived two lives' (*Giovinezza*, p. 28). The writing of Neera marks the drama of transition and adjustment which Italian society experienced in those years, torn between the old and the new. In her theoretical, polemical work Neera writes from an inflexibly traditionalist and anti-feminist philosophical position which would find favour with the most reactionary elements of Italian society; yet, paradoxically, her fictions offer an oblique critique of personal relations and family life which would not have been out of place on any feminist platform.

With the achievement of Unification in 1860, the question of the role that women were to play in the new nation-state emerged into the public and political arena. Thoughts on writing by women – almost always written by men – focused on women's work as analysis of sentiment and the most intimate affairs of the heart. Carlo Cattaneo articulated prevailing opinion in his belief that when women emerged into the public sphere it was to be as nurses and missionaries, roles for which, latching on to a polite compliment by Florence Nightingale, he deemed Italian women particularly well suited. The mission of women writers – although in his opinion women did better to inspire lofty emotions of love, faith and virtue rather than ruin themselves in dusty libraries – was to minister to the soul, to be the civilizing spirit of the new society; their purpose was to lend gentility and delicacy to the more masculine military and political achievements of recent times.[2]

There were few dissenting voices in the early days of the new Italy. What is striking about Neera is that in her stories and novels aesthetic practice wins out over dogmatic orthodoxies, as she writes out of directly observed and pragmatic experience rather than idealist intentions. Her fictions bore witness in particular to the condition of women, to the structures of family life, private and public authority over women's lives, and to the aspirations, hopes, dreams and disappointments of women in the newly united country. While the focus of her fiction remains an acute analysis of love, marriage and maternity in a society which promotes these activities as the woman's exclusive and only sphere, she engages polemically with the rising feminist and Socialist movements, which she sees as a betrayal of women's role in society and in the family. Neera presents us with the striking paradox that while her theoretical writings on the proper aims and ambitions of the female sex express a conservatism which allies itself with the theory of 'separate spheres' – the respective public and private worlds beloved of so many nineteenth-century writers on gender roles – her narratives systematically and ruthlessly expose woman's lot: the discrimination practised and the injustice imposed on women in the name of law and convention, and the oppression they experience in both the public and the private realms.

As Neera looks back over her own life, her forthright assertions as to women's proper sphere of activity and influence are shot through with an almost palpable sense of anxiety and unease. With the ending of formal schooling at the age of fourteen, Neera embarked on the life of rigid domesticity reserved for women of the bourgeoisie, 'methodical and regular as in a convent. . . . When somebody wants to know about preparatory studies I made for the thirty or so volumes I have published, I always answer: stockings and shirts, shirts and stockings (*Giovinezza*, pp. 55, 100).

Neera does not rebel against the social code which ties her to the domestic arts; indeed, she flaunts her feminine skills, insisting not just on duty but on the pleasure to be found in those household tasks which the younger, flighty women chasing after jobs in the early years of the new century no longer experience. Young mothers who cannot make clothes for their own children earn her pity, but also her contempt, for Neera has 'long been familiar with the pleasure of remodelling an old skirt and piling up in the drawer pair after pair of stockings' (*Giovinezza*, p. 100)

The protestations of domestic bliss and the joy of plying her needle are undercut, however, by Neera's description of the terrible boredom and frustration experienced by the young girl, enclosed with her middle-aged aunts, for whom the only escape was through her imagination. The young Anna read Sterne, Byron and Swift, composed stories which she related only to the servant who had come to do the ironing, and dreamed of adventures and love.

Just as the tedium of unvarying routine is pointed to, but not challenged, so the gulf between the physical and intellectual limitations of Anna's restricted, enclosed life and that of her brothers is outlined, but never overtly criticized. Anna protests her perfect accord with her brothers. Her description of their lives is remarkable for what it – just – conceals about her own situation, and barely resists being read as a feminist demand for equal opportunities:

> Between my brothers and me there was never the slightest false note. But they lived the free lives of men; they were not obliged like me to remain night and day under the watchful eyes of our aunts. They had their studies, their pastimes and their inclinations in common. As soon as they emerged from adolescence they enrolled at the university; their return home was always celebrated as a feast. (*Giovinezza*, p. 95)

A slight shift in tone would ally Neera here with Maggie Tulliver's demand to be allowed, along with her slower-witted brother, to study Latin and Euclid. In an even more telling comment, she concedes: 'my brothers had their studies, their walks, their friends; and then they were at the University for a number of years. Sometimes they laughed. Not I' (*Giovinezza*, p. 129). Neera explicitly refers to herself as the solitary Cinderella whose brothers have gone to the festivities offered by education, liberty, freedom of thought and action. The young girl never lost her reverence for the figure of her father, despite his unwillingness to guide her own education as he did that of her brothers; his status, 'unique, luminous, sacred', is never challenged even while it is narratologically juxtaposed to her own lost and imprisoned youth, her 'buried treasure'.[3]

Neera's descriptions of the social structures and customs which delineate her life are marked by a similarly ambiguous tension. She extols the harmony and tranquillity to be found in life in the provinces, 'when it is not spoilt by gossip or found wanting through particular aspirations of the intellect' (*Giovinezza*, p. 71), writing in praise of 'those dear provinces which are fast disappearing' (*Le idee*, p. 30). In the idealized countryside of Neera's youth, even the brigands are gentlemen; their deeds are recounted by an admiring aunt who lingers over the legendary courtesy and romantic gallantry of one Strigelli, whose reputation with the fair sex was fuelled by tales of unrequited love, and who rode into the attack on coaches and travellers armed with *eau de Cologne* with which to succour young ladies who took fright. Neera remarks that 'artistically' she adores the provinces, finding them more intimate than the big cities, 'where by dint of always bumping into each other, people all finish up the same, where corners and edges are blurred, where colours lose their brightness' (*Le idee*, p. 30). Perhaps 'artistically' is the key word here, for personally Neera chafed against the restrictions and limitations of provincial life.

Neera demonstrated unremitting hostility towards nascent feminist and Socialist movements in Italy. In her autobiographical and diaristic writing she never questions the prevailing social order of tradition, maintaining an austere and anti-democratic conservatism based on a moral code of duty and *noblesse oblige*. Morality is based not on modernity and progress but on established tradition; beauty is found in the refinement of the centuries; harmony lies in the willing acceptance of one's allotted role in life. She asserts a higher, idealist ethic rather than vulgar economics as the spring of human happiness, and her hostility to both Socialism and feminism derives from a rejection of a materialist basis to either personal or public life.

Neera's is not the optimistic, utopian vision of the reformer but a dystopian conviction of the imperfectibility of mankind, a renunciation of the possibility of human happiness in a fallen world. She remains unpersuaded that access to education and to work will bring women the satisfaction they seek; to push women out of the home, away from husband and children and into paid employment is to alienate them from their own nature and source of pleasure:

The injections of masculinity they want to give women, even if they offer some occasional and exceptional fruit to those few who are able to take advantage of it, would inflict far greater damage on woman and on society, needlessly stirring up thousands and millions of small souls who are easily persuaded that they can rise up further by swishing their skirts around public offices than by watching silently over a cradle. (*Giovinezza*, p. 78)

Neera scorns the idea of economic independence for women through work; as the bearers of children, women's work is already defined for them. She curiously anticipates some disillusioned voices of the 1970s in her assertion that a woman who does a 'man's' work does twice the work, for she has her own work to do as well, which will not be taken from her. She shares the apprehension of the Church that women's virtue will not withstand the easy pleasures placed within her grasp once she leaves her proper sphere. Drunkenness, already a scourge of the male working class, would become rife among women too, and the numbers of 'delinquents, idiots, epileptics and neurasthenics' (*Le idee*, p. 134) born to alcoholic parents would inevitably increase. Alcoholic working-class women (and for alcoholism one might here substitute syphilis), neurasthenic middle-class girls struggling with a university education, the destruction of home and hearth: this, for Neera, is the brave new world of feminism and socialism.

What Neera objects to in feminism is the desire for emancipation, for freedom from husband, house and children. This is not what the majority of nineteenth-century feminists were advocating, and she is clearly overstating the case. But hers is a dramatic call for women to hold on to that which is most precious to them – in other words, maternity, echoing post-Risorgimento assertions as to women's role in society, exhortations to women to become the mothers of the new nation. Maternity was idealized not only by politicians but also by writers. Writers such as the Marchesa Colombi may have let a note of irony creep into their work, but before Sibilla Aleramo the fundamental nexus of women and maternity was never seriously challenged.

There is, however, a sting in the tail. If children are the flower of a woman's life, marriage and a husband are, somewhat reluctantly, the necessary fecundating seed, an indispensable step on the way: 'It would be a gross misjudgement to believe that a woman's happiness should depend on the single material act of joining together with a man; her happiness depends on a logical concatenation of things, but it is true to say that her desire for the flower implies the search for the seed' (*Giovinezza*, p. 76). Motherhood is not only the sublime duty of women, it is their sublime joy, source both of their own satisfaction and of the continuation of the species, which, sighs Neera, would rapidly head for disaster if it were left to the male ego in search of more transient pleasures. Maternity is the goal, marriage just the means. Woman's role, her 'exalted mission . . . which only the intellectually short-sighted believes consists in nothing more than knitting stockings' (*Giovinezza*, p. 82), is that of education rather than creation: 'it is not school which educates, it is the home; it is not the book which teaches, it is life; it is not teachers who make the man, but the mother' (*Le idee*, p. 81). It is not simply that 'the male quality is the creative gift': that part of a woman's abilities which is not dedicated to the child is stolen from him; better to be the mother of Beethoven or Verdi than some second-rate hack writing on a provincial newspaper. Neera does not deny women talent, or even genius – as a writer she could hardly go so far – but she does require them to instil their own learning and intelligence not into works of art, but into their offspring. From similar basic premises she draws the opposite conclusions to those of her contemporary Olive Schreiner, who, while she shared the view of women's role as educators of the young, demanded that women be allowed greater access to culture and work in order the better to be able to fulfil that duty. For Schreiner: 'There was never a great man who had not a great mother – it is hardly an exaggeration. The first six years of our life make us; all that is added later is veneer; and yet some say, if a woman can cook a dinner or dress herself well she has culture enough'.[4]

Feminists from Sibilla Aleramo to Anna Maria Mozzoni tried to persuade Neera – after all, one of the most widely read authors of her day – of the justness of their cause, for on many points their views did, in fact, overlap.[5] Historians and critics have remarked that, after Unification, the greater part of literary production by women is pedagogical in its intentions: women are given the task, both within the family and within their growing roles in public elementary education, of educating the nation. Women's desires to 'change the world', to contribute to the construction of the new Italy, were in this way channelled and contained; they were indeed to be given a role to play – and Neera was not the only one to be convinced of women's absolute superiority in this field – but it was not to take them outside the home.[6]

Neera's work was much admired by the philosopher and critic Benedetto Croce as well as the leading theorist of *verismo*, Luigi Capuana. Croce admired her consistently anti-feminist, anti-materialist stance; modern readers are beginning once more to admire her for her narratives, which reveal the opposite. Her short stories offer a window on to some of the problematic choices to be made by women in the post-Risorgimento period. 'Un giorno di nozze' ('A Wedding Day') anticipates what Tina, a young countrywoman, can expect from her impending marriage: a life of penury, drudgery and servitude to both her husband and her father-in-law. Nowhere does Neera come closer to John Stuart Mill's view of marriage as the only legal form of slavery.[7] In 'Paolina', the eponymous protagonist seeks to escape the family home where her father has made a second marriage to the beautiful and charming Aurora, an image of warm perfection worthy of her namesake in the paintings of Guido Reni. Paolina's feelings of rejection – this second marriage has produced a second child, adored by her mother – lead her to seek paid employment: "'Let her get it out of her system'', said my father, "this whim of emancipation won't last long. Our house is always open to her, as are our hearts, is that not right, Aurora?''"[8] Neera gives her character little room for manoeuvre; Paolina is helplessly caught between conflicting desires, and leaves us with a clear impression of the sense of suffocation experienced by unheroic women faced with partial but equally undesired choices.

As a moral and social thinker, Neera proclaims the role of women to be at the heart of the family, surrounded by children; yet as a writer, she obsessively explores the fate of women who do not achieve this goal, and are marginalized from the rhetoric of post-Risorgimento ambitions for women as mothers to the nation. The young, *petit-bourgeois* and provincial Teresa (*Teresa*, 1886) is crushed by her family: by her imperious and dominating father; by her brother, whose future outweighs any thoughts of her own prospects; by the younger sisters she is obliged to care for; by a mother whose only consolation is to shed tears. Loaded down with the restrictions and compulsions of *petit-bourgeois*, provincial life and the marginalization of female sexuality, Teresa experiences the female condition as one of utter subordination. Neera is careful in her disavowal of emancipation as a worthy goal for women, but her own material sweeps her along:

> She suffered alongside that healthy, happy young brother, that contented young man, before whom all doors were opened by the privileges of his sex. Teresa did not reason in this way, but she had an intimation of a profound injustice, while her woman's instinct pushed her blindly towards her masters.

> What could she do? Rebel against her father, cause that angel, her mother, to die of grief, break with all the traditions of the family, fail in her duties as obedient and willing daughter? She was enslaved whichever way she looked. Affection, habit, society, example, each only bound her more tightly.[9]

Neera's characters are antiheroines, and it could be argued that her narratives are thus all the more powerful in the obliqueness of their criticism, their examination of a social system from within. Teresa's hopes of marriage vanish, and her acceptance of the subordination of her own wishes to those of others 'only serves to underline the denunciation: not only does injustice exist, but society obliges the woman to acknowledge it as a sacrament'.[10]

Teresa's remaining youth is spent nursing a sick father. With the death of both parents, her brother's marriage and her sister's departure for a remote schoolroom, she finally breaks out of her inertia and escapes her closed world. Receiving a letter from the man she had once loved and who is now, like her, alone, she decides to flout bourgeois public opinion and join him in a final attempt to reappropriate a sense of self and self-determination. She has, she says to her friend, paid her dues to social decorum and expectation:

> 'What will your sisters think, or your brother?' She shrugged. 'People?' 'Oh, as for people . . . ' She smiled with that melancholic smile of hers, in which there was this time a touch

of irony. 'What am I to say if they make any comment about it all to me, your friend?' 'Well, you can tell the zealots that I have paid for this moment of freedom with the whole of my life. It's rather a high price, don't you think?' (*Teresa*, p. 202)

L'indomani (The Next Day, 1890) gives a brutally clear account of a marriage marred by neither poverty nor cruelty, but one which is based on economic contract rather than mutual love and respect. Marta finds herself in a strange province with a husband she barely knows, and who is more indifferent than unkind. *The Next Day* exposes, as lucidly as any feminist could desire, the extent to which a social system which is wholly disadvantageous to women is simultaneously dependent on their sacrifice, which is presented to them under the wrappings of romantic illusions.

As Marta approaches her twenty-third birthday, time is seen to be pressing and marriage becomes a matter of some urgency. The choice of a husband for her is depicted in a passage of high comedy; as more or less eligible bachelors are put forward by the council of family and friends gathered to settle Marta's future, the matter of the young girl's happiness is held to be of *prima facie* concern:

De Martini – tall, slim, fair, a touch bald, very well mannered, calm and well educated, should please Marta. Valdranchi – small, lively, known to keep somewhat dubious company but with the fire of genius in his eyes, restless, agreeable, should also be attractive to her, and there was no reason why she should not like Anselmo Bianchi – no longer in the bloom of youth to be sure, but he was healthy and owned that almost princely villa endowed with an enormous garden, where Marta could indulge her passion for flowers.[11]

Marta at least has a choice and is encouraged to count her blessings, her

singular good fortune compared to most girls, many of whom marry late when they have lost their poetic charm and are already a bit withered. Others do not marry at all; some have to be satisfied with an old man, or with a widower, or somebody not quite right in the head, or a man who stammers or has a touch of tuberculosis because – as wise people will always tell you – you can't have everything. (*The Next Day*, p. 11)

In her marriage, Marta faces barrenness not of the womb but of the emotions. Her elevation to the status of married woman makes her the unwilling confidante of her neighbour, the mournful Signora Merelli, and privy to her numerous difficult pregnancies (five children and four miscarriages in ten years, the normal lot of the wife), but she remains excluded from the cosy intimacy of her husband with his friends, his servant, even his horse. The sexual indiscretions and infidelities both of the men of the village and of her own husband reveal the double sexual standard at the sharp edge. Marta discovers letters written by her husband some years before to one Elvira. Confronted with the discovery, Alberto, rather than revealing himself as heroically scarred by a passion thwarted or lost, is simply indifferent to the discovery, as of an event which barely causes a ripple in his easy existence.

Like Emma Bovary before her, Marta soon discovers that the love and passion held out by the poets and novelists is illusory, a childhood sham. It is the doctor who takes it upon himself to articulate the contractual nature of marriage, and to confirm that women get the worst of the bargain. The clever man, says the doctor, idealizes the notion of love as duty and thus, at a stroke, deprives women of their natural birthright:

> 'He says to his victims: – You are the joy of our hearth, the repository of our name and our future, the queens of our home: you are peace, you are stability. He might as well add: you are the least of all evils which we choose after all the others we have known, you are the panacea for all our ills, the bed of rest after a day in the fields. In exchange for your youth, your candour, the ideal in your young lives, we who no longer have youth, nor candour, nor ideals, offer you something which is so common, so straightforward, something which you could find on every street corner if we hadn't granted ourselves an exclusive monopoly of it, increasing its value by denying you access to it, substituting decorum, a sense of shame and human virtue for the divine laws of nature.' (*The Next Day*, pp. 47–8)

The views expressed by the doctor are common enough in *fin-de-siècle* fiction and theatre. But while they come as no surprise in Ibsen, Shaw or Pinero, they are rather more startling when enunciated by the self-appointed spokeswoman of Italian female decency. Neera could hardly come closer to condemning the emotional and sexual frustrations foisted on women by a self-serving male-centred culture and sexual economy, ably assisted by the sugary dreams of romantic literature. Her answer to the discontent of Madame Bovary would be to have her accept the reality of marriage and seek satisfaction and fulfilment in motherhood, to preserve at whatever price the unity of the family, the bond between mother and child. Emma's neglect of her daughter and her eventual suicide, and Sibilla Aleramo's abandonment of the conjugal home and of her own son at the dawn of the new century, would only prove Neera's point – that if happiness is rarely to be found within marriage, outside it women are even more wretched: she might concur with Dr Johnson that if marriage has many trials, celibacy has few joys. A heavily pregnant Marta confesses her disappointments to her mother, for whom all artistic and social activity is mere sublimation, compensation for the void left by the youthful ideal of 'love':

> 'Love is an illusion! Do you think there would be all this activity in the world, that art would produce its masterpieces, that holy pity would raise its monuments, that patriotism would give us its heroes and religion its martyrs, if love as you understand it existed? Why do we cultivate flowers in pots and keep canaries in cages, why do we fill our homes with embroidery and needlework, why do we read novels and fashion journals, why do we go to concerts, why are there so many charitable institutions where women are patrons, inspectors, visitors, if love is a reality, if it is enough for one woman's life?' (*The Next Day*, pp. 140–1)

If Neera is hard on women, she spares men even less. In *The Next Day*, Signor Merelli gives his wife a new child each year, but keeps young and attractive servants; Gavazzini, despite the romantic tales about his passion for his young wife, ogles other women; Toniolo, the widower, marries again on the promise of a good dowry. 'Women', sighs Neera, 'have good reason to say that the love of men is made up half of pride and the other half selfishness – it is an unusual man who has anything left over which he can give to pure affection'.[12]

Duello d'anime (Battle of Souls, 1911)[13] has been described as 'one of the most striking analyses of false conjugal consciousness as the condition of the woman tilts dangerously towards the subjection of Fascism'.[14] In this novel the protagonist, Minna, is a timid orphan completely overwhelmed by her husband Filippo, an arrogant man who subjects her to constant humiliation. When she falls pregnant he marries her out of concern less for her reputation than for his own political career. This is perhaps the bitterest of Neera's works, where even the minimal consolations available in the other novels no longer assuage the damage inflicted by unequal relationships of power, and the façade of normality hides not just indifference but cruelty. Unlike Teresa, Minna no longer has a self to assert, and even after Filippo's death she continues to keep up appearances and conceal her husband's illicit and disastrous financial dealings.

By the time of Neera's recollections of her youth, written in the second decade of the new century, what Bernard Shaw called 'the modern woman' was rejecting the traditional values of home and hearth, domesticity and the harmony of provincial life which she defended in her writing, even if these same sources of happiness and contentment for women were considerably more problematic in her fictions. Neera's novels and stories offer a profound and ironic vision of life for middle-class women at the end of the nineteenth century, the same life which Aleramo was to walk out of so decisively just a few short years later, staking her dramatic claim for emancipation even at the cost of her own son. Neera's narratives, which in recent years have begun to resurface and to be made available to a new reading public, demonstrate the philosophical pessimism of this woman who ruthlessly exposed the banality and emotional sterility of most marriages even while wishing it for all women; who remained sceptical as to the possibility of real communion between the sexes, but none the less tied them together; who was convinced that fulfilment for women was to be found in motherhood alone, and everything else was to be borne for that purpose and that one satisfaction.

Neera never discusses her own marriage, never reveals her own

private, 'second' life to her public. Any references are obliquely
negative: 'It is certain that if I had been less sensitive I would
not have noticed the offence to my conscience and to my
feelings, I would not have withdrawn into myself to reflect,
perhaps I would not have written or perhaps I would have
written differently' (*Giovinezza*, p. 123). A modern reader can
only pruriently speculate on the extent to which her marriage, to
the Milanese banker Adolfo Radius, contributed to the disillusion
consistently expressed by her characters. To what extent does
Neera exercise self-censorship? The apparently contradictory conservatism of other nineteenth-century writers in Britain, such as
Mrs Gaskell, can be tentatively understood as self-defence and
expiation of a sense of guilt. Rather than confronting the values
of their society, these women novelists were competing for its
rewards: they 'publicly proclaimed, and sincerely believed, their
antifeminism. By working in the home, by preaching submission
and self-sacrifice, and by denouncing female self-assertiveness, they
worked to atone for their own will to write'.[15] Neera only hints
at the very undemure and unfeminine struggle – 'scratching myself
on the thorns, lacerating myself against the stones and rocks' –
necessary to achieve literary fame and fortune (*Giovinezza*, p. 86),
and she explicitly denies that writing is a suitable job for a woman
even as she acknowledges her own vast reading public. What we
might conclude from Neera's experience and career is that, in the
final analysis, it is not maternity but writing itself which offers the
only refuge.

3
The Sentimental Democracy
of Matilde Serao (1856–1927)

> Learning from books is a capricious business at best, and
> the teaching so vague and changeable that in the end, far
> from calling books either 'romantic' or 'realistic', you will
> be more inclined to think them, as you think people, very
> mixed.
>
> (Virginia Woolf, *Anatomy of Fiction*)

When Edith Wharton met Matilde Serao in Paris, the American
was as intrigued by the Neapolitan's unabashed and striking
difference from the fashionable ladies of the salons as by her
acute and generous intelligence. Serao's eccentric appearance was
accompanied by a readiness of wit, a depth of insight and a practical
experience of life rarely to be found even in the cultural Mecca
of Paris:

> This strange half-Spanish figure, oddly akin to the Meninas
> of Velásquez, and described by Bourget as 'Dr Johnson in a
> ball-dress', was always arrayed in low-necked dresses rather in
> the style of Mrs Tom Thumb's – I remember in particular a
> spreading scarlet silk festooned with black lace, on which her
> short arms and chubby hands rested like a cherub's on a sunset
> cloud. With her strident dress and intonation she seemed an
> incongruous figure in that drawing-room, where everything was
> in half-shades and semi-tones, but when she began to speak we
> had found our master. . . . Her training as a journalist had given
> her a rough-and-ready knowledge of life, and an experience
> of public affairs, totally lacking in the drawing-room Corinnes
> whom she outrivalled in wit and eloquence.[1]

Matilde Serao was at one point the most celebrated woman in
Italy, revered writer and observer of her native land, but hers was

a reputation swiftly lost within a few short years of her death. When Anna Banti published her biography of Matilde Serao in 1965, she recalled her sense of shock on discovering a woman who, less than forty years after her death, was already in the grip of myth, 'but was by this same myth cancelled out and obliterated. The legend which surrounded her name was not a benign one, but a sort of anthology of the same banal, endlessly repeated episodes, at the centre of which gestured and joked a merry, squat, ugly woman'.[2]

Serao seemed to have fallen victim to the process of dis-remembering, or dismembering, women's writing identified by feminist criticism: the long-term failure to establish a female literary tradition and heritage. Serao was an indefatigable portrayer of life and customs in Naples, and put her name to works of the utmost Naturalist severity as well as of late-Romantic, sentimental fiction, drawing on genres such as the Gothic and detective fiction. The work of the complex, contradictory, exuberant, populist Neapolitan writer, known to all her fellow citizens in the metropolis as 'a signora, a woman writer coming from the South, influenced by French literary tradition but keenly in tune with her native city, who pronounces herself ambivalent on feminism and writes of love and passion but lives a vigorously intellectual life herself, provides a fascinating glimpse of life and letters in a country where Unification appeared merely to point up diversity, where socialist and feminist theoretical models were beginning to articulate the failures of the democratic system, and where intellectuals were struggling – and failing – to forge a national literature in which Italians could recognize themselves as such.

Matilde Serao was born in Patras in 1856: her father, Francesco, had left Naples during the anti-Bourbon disorders of 1848. The figure of Francesco is markedly absent from Serao's work; she reserves her fascination for her Greek mother Paolina, the delicate, fragile woman who wore herself out giving French and English lessons. The elevation of the mother figure at the expense of the father is perhaps unsurprising in the light of Serao's own vision of herself as a '*maschietto*', a little boy, 'unfeminine' in all her ways. Intellectual and literary activity was still a primarily male sphere, and her ambition to succeed leads her to identify with male rather than female characteristics: 'everywhere and about everything with a singular audacity, I am making my way by pushing and shoving, with nobody or almost nobody to help me, just a burning desire to succeed. But you know I pay no heed to the weaknesses of my sex, and I go on my way as if I were a young man' (in Banti, *Serao*, p. 22).

With the fall of the Bourbons in 1872, the family returned to Naples, where Serao gained her teacher's diploma, after which she worked for the State Telegraph Company. These were two areas of growing employment for middle-class women, and provided material for a number of Serao's stories, the best of which are collected in *Il romanzo della fanciulla* (Novel of the Young Girl, 1886). She also began to collaborate with a number of journals and papers, and it was to work for the paper *Capitan Fracassa* that she left Naples for the capital in 1881. Serao's difficulties in integrating into Roman society are explored indirectly in *La conquista di Roma* (The Conquest of Rome, 1885). The novel – which also mirrors the fascination exercised by the new Parliament over the imagination of numerous contemporary writers – describes the newly elected Southern deputy Francesco Sangiorgio's first political and amorous encounter with the new capital, the dominant city in unified Italy. In a conceit reminiscent of Balzac's *Lucien de Rubempré*, both city and woman prove hostile: the city, indifferent and treacherous to the ardent male, conquering spirit, is finally scorned as 'the woman who could not love'.

Rome is, inevitably, a disappointment, and Sangiorgio's idealistic fervour at the opening ceremony of Parliament rapidly tarnishes. The deputies are almost to a man involved in the political *trasformismo* or power-brokering, corruption, and failure to address fundamental economic problems which have dogged Italian politics in all its democratic phases. Serao's most bitterly hostile criticism, however, is reserved less for the deputies than for their wives. The women, too, attend the investiture ceremony, 'these women who have invented every kind of false oath, overcome by emotion at those solemn promises which five hundred made to a single man' (*Conquest*, p. 78). The working woman Serao can barely hide her contempt for these fluffy-headed creatures who consider themselves to be close to the source of power, who believe they are talking politics when in fact they are talking gossip.

In Rome, Serao met and fell in love with Edoardo Scarfoglio, fellow Neapolitan and journalist, follower of the poet Carducci, would-be writer and virulent polemicist. Scarfoglio's move to Rome was one more example of the fascination the capital exerted over young provincials who had grown up under Bourbon rule. Scarfoglio shared the disillusion felt by the post-Risorgimento generation, and their strong sense of disgust at the scandals and vice which appeared to accompany parliamentary democracy.

Scarfoglio wrote scathingly of the current French fashion in literature, and urged Italian writers to turn to Boccaccio rather than to Zola or Balzac for their models. Matilde herself was not spared his splenetic and occasionally scatological pen, for he was as harsh in his criticism of her second novel, *Fantasia* (1883), as of other acclaimed novels of the day:

> All the critics huddled together like a pack of sheep and proclaimed *Fantasia* the only Italian novel with real life in it, and everybody clapped their hands. Nobody stopped to think that exactly the same thing had been claimed for *Eva*, then for Verga's *I Malavoglia*, Capuana's *Giacinta*, Fogazzaro's *Malombra*, Rovetta's *Mater Dolorosa*: and with fanfare after fanfare our novel is heading triumphantly straight for the cesspit.[3]

The two were drawn together by an instinctive sympathy, a shared passion for journalism and also a shared literary taste which inclined to realism, if in a rhetorical manner which owed more to Luigi Capuana than to Giovanni Verga. Serao admired her husband's better education, the privilege of his class, and for many years faithfully followed his political line in her journalism. Their marriage produced four sons and a number of new newspapers, but stormy scenes and Scarfoglio's notorious infidelities – which, together with their lavishly furnished house and Scarfoglio's extravagant tastes, made the couple the centre of attention in Naples – led to a legal separation in 1902.

In the meantime, however, Scarfoglio and Serao had combined their talents and set up a new daily, *Il Corriere di Roma*, intended to be a modern broadsheet, well illustrated and with effective and accurate reporting. Their resources did not match their ambition:

threatened with bankruptcy, they returned to Naples to set up *Il Corriere di Napoli*, financed by the Jewish banker Matteo Schilizzi. In Rome, Serao and Scarfoglio had become close to the poet and writer Gabriele D'Annunzio. When D'Annunzio's publisher, Treves, rejected *L'Innocente* (The Innocent) on grounds of immorality, it appeared first, in instalments, in the *Corriere di Napoli*. D'Annunzio collaborated enthusiastically with the *Corriere* and then with *Il Mattino*, Scarfoglio's own paper, which first appeared in 1892.

As a journalist, and under the customary variety of pseudonyms (D'Annunzio used the names Happlemouche and Biscuit, among others), Serao wrote on anything and everything, touching subjects as diverse as fashion and customs, literary criticism, Franco–Russian relations, Neapolitan painting and the novels of Rovetta. Her duties as a reporter took her to the salons, 'those elegant meeting places where her fame as an independent woman aroused perhaps more curiosity than admiration . . . those beautiful, idle women with their delicate nerves, their exquisite gowns, must have looked upon her with something like amused condescension, as upon a strange, clumsy little animal' (Banti, *Serao*, p. 38). Serao's version of her encounters with the upper classes suggests a much more defiant attitude, despite the fascination which the leisured classes continued to exercise on her imagination: 'Those elegant ladies don't realize that I know them inside out, that I hold them in my mind, that I will put them in my books: they have no idea of my strength and power. They find me absolutely *charmante*'.[4]

For many years Matilde Serao faithfully followed her husband's political line, which was anti-Socialist, imperialist and meridionalist. Post-Unification agrarian reforms in the South had failed disastrously, and Scarfoglio was a vigorous campaigner for Italian expansionism, for the move into Africa that was to lead to war with and eventual bloody conquest of Abyssinia and Libya. Such an imperialist attitude was to be found right across the political spectrum in Italy. The poet Giovanni Pascoli considered himself a Socialist, yet he was passionately in favour of the Libyan war, as post-Risorgimento nationalist fervour fuelled the desire to match countries such as France and Britain in the acquisition of Empire.

It was a mixed time for Serao. Her personal life was turbulent;

melodrama threatened to become a way of life when one of her husband's rejected lovers killed herself at their front door. With the final breakdown of her relationship with Scarfoglio, Serao left *Il Mattino* and set up a rival news-sheet of her own, *Il Giorno*, where she published short stories by writers such as Kipling, Capuana and Panzini. Serao's political line began to change; in part, at least, to contradict publicly the voice of *Il Mattino*. But she was genuinely anti-war, and came out strongly against intervention in the First World War. With the advent of Fascism, she spoke out vehemently against the occupation of Palazzo Marino, Milan, in August 1922. Despite her newspaper offices being raided and almost destroyed by Fascist *squadristi* in December that year, she continued to protest. On 9 March 1924 she wrote an article declaring: 'Napoli non è fascista', and on the 22nd of the same month she printed the text of a speech by the Liberal leader Giovanni Amendola; in June that year, after the murder of Giacomo Matteotti for accusing the Fascists of falsifying election results, Cesare Sobero published an article calling for the overthrow of Mussolini, widely held to be personally responsible for ordering the removal of the troublesome Socialist deputy. Serao later became more reconciled to Mussolini, however, meeting with him a number of times, although rumour had it that the 1926 Nobel Prize for Literature was not given to Serao (it went instead to Grazia Deledda) because of her paper's non-alignment with the regime. Serao died a year later in 1927, of a heart attack, at her writing table.

As writer and journalist in Naples at the turn of the century, Serao had a role to play in her native city which for some commentators has never been matched. She became a living legend, a social institution. She was perhaps an exception to Antonio Gramsci's general observation that French literature in the nineteenth century was more 'popular' than Italian literature; Gramsci points out that while ordinary people read the Gothic potboilers of Carolina Invernizio and the work of Serao's fellow Neapolitan Francesco Mastriani,[5] these were exceptions: 'in Italy the intellectuals are distant from the people, i.e. from the "nation". They are tied to a caste tradition that has never been broken by a strong popular or national political movement from below . . . the indigenous intellectual element is now more foreign than the foreigners',[6] leaving a chasm between the educated, cultured classes and the 'nation-people'. Gramsci might have mentioned Serao, too, at this point, for she was closely identified with the people of her city. Antonio Ghirelli comments that Serao's psychology, her contradictions and her cultural limitations, correspond exactly to those of her bourgeois or *petit-bourgeois* reader, to the Neapolitan women of her day: 'Like her, she is sentimental and romantic, like her she is readily moved by the fate of the poor, easily roused to indignation by the tricks of the powerful. . . . She writes in Italian and thinks in dialect. She is rich to overflowing with powers of observation, but impoverished in imagination'.[7]

Serao's last contribution to her husband's paper, in 1901, was called 'I figli', 'The Children', and was a polemic against the idea of divorce. While this article shows that Serao was acutely aware of the difficulties of finding a satisfactory and fulfilling role as a woman at the turn of the century in Italy, her relationship with emerging feminist and Socialist movements was a stormy one.[8] In newspaper articles she stood out consistently against suffrage for women, against divorce, against Anna Kuliscioff when she was dismissed from her hospital post for political activity. Like Neera, she pronounced herself determinedly anti-feminist, excoriating women such as Mozzoni, Mario and Beccari for looking beyond the borders of Italy to Britain, America and Scandinavia for models for women's participation in national life, and accusing them of a failure of love for their own country: let them learn, rather, from the patriotic resignation of those mothers whose sons had died in Africa. Kuliscioff and Mozzoni's response was to reject any comparison between the wars of national liberation and those of colonialism: the massacres in Africa could never be regarded as the legitimate offspring of the Risorgimento.

The case of Serao is another instance of the uneasy discrepancy between ideology and the practicalities of life, the failure of conviction and purpose to coincide. Before Serao, the novelist Neera proclaimed her hostility to and distaste for the idea of a woman writing. Their ambivalence is remarkable, but perhaps not surprising. The grip of Catholicism was tight, and late industrialization meant the late development of the proletarian and egalitarian consciousness which was vital to the formation of an early feminist position.[9] The novel as genre had a short history in Italy, and there was no Mary Wollstonecraft, Mary Shelley or

Jane Austen to serve as model. Female novelists had had little time to explore the possibilities and challenges presented by a non-romantic heroine. It is possible that these women experienced the same sense of guilt in writing as did, for example, their English counterparts in the earlier part of the century, the guilt at usurping what was still principally a male activity; Anna Banti concurs, suggesting that Serao's avowed hostility to women is defensive, her alignment with the stronger sex a shield against criticism for usurping traditional male prerogatives. Besides: 'in those years the English suffragettes were exposing themselves to all kinds of ridicule, and it did not take much to slip into the grotesque and make enemies of men such as our dear Edoardo' (Banti, *Serao*, p. 125).

While Serao's hostility towards the term 'feminism' gradually diminished, she never loses her reservations about the ability of feminism to bring about sweeping social change, nor her romantic notion of passion as the prime mover in social affairs. Women, she states, will find it hard to forget that their primary role is to please men. She is, of course, speaking here of women of leisure:

It will never be possible, never, to convince a woman's heart that love is not the most important event in her life, the *grande affaire*, as our brothers say in Paris. . . . Feminism will never find anything equivalent to love to fill a woman's life. Thousands upon thousands of women live in this truth which is as ancient as the world, and we have seen no other dazzling and powerful truth which can similarly illuminate the hearts of women.[10]

Serao's narrative output is as resistant to neat categorization as are her social and political views. She is at heart a professional writer, who adapts to the shifting tastes of her public. The sobriety and acute social observation of *Il paese di cuccagna* (*The Land of Cockayne*, 1891) and *Il ventre di Napoli* (The Belly of Naples, 1884) stand beside other texts which borrow from genres of romance, Gothic, thriller and even the supernatural, such as *Fantasia*, *Castigo* (*Punishment*, 1893) and *La mano tagliata* (*The Severed Hand*, 1912). It would be reductive to assign Serao's work to a specific genre, just as it is difficult to discover a consistent stance on social and political issues consonant with the interests of any one specific group.

A widely shared critical view is that Serao's best work is that which springs from direct observation of the life and manners of her native city, work in which she neither tries to imitate French models nor slips into the easy familiarity of popular romance. While Serao's version of realism is closer to Capuana, whose psychological and pathological approach to the observation of society left room for individual subjectivism, she shared with Verga a deep and passionate commitment to the South. In the new Italy of the Risorgimento, writers such as Verga and Serao expose the fallacy of the unified tradition of Italian literature:

> After the facile idealism of one type of romanticism, art turns to look at brutal facts, at the lower classes, at a bourgeoisie with no more concern than for money, to peasants with the bleakest lot, to the dregs of society. Now we shall see the world of the peasant without Manzoni's rosier tinting: something harsh, yet maybe more acceptable, because more genuine. (Whitfield, p. 245)

The Belly of Naples is considered by many to be the authentic voice of Serao. This work, written in fact in Rome rather than Naples, first appeared as a series of articles in *Capitan Fracassa* during 1884, when Naples was ravaged by a violent cholera epidemic which claimed many thousands of lives. The epidemic inevitably hit hardest in the poor quarters of the city, and the response of Prime Minister Depretis – 'bisogna sventrare Napoli' ('Naples must be gutted') – was the source of heated debate as to what should be done to relieve the misery of the Southern city.[11] Serao's purpose in her articles was to influence public opinion, to oppose the deadly uncertainty and hesitation of the government and propose a more radical solution than politicians put forward. Her aim is to rehabilitate a city in physical and moral decline, both literally ('bisogna rifarla' ['we must make it anew']) and semantically, in the way that Naples is habitually described, viewed and presented to the outside world. It is probable that *The Belly of Naples* was written in response not simply to the cholera epidemic but also to Renato Fucini's travel documentary of 1878, *Napoli a occhio nudo* (Naples to the Naked Eye).[12] Serao combats the racist rhetoric of the Realist writer which speaks of the Neapolitan people in bestial, grotesque metaphors. She guides the reader through the sullied, winding streets of the slums, through the human misery and the inhuman living conditions; shows the dreadful housing, the numerous expediencies such as usury and the lottery to which people are forced to resort in order to survive. Serao sustains the physiological imagery of the *ventre*, the belly, in a rhetorical image designed to shock the *bien-pensant* comfortable bourgeoisie of the capital; her description of via dei Mercanti gives a graphic image of Naples at the end of the last century:

> It is maybe four metres wide, so carriages cannot pass along it, and it twists and winds like an intestine. Even on the most sunny days, the high buildings permit only a pale, lifeless light; in the middle of the street runs a sluggish, black, foetid stream of evil-smelling soapy water, water from the pasta and the soup, a rotten, stinking mixture. You can find anything in this via dei Mercanti, which is one of the main roads of the Porto district: dark shops where shadows move around selling everything, pawn-shops, lottery counters, here and there a black doorway or a muddy sidestreet, a fryer giving off the stink of bad oil, or a salami seller whose shop stinks of mouldy cheese and rancid lard.[13]

In her denunciation of the appalling social hygiene of the city, this self-proclaimed anti-feminist shows an understanding of and sympathy with working women 'which could not be matched by a social worker in our own times' (Banti, *Serao*, p. 98). If they are lucky, women find work in the tobacco factories or as flower girls or seamstresses, but most of them are destined to the slavery of domestic labour, wretchedly paid like all other work in Naples:

> These work-horses also find the time to give milk to a baby and mend their stockings, but they are monstrous creatures and inspire pity and repugnance in equal parts. At thirty years of age they already look fifty: they are bent over, their hair has fallen out, their teeth are yellow or black, they walk as if crippled, they wear the same dress for four years, the same apron for six months. They do not complain, or weep: before they are forty years old they go to the hospital to die, of pneumonia, or pernicious anemia, or some other horrendous disease. (*The Belly of Naples*, p. 16)

If *The Belly of Naples* recalled Zola, *The Land of Cockayne* echoes

Balzac in its desire to paint a wide canvas which will include all sections and levels of society. Serao's Ariadne's thread, leading the reader through the whole of Naples, is the city-wide passion for the lottery, defined uncompromisingly as 'an infamy which led to sickness, to destitution, to prison, to every kind of dishonour, to death'[14] and a running sore which drew the wrath of many early Socialists. Serao is vivid in her account of this obsession which focuses all the passions in crowded, hectic Naples, transcends class barriers, and is indiscriminate in its destructiveness – a plague all the worse for being man-made.

Serao describes in detail the anatomy of a disease which corrupts an entire city, which leads a man to ruin his family, or a father to imprison his daughter until the winning numbers are revealed to her in a vision.[15] Some of the most striking scenes in the novel take place between the usurious Esposito sisters and their wretched, cringing but insistent clients, while the upper classes have recourse to a ruthless, faceless aristocrat, all the more threatening for his deadly calm and poise. The lottery is

a problem of organized crime, but difficult to unravel. The excuse for the Lottery, its initial pretext, is a thirst for dreams, exacerbated by a cruel reality from which there is no apparent escape; but the reasons for its power are numerous. The Lottery brings in its train innumerable ways of exploiting hope and need, and of orchestrating superstitions.[16]

Yet while Serao observes the destructive psychological drive which pushes people to gamble away their lives and fortunes, her analysis stops at this point. Anna Banti comments: 'for human passions Serao always showed a comprehension which verged on complicity: love, gambling, vanity and pride were for her so many diseases: she does not judge them, but observes their symptoms with an almost short-sighted obstinacy; and then she absolves them, tilting her chin in that very Southern way of hers, as if to say, what can you do?' (Banti, *Serao*, p. 134). While she accuses the government of complicity, she is mild in her criticism of a system which generates huge profits for the few and permits, even encourages, the bleeding of the citizenry.

Neither Serao's sense of outrage nor her acute observation of detail leads her to uncover and denounce the real centres of

power in the city – legitimate and illegitimate power embodied
in the same powerful few – by which its people are undone.
In the extraordinary set piece of the novel, when the crowd is
waiting for the Miracle, the biannual liquefaction of the blood of
San Gennaro, the tension is intense, but to some extent misplaced.
The crowd, obliged to repeat the Credo thirty-eight times before
the blood finally liquefies, becomes first sullen, then angry, then
positively dangerous; the priest, at first anxious, becomes seriously
alarmed. Failure of the blood to liquefy is an ill omen for all
onlookers alike; for the believers it heralds a time of divine
retribution and punishment, while for the forces of law and
order it signifies a period of social unrest and dissatisfaction in a
city always verging on eruption. The real tension of the moment
lies in these two diametrically opposed interpretations of events,
but Serao focuses on the individual experience of hopes raised
and dashed against a background of misery and despair, rather than
untangling the complex web of political and criminal power which
enmeshes them.

In a later story, 'Trenta per cento' ('Thirty per cent'), the protagonist's husband becomes involved in an enormous confidence
trick whereby false banks fraudulently offer unheard-of rates of
interest, make swift and vast profits, then collapse dramatically,
ruining thousands. The hope for quick returns, through the bank
as through the lottery, again seizes not only the city but the entire
province. Serao comments ruefully: 'in a hot Southern country
with a fiery imagination like ours, it is so difficult to keep one's
distance from madness, from getting carried right away!'[17] Thus
she exonerates her people in their resurgent dream of the Land
of Plenty even while she gives in this story one of the few hints
that she is aware of the level of corruption which gripped the city.
Warned by his desperate wife that he will be imprisoned for his
illegal activities, Carlo shows the cynicism of a man who knows
that power and authority have a price tag: 'Judges, presidents, the
king's prosecutors – they're all our friends. Money can do anything.
What can't you buy with money? . . . We've fixed everything up.
There are so many interests tied up with ours, we can't collapse; too
many people would go down with us' ('Thirty per cent', p. 253).

This is a rare moment for Serao. Like other writers of her time,
either in the South or on the islands of Sardinia or Sicily, she

was unwilling to describe the malignant presence of the Mafia or the Camorra, and while she wrote a series of articles on women teachers, for example, she maintained a similar silence on the notorious problem of prostitution. She was largely silent on the discontent which followed the unification of the Bourbon city to the rest of Italy, the disillusion and resentment which led Cavour to comment that harmonizing North with South was more difficult than dealing with Austria or with the Church. Serao is an observer of life and manners, but features of social and political life such as the endemic problem of brigandage find little space in her work. Later writers and intellectuals have castigated Serao – and many others with her - for failing to tell the truth about Naples, for colluding in the abyss between the real Naples and the Naples portrayed in literature and music, for neglecting the underlying dynamic of the city in favour of a little local colour, for failing to connect the social and human reality they saw to any wider political or ideological discourse:

> In literature we find only traces of the gestures and colours of the real Naples. The real Naples is brutal, yes, but more historic and more deserving of comprehension. . . . It seems incredible that in writing *The Belly of Naples*, Serao, the most important woman writer in Italy, could not produce a work capable of going right to the heart of things.[18]

Writers such as the Sicilian Leonardo Sciascia and the Neapolitan Domenico Rea, coming half a century later, were to break more than a hundred years of literary *omertà*, a self-imposed code of silence. Southern writers had no desire to present a negative picture of their lands and city to a centralized power already prepared and willing to believe the worst, while a long-instilled inferiority complex resulted in a silence which it took extraordinary courage to break.

Serao's last major work to deal with a social 'issue' is *Suor Giovanna della Croce* (Sister Joan of the Cross, 1901).[19] This sober, measured work deals with the government's decision to reduce the temporal power of the Church by confiscating lands and buildings belonging to religious orders. The decision was clearly a consequence of the Vatican's refusal to recognize the newly formed State (Catholics who stood for public office were excommunicated), but the implications in human terms were dramatic. Women who had spent years, decades even, 'buried alive' in closed orders were suddenly forced back into the world. Suor Giovanna's hard-won peace and tranquillity, found in the cloisters, is shattered by her brutal return to a family who will tolerate her only as long as there is hope of the nun's original dowry to the convent being returned by the government. With this hope finally gone, the now destitute Suor Giovanna is reduced to fending for herself as best she can. Edoardo Scarfoglio had written numerous polemical articles condemning the cruelty of the government's move, but Serao resists any temptation to exoticize or glamorize the situation: the nun who is the protagonist of the story is neither a beautiful young creature of Gothic romance nor an exalted mystic; there are no thrillingly beautiful heroines after the manner of Audrey Hepburn. Serao's narrative restraint in this novel reveals itself in its refusal to indulge in and exploit romantic novelistic conventions and situations. Her rejection of sensationalism, her delicate treatment of carefully husbanded sensibilities, place this novel apart from the dominant trends of the day, the psychological complexity, sultry decadence or romantic sensuality of Fogazzaro or D'Annunzio.

This sober, austere output of Serao, which shadowed the work of Giovanni Verga in the last two decades of the nineteenth century (Verga's *I Malavoglia* appeared in 1881, the *Novelle rusticane* in 1883 and the first edition of *Mastro don Gesualdo* in 1889), was framed by a further extensive production which followed on from Romanticism and from the tradition of the Gothic novel. Here Serao can give free rein to her emotions and her imagination without looking over her shoulder at her French masters. While these novels may not be masterpieces, Serao would be more sympathetic to G.K. Chesterton's view of popular literature – that 'literature and fiction are two entirely different things – literature is a luxury; fiction is a necessity'[20] – than to the elitist view, represented by Q.D. Leavis, that popular fiction meant an inevitable debasing and coarsening of aesthetic taste.[21] Serao adopts the conventions of romantic, sentimental popular fiction, with its emphasis on obstructed love, adultery and triangular relationships, but she radically alters the emphasis of the traditional triangular structure to focus less on heterosexual relationships than on relationships between women.

The woman may still be caught between husband and lover, or the man between lover and wife, but passion, closeness and betrayal are experienced less in the conventional heterosexual relationship than in the relationship between two women.

The triangular relationship of Serao's first novel, *Cuore infermo* (The Ailing Heart, 1881) follows Beatrice's refusal fully to love her husband; her weak heart leads her to a moral as well as physical coldness which she summons up in self-protection. Beatrice's name, as well as her coldly chaste and distant demeanour, inevitably recall the ethereal and similarly chaste lover of Dante's dreams in the *Vita nuova* and the *Divina Commedia*. But fashionable late-nineteenth-century Italian society is secular in its habits, and Marcello turns to the warmer charms of the extravagant Lalla d'Aragona for comfort. Lalla represents the 'modern woman, the passionate woman, strange, superficial perhaps, delicate, sick, nervous, capricious . . . the woman made to please restless and refined modern youth'.[22] When Beatrice finally allows herself to fall in love with her husband, their passionate idyll is made all too brief by her sudden death: happy marriages are not the stuff of romantic drama.

Serao combines the romantic convention of adultery, the dynamic triangle of emotions, with the dyad of the two women as doubles, as a splitting of the female figure in the text. Lalla herself recognizes this: '"You are in love,"' she tells Marcello, '"but you come here, to my house, to love the woman who will not love you in your own home"' (*Ailing Heart*, p. 99). The split, divided woman (a metaphor for Serao herself, perhaps) appears in literature from Choderlos de Laclos's *Les Liaisons Dangereuses* to Charlotte Brontë's *Jane Eyre*, Igino Ugo Tarchetti's *Fosca* (1869) and Thomas Hardy's *Jude the Obscure*, with the good, pure woman (Madame de Tourville, Jane Eyre) set against the woman who is bad (Madame de Merteuil), mad (Mrs Rochester) or vulgarly sensual (Arabella and Fosca). The purity of Beatrice is confronted with the dark, mysterious, dangerous and diabolically unwholesome Lalla. Serao, too, turns her hand to the Gothic convention whereby the woman is split between 'the angelic creature of the Provençals and the poets of the Dolce Stil Nuovo translated into bourgeois terms, a cherub or seraph who for wings unfurled long silk gloves and crinolines' and the woman 'who finds in sickness and in death two magnificent opportunities to express her emotional turmoil'.[23] But just as Jane is curious about the creature locked away in the attic, so the primary fascination of *The Ailing Heart* is not the heterosexual relationship between Lalla and Marcello, even less that between Marcello and his faint-hearted wife, but the attraction felt by the two women drawn to each other, the obsessive interest and curiosity each feels for the other. The shock of recognition when they finally meet suggests a collision not between opposites but between two selves which inhabit the one woman, a culturally divided female sexuality and identity.[24]

Fantasia similarly presents us with the classic figure of the *femme fatale*, Lucia Altimare: her affair with Andrea Lieti, husband of her old friend Caterina Spaccapietra, leads to the flight of the lovers and the suicide of the abandoned woman. Lucia, like Lalla and Dumas's Lady of the Camellias, harbours within her body both irresistible love and death, Eros and Thanatos; it is in this conflation of two primary drives that the *femme fatale* is the ultimate creation of Romantic fiction.

Serao shows her pragmatic irritation at this self-invented, narcissistic creature, even while the conventions of the genre compel her to describe the seductiveness of a passion which is literally outside the lexicon of pedestrian, bourgeois marriage. If Caterina has no words to express any emotion other than placid contentment, Lucia has an abundance of them; she is even, it seems, writing a novel, and Serao almost seems to be mocking the romance genre, although she nevertheless concedes to its superficial conventions. The source of Lucia's unidentified sickness, her weakness, is located by her author in her reading matter – Italy is the land of poets, and Leopardi is Lucia's undoing. If, like that of Emma Bovary, Lucia's sensibility is a very literary – even an operatic – one, her self-image is equally a copy – of a portrait once seen of 'an unknown woman, with drawn face, dressed in white. Lucia liked to imagine that the stranger had suffered a great deal and then died, unknown, in the shadows of the unknown'.[25] Serao, like Thomas Hardy, blames the modern age for its invention of 'false modern neurosis' (*Fantasia*, p. 80) afflicting women.

Although *Fantasia* remains firmly within the structures of romance, it takes *The Ailing Heart* a stage further in its investigation of the relationship between two women. Serao's rather negative view of romantic love leads her to stress friendship with women as more than a simple prelude to the more significant and permanent heterosexual relationship. Some critics have also suggested a latent lesbian subtext in these novels, which appeared at a moment of increasing knowledge and social concern about homosexuality and lesbianism.[26]

The novel opens with a scene reminiscent of the early chapters of *Jane Eyre*. Two girls, very different, are fast friends: the plain, conventional one has to stand by as her more exalted colleague is punished. But unlike Helen Burns, Lucia does not die, and her exaltation is sentimental rather than religious. About to leave school, she takes the bemused Caterina into the college chapel, and there makes her swear dramatic and eternal fidelity. A broken and divided rosary is the symbol of this friendship made in heaven.

As in *The Ailing Heart*, the adulterous relationship is secondary to the fascination the two women exercise over each other. When Lucia is tempted to sin, it is a sin against their friendship rather than against the sacrament of marriage. It is Lucia who writes to Caterina to inform her of the lovers' elopement. Caterina, good housewife in death as in life, calmly puts her affairs in order before taking her own life: 'The eyes of this little dead woman are open wide, but glassy, as if amazed at some incredible spectacle. And around her grey hands and purple fingers was the blue flash of the lapis lazuli rosary, half broken' (*Fantasia*, p. 368). The incredible spectacle is clearly the betrayal not of Andrea, by now a cipher in the novel, but of the other woman. This emphasis on female relationships, new to Italian fiction, turns the novel from yet another romance about adultery to a more mixed genre, and opened up new areas to be explored by women writers.

Other novels show an increasingly eclectic use of genre. With *Punishment* Serao hovers on the border between Gothic romance and psychological drama. The device of the double is transformed from an element of romance to a feature of the thriller, as the Gothic slides into detective fiction. In the later work *The Severed Hand*, elements of the thriller (the search for the woman to whom the hand belongs) are turned from hints into structuring features of the novel, whose robust and unashamedly entertaining plot moves from Gothic beginnings to a detective story set in England, employing its own detective by the name of Dick Leslie.

In her shifting and eclectic use of genre Serao reflects and magnifies the turbulent state of Italian life and letters at the end of the nineteenth century. In recent years critics have been drawn back to her, to reconsider the relationship between her extraordinary life and her erratic literary output; between her work, which draws on all genres, and the literary and cultural debates of the day. If in England in the later half of the nineteenth century female novelists were more advanced than political activists in their demands for women's rights, in Italy the opposite was probably the case. But Matilde Serao, straddling the nineteenth and twentieth centuries, romance, Gothic and realism, her feet planted firmly in Naples even if her head was in Paris, captures a society in turmoil and flux, the contradictions, tensions and impossible dreams of post-Risorgimento Italy.

4
Taboo and Transgression
in Grazia Deledda (1871–1936)

> Where shall be found
> This dim seen track-mark of an ancient crime?
>
> (Sophocles, *Oedipus Tyrannus*)

In 1926 Grazia Deledda received the Nobel Prize for Literature, only the second woman ever to do so after the Swedish writer Selma Lagerlöf in 1909. The award remains controversial to this day, as suspicions linger on that Mussolini regarded Deledda as a 'safer' choice than the novelist and dramatist Luigi Pirandello, and that the Sardinian's passionate tales of guilty love played out against the barren and evocative landscape of Sardinia were more congenial to the Duce's taste than the abrasive and outspoken novels of the more urban 'a signora, Matilde Serao.[1]

In her last, posthumous, semi-autobiographical novel *Cosima* (1937), Deledda gives an account of her early years in Nuoro, Sardinia, and of her determination against all odds to become a writer. Under the light guise of fiction the 'c'est moi' is clear; while to write for pleasure and in a strictly dilettante fashion was acceptable (her brother even sent her to have lessons in Italian, the language of high culture), to write for money was frowned upon by her bourgeois family as severely detrimental to both her own and her sister's chances of a suitable marriage. Deledda, 'a kind of rebel against all the habits, traditions and customs not only of her family but of her race',[2] swiftly felt the force of the family's 'unanimous and implacable execration. My aunts, the two old maids who did not even know how to read and who would burn any papers with images of sinners or fallen women on them, came rushing over to the cursed household, spreading utter terror with their criticisms and their worst prophecies' (*Cosima*, p. 751).

'In many countries, and not only in Sardinia, people believe a woman writer to be a none too virtuous woman'.[3] Women writers, like ladies of easy virtue, were beyond the pale of the traditional social order. Cosima's experience recalls that of Charlotte Brontë, advised by an alarmed Robert Southey to put down her pen and return to her pots and pans. Cosima's work, submitted to an unnamed but hostile critic, is torn to shreds: she is invited to use the scraps to light the kitchen fire, and to prepare herself for a future more fitting to a young girl of her class: 'Let her go back home, the little scribbler, back to her father's orchard, to grow her carnations and her honeysuckle, to make her stockings, grow up and wait for a good husband, to prepare herself for a healthy future of family affections and maternity' (*Cosima*, p. 772).

Despite such determined discouragement, Cosima/Deledda persisted in her chosen career, moving first to the Sardinian capital, Cagliari, and from there to Rome with her husband, a Ministry employee. Deledda's reluctant anticipation of 'this Rome which I hate, loathe and detest, whose ugliness I can feel even before I have seen it, the city to which my destiny binds me with irons and chains, with all those stupidities of life called love, friendship, art, and who knows what else'[4] is modified by her professed adjustment to a new way of life whose seclusion could barely have been more complete. The direst predictions of Deledda's family were unfulfilled, as biographers and critics have repeatedly stressed her domestic contentment and her refusal to enter the social circles of the opinion-forming cultural elite, praising (perhaps with the rebellious Sibilla Aleramo in mind) her lack of narcissism or self-dramatization. Deledda's self-effacement as a writer appears almost as welcome to biographers and critics as it would have been to her family. Roberto Branca writes that Deledda, who 'in her home life and her sober conversation was a perfectly normal woman, for two or three hours each day fell back into the dream of a distant land, reliving it in an artistic rapture'.[5] Disturbing as it may be to see a woman who writes as a woman who disrupts the 'normality' of home life, and can be allowed to do so only in a kind of hallucinating rapture, Deledda's relationship to her native Sardinia, the land of which she wrote almost exclusively but to which she never returned, remains an extraordinary one.

More familiar with the rhythms and cadences of the Sard dialect, whose stories and tales formed her first imagination, Deledda, like Serao, struggled to write in Italian.[6] Her work, like that of Matilde Serao and Neera, resists the bonds of literary categorization; she was claimed for the Realist school of the *veristi* (by Luigi Capuana), and variously located by other critics within the ambit of Decadence, late Romanticism, psychological realism and folklore.[7] Deledda is much more than a regional writer. More than any she recalls the Russian writers Gogol and Goncharov in her descriptions of daily life, Tolstoy and Dostoevsky in her depiction of inner moral life and moral crisis.

Coming from the wild lands of Sardinia, isolated from and unknown to Italians as well as to Europeans, Deledda was an outsider to literary tradition. Her work can most fruitfully be seen as an instance of the split at the heart of Italian social and cultural life as the country moved awkwardly into the twentieth century. Literary criticism which seeks a unifying history risks being centrist and nationalist in its aspiration to erase difference. It is possible to read Deledda's narratives of the clash between the individual and the social order as the literary correlative of the relations between an island which is only in theory part of a post-Unification reality, torn between the old world and the new, and the newly formed nation-state, the Kingdom of Italy. Deledda's tales of passionate and illicit love, her narratives of taboos and transgressions, speak not, as in Pirandello, of the irredeemable existential alienation of the individual, but of a whole set of parameters – social, historical, cultural and psychological – which were being tested and strained by Sardinia's sudden emergence into the modern world. What is still worth exploring in Deledda is less the resolution of psychological or moral conflict than the collision of the ancient and the modern, the rupture between the individual and the social order, Sardinia and the 'continente', ethnography and fiction; the contradictions and paradoxes of Deledda's work, and indeed her very ambition to become the creator and writer of the Sardinian popular epic, illuminate a critical point in both Italian and Sardinian history.

Sardinia, long isolated from the rest of the world, was a land which had been subject to repeated and brutal invasion. Before the start of Unification in 1860, the Kingdom of Sardinia was kingdom in name only, in reality annexed as a colony to Piedmont. For D.H. Lawrence it is 'this old Sardinia, at last being brought to heel', which is the real theme of Grazia Deledda's books.[8] The 'old Sardinia' had been subject to countless invaders - Phoenicians, Greeks, Romans and Catalans as well as, more recently, city-states from the Italian mainland – who brought with them no technical or agricultural skills; for centuries the land continued to be worked as in Roman times. Sards knew little of industry and less of commerce, province of the foreigner, and there was little opportunity for the development of a trading middle class with an interest in technological innovation. Endemic malaria and an inadequate diet meant susceptibility to disease; yet even at the end of the nineteenth century, doctors and hospitals remained virtually unknown.[9]

Popular uprisings by the Sards against their foreign rulers throughout the eighteenth and nineteenth centuries were crushed by the punitive expeditions of the Piedmontese Viceroys, and with the greatest of brutality. The new central government regularly despatched large numbers of armed forces to both Sicily and Sardinia to quell the unrest created by their own policies, while the later 'Partito Sardo d'Azione', the Sardinian Action Party, was frequently referred to as the Italian Sinn Féin. Rebels were torn to pieces by savage dogs, burnt alive, hanged from the gallows which dotted Sardinian plains, and mass arrests, imprisonment and execution continued to be the style of rule. Each era had its bandit hero, who became the stuff of legend among the people and the focus of rebellious sentiment. Despite attempted agrarian reforms, land was concentrated in the hands of a very few. Land enclosures over this period meant the end of common pasturage, while protectionist tariffs against France blocked a traditional outlet for Sardinian grain sales. Many died from hunger as a result.

Social relations in Sardinia were moulded by this context of millennial oppression. Sards eked out a living on small plots of barren land insufficient for their needs, with no technological innovations to offset the inherent difficulties posed by poor soil and harsh climate. This was the land which was still only just beginning to change by the time the Taviani brothers made their remarkable film *Padre padrone* in 1977. Christian doctrines made little headway in a land where vengeance was the basic law, and both the social and the natural world offered little hope of justice. Antagonism towards the foreigner, and hostility towards the 'continentali', as Gramsci pointed out, remained stamped into the minds of all.

With the political integration of Sardinia into the newly formed Italian nation-state, the question of the cultural relationship between the centre and the margin, of how Sardinia was to be represented and to represent itself within a larger sociopolitical entity, began to arise. Deledda's Olympian ambition was to become the epic singer of Sardinian life: 'By the time I'm thirty,' she wrote, 'I want to have reached my marvellous goal, which is to create all by myself a literature which is completely and exclusively Sardinian.'[10] Deledda's ambition is an affirmation of Sardinian cultural difference, with a simultaneous desire for an acceptable representation of Sardinia to the centralized state. Hers is the cultural paradox of all smaller societies faced with larger and more powerful ones, the delicate dialectic of identification and alterity. Her reference to the mainland as the 'terre civili', the 'civilized lands' where she wished Sardinia to take a higher and more noble place in the public imagination, reveals the deeply ingrained feeling of inferiority of small communities deprived of power.

Deledda had no need of a Sardinian Pitré, the anthropologist and chronicler of rituals and customs in Sicily on whom Verga had drawn heavily for his narratives. She herself collected and published material on the language, customs, habits and rituals of her people, and she takes an unfailingly sympathetic – if unsentimental – view of the lower classes of Sardinian society, driven by need to lay hands on the property of others and to be economical with the truth. Deledda recounts with amused irony the story of the 'famous peasant who tried to deceive the father confessor telling him he had stolen a rope, and who on the insistent questioning of the good priest finished up admitting that the rope had an ox attached to the other end' (*Cosima* p. 751).

Deledda finds herself, as mediator between two cultures, caught between conflicting demands. Marxist critics have reproached her for failing to take up the position of the Gramscian intellectual, for interposing an ambiguous personal ideology between Sardinian reality and her representation of it, for avoiding the real issue.[11] To some readers, her tales of patriarchal society, sexual taboo, violent and illicit passions, remorse and penance seem at times curiously dislocated from contemporary social and cultural structures. Deledda's work lies outside the intellectual sphere of Marx or Taine, in that it sets out to present not an analysis of specific social configurations but a synthetic, tragic and pessimistic vision of mankind beset by the moral problem of evil, sin, suffering and remorse. In Deledda's fictional writing, the landscape of Sardinia becomes transformed, transfigured almost, into a stylized, virtually ritualistic backdrop which both reflects and participates in human vicissitudes.

Deledda's work is not objective social documentary or ethnographical enquiry, but a subjective vision formed by the cultural and sociopolitical complexities of her age. If Deledda can be seen as a writer whose narrative strategies are both Realist and Romantic, her work simultaneously addresses another paradox in that personal dilemmas and passions are seen in terms of both identifiable social constructions and more ancient laws of the blood. In the novels, a traditional Mediterranean code of honour combines with a Catholic sense of sin to produce works whose ethical dilemmas point to the diverse levels of social code laid down in Sardinia over the centuries. It is the clash between the old and the new, the individual and the moral order, the margin and the centre, the male and the female, which constitutes the core of her work, and the consequences of transgression of rigid codes which form its drama.

The fundamental theme in Deledda's work is love: not dallying romance, but a love which is passionate, all-embracing, irrational, consuming and invariably transgressive. Incestuous or oedipal, breaking the sacrament of marriage, the barrier of class or the vow of celibacy, love in Deledda's work presses against social and sexual parameters, and always stands in contrast to the Law (of the Church, of public seemliness, of deeply ingrained incest taboos). Deledda goes some way towards questioning social and religious laws which legitimize some objects of desire and place others beyond acceptable reach, or make all women subject to all men. However, the centre of her work is neither social criticism nor psychological pathology but an investigation of the conflict between different ethical orders. If transgression is the crossing of a boundary, it is the moment when the individual reaches that boundary that interests her. Transgression in her work is a moment of rupture, a nexus of psychological, social and historical collision.

Deledda's classical, fatalistic notion of love as blind, unstoppable and irresistible passion is seen clearly in her first masterpiece, *Elias Portolu* (1903). Returning to Sardinia and to his family after some years spent in a mainland prison, Elias falls in love with Maddalena, his brother's fiancée. His feelings are reciprocated, but he is incapable of taking any action to relieve their desperation. The marriage goes ahead, while their continuing affair produces a child. Elias fails to follow the advice of Zio Martinu, for whom proof of manhood would be to transform Maddalena into a legitimate object of sexual desire by marrying her: he will then tire of her soon enough. He decides to study to become a priest, and even on the death of his brother is unable to stop the slide towards disaster by marrying Maddalena himself. The child dies and his vows are confirmed: Maddalena marries another man.

Elias's state, the moral weakness pointed to by his effeminate, pallid appearance, and his now impure dialect after years in a mainland prison, finds its corollary in nature, which serves as an anthropomorphic mirror-image to his own intensity of feeling. Passion is suggested in the darkness of the night, the brightness of the moon, the sweet and heady intensity of night-time fragrances. The landscape in *Elias Portolu* both bears witness to and participates in his suffering. Like Dante's illicit lovers Paolo and Francesca, Elias is buffeted by the winds of guilty passion, desire and pain, and Deledda leans towards an extreme Catholic Manichaeism, whereby love becomes inverted into an emotion which is wholly depraved. She carefully delineates every vacillation, every shift in emotion. Elias's passion makes him not stronger but weaker; he is dominated by feelings of rage, anger and jealousy. His kindness towards his own child, Berto, is inspired not by paternal affection but by an irrational hope that the child will prefer him to Maddalena's new suitor. His decision to become a priest is an attempt to shore up the broken barrier of kinship with a further social taboo, to seek protection from temptation in the sacramental vow of celibacy. In consciously - almost deliberately – avoiding the resolution of his dilemma, he fails to escape the double bind of passion and guilt. This is not sententious moralizing but a fatalistic, pessimistic conviction that mankind is fragile and almost always doomed to fail.

Cenere (Ashes, 1904) inspired the film of the same title which saw Eleonora Duse's only appearance on the big screen.[12] *Ashes* explores a psyche torn between ambitions in the world and an interior life which is damaged, stunted, and unable to develop. In this novel, the young woman Oli (the part played by Duse) falls pregnant after an affair with a married man. Disowned by her family and sent to a remote village, she later takes her son to his father, abandoning him to an environment which offers him the social and educational advantages she cannot herself provide. The separation from and loss of the mother haunts the boy Anania, notwithstanding the favour he finds with his new, wealthy *padrino*, who sends him to Cagliari and then to Rome to study. A number of years later the longed-for meeting with Oli takes place, but it is, of course, a disaster. Oli's wretchedness (she has been wandering the island as a beggar) mocks Anania's desire for reunion, even though his humiliation of and contempt for his mother suggest his own disillusion and uncertainty, the cultural dilemma which would have the flesh-and-blood mother as iconic source of life and purity. In this scheme of things Oli must inevitably die – to free her son into a better material and economic way of life, but also to cut the umbilical cord of regressive fantasy. Oli commits suicide, cutting her own throat. Anania opens the locket she placed round his neck before leaving him as a child; it turns out to contain nothing but dust. It is only with the self-erasure of the woman, her second sacrifice, that Anania is freed from his incestuous, destructive obsession with his mother's body which will now, like the talisman he has worn round his neck all these years, turn to nothing but dust. In his brutal domination of his mother, his adoption of the role of *paterfamilias,* Anania also adumbrates a massive Sardinian inferiority complex in which personal identity, in the face of adversity and repression, resides in the forms and roles sanctioned by patriarchy.

Ashes, then, is a remarkably restrained but subtle account of an oedipal obsession, written in the key not of fashionable psychoanalysis but of moral tragedy. Anania bears the name of his father, who is the object of his fervent imagination and fantasies during his early years with Oli. The coincidence of names underlines the parallel search of father and son for what is lost and hidden. Anania *père*'s original seduction of Oli takes place in the context of his search for buried treasure, a fantasy with obvious Freudian overtones, and the erotic connotation of treasure is repeated and extended in the boy's increasingly obsessive imagining of his mother, his intense desire to 'penetrate into the fantastic world of that mysterious continent where his mother was in hiding!'[13]

Oli herself can clearly be seen as the victim of a society where women as sexual prey are then brutally abandoned to the consequences of their passions, where unsanctioned sexual activity means ostracism from both society and family. She is taken to live with the widow of a bandit; both women are placed outside the law by the actions of their men. Deledda is conscious of the injustice and inequality suffered by women, but she adheres to no utopian social or political creed which would contemplate change or progress. While her instinctive compassion for the poor and oppressed may point her in the direction of Socialism, her historical sense is very different from the one which would take class struggle and control of the means of production as the primary spring of an inevitably linear and progressive human history. Deledda's representation of history as cyclical, reiterative, reflects a Sardinian mentality born of more than a thousand years of repression, and her character Anania reflects this ideological disjuncture between a traditional understanding of human affairs and a desire for integration and change, embodying the difficuties of a culture coming to terms with its own tormented past.

We never discover what the locket originally contained. Anania's bitter entry into adult life is expressed in an image which reiterates the underlying pessimistic theme of the novel: "Now I understand what man is: a vain flame which passes through life and turns everything it touches to ash, and is extinguished only when there is nothing else to be destroyed" (*Ashes*, p. 250).

Canne al vento (*Reeds in the Wind*, 1913) is again the story of incestuous, misdirected desire, of decadence, of a past crime which continues to undermine the social and psychological order. The three Pintor sisters live in increasingly straitened circumstances, their wealth reduced to a small patch of land worked by the faithful servant Efix. Into this atmosphere of repression and decline comes Giacinto, son of a dead fourth sister, Lia, who escaped the oppression of their father, Don Zame, by running away to the mainland. Lia's scandalous disappearance, followed by her marriage to a man not of her own social class, was clearly provoked by the young woman's emotionally repressive education. As well as being compelled to sew, cook and make bread, the sisters were forbidden 'to raise their eyes in the presence of men, nor could they turn their thoughts to any man who was not destined to be their husband. But the years went by and the husband never came.'[14]

Lia escaped with the help of Efix, secretly and guiltily in love with her. Her son Giacinto, far from fulfilling vaguely expressed hopes that he will save the family from final ruin, takes to drink and signs false money orders in his aunt's name. Meanwhile Efix, unable to relay Noemi's (another of the sisters) refusal of marriage to her suitor Don Predu, and overcome with the burden of guilt at the family's ruin (for it was he who, albeit in self-defence, murdered the tyrannical Don Zame), runs away from the family to wander the island as a beggar. This penitential pilgrimage from one religious festival to another is perhaps the least successful part of the book in that it distracts from the tight story line, but it does give Deledda a chance to explore what remains, for her, one of the most fascinating aspects of Sardinian life. Efix eventually returns, seriously ill, to the Pintor family, where his death becomes a symbolic sacrifice that enables the family to rise again through the marriage of Noemi, who finally consents to wed the wealthy Don Predu.

The family drama, with its conflicting elements of passion and crime, is played out against a Nature in which man finds an image of his own existential condition, a reflection of his own painful, suffering sense of reality, which recalls the work of Thomas Hardy. The late-Romantic pathetic fallacy is juxtaposed to a conception of justice which glimpses, but finally draws back from, a Socialist sense of justice. At the end of a working day Efix surveys the land which, the text half suggests, should be his by virtue of his labour, 'the little farm which Efix considers more his than his mistresses': thirty years of living and working on the land have made it his' (*Reeds in the Wind*, p. 171). But the Sardinia of Deledda's novels is a land at a crossroads, where the new is struggling to be born, where modern political ideologies are just beginning to be heard. Efix's claim on the land – and, indeed, to his years of unpaid wages – would find little political or ideological support in an island only recently released from its feudal bonds. In Deledda's work a modern egalitarian sympathy makes a strange bedfellow with ancient codes of honour and vengeance.

It is not only ethical codes which are underlined by paradox. Sardinia is a world as old as Virgil's; a parallel world of spirits and phantoms lives alongside not only mankind but the guardian angels of the Catholic faith. This is the same 'civiltà contadina', 'peasant civilisation', described in Carlo Levi's *Cristo si è fermato a Eboli* (*Christ Stopped at Eboli*, 1947). Peasants work the material land, but know that it is also spiritual and magical: 'Especially on moonlit nights, this whole mysterious life animates the hills and the valleys: man has no right to disturb them with his presence, just as the spirits have respected him throughout the course of the sun: and so it is time for him to retire and close his eyes under the protection of the guardian angels' (*Reeds in the Wind*, pp. 173–4). In this land of spirits, the laws of morality are as solid and inevitable as Newtonian physics. In murdering Don Zame, and in loving Lia, Efix has disturbed an order more profound than that of the distribution of property, and due retribution must be made. Indeed, the ghosts of the past, and the murdered Don Zame, hover over this landscape of spirits, haunting any idea of escape from past wrongs, any idea of progress, and undermining historical, linear time. Efix's years of unpaid service, his lengthy pilgrimage and his eventual death make some reparation for the original transgression and mark a (temporary) return to order.

The tone of *Reeds in the Wind* remains deeply pessimistic. Death and decay are present throughout the novel; the sisters' house overlooks the now disused cemetery, and while death can offer some sort of peace, the underlying disintegration and collapse cannot be halted. In the final analysis, Efix's sacrifice is a vain one, and in dying he foresees that Noemi's sacrifice will paradoxically continue the circle of crime and expiation. The sisters, Ruth, Esther, Lia (Leah) and Noemi (Naomi) all have Old Testament names, hinting at the impossibility of forgiveness; the sense of fatality and destiny at work suggests a pre-Christian code, where Jehovah, too, seeks vengeance. Noemi's marriage to Don Predu is doomed to continue the cycle of misery and transgression, as she sacrifices herself to the advantage of her family. As she leans over the dying Efix to show him her wedding dress, 'she was pale, in her brocade dress, her angry eyes full of tears' (*Reeds in the Wind*, p. 383). She has sacrificed herself to the family fortune, but there will be a heavy price to pay, as Efix himself half realizes: 'She will be like the Queen of Sheba. But even the Queen of Sheba was not happy. . . . Noemi, too, will tire of her golden cross and will want to go far away, like Lia, like the Queen of Sheba, like everyone. . . .' (*Reeds in the Wind*, p. 384). The uneasy truce achieved at the end of the novel rests on a deeper belief that mankind is doomed to tread for ever the same paths of sorrow and suffering. Men and women are simpy 'reeds in the wind': 'some bend and some break, some resist today but will bend tomorrow and then will break' (*Reeds in the Wind*, p. 370).

The eponymous protagonist of *Marianna Sirca*, (Marianna Sirca, 1915) brought up in the house of her uncle, a priest, has become his heir after looking after the sick man for the last few years of his life. Visiting her father's lands she meets Simone Sole, a bandit whom she knew as a servant in her house many years before. *Marianna Sirca* evolves with the tragic inevitability of Greek drama. Once feelings have been released, they cannot be recalled; the novel concentrates on the dark emotions which hold sway over all else. Both are seized with the violent passion typical of so many of Deledda's characters. They decide to marry; but their passion is tinged less with romance than with the desire for self-affirmation. Marianna wishes to show that she is a free and independent woman, a *padrona*, by marrying whomsoever she chooses, even a bandit, while marriage to Marianna would legitimate Simone and enable him to enter the social class which has hitherto rejected him. Marianna's agreement to marriage is accompanied by the *sine qua non* that Simone give himself up to the legal authorities and serve out any imposed prison sentence, thus reconstituting himself as a member of the legitimate social order.

Simone is approached by other bandits more ruthless and vicious than himself. Mocked by those he admires for giving in to a woman, for letting himself be talked into losing his most valued possession, his liberty, he sends his servant Costantino to inform Marianna of his change of heart. Marianna's response of scorn and contempt is a challenge to Simone's courageous virility, and he visits her once more to persuade her to agree to his terms. Marianna's cousin Sebastiano, meanwhile, in the absence of any positive resistance to her affair by her father, has taken upon himself the role of *paterfamilias*. He challenges and fatally wounds Simone as he leaves his encounter with Marianna. Brought inside, about to die, Simone slips a ring on to Marianna's finger; this is their only wedding.

The relationship of ruling to subservient class underlies the love between the protagonists. Simone justifies his banditry as the only way out of poverty for his family in an archaic society with a rigid class structure; he simultaneously claims innocence for himself as a victim of the law, insisting that he has never shed human blood. Deledda effectively defuses any romantic interpretation of the story, whereby young girls secretly fall in love with the glamour and swagger represented by the male who successfully and courageously defies the law. What he half-consciously seeks in marrying Marianna is revenge on the social class from which he has been excluded by birth, an exclusion for which he has been unable to compensate through brigandage. Marianna is seen as the equivalent of property: 'Marianna, who used to order him about, who wouldn't even look at him, Marianna loved him and had promised to wait for him. . . . Taking hold of her was to take hold of all the things which she represented.'[15]

Marianna Sirca is in many ways a interpretation of Giovanni Verga's short story 'L'amante di Gramigna', 'Gramigna's Lover', in which the girl leaves her family and community to live with the bandit-hero, attracted by the ancient tradition of maleness and virility which he represents. If Simone is less than heroic, then Marianna likewise seeks escape from a role imposed upon her. Refusing the position of woman as exchangeable currency or goods (which Simone would ironically impose on her afresh), an item of value in a patriarchal society, she will dispose of her wealth – and her body – as she wishes: '"You used to shut Marianna up, like a coin inside a box, but she has got out. Yes, I will marry a servant, a bandit: what do you care? But at least he does not look on me for my possessions. Yes, I will marry him. I am my own mistress"' (*Marianna*, p. 855). With the death of Simone, for the first time in Deledda's work a murder committed by a member of the ruling class, both Marianna's aspirations to self-determination and Simone's hope to erase class difference are destroyed. Sebastiano represents traditional, patriarchal power, and his function in killing

Simone is to stamp out any sexual or class rebellion. Marianna renounces love, the instinctive demands of the body, and is restored to the legitimate social order.

La madre (*The Mother*, 1920), introduced to the British public by D.H. Lawrence, focuses on a triangular relationship between Paolo, Agnese, and Paolo's mother, Maria Maddalena. Paolo is a priest; his love for Agnese therefore breaks the law of celibacy to which he has sworn allegiance. Aware of the temptation to which her son is succumbing, the mother urges him to break off the affair. Much of the novel is taken up with Paolo's inner conflict as he struggles between the instinctive sexual drive, the bodily need for life and love, and the denial of the flesh demanded by his priestly functions and his mother as representative and reminder of the Law. His mother, and the Church, finally win out, and Paolo reluctantly and unwillingly resists Agnese's entreaties for them to run away together. In a spirit of revenge, Agnese threatens to reveal their relationship to the crowd attending Mass the next day. In the closing scenes of the novel, set dramatically in the church itself, Paolo's fear is allayed at last when Agnese fails to carry out her threat, instead falling on her knees at the altar. The mother, aware of the risk to her son, has been watching from the back of the church: with the danger of revelation passed, Paolo emerges from the sacristy to find his mother dead.

It is less morality than the moral dilemma which engages Deledda, and takes her close to writers such as Dostoevsky and Gide. The mother, Maria Maddalena (Mary Magdalene), spent years slaving in a seminary in order for her son to receive his religious training. Paolo feels neither pride nor gratitude, but the less lofty emotion of shame for his mother, a mere kitchen servant. His lukewarm vocation is coupled with the lost right to live as other men, even the most humble or criminal. The mother's delicate questioning of the enforced celibacy of the priesthood suggests Deledda's fascination with this ultimate taboo, which goes against the sexual laws not only of society but of God. Her concern is with the struggle between the individual and society, law and instinct; between order and desire, the ethical code and a desire for gratification and fulfilment.

The novel is set in a remote village where Paolo and his mother are sent following his ordination. His congregation are unaccustomed to seeing the application of moral rigour either in themselves or in their priest: the previous incumbent, alcoholic and degenerate, could not be replaced while he was still alive for fear of his revenge on any successor. In this wild place, where even the priest shuns faith in favour of ancient moral codes, Christianity has laid only a thin veneer over more pagan beliefs: a sick man escapes from his house in order to go and die alone; Paolo guiltily gains much respect from the people for a knowingly fake exorcism. Against this background, the new priest's struggle with himself takes on an edge of primitive, instinctive passion removed from the domain of social morality. Passion is here laid bare in a rugged and harsh landscape which is as inhospitable to refinement of feeling, as ferocious and starkly instinctual, as Emily Brontë's wild Yorkshire moors.

But the mother, who has sacrificed herself in order to make her son a priest, now demands a sacrifice in return. Paolo's dilemma, between desire and conscience, is also the choice to be made between mother and lover, dependence and adulthood, Christianity and paganism. His sacrifice not of himself but of Agnese, his immolation of one woman to another, has overtones of Lawrence's own *Sons and Lovers*. Deledda, Catholic as she may be, is engaged not in moralistic propaganda but in exploring a deeper sense of the justice of pagan sensuality than Pauline theology which would annihilate the body. Agnese is prevented from taking her revenge on her faithless lover by another kind of law, that of her class. Sitting in the church watching Paolo celebrate Mass, she experiences a more authentic sacrifice, to a social order whose roots go deeper than Christian feeling in the village. Agnese's decision not to denounce the priest is made not out of the same fear felt by Paolo, but out of adherence to the ancient law of blood caste which has governed and formed Sardinian society over the centuries.

While in *Reeds in the Wind* the names of the Pintor sisters are Old Testament, those in *The Mother* are New Testament: St Paul, the apostle of chastity; St Agnes, the virgin martyr; and, perhaps ironically, Mary Magdalene, the converted whore. The earlier novel shows an almost Sophoclean sense of fate, an Aristotelian *hamartia* which must be expiated before order can be restored in a land inhabited by spirits. *The Mother*, on the other hand, perhaps demonstrates the impossibility of a Christian tragedy; the death of the mother has nothing of the same symbolic power of inevitability as that of Efix. This is also a narrative in which, like the land it depicts, one ethical code is laid over another, one social order is beginning to displace another; where a strong Catholic sense of sin is combined with a pagan sense of morality, where angels and spirits live side by side and fight for the souls of men.

Many more examples could be adduced from Deledda's work of the rupture between the ancient and the new, progressive and fatalistic visions of the human condition. Her seemingly paradoxical pluralism is symptomatic of the complex social and political culture in which she worked, and the taboos and transgressions which she explores in her novels mark the moments of contact and collision between individual desire and social ethics, between a pagan and a Catholic view of the world, between an ancient culture and a new political reality.

5
Breaking the Chain:
Sibilla Aleramo (1876–1960)

It is the woman who must speak. And it is not only the woman Anaïs who must speak, but I must speak for many women.

(Anaïs Nin, *Diary*)

When Sibilla Aleramo's *Una donna* (*A Woman*, 1906) was reprinted in 1973, Maria Antonietta Macciocchi celebrated the reappearance of a book 'which pushes forward the battle for female emancipation', and speaks not to the past but to the present: 'It is not the book which belongs to the past, but the world which surrounds us, a world crushed by bourgeois and petit-bourgeois moral hypocrisy.'[1]

Aleramo engaged with feminism in its most expansive moment at the end of the nineteenth century and beginning of the twentieth. The tensions she attempted to resolve in her own life are those which occupy her theoretical writing; the private sphere is also recognized as political moment. Emerging into the ferment of the neo-feminist movement in Italy, Aleramo's novel, almost seventy years on, compelled a rather depressing evaluation of the achievements of women in Italy since Aleramo first walked away from the domestic hearth and became famous by telling her tale, and Macciocchi sounds a note of despair that the regressive social order of the 1970s would have been instantly recognizable to the older author. With its devastating critique of the moral hypocrisy and intellectual sloth of small-town, small-minded bourgeois Italy, the novel provided a crucial link between Italian feminists from the early and late twentieth century, a history disrupted by the hiatus of Fascism and decades of reactionary politics – a link of political solidarity and common interests which was to displace the 'monstrous chain of servitude', the subservience imposed by a patriarchal society which

Aleramo diagnosed as restraining both the lives and the creativity of women.

When it was first published, in 1906, *A Woman* was an instant success both in Italy and abroad. Aleramo was not the first woman writer to achieve public and critical acclaim in Italy, but she was the first to do so with a novel which strongly challenged the social, moral and legal condition of the new State, one in which the condemnation of women's oppression is accompanied by a lucid analysis of social and family structures which underpin the stability of the dominant order and keep women in their allotted roles. Aleramo dissects the condition specifically of middle-class women, uninformed, unemployed, undefended by common class interest, subject to the prevailing moral and social hegemony of a patriarchal society backed by a strong Catholic Church. The exalted rhetoric of noble womanhood, wifely and maternal duty and self-sacrifice, was held in place by a legal, scientific and religious establishment which proclaimed with one voice woman's inferiority, her unsuitability for intellectual activity, her delicacy which enabled her to bear repeated enforced pregnancies and to act as guardian angel to the weary husband and innocent child, but not to administer her own property, vote, or have any say in family, let alone national, matters. In the barely disguised autobiography of *A Woman*, Aleramo exposes the family as an oppressive institution rooted in a misogynistic social and legal culture, and recounts her own search for an alternative to the manifold public and private constraints on femininity which is neither the madness into which her own mother sinks nor the death which she herself contemplates. For Aleramo to write is an act both of personal catharsis and of cultural revolution.

Sibilla Aleramo was born Rina Faccio in August 1876, the eldest of four children. *A Woman* gives an account of Rina's childhood, and particularly of her fascination with her father Ambrogio, atheist, nonconformist, a positivist and a scientist. Rina's mother at this point is merely a shadowy figure eclipsed by the strength of her feelings for her father: 'My exclusive passion for my father completely dominated me. I loved my mother, but my adoration for my father was without limits. I was aware of this difference, but I did not dare try to ascertain its cause' (*Una donna*, p. 10). When Rina was barely a teenager the family made a fateful move from

Milan to the provincial town of Porto Civitanova Marche, where
her father was to take over the management of a glass factory.

The father–daughter bond was, if anything, strengthened as the
urban, modern, Northern family encountered more archaic forms
of social organization. Local women were astonished when the
new Director refused their chickens, offered in favour of their sons,
and local dignitaries were offended when he refused to take on the
trappings of the ruling class, turning down the presidency of this or
that association or club. If the father did not act like a member of
the ruling class, neither did the daughter act like a woman: 'The
servants must have told some dreadful stories about me in the town:
I never picked up a needle, never paid any attention to the housework' (*A Woman*, p. 31). Difference from local customs swiftly slid
into suspected deviance, with insidious rumours circulating about
the unnatural relationship between father and daughter.

Given the lack of any provincial schooling beyond the age of
twelve, the young Rina was sent to work in her father's factory;
here she was courted and seduced by one Ulderico Pierangeli,
tempted perhaps as much by the idea of the boss's daughter as
by an attractive young woman. In *A Woman* Aleramo treats the
seduction scene with depth and discretion. While Pierangeli clearly
takes illicit advantage of a young and inexperienced girl, Rina is
made more vulnerable both by her ignorance of her own sexuality
and by the headlong disintegration of family life, compounded by
her knowledge that her beloved father is betraying his wife, and
his daughter, by having a none-too-secret affair which is the fount
of common gossip. Rina, believing herself less in love than now
belonging in some way to Pierangeli, marries him, still only sixteen
years old.

Rina's married life is marked by the sexual brutality and lack of
delicacy of her husband, her mother's despair, attempted suicide,
madness and subsequent institutionalization, the distraction of her
now openly philandering father and the social and intellectual
limitations of provincial life, where 'women for the most part
never went out of the house, were ignorant, lazy and superstitious'
(*A Woman*, p. 12). The narrowness of the customs, restrictions
and expectations of provincial life become an increasing burden
for a young woman with rapidly expanding cultural and literary
horizons, and a growing interest in culture and politics both in Italy

and abroad. Aleramo is relentless in her exposure of the dishonesty of both public and private life:

> There was enormous hypocrisy in the town. In reality parents, among both the bourgeoisie and the workers, were calmly exploited and ill-treated by their children; many mothers in particular took beatings in silence. Not a single wife was honest with her husband about the housekeeping money, not a single husband took the whole of his pay-packet home. Few couples remained faithful to each other. Just a short time before, a vicious parricide had plunged one household into mourning: the son had caught his father with his own wife. Many girls sold themselves, without the compulsion of hunger, for some bauble; by the age of fourteen none of them was totally innocent. But there they were in their homes proclaiming their candour, daring the town to prove otherwise. Hypocrisy was considered a virtue. Woe betide anyone who spoke against the sanctity of matrimony or the principle of paternal authority! (*A Woman*, pp. 68–9)

Her wretched marriage, a jealous husband who proposes that she should commit suicide when there are whispers that she has responded to the attentions of another man, and a widening gap between her sense of her own potential and her inability to conform and unwillingness to succumb, make Rina's 'instant and irresistible' sympathy with nascent international feminist thought almost inevitable:

> Almost without my noticing, my mind had lingered a little longer each day around that word 'emancipation' which I remembered hearing when I was a small child, pronounced seriously by my father and then with increasing derision by all manner of men and women. . . . And I experienced something approaching a religious conversion. (*A Woman*, p. 115)

While Rina's intellectual horizons begin to broaden, her emotional sensibility is marked indelibly by the experience of maternity. The experience of creativity, in motherhood or in writing, is – curiously – seen to have a single source: 'he belonged to me, because I alone gave myself to him. His father, his grandmother, all the others enjoyed the spectacle, but it was I who *authored* it' (*A Woman*, p. 19, emphasis added).

The significance of *A Woman* lies less in its potential as socio-logical document or radical feminist tract than in its representation of a woman struggling to establish a separate identity in the face of a culture which would define her in functional terms as wife and mother, in its clear depiction of the high price exacted for her freedom, in the struggle to claim a subjective speaking voice whereby an achieved separate identity means the loss of all that had previously defined her situation in the world, as well as that which she held most dear. Aleramo's feminism, like that of her peers, aimed not at the dissolution but at the reform of the family. She leaves the reader in no doubt as to the depth of her passion for her small son, Walter; she is convincing in her jealousy when she is unable to feed him herself, and eloquent on both the joys and the responsibilities of the bond between mother and child.

The 'woman question' had become increasingly pressing in the second half of the nineteenth century, following Unification. It was given enormous impetus by the entry of women into the factory workforce, a move which happened on a massive scale in Italy. The nascent Socialist movement allied women with workers, and the first union was organized by Paolina Schiff in 1883 in Milan. In the golden years of Italian feminism there were numerous journals, associations, surveys (on prostitution, divorce, suffrage). Rina began contributing to journals such as the feminist *Vita Moderna* (Modern Life) and the cultural and political magazine *Vita Internazionale* (International Life), whose contributors included Ada Negri, Neera and Emilio De Marchi (1851–1901), and leading political and sociological thinkers such as Cesare Lombroso. As well as reviews of writers such as Grazia Deledda, Rina offered sociological articles describing the lives of women as she saw them. Paolina Schiff, one of the leading figures of the emancipationist movement at the time, asked her to form a Women's League in the Marche. The project floundered, but in 1899 an offer to direct *L'Italia Femminile*, set up in Milan by Emilia Mariani, journalist, feminist activist, and worker for women's suffrage, coincided with her husband's dismissal from his job after an altercation with her father. Her job with the journal was hampered by her husband's insistence that she work largely

from home, but during the brief months in which she controlled
L'Italia Femminile it became more attentive to cultural and political
matters, and gave a considerable amount of space to information
on feminist movements abroad. In this position Rina made contact
with writers and activists such as Paolina Schiff, Matilde Serao, Ada
Negri and Emilia Majno, founder of the Women's Union, as well
as Filippo Turati (1857–1932), leader of the Socialist movement in
Italy, and Anna Kuliscioff. Rina became closely involved with the
Women's Union and its struggle against the slave trade in women;
the Union also expended much time and energy on philanthropic
missions which drew in women from the middle classes to work
in conjunction with local authorities and organizations.

In the meantime, Rina Faccio's father had been displaced as
manager of the glass factory. Ambrogio exploited the low cost
of local labour and took on more underage employees than
was permitted by law. Workers were, it seems, dismissed on
the slightest of pretexts, and protection in the workplace was
minimal. Ambrogio's authoritarian rule had unwittingly been a
significant factor in the rise of local Socialist groups – strikers
were as likely as not to be greeted by Signor Faccio brandishing
a pistol. Rina was compelled to return to the provinces following
her husband's appointment to replace her father, although her
departure was delayed as she watched over the death of her
closest friend, a young Norwegian designer whose imported ideas
on feminism went much further and deeper than the somewhat
limited emancipationism of the Italian movement, embracing an
ill-defined – if all-embracing – reform of consciousness. Just one
year later she abandoned her house and her family, and headed
for Rome. She was not to see her son Walter again for more than
thirty years.

The search for autonomous identity described in *A Woman*
is paralleled and reflected by the search for a speaking voice.
Aleramo begins her literary career as a reader, eagerly subscribing
to national and international journals. Her early writing, she tells us,
is solipsistic, introverted, designed for no other reader than herself,
diaristic – the most common form of women's writing. Gradually
she moves from the introspective diary to articles and features for
social and cultural journals, finally taking the enormous step of
claiming autobiographical subjectivity, inviting the reader to adopt

her perspective and share her experience in the first person. While the book is a powerful challenge to women readers to engage in the analysis of family and legal institutions in relation to their own lives, the book's addressee, we learn on the final page, is indeed Walter, her son. The personal and the political fuse: if she cannot tell her son of her love, she will write it, while the very need to write is an indictment of a social system which wrenches her from him.

Few observers have failed to acknowledge Aleramo's extraordinary step in distancing herself from her husband, from her domestic role, from the constricting *petit-bourgeois* expectations among which she lived, and, in particular, from her son. That to win her own life entailed losing her child was the clearest of demonstrations – were any needed – of the impossibility for her and her contemporaries of evading the limitations of prescribed subject positions, being both independent woman and wife, writer and mother. Aleramo's revered Ibsen might almost have written the script of her life as she finally leaves, for Nora's departure anticipates Sibilla's own:

> HELMER: Before everything else, you're a wife and mother.
> NORA: I don't believe that any longer. I believe that before everything else I'm a human being – just as much as you are. . . . Or at any rate I shall try to become one. (*A Doll's House*, Act III)

Such, then, are the events related in sober, spare style in *A Woman*. The novel ends with Aleramo's marginalization by the law: once she distances herself from her family, the law proclaims itself against her. She is given no access to her son, let alone custody. Divorce is not an option, and she is encouraged to regard herself as fortunate in so far as Pierangeli does not force her return to the family home, an option legally available to him. Left money by a relative, she cannot inherit without Pierangeli's permission, which is denied. The book is extraordinary even today as an assertion of emancipationist feminism, in its powerful demand for legal guarantees and economic parity, for the regeneration and reform of personal and family life. The enduring power of *A Woman* lies in its overlapping of the protagonist's dramatic consciousness of her own intolerable position with an increasing awareness that this is the story not of 'a woman' but of women, that the moral squalor of women's lives is the price of a social and political order based on property, exploitation and exclusive ownership. In her writings on feminism Aleramo gives a lucid account of the social, legal and cultural subordination of women, and to this extent the 'woman' of the title is Everywoman – or at least, every bourgeois woman in provincial Italy.

While *A Woman* was an instant success not only in Italy but also in France, Britain and Germany, the mixed response of contemporary reviewers was itself an indication of prevailing opinion and morality – including that of many women – which Aleramo sought to challenge. While several critics noted the book's modernity, others castigated the writer for abandoning both the conjugal home and her son. Female critics in particular accused her of unwomanliness: 'this woman, who becomes a rebel, lacks simplicity of heart, any sense of woman's highest virtue. She lacks faith . . . and flees the cradle of her child', reproaches one.[2] Laura Gropollo, while accusing Aleramo of making a fuss about nothing, gives an unintentionally gruesome glimpse of conjugal expectations at the turn of the century, when venereal disease was rife. 'Ibsen's Nora', she snorts, 'has spawned. . . . But the straw that broke Sibilla's back is the illness which her husband contracts when his wife is absent for some weeks. A malicious argument, because if all wives were to abandon their husbands made ill by human weakness it is plain to all how many hearths would remain deserted.'[3]

For Gina Lombroso, writing in 1907, 'the drama of Sibilla Aleramo's life as she presents it is not so much between this man and this woman but the struggle which the woman carries on with her own mother'.[4] Sibilla's discourse on motherhood in *A Woman*, more than a rationalization of her decision to 'break the chain' of maternal enslavement by leaving her son, can be read as a dialogue with her own mother, and with a submerged female tradition of despair and insanity. Sibilla's fear is that in failing to embrace the male hegemonic world-view, the only road for her to travel is that of madness. Early in the novel the unhappy solitude of a gifted woman deprived of intelligent love is equated with madness in the person of Sibilla's mother. Even the socially prescribed roles of daughter (she has cut off her own family ties), wife (her husband is having an affair) and mother (her own children disregard her) are barely available to her. The mother's fate can be seen as the result not of a psychological dysfunction but of social structures which deny the woman access to any role and purpose outside the domestic sphere.

The mother, Sibilla states clearly and repeatedly in *A Woman*, should act as teacher, guide and source of moral value, and she protests against a simultaneous lack of role models for her own life and for her art. The mother–daughter relationship adumbrated in *A Woman* anticipates Dacia Maraini's recent hugely successful novel *The Silent Duchess*[5] as it describes the initial favouring of the fascinating, powerful father over the shadowy mother figure; the mother's attempt at self-obliteration; a gradual, profound and shocking identification with the mother. Towards the end of *A Woman* the protagonist discovers that her mother, too, had considered abandoning husband and children, and it is no accident that this recognition of herself in her mother is coupled with the fear of a new pregnancy, of being pushed once more into the maternal role. If motherhood is socially and ideologically framed as sacrifice by a powerful clergy and a compliant bourgeoisie, existentially it can lead to 'crime and madness' (*A Woman*, p. 195), an attempt to erase the body which bears the crushing weight of patriarchal discourse.

A Woman is a lucid representation of its own times, and of the repressive social and political forces brought to bear in a fast-industrializing new Italy. Aleramo deplores such obvious outrages as enforced prostitution, the common practice of seizing women who are then compelled to marry in order to preserve the family honour (right up to the 1960s the crime of rape in Italian law was erased by a subsequent marriage of 'reparation'), and the blatant injustice that unfaithful men can pass on veneral disease to their wives without social condemnation, a situation which Anna Franchi had similarly denounced. Where Aleramo marks her difference is in her refusal to acquiesce, to conspire with her own degradation and to linger in the twilight of consciousness, like her peers who 'vegetate in somnolent self-satisfaction, feeling themselves caressed and adored and even, greatest indignity of all, pitied and consoled . . . and whom men praise to the skies as living proof of the sanctity of the old ideas'.[6]

Aleramo scorned the intellectual sloth of the Italian female bourgeoisie, their acquiescence to a comfortable status quo. Yet despite her sense of frustration, she is convinced that the participation of middle-class women is crucial to the success of the feminist movement. The aristocracy, on the verge of extinction, is no longer a force to be reckoned with, while working-class women have learnt of a better future from their alliance with Socialism; only middle-class women remain desperately stuck in old patterns of thought and life. The bourgeois woman is, for Aleramo, the one most in need of emancipation and, simultaneously, the one whose move towards liberation would sweep away the old system: 'the one to strike the hardest blow against the barbaric and rotten social system which has until now caused the misery of the human race' (Conti and Morino, p. 133).

Aleramo locates the reason for the absence of a coherent feminist movement in the power of the Catholic Church, and the lack of a strong lay intellectual class. Catholicism sidelined women's energy into philanthropy and charity work rather than political analysis. Freethinkers in Parliament sent their daughters to be educated by the nuns, just as the men in the South sent their wives to Confession. She is also fully aware of the near-impossibility of achieving a national movement in a country so fragmented by history, experience and class. Aleramo points to the 'economic, moral and social unevenness which has been the scourge of the country for the past ten years' as the root cause of the absence of a real feminist movement on a par with that to be found elsewhere, and she was acutely aware that a united Italy held within its borders a wide diversity of temperament, history and experience.

Aleramo reserves a polemical contempt for women writers who hold on to the tailcoats of a male model of literature, who regard literature as some sort of fashion accessory designed to please and flatter men: if, so far as feminism as social and political movement was concerned, 'the fashion had blown in from France, just like for our hats' (*A Woman*, p. 75), neither was there a radical tradition of women's writing, even a suppressed one, on which to call, as there was in England or France. Like feminist critics many years later who saw in male texts an 'image of women' which confirmed and vindicated the female role prescribed by patriarchy, Aleramo pointed to the idealizing presentation of women in literature which had little to do with the real lives of real women. Petrarch and Dante spoke of Laura and Beatrice, not of the women they lived with and who bore their children. This, for Aleramo, is as hypocritical as the bourgeois mentality she despised: 'Why carry on contemplating in poetry a metaphysical woman and dealing in prose with a serving girl even if she has been legally wed?' (*A Woman*, p. 150). She decries the failure of women writers in Italy to forge what, in more contemporary parlance, might be called an *écriture féminine*, their willingness to adopt masculine models – to write, effectively, in a foreign idiom. She is indignant at the sight of 'mediocre' books signed by women which flooded into the journal, 'real parodies of the most fashionable male books. . . . How on earth could all those "intellectuals" not understand that woman cannot justify her entry into the already overcrowded field of literature and art, unless with works which bear her own stamp and imprint?' (*A Woman*, p. 135).

Aleramo recognizes that different linguistic registers and styles are not autonomous or equal in value, but reflect a complex web of intricate and hierarchical power relations, and that the dominant cultural and intellectual discourse in a patriarchal society is inevitably shaped and fashioned by that masculine power. She perceives the cultural language at her disposal to be that of a dominant male culture – in order to speak to men as an equal, she has had to learn their language. The task is a slow, painful one of accommodation: the woman writer is almost schizophrenic, experiencing a dramatic gulf between a verbal expression or form, and an inchoate inner sense of self: 'To understand man, to learn his language, has been to move away from my own self. In reality I do not express myself, nor do I even translate myself. . . . You will have to listen to me as if I were dreaming.'[7]

Aleramo takes pride in her ability to manipulate male discourse as well as any of her masculine colleagues. But to enter male discourse is to risk the disenfranchisement of female forms of expression which, for her, have yet to be realized. The world has to be renamed, rethought, in the feminine. Sibilla clearly anticipates the radical view expressed decades later by the feminist theorist and philosopher Adriana Cavarero, who writes: 'there is no mother tongue, since there is no language of woman. Our language is a foreign language which we have not learned by translation from our own tongue. And yet, it is not ours, it is foreign, suspended in a faraway place that rests upon the missing language.'[8] She would similarly recognize her own position in that taken up by French feminist theory and writers such as Hélène Cixous, and is remarkably close to their call for the emergence of new feminine discourses, for a linguistic utopia, and the dream that 'there will not be *one* feminine discourse, there will be thousands of different kinds of feminine words, and there will be the code for general communication, philosophical discourse, rhetoric like now but with a great number of subversive discourses in addition that are somewhere else entirely'.[9]

Aleramo rejects feminism as simply emancipation and equality, a kind of social and psychological transvestism whereby women ape the opposite sex as lesser writers ape male cultural form. She anticipates the feminist debates of the 1960s and 1970s, when the struggle was shifted away from the grounds of economy and independence to that of (self) representation. Aleramo's view of the socioeconomic goals of emancipation as too limited recalls the shift in the intellectual focus of neo-feminism. 'Woman', she states unequivocally, 'has never had real individuality: either she has accommodated herself to please men, not just physically but also morally, giving no credence to the imperatives of her own organism and her own psyche, or she has rebelled by copying him, distancing herself even further from the conquest of her own subjectivity.'[10]

The repressed, unformed feminine is that which does not express itself, which is silenced and hidden. These are the inner, bodily rhythms, forerunner to Julia Kristeva's semiotics, to which Aleramo sought to turn in her search for a truly feminine discourse which was not simply a travesty of male culture:

> We know now that human language is one, and has been from its remotest origins and in all parts of the world. But perhaps the secret laws of rhythm have a sex. If we are convinced of a deep spiritual differentiation between man and woman we must be persuaded that this implies a profound expressive diversity, and that an autocthonous mode of feeling and of thinking necessarily has its own style, and no other, however barbarous it may initially appear.[11]

Aleramo believed she came close to new forms of 'feminine' writing in works after *A Woman*, and it is worth while considering to what extent she achieved her aim. Her identification of new potentialities in her own writing, her statement of a substantive difference in style and technique between her first and subsequent works, is seen as liberation and mystical enlightenment. Her claims demonstrate a refreshingly unfeminine lack of modesty, as she speaks of 'a great astonishment, a sense of benediction which I called a rediscovered childhood when I felt within me an unhoped for secret harmony. And after that everything I wrote, in prose as well as poetry, was marked by an airy grace, and a musicality, which are missing from my first novel'.[12]

Aleramo produced more than twenty volumes of prose and poetry as well as publishing extensive diaries and collections of journalism. The greater part of her work, including that written in the third person, is autobiographical, an attempt to transform the material of her life into art, to live as the heroine of her own novel. Having cast off the roles of wife and mother, Sibilla takes on the mantle of tragic poet. She has little time for those women who regard her with admiration and awe while remaining confortably within their bourgeois niche, those women whose dreams and fantasies are anaesthetized by ether and morphine.

Aleramo's later autobiographical works, *Il passaggio* (The Passage, 1912) and *Amo dunque sono* (I Love, Therefore I Am, 1927), as well as her diaries, speak clearly of one woman's doomed search for love, for a reciprocal sense of sacrifice and heroism that she has experienced in her own life. Having broken free of social constraints and made the sacrifice demanded by the society and culture of her time, Aleramo was faced with an acute dilemma in both her life and her art. The difficulties of a woman both alone and with a 'past' were not necessarily mitigated by a feminist ethos still eager to proclaim the centrality of the family in social structures, and with the consolidation of Mussolini's Fascist state, feminism all but disappeared from Italian intellectual discourse. Sibilla sought – and failed to find – an all-encompassing love which would sweep aside the dictates of bourgeois morality. Despite her acute analyses of culture and women's part in literature, she found no direction to move in other than to be absorbed into the prevailing Decadentism.

It would be too much to demand of one woman that she be both social and cultural exemplar, that both her life and her art should be revolutionary, but there was in Aleramo a striking gulf in her later works between theory and practice, between 'life' and 'art', made all the more poignant by her own belief that she could fuse the two. While she anticipates literary and feminist theory to come fifty years later, the very need to restate the theoretical position is an admission of an earlier failure in practice. The large claim made by Virginia Woolf for Dorothy Richardson – that here at last was a woman who could write a 'woman's sentence' – would not seem to be translatable to Aleramo's own artistic practice and aesthetics. Aleramo claims more than is the normal lot of a woman of her times; but, rather than develop genuinely new forms for women's writing and consciousness, she is led to appropriate for her own gender a *fin-de-siècle* aestheticism quite at odds with the radical style and technique of her first novel. Sibilla's desire to write 'from the body', to develop a language and expressivity which springs not from (male) rationality but from the more complex, multiple and diffuse female physical experience, becomes submerged into a rhetorical, D'Annunzian mysticism closely related to the ethereal ambitions of any number of writers at the turn of the century.

While the dramatic modernity of *A Woman* was widely acknowledged, not all Aleramo's readers and critics were convinced by her efforts to turn herself into a work of art, to become both artist and muse in a mutual and reciprocal immolation to a higher transcendental, mystical principle of art. For the philosopher Benedetto Croce, this failure – or refusal – to differentiate between 'life' and 'art', far from heralding a new age, is a symptom of contemporary sickness, the affliction of aestheticism, the literary virus which had, for him, corrupted Italian cultural life. Sibilla's (all too brief) affair with the Futurist artist Umberto Boccioni brings into conflict two opposing visions of modernity. She offers herself as Boccioni's Muse in an image of fertility which is transcendental rather than physiological: from their union, male and female, intellect and passion, will spring forth not a child but a superior art form, a 'work of life'. Boccioni rejects her overdramatization of a coupling which he prefers to take more lightly: 'the catastrophic and literary character you give to this gay and, if you like, highly intelligent meeting of ours makes it impossible for me to approach you,' is his laconic response to Aleramo's pleading, and he taunts her with being 'a traditional plotter of amorous complications',[13] chiding her for living their affair as a tragic and melodramatic heroine, as an aspiring *femme fatale*, and for entertaining sentiments consonant not with the modern age at all but with the literature of degenerate Romanticism. In her attempt to forge a feminine aesthetic, Aleramo paradoxically turned to the most masculine of men, such as D'Annunzio and Giovanni Papini (1881–1956). With Dino Campana (1885–1932) she had a turbulent affair, frequently violent in its passion, which ended with Campana's madness.

Aleramo's reputation as a writer has always rested on her first work, *A Woman*. While in this early novel Aleramo describes her triumphant emergence from the social roles allotted to her, her transcendence of the mediocrity which taints bourgeois femininity, she attempts in subsequent works to retain her status of heroic individuality. The emancipationist feminism of the day could take her only so far, and could not conceive of the formation of new identities outside traditional gender structures. With the failure of feminist and sociocultural theory to carve out space for women such as Aleramo (and who knows how Ibsen's Nora fared?), the only models of self-representation available to her were the literary ones – the ethos of Romanticism, the philosophy of Nietzsche, the aesthetics of Decadentism. In denouncing the mediocrity of the lives and literature of bourgeois women, Aleramo veered dangerously close to adopting a Nietzschean position of innate superiority. Lucid in her analysis of the position of women in contemporary Italy, she was perhaps less articulate in the synthesis of her own artistic response. With the advent of Mussolini's Fascism the emancipation movement in Italy fell virtually silent for over twenty years. Aleramo's compassionate intelligence no longer found the supporting discipline of a sympathetic movement which could channel her energies. For many decades she lived on the twin margins of fame and starvation, revered for an achievement she could never repeat. With the arrival of the mass culture which was to typify the modern age, her increasingly exalted tone became less relevant to the daily lives of the majority of Italian women. Sibilla was left to pick up the crumbs of cultural rewards. Her contemporary Ada Negri, one-time fiery Socialist poet and in later years considerably more subdued in her political opinions, was awarded the Mussolini Prize by the Academy of Italy in 1930, and in 1940 was finally made a full member: 'After that, Negri too had the right to be called "Your Excellency", receive a monthly stipend, travel first class on a pass, carry a sword, and wear a plumed hat.'[14] Aleramo, too, was granted a small monthly pension by the Fascist state, but had to beg for it, her position not helped by the fact that one of the many assassination attempts on Mussolini's life was carried out by a lover, Tito Zaniboni, in 1925: Aleramo was promptly arrested and, albeit briefly, imprisoned. The real disaster of Sibilla Aleramo's life was perhaps less her marriage than her long, long search for something to replace it, and the arrival of a political culture which reinforced precisely those conceptions of women's roles and lives against which she had rebelled. Sibilla Aleramo died as late as 1962, an impoverished but proud old lady, just a few short years before her demands for political, social and cultural autonomy, silenced for half a century, were to be taken up again by a younger generation.

PART II
1922–64

6
From Fascism to Reconstruction

MUSSOLINI'S FASCIST STATE

After secret negotiations with both sides, Italy finally entered the First World War in 1915 on the side of the Allies. Despite a disastrous series of military operations, including the defeat at Caporetto in 1917, the Italians were able to share in the post-war spoils. Not all Italy's claims, however, which included large stretches of the Dalmatian coast, were met, and nationalist, irridentist sentiment was duly outraged at the failure to secure the Italian-speaking Fiume. The settlement was not in fact especially disadvantageous to Italy, but dissatisfaction was to be deliberately fostered in order to create a consoling and defensive myth of an Italy cheated by her European partners.

The battered economy of post-war Italy, inflation and unemployment, led to a high level of civic unrest. Although strikes tended to be spontaneous rather than organized by national unions, 1919 and 1920 saw the occupation of the factories in Turin, and some believed conditions were right for a Russian-style revolution. In fact, sporadic and half-hearted Socialist activism merely succeeded in provoking right-wing reaction. Labour leagues around the country – and not a few Socialist heads - were smashed by the emerging Fascist squads, who soon found they could destroy printing presses or deal out beatings and castor oil with little or no intervention by government or police. The Fascists' self-proclaimed task was not just the protection of property rights but the restoration of law and order. Disturbances were used by the Right as leverage on public opinion, to facilitate the imposition of authoritarian rule.

Benito Mussolini (1883–1945), former socialist, journalist, editor of the socialist newspaper *Avanti!* and self-proclaimed war hero, swept into power in 1922 with the notorious March on Rome, the beneficiary of an anxious capitalist class who feared a Bolshevik revolution in Italy, and willingly believed in Mussolini's promise to produce a strengthened state which would suppress the Red threat. Fascism emerged from the war as an opportunistic rather than ideological party, exploiting middle-class fears and socialist ineptitude, finding its constituency in patriotic sentiment and a growing cult of personality.

Once in power, the Fascists moved towards establishing a dictatorship. The intimidation of opposition deputies culminated in the murder, in 1924, of the socialist Giacomo Matteotti, for accusing Mussolini of electoral corruption. Even now, constitutional opposition proved ineffective and Mussolini survived the scandal, aided by the public support of liberals such as Benedetto Croce (1866–1952). Other writers and artists supported Mussolini, too: D'Annunzio was regarded by many as a proto-Fascist; the Futurists, led by Marinetti (1876–1944), proclaimed themselves Fascists, and the writer and dramatist Luigi Pirandello (1867–1936) also joined the Party in the aftermath of the Matteotti murder. By 1925 Mussolini's government had blatantly become a regime. Opposition deputies were routed, many of them fleeing abroad. The totalitarian, one-party state, Italian style, had arrived.

Mussolini's flair for self-publicity, however, outstripped his economic grasp. Modernization was piecemeal, and the state of Italian industry remained precarious, as totalitarianism led not to greater efficiency but to corruption. Neither did wages and conditions of employment improve. By the end of the Fascist era many Italians were still living in appalling housing and surroundings, while expenditure on social services was minimal. Standards of living generally declined, and as the traditional route of emigration gradually ceased to become an available option, overpopulation and insufficient employment continued to exacerbate social tensions.

FASCISM AND POLITICAL CONSENSUS

A number of more or less effective measures were introduced to achieve consensus and political legitimation of the regime. While there was clearly a gap between rhetoric and practice, between ambition and achievement, Fascism set itself the task of completing the Risorgimento, of transforming a disparate and fragmented nation into a single, unified and coherent state.

Rigid censorship was imposed on an already obeisant press,

which had for some years already been in the hands of large firms and banks with strong political links and vested interests to protect. As a former journalist himself, Mussolini was fully aware of the importance of controlling public opinion. In 1919 the offices of the Socialist Party's *Avanti!* in Milan were burned. With the establishment and consolidation of Fascist power, the paper was subject to repeated sequestration and eventually driven underground. The Communist Party's paper, *L'Unità*, met a similar fate. The level of political intervention in the press extended from the enforced reporting of the Duce's speeches and persuasion to what might be called a 'feel-good' factor: there was to be no reporting of events which would disturb the image of a country at peace with itself, while traffic accidents, murders, suicides and petty crime were deemed, officially, not to exist. Vigour and authority were the order of the day. No mention was to be made of the Duce's birthday, or that he was a grandfather; photographs of the Father of the Nation smiling were not to be printed.

By 1937 the so-called 'Miniculpop', the Ministry for Popular Culture, was in place. The Fascist era coincided with the arrival of mass-media entertainments, and Mussolini recognized the potential of cinema and radio as organs of Fascist propaganda. There was censorship of film, theatre and publishing, although the imperative of commercial success frequently won out over political ideology.[1] Fascism's nationalist and culturally introverted programme had to contend with the widespread internationalizing of popular culture as Hollywood saw off Italian and European competition, and Lydia Borelli was displaced by Mary Pickford in cinemagoers' hearts. While Fascist cultural nationalism attempted to legitimize the Fascist state by dramatic rereadings of literary works from Dante to Manzoni, Italian publishers continued to produce numerous translations of foreign literature, and contact with American culture was to be crucial for writers such as Cesare Pavese (1908–50) and Elio Vittorini (1908–66); in the American writers the young intelligentsia perceived moral, civic and stylistic liberties unavailable to them under Fascism.

A more pragmatic move to organize the masses and gain the allegiance of the working classes – not, after all, Fascism's natural constituency – took the form of mass leisure schemes, and particularly the 'dopolavoro' (literally 'after-work') schemes.

These were to be community-based centres of recreation and instruction, with programmes designed to promote the moral, physical and intellectual improvement of the people outside the structures and associations of traditional class politics.[2]

FAMILY POLICY AND IMAGES OF WOMEN IN FASCIST ITALY

Despite rural overpopulation and the consequent drift towards towns ill-prepared for any rapid increase in numbers, Mussolini decreed that there should be a demographic campaign to steady the falling birthrate. This aim, together with the traditional, patriarchal views of Fascism, led to a high degree of intervention in family law, and in the lives and work of women. According to this ideology, women's social and cultural identity was restricted principally to their biological, reproductive function. For the Fascists, maternity was to women what war was to men. They were to be mothers, 'reproducers of the nation',[3] and the bearing of as many children as possible was to be their contribution to the national effort to achieve a modern economy capable of competing with more established colonialist and imperialist powers. The demographic campaign, intended to reverse the long-term decline in the birth rate and reach a population of sixty million by 1950, was a clear failure, much to Mussolini's disgust, but it had specific consequences for women's legal position and status.

In order to encourage marriage and children, bachelors were taxed and married men given preference in terms of jobs, promotion and housing.[4] Loans were given to newlyweds, repayable only if there were no children. The officiating priest also gave out favourable insurance policies, along with a copy of Pius XI's anti-birth-control encyclical *Casti connubi*. Abortionists were prosecuted, although large numbers of women continued to seek dangerous clandestine abortions; the size of families continued to decrease as industrialization, urbanization and the shift towards nuclear rather than extended families continued slowly but inexorably.

Mothers who managed twelve children were awarded medals at annual ceremonies;[5] those who reached seven qualified for tax exemptions. Fascist rhetoric was clearly echoed by the position of the Catholic Church. The Lateran Pact of 1929, which provided for closer relations between Church and State than at any time in the nation's short history, gave the Church comparative freedom to organize and a great deal of moral authority in social and family affairs, reinforcing a traditionalist policy. Ettore Scola's remarkable film *Una giornata particolare* (*A Particular Day*, 1977) is a clear representation of the drudgery of the lives of women compelled into motherhood against a background of strident declamations of national virtue. In the relationship between the woman left at home on the day Hitler visits Rome in 1938 and the homosexual who has just lost his job (Marcello Mastroianni), Scola delicately suggests that both are victims of rigidly patriarchal definitions of sexual roles. The film ends with the mother, played by Sophia Loren, being led into the bedroom to make the seventh child, the one who will trigger financial reward.

The dominant female image of Fascist rhetoric was rural rather than urban and domestic; even her ideally rounded physical shape was defined for her, to accord with her supposed maternal, strictly unerotic biological function, in stark opposition to international fashions of the day. Censorship decreed that the ideal of robust, maternal womanhood was to be promoted even on the fashion pages of women's magazines: 'It has been recommended that we should avoid the reproduction of figures of snake-like women who represent the negation of true women, whose function is to procreate healthy children. We have therefore issued invitations to write articles against the silhouette fashion.'6 The glamorous film stars and models who were the product of an increasingly commercial and circulating culture were condemned by the Fascists as the *donna-crisi*, the 'crisis-woman'; elegance was deemed a hindrance to fecundity, and slovenliness was officially regarded as more promising for procreation.

FROM RHETORIC TO REALITY: THE PROBLEM OF CONSENT

While the rhetoric is well known, the complex and multiform nature of women's experience in a country so diverse not just on the grand scale between North and South but locally, between town and countryside, is just beginning to be uncovered.7 The monolithic nature of Fascist ideology had a variable impact in a country which, although united politically, was still fragmented in its customs, working practices and level of modernization and industrialization. Lesley Caldwell comments that Fascist leaders attempted to 'argue for a dominant set of representations that would signify Fascist womanhood through a rhetorical appeal designed to minimise differences', while in practice 'it was always particular groups of women who were legislated for, appealed to, complained about, argued against'.[8]

Fascist employment policy did little to reduce the numbers of women working, although it probably affected attitudes to work; whatever the theory, in practice employment legislation was designed to protect specific interest groups rather than put into practice a misogynist ideology of work. In 1927 women's salaries were reduced to half that of men. The following year they were banned from administrative positions in secondary and tertiary education, and five years later they were excluded from Civil Service examinations, while tuition fees for women were half as much again as they were for men. While Fascist ideology would have women safely at home, in practice many continued to work. Women working in factories represented a cheap source of labour, and the principal aim with regard to middle-class women was less to oust them from the labour market altogether than to prevent them usurping male supremacy and privilege (and wages) in the workplace. From 1923 women could not work as heads of middle schools, nor could they teach history, philosophy or economics in the *licei* (grammar schools). Legislation on women's work frequently proceeded by imposing quotas rather than outright bans: from 1933 the maximum quota for women in the state sector was down to ten per cent. Yet from 1934 women could begin lawful work at the age of twelve rather than fourteen, pointing to an unskilled female workforce who left young to get married.

The issue of female consent to the regime has been a particularly controversial point for historians of the period. Much Italian historical writing since the Second World War has tended to give the image of a working class which was spontaneously anti-Fascist, highly organized and politicized, their adherence to workers' traditions uncompromised by the new Fascist regime. Maria Antonietta Macciocchi (former PCI deputy, political and cultural observer), while accepting that in Fascist ideology woman is 'nothing more than an abstract entity, a principle whose role is to encourage the man to fight, to exhort him to do his duty',[9] attempts to establish to what extent women complied with the regime, and why. She points to the appropriation by Fascism of religious, liturgical language and imagery, a discourse to which women were particularly vulnerable. According to Macciocchi's psychoanalytical account, the Duce becomes a semi-divine spiritual leader to whom women owe their primary allegiance. She reminds us that in 1936 women were asked to surrender their wedding rings in order to assist the war effort in Ethiopia, in return for which they were given rings of iron, and she cites this incident to illustrate her thesis that Mussolini was represented as the transcendental 'marito' (husband). Macciocchi also cites the first congress of Fascist women in Venice (1923), as an example of the extraordinary discourse of submissive and sacrificing sexuality generated by the appeal of Fascism to women.[10] The feminist and historian Elsa Emmy agrees that the rhetoric of Fascism engaged in a forced mysticism which drew on women's experience of a rigidly Catholic and patriarchal society, commenting: 'every sexual instinct in women had to be extinguished in order to consolidate the link with the authoritarian family. Mussolini was always present, even in bed, because there women would evoke his magnetic gaze, and men his virile potency.'[11]

Macciocchi is in no doubt as to the importance of assessing women's role in Fascism and Nazism, and she is suspicious of the authoritarian and revisionist tendencies of political and feminist movements which would gloss over twenty years of history, whether from a phallocratic position which would barely question the Fascist ideal or from a facile feminism which is interested only in apologias for women; both are ways of excluding women from the real processes of history. Her fascinating – if slightly lurid – account of women's erotic response to Fascist rhetoric explains the mass consensus as a projection of their masochism, appealing to their sense of heroic self-sacrifice and the sacrifice of their husbands and sons. The repressed sexuality of Italian women in a bigoted moral climate is redirected by Fascist rhetoric towards the other drive dear to psychoanalysis, that of death.

Other historians prefer a more materialist analysis to the one offered by Macciocchi, and consider the impact of Catholicism, of war and of nationalist and Futurist ideology on Italian society.[12] As a pre-political avant-garde movement, Futurism tackled head-on traditional bourgeois values and the stifling Victorian morality peddled by a small-minded and self-regarding society. While it had the intellectual energy to sweep a new broom through Italian thinking on the relations between the sexes, Futurism was firmly rooted in virulently male, elitist thinking, anti-democratic, ultra-nationalistic, fascinated by war, speed, technology and violence. Their affirmed belief in free love seemed to be something of a one-way process, and the role of reproducer rather than producer, the Maker of Heroes, assigned to women in the new Futurist society was almost indistinguishable from that proposed by Fascism.

WHATEVER HAPPENED TO FEMINISM?

Fascism did make some attempt to mobilize women, setting up women-only organizations such as the *fasci femminili*. There is something of an irony in such organizations which made the role of women more visible, opening up new spaces for them in the public sphere, even while their propagandistic purpose was to tie women ever more tightly to a domestic role. Such an unprecedented amount of attention to defining the female contribution to the state meant that women were brought on to the national stage for the first time. In this respect, Fascism could be considered a watershed in Italian women's history. But this venture was clearly fraught with contradictions as the Fascists tried to mobilize women in a manner that was shorn of any potentially feminist or democratic overtones about female citizenship and equality.[13]

Contemporary historians stress the dangers of Macciocchi's generalizing psychoanalytical thesis about female consent to Fascism. The capitulation by prominent, particularly middle-class feminists was, however, remarkable. Reasons for conversion to Mussolini's cause were numerous. Some joined the nationalist cause during the First World War, others joined later. Their move was made more probable by the failure of pre-war feminist movements to define a role and social place for women, in direct contrast to the Fascist propaganda of the domestic child-bearer, and their shared belief in motherhood as principal index of social and cultural identity. The historian Enzo Santarelli comments: 'In Italy, like England, a whole section of the feminist movement, those who called most strongly for women's suffrage, with the war had moved to positions of national concord in order to win civil and political rights; but this was to lead to a break with working class women and, unlike in England, to a very notable turn to Fascism' (Santarelli, p. 84). The writer and political activist Joyce Lussu (b. 1912) is even more uncompromising in her condemnation of these women, in Italy and abroad, who gave 'feminism' a bad name, as she recounts her experience as a partisan in the Second World War:

> The ancestors I traced myself back to were the women of the Paris Commune, the peasant leagues, the workers' movement; and not the feminists and the suffragettes, structurally antiproletarian as they had demonstrated by their reactions to the October Revolution and the rise of Fascism . . . I think that if the feminists of recent years had known the history of the last few decades they would have chosen another name, other mothers.[14]

FASCISM AND LITERATURE

Writing in his Prison Notebooks, Antonio Gramsci laid bare the gulf between the intellectuals and the people, pointing up the failure of the lay forces to fulfil their 'historic task as educators and elaborators of the intellect and the moral awareness of the people-nation', because they were 'tied to an antiquated world, narrow, abstract, too individualistic or caste-like'.[15] Writers in the Fascist era did little to bridge the gap between an exclusive artistic and cultural elite and a mass public, although on the whole their failure was due less to a genuine commitment to Fascist principles and doctrine than to a limited and partial view of the role of culture in society, a traditional belief in the disengagement of 'art' from 'politics'.[16] The poet Eugenio Montale, although hostile to the regime, articulated the abstention of writers and producers of 'high' art from the business of social and political involvement:

> I never was a Fascist, nor did I sing to Fascism. Nor however did I write poems that might appear to oppose that pseudo-revolution. Certainly, it would have been impossible to publish poetry that was hostile to the regime, but the fact is that I would not have tried it, not even if the risk had been minimal or non-existent.[17]

Fascism easily tolerated the cultural elite as a separate and exclusive club, more interested in the existential and the philosophical than the banally social and political, and its practitioners were all too susceptible to the honours and rewards lavished on them by the regime. Literary disengagement and intellectual aloofness were underpinned by the idealist philosophy of Benedetto Croce, who theorized the transcendental autonomy and abstraction of art from immediate circumstances, its universality and timelessness. Croce's 'Manifesto of Anti-Fascist Intellectuals', swiftly produced in response to the 'Manifesto of Fascist Intellectuals' published by Giovanni Gentile, leading theorist of Fascism, was remarkable less for its political dissent than for its utter refusal to let literature and art have anything to do with politics at all. 'High' art was vital for the international prestige of Fascism, and the public endorsement of Mussolini by such as Luigi Pirandello, one of the fathers of modern experimental theatre, was crucial in establishing the legitimacy of the regime. Alberto Moravia (1907–88) and Italo Svevo (1861–1928) achieved international recognition in the 1920s, with work which was more hostile to bourgeois morality and corrupt cynicism than to Fascism itself. The prestigious poetry of Saba, Ungaretti and the 'hermetic' school effectively insulated itself from current events, preferring the transcendental to the contingent.

With the passing of the 1930s, the Italian involvement in the Spanish Civil War in 1936 and the implementation of racial laws two years later, the climate of opinion suddenly began to change. Writers and thinkers who expressed open dissent were dealt with increasingly harshly. Carlo Levi, Cesare Pavese and Emilio Lussu were banished to remote parts of the country (source for Levi's *Christ Stopped at Eboli*); Ignazio Silone (1900–78), author of *Fontamara* (1930), was driven into exile; Giorgio Bassani (b. 1916), Antonio Gramsci (1891–1937) and Leone Ginzburg (1909–44) were all imprisoned; Gramsci and Ginzburg died at the hands of the regime.

Fascist cultural policy led in practice to the complete separation and self-sufficiency of 'high' and 'popular' art. If a free but largely obeisant intellectual literary class served to embellish rather than challenge the regime, the widening readership for popular fiction was fed an unremitting diet of predigested Fascist beliefs and aspirations. Women were substantial contributors to this level of production. Excluded by a masculinist ethos from the trappings of high culture, such as membership of the Academy (with the exception of the illustrious and fascinating Margherita Sarfatti, the Duce's mistress) and the rewards and opportunities of cultural patronage, women none the less established their own spheres of influence, such as women's magazines (some of which, such as the *Almanacco della donna italiana*, regularly carried columns on women writers) and cultural clubs. These cultural circles were an exclusively middle-class affair, but they did develop a national organization of women and promote women's self-awareness as 'Italians': Fascist cultural policy, like its social policy, was intended to foster a sense of national unity and national pride.

The Fascist attempt to complete the political aims of the Risorgimento, by reaching for political consensus and fostering a national cultural sense of identity, had some unexpected spin-offs. Apart from the establishment of the Academy (to which women could not belong) and the first encyclopaedia (to which women barely contributed), cultural policy attempted to bring women into the body politic, if not out of the domestic sphere. Books were written about Italian women writers, such as Mario Gastaldi's *Donne, luce d'Italia* (Women, Light of Italy, 1928) and Jolanda De Blasi's less reverential but more informative *Le scrittrici italiane dalle origini al 1800* (Italian Women Writers from The Origins to the Nineteenth Century, 1930). Heroines and martyrs of the Risorgimento cause, such as Eleonora Fonseca Pimentel, Luisa di San Felice and Teresa Confalonieri were celebrated, as women once more took pride in the role they had played over the generations in the developing nation-state.

A great deal of work by women was published, and their growing confidence led Daria Banfi Malaguzzi to proclaim, in curiously militaristic imagery, that women's literature in Italy was 'by now so vast and so rich as to impress even the most obstinately misogynist spirits. . . . The troops are becoming ever more numerous, ever bolder.'[18] Certainly some of their male colleagues watched with alarm what they saw as the 'feminization' and 'emasculation' of Italian letters. Some of the production by women was pure propaganda, pandering to Fascist gender role models of the brave hero and the self-sacrificing mother. Such was Fanny Dini's prizewinning *La madre e il figlio* (Mother and Son, 1938), which recounted the nobly borne grief of an archetypal *mater dolorosa* when her son meets his death in the new Italian colony of Ethiopia. Margherita Sarfatti's only novel, *Il palazzone* (The Big Palace, 1929), was a clear allegory of emotional satisfaction and intellectual self-fulfilment within the new Fascist order. Numerous women, such as Maria Chiappelli, wrote domestic and psychological dramas centring on the woman's role as mother. Gianna Anguissola (*Romanzo di molta gente* [Story of Many People], 1933) and Bianca de Maj wrote narratives of love, maternity and social customs. Regional novels of rural life were popular: Lina Pietravalle (1890–1956) took her characters, customs and passions from the peasant world in a prose open to dialect rhythms and forms.[19] Most common – and most widely read – was the so-called 'romanzo rosa' or 'pink novel', sentimental fiction written for women and written by such as Milly Dandolo (1895–1946), Carola Prosperi (1883–1966), Anna Zara Magno (b. 1913), Marise Ferro (b. 1907), Luciana Peverelli, Flavia Steno and the young Liala. Their writing, like that of many of their nineteenth-century forebears, was tailored to a growing but not especially sophisticated readership, provoking abuse against 'female literature consisting of chlorotic women, latter-day Bovarys, the misunderstood, the confused' (De Grazia, p. 256).

It is possible to take the revisionist view that women writers, barred as they were from patronage and easy routes to success, depended entirely upon sales and upon an immediate appeal to their public, and thus maintained closer links with their readers than their more intellectually aloof male counterparts. But women writers were clearly not as close to the sharp edge of Fascism as were men, and it would surely be rash to claim that 'a socially constructed female sensibility . . . caused women writers to be "more modern"' (De Grazia, p. 252), or that these narratives of frustrated love, maternity and social customs were any closer to anticipating new literary styles than were those of nineteenth-century writers such as Marchesa Colombi. While Anna Banti considered the development of popular literature, and the 'romanzo rosa' in particular, to have been openly tolerated by a ruling class who preferred their women to read Marie Corelli rather than the scandalous George Sand, she is harshly critical of the banal conformism which marked so much writing by women under

Fascism, and remains unconvinced by its veneer of internationalism and its superficial – certainly not subversive – treatment of women's lives and choices.[20] Banti strips away the chameleon hypocrisies of the writers who buy into contemporary myths and shibboleths in order to earn a living, and notes uncomfortably that women's education, their ability to adapt and desire to please, make them particularly successful at this kind of writing. Banti attacks not popular literature – indeed, she admires Daphne Du Maurier and Rosamund Lehmann – but narratives which support those myths of aggressive heroism and redeeming maternity which can only exploit women themselves; she cites Vanda Bontà's 'nauseating' *Diario di Clementina* (Clementine's Diary, serially published between 1940 and 1943), story of the patient wife and mother awaiting the homecoming of her soldier-husband so that she can return to the domestic sphere. Such work, Banti eloquently argues, is more damaging to women than pornography, and more immoral and detrimental to their already fragile dignity for being penned by women themselves.

A small but fascinating aspect of production under Fascism was the work of Futurist women. The Futurist movement under Marinetti was unremittingly misogynistic; its glorification of war, its unabashed militarism and patriotism, were linked to a profound contempt for women and for feminism in particular, and it is notable that Marinetti's founding manifesto came out in 1909, just one year after the first National Women's Congress in Rome. The anti-female bias of Nietzsche, Darwin and Weininger resonated through Marinetti's determination to destroy 'moralism, feminism, every opportunistic or utilitarian cowardice'.[21] Woman, slave to sentimental passions and to the family, was identified with the natural world, symbol of the earth to be abandoned, while Futurism embraced technology and the machine, speed and flight, in a conception of modernization as 'a relentless overcoming of resistance, a destruction of those differential and dialectical formations in culture which threatened to impede the homogenizing movements of capital'.[22] As the 'obstacle to be confronted, barrier to be cast aside, whose justification lies in the antagonism she is able to evoke and in which male aggressivity and supremacy finds its measure',[23] woman was the antithesis of the Futurist technological, mechanical and bellicose dream, symbolized in Marinetti's novel *Mafarka il futurista* (Mafarka the Futurist, 1910) by the ultimate sexual fantasy which would rupture the nexus of woman/sexuality altogether and produce the 'figlio meccanico', the 'mechanical son'. Man is multiplied, no longer by woman, but by the machine.

Futurism's vitally irreverent, anticonformist attack on the bourgeois family and sexual hypocrisy (which won the admiration of Antonio Gramsci for being more radical than anything the Socialists had achieved), its totalizing aim to revolutionize private and sexual relations as well as public and cultural institutions, might have been expected to hold out some promise of liberation for women. Indeed, Marinetti recognized the historical conditioning of women's intellectual, social and erotic status, while the 'Manifesto of the Futurist Political Party' (1918) proposed the introduction of a divorce law, universal suffrage and equal pay. Marinetti's attack on women was 'aimed at the late-Romantic and decadent clichés of woman as on the one hand *femme fatale*, vampire, adulteress – the eternal object of man's desire and agent of his damnation – and on the other hand woman as muse, Beatrice' and as 'cultural icon of decadence in *fin-de-siècle* Europe'.[24] Woman – as symbol and representation – was seen as anti-modern, denoting psychological and social formations resistant to the new.

In the journals *L'Italia Futurista* (1916–18) in Florence and *Roma Futurista* (1918–20), Futurist women engaged in a lively debate about women's role in the brave new world, in which the paradox of their position becomes clear. The modernizing drive of Futurist theory, the potentially politically progressive attack on the family and demand for a free erotics, is undermined by a continuing subservience to the masculine, virile ideal. War was seen to be a prime mover in changing the condition of women: as a result of war, declared Rosa Rosà in 1917, 'women are about to conquer something new . . . the consciousness of a free and immortal "I" which owes nothing to anybody or anything'.[25] Maternity remained a stumbling block, however, for this new 'I' was inimical to motherhood, with its decentring of female identity across the family. Valentine de Saint-Point, the Frenchwoman who became the leading female theorist of Futurism's early days, does not move beyond acquiescence to the male libidinal economy which would divide women into mothers and lovers: 'Women must be either mother or lover. Real mothers will always be mediocre lovers, just as lovers will be no good as mothers. Equal in the eyes of life, these two women complement each other'.[26] For de Saint-Point, women should undermine the current repressive social order from its very heart, from within the family: despite her deconstruction of sexual identity, she was unable to move towards any progressive or radical political position with regard to women's social role.

Creative writing by Futurist women similarly exhibits an ideological conformity underlining the extent to which Futurist aspirations merged into Fascist orthodoxies. Their writing is fascinating for the uncertainty it exhibits, caught between a desire for freedom from traditional bourgeois custom, the decadent, post-Romantic erotics of Futurism and the increasingly strident Fascist obsession with race. Rosa Rosà portrays her female characters trapped within the coercive structures of patriarchal society, marriage and the family. Her visionary *Una donna con tre anime* (A Woman with Three Souls, 1918) portrays a very ordinary woman three times suddenly and unexpectedly metamorphosed, becoming in turn sensuous and glamorous, a scientist, and a poet. The revolutionary potential of this engagingly constructed fantasy of liberation is, however, defused by turning the heroine into a surrogate Futurist male, and Rosà has little to say to the vast majority of women whose lives resemble that of the heroine before her fantastic transformations.

While Futurist women attack the family as institution, maternity is defended as woman's sublime mission in a stance which is almost indistinguishable from Fascist ideology. If Rosa Rosà calls for a new female identity, she ends up in a sentimental panegyric to maternity. Enif Robert's *Un ventre di donna* (A Woman's Womb, 1919), while based on Robert's own experience of surgical intervention, equates creativity, art and poetry, as well as the glorious art of war, with maleness, while the reduction of the woman to 'suffering uterus' is a catastrophic admission of failure.[27] Yet Robert, too, celebrates the life-giving womb and female fecundity. The Futurist attack on bourgeois family structures and Romantic iconography was paralleled by an impassioned defence of the maternal role, and as Fascism's political and ideological grip tightened throughout the 1920s and 1930s, Futurist women and apologists for Fascism such as Benedetta Cappa Marinetti and Maria Goretti increasingly stress motherhood as the only option for women. With *La donna e il futurismo* (Women and Futurism, 1941) Goretti closes the circle by denouncing the early libertarian manifestoes of Valentine de Saint-Point, and marks the end of Futurism.

There were a few writers, however, and women writers, more prepared to be innovative, radical and unorthodox. The impact of Maria Messina's *Casa paterna* (Paternal Home) and *La casa del vicolo* (House in the Lane), first published in 1921, has been realized only *post factum* with their reissue in the late 1980s, and they are extraordinary tales of contemporary patriarchal Sicily and women's struggle to establish an autonomous identity. *Nascita e morte della massaia* (Birth and Death of a Housewife, 1938) by Paola Masino (companion to Massimo Bontempelli and editor of his works after his death) was censored for its parody of the Fascist regime.

Remarkable, too, was the experimental, modernist prose of Gianna Manzini (1896–1974), a much underrated writer yet to be fully rediscovered. Labelled 'difficult' and 'elitist', Manzini's lyric prose and constant attention to style provided a vivid contrast with much of the more transient work produced under Fascism. Her art remains aloof from social and political engagement, and from realism; instead, her works are allusive, associative, and she employs a diffuse narrative voice which permits the interweaving of multiple narrative levels and techniques. Manzini was a regular contributor to the influential periodicals *Solaria* and *Letteratura*, which worked to open up Italian culture to influence from abroad; like Anna Banti she was a great admirer of Woolf, and the influence is clear even if she cannot match Woolf's achievement. Manzini began publishing in 1928 with *Tempo innamorato* (Enamoured Time), while *Lettera all'editore* (Letter to the Publisher, 1945), a self-reflective and open-structured text after the manner of Luigi Pirandello's theatre or André Gide in *Les Faux Monnayeurs*, is a statement of her very modern poetics.

Manzini has yet to be credited with being one of the innovators of form and style in the Italian novel. What can be argued is that in her intense seriousness of purpose, her belief in literature's ability to illuminate reality rather than its obligation merely to reflect it, and her meticulous attention to style in the face of a prevailing grey realism or rosy romance, she paved the way for the extraordinary achievements of women's writing in the post-war period.

WOMEN AND THE RESISTANCE

While the impact of Fascist rhetoric on women's lives was patchy at most, the advent of war affected all to a greater or lesser degree. As during the First World War, women took over the jobs of their male counterparts in the factories; in the last stages of civil war following the establishment of Mussolini's puppet Republic of Salò, some even donned the uniform of the Italian army. These were traumatic times for the country; with the fall of Mussolini the Nazis poured reinforcements into Italy – now an enemy state – from the north, while the progress of the Allies up the peninsula after the landings in Sicily and at Salerno was painfully slow. Moreover, Italy was at war with herself as the rump of the Fascist regime struggled against the growing tide of anti-Fascists and partisans, organized in large part by the Communist Party.

The Italian Resistance numbered, probably, around 100,000 active members: of these over one-third died, one-quarter were wounded, and many thousands were deported to Germany. The undoubted courage of the partisans, who refused to limit their activities to the occasional acts of sabotage but determined to take the fight to the Germans, and who thus bore the full brunt of German reprisals, did much to restore Italy's tarnished image in the eyes of the international community; the Allies, too, acknowledged the pivotal role of the Resistance fighters in liberating their own country. Yet it is questionable whether the activities of the Resistance, notwithstanding its undoubted heroism and high ideals, brought about any profound break with the past; despite Allied anxiety at the degree of independence achieved by the partisans, particularly in the North, and their fears of a social revolution and new totalitarian state – red this time rather than black – the dreams of the partisans were not realized. With the collapse of Germany, the Allies succeeded in disarming Resistance fighters swiftly, and rapid economic measures and security of employment – temporarily at least – diffused tensions among the working classes.

Many women joined the fast-growing Resistance movement, particularly from 1943 onwards, after the fall of Mussolini. There is an enormous body of heroic literature about this period, which has received a vast amount of fascinated, if not always critical, attention.[28] Up to 35,000 women were involved in the partisan movement, while twice that number enrolled in the *Gruppi di difesa della donna* (Women's Defence Groups) established in 1943. Yet while a whole aspect of the Resistance was a debate on the future shape of Italy, and a passionate vision of future democracy, militant female participants did not, on the whole, add a specifically feminist slant to these deliberations. The importance of women's contribution to the Resistance effort was, however, recognized. It brought large numbers of women into a collective struggle for the first time, either as active militants or in a wide network of communications and support, and it undoubtedly contributed to Italian women winning the vote. Estimates of the number of women involved vary hugely. Rossana Rossanda, one of the founding members of the far-left daily *Il Manifesto*, makes the point that women's daily lives and routine made them particularly suited to clandestine activity: 'Nobody expects a woman to express political opinions, and who could imagine that when she goes off to the market she has a revolver in her shopping bag?'[29]

WINNING THE PEACE: 1945–64

When Italian women finally gained the vote in 1946, it was evident that their contribution to the national struggles of the previous few years played a considerable part in this long-overdue acknowledgement of their rights to full citizenship. But while the Constitution of the new Republic (with the discredited monarchy ousted by referendum) guaranteed equal rights to women, these rights were, once more, defined in terms of maternity; the rhetoric of woman as Mother to the Nation had not been dispelled. The family unit was still seen as the fundamental unit of society, and the woman at the hearth as vital to its proper functioning. The struggle for emancipation was countered not only by a reactionary Church which feared the consequences of emancipation both for women's fragile morals and for traditional family structures, but also – and perhaps more insidiously – by a political Left worried that women's instinctive conservatism and political backwardness would hamper the drive to Socialism: to give women suffrage would, it was feared, be to hand votes to the Right on a plate.

But the 'woman question' refused to go meekly away, or to submit itself to any political imperative. The Unione Donne

Italiane (Union of Italian Women, referred to hereafter as the UDI) was formed in September 1944 to take up the struggle for emancipation after twenty years of Fascism. Civil rights were the primary objective. The UDI, a flanking organization of the Communist Party (PCI), achieved substantial membership in its early years (three and a half thousand local circles by 1954, and over one million members) and much influence through its journal, *Noi donne* (We Women). With the backing of the unions and the political parties of the Left, women made definite advances towards emancipation in terms of civil rights, despite the slowness of the state. The state was very slow, for example, to abrogate law which made women more liable for punishment for adultery than men, or gave men the right to dispose of their wife's possessions. Women gradually achieved equality of access to education and professions, extensive state-run nursery provision was established, and women's right to work was defended. The UDI was reformist and gradualist, focusing on specific issues and bringing pressure to bear on the ruling parties, hoping to wrest a fair deal for women from the new Constitution.

The battle for emancipation under the aegis of the Left – and Palmiro Togliatti, leader of the PCI, wrote many articles on the subject - was still conducted in terms of an ideology which saw women as primarily reproducers rather than producers; hence the struggle for protection for pregnant women, the constant foregrounding of the problems of the family, and the development of social services to assist families of the poorer classes. Nor could the Left risk being seen to support any move which might be interpreted as an attack on the family as an institution. The UDI involved itself with assistance and welfare, supported the post-war struggle for agrarian reform of the infamous *latifondi* (vast landed estates) of the South, and concerned itself with the education of children. Women's rights were supported by the Left so long as they did not conflict with traditional thinking about the family and gender roles within the family, or with the interests of male workers. The problem of female emancipation was viewed on the Left as part of an overall strategy for the renewal of Italian society, and analysed in terms not of relations between the sexes but in terms of political and economic relationships between the classes. Issues such as divorce and abortion, which addressed a specifically female condition, were not raised; women of the Left found themselves caught between the rigid morality of Russian-influenced Communism, with its idea of the 'proletarian family', a powerful Catholic Church, and the legacy of Fascist ideology.

THE 'ECONOMIC MIRACLE'

The 1950s and early 1960s saw a rapid transformation of large sections of Italian society as the economy went through a boom period, commonly described as the 'economic miracle'. In the mid-1950s Italy was still largely undeveloped, its principal production and source of employment still agriculture or traditional small-scale, labour-intensive firms; standards of living were low, and industrialization was limited to a few small pockets in the North. Emigration remained one escape route – to the Americas or to Northern Europe, particularly from the South, where growth rates were minimal.

In the post-war period, a principally agrarian economy fast became a primarily industrial one. Companies such as Olivetti and Fiat competed successfully on the international stage, and the export market for Italian domestic electrical appliances, the 'elettrodomestici', expanded hugely. The development of industry was boosted by the discovery of methane gas, and Italy no longer needed to depend exclusively on fuel imports. Individual incomes and standards of living rose to unprecedented levels. Italy turned herself into the new 'consumer' society as economic and cultural traditions were increasingly challenged.

Expansion of the industrial and manufacturing base was matched by a substantial growth in educational opportunity, as the universities increased their intake of both male and female students. Meanwhile, as burgeoning industrial development resulted in a shortage of skilled labour in a country where labour had traditionally come cheap, workers were gaining a confidence they had never had before. The changing face of education and employment, mixed with the ideological ferments seething across Europe as well as the United States, were to lead in the 1960s and 1970s to dramatic disturbances, the rise of alternative ideologies such as the youth movement, far-left political groups and feminism, and, most dramatically of all, terrorism of both Left and Right.

POST-WAR CULTURE: NEOREALISM AND FEMALE AESTHETICS

Despite Fascist censorship and the drive to a cultural nationalism, Italy had probably never been so swamped with foreign products, whether in the form of the printed word or celluloid. Foreign cultures, particularly American (Faulkner and Steinbeck, for example), were considerably to influence the Neorealist aesthetic of the early post-war years. Neorealism was an attempt by writers and film-makers to take up Gramsci's challenge to the intellectuals to close the distance between themselves and the working class, and addressed the gap left in Italian culture and the portrayed experience of the Italian people by a triumphalist Fascist rhetoric. Neorealism, which followed on directly from the experience of Liberation, was an attempt to revitalize political culture and recover sections of the nation which had been absent from Italy's self-representations for the past twenty years.

Films such as Rossellini's *Roma, città aperta* (Rome, Open City, 1945), Visconti's *La terra trema* (The Earth Trembles, 1948) and De Sica's *Ladri di biciclette* (Bicycle Thieves, 1948) were revolutionary in their use of non-professionals for greater authenticity (De Sica refused to use Cary Grant in *Ladri di biciclette* in favour of a completely unknown factory worker), their realistic and natural settings and their efforts to present a more democratic and less alienating cinema. The results are striking even today, when spectators can see more clearly the artistic and aesthetic achievement of these films, as well as appreciate the break they represented with more prevailing cultural forms. In the field of literature, Cesare Pavese, Carlo Levi and Elio Vittorini all produced work which aimed to address this new concern for literature to be inclusive and, above all, *engagée*.

What this meant for women, however, is more problematic. Just as the emancipationist politics of the Left were bound up with a less than revolutionary vision of women's role in society, so Neorealism revealed itself to be fundamentally conservative in its vision of sexual roles. The search for 'traditional' values embraced by the Neorealists as they turned to disenfranchised – and hence uncorrupt - sectors of society held out little hope of anything new for women. The critic Lucia Re comments: 'Neorealist narrative tends in general to employ a basic framework of values taken entirely from the traditional conventions of Italian patriarchal culture. . . . By appealing to the most deeply sedimented and universal truths of the Italians, Neorealism sought a "catholic" consensus above and beyond party differences.'[30]

Women's reponse to the post-Resistance culture of Neorealism was somewhat more ambivalent. In her novel *L'Agnese va a morire* (Agnese Goes to Die, 1949) and her collections of short stories such as *Donne della resistenza* (Women of the Resistance) and *Matrimonio in brigata* (Brigade Wedding),[31] Renata Viganò celebrated both the courage of ordinary women during the Resistance, and the consequent loosening of the traditional ideological grip on women's sense of their own role and value. Yet Neorealism remained a largely male enterprise. Already defined and prescribed for by the various ideologies of post-Unification liberalism and Fascism, women showed themselves in no hurry to line up behind another flag, of whatever colour.

The most important woman poet of this and probably the whole post-war period is Amelia Rosselli (b. 1930). Rosselli's focus on the intimate register of the everyday in free psychological flux marks a distance both from the social thrust of Neorealism and from the more abstruse experimentation of the neo-avant-garde. Rosselli's own personal history – daughter of Carlo Rosselli, an anti-Fascist exiled in Paris, and an English mother, her plurilingualism, as well as her musical training, emerges into the organization of her poems, which are closer to other traditions than the Italian, such as French Surrealism or the English Metaphysical poets.

Rosselli subverts the norms of written Italian at all levels, syntactic and lexical as well as graphic and morphological, incorporating Anglicisms and deliberately ungrammatical usage as well as quotations from other poets such as Dino Campana and Eugenio Montale. Rosselli's linguistic experimentalism, her alienation of the Italian language from itself, is grounded not in a formalist aesthetics but in personal and historical experience, in a distancing from the 'barbaric' land of Italy which had her father killed and, she claimed, continued to persecute her. In her aesthetic violation of language, her linguistic alterity, she suggests both the 'historicizing' of poetry and the 'poeticity' of history as form, rhythm and flux. Writing at the margins of both linguistic and sexual difference, Rosselli rewrites poets such as Rimbaud in a female key, adding a subversively feminine note to an Italian poetic tradition which has been unashamedly male-dominated.

Writers of fiction such as Fausta Cialente (b. 1896), Alba De Céspedes (b. 1911) and Milena Milani (b. 1922) were beginning the task of assessing women's social role in a manner which increasingly approached that of feminism. While Cialente's early, pre-war novels are set in an exoticized Egypt, where she lived with her husband, the composer Enrico Terni, her later work is less romantic and more concerned with the pragmatic, practical details of life. Cialente shows an increasing consciousness of history and of women's roles within it. In line with the emancipationist movements of her day, she shows an acute awareness of women's need for financial independence, and in *Ballata levantina* (Levantine Ballad, 1961) as well as an earlier short story, 'Marcellina', she plays with the idea of economic and domestic role-reversal. *Un inverno freddissimo* (A Very Cold Winter, 1966) takes up other themes of the emancipationists as it considers a woman's role within marriage and questions their enforced emotional as well as economic dependence on men through the institutions of marriage and the family. Cialente's protagonists can find few real alternatives to the traditional typology of woman as mother or woman as lover, but *A Very Cold Winter*, set against the background of the Resistance in Milan, has as its goal women's intellectual emancipation, as her protagonist seeks escape from the restricted world of women through writing itself.

Cialente's last and probably best work, *Le quattro ragazze di Wieselberger* (The Four Wieselberger Girls, 1976), is the most autobiographical, with numerous details of her childhood in Trieste amid the same political and cultural context which so influenced the work of Italo Svevo, and her private revolution: departure from the conjugal home and public involvement in anti-Fascist propaganda with Radio Cairo during the Second World War. Yet while Cialente, like her life-long friend Sibilla Aleramo, seeks emancipation for women and a productive role outside the home, she is only too aware that the vast majority of Italian women are not yet ready for such a move. Like Aleramo, she expresses condemnation and pity in equal measure for women 'who will never learn that it is not worth while to suffer so much, not even for the children's sake, [and who] in spite of their own wretched experience will educate their own children – and especially their daughters – to renunciation and sacrifice'.[32]

The novels of Alba De Céspedes are similarly centred around a female character, and her sense of alienation and marginalization within her family and social context. Her characters, more self-consciously lucid and analytical than Cialente's, clearly prefigure the feminist awareness to be found in novels of the 1960s and 1970s. De Céspedes was also politically active, broadcasting during the Resistance under the code name 'Clorinda'. *Nessuno torna indietro* (*There's No Turning Back*, 1938), a minute examination of the lives of eight women, was an international bestseller, translated into twenty-four languages: it was banned by Fascist censorship, as was her subsequent collection of short stories, *Fuga* (Flight, 1940). *Dalla parte di lei* (*The Best of Husbands*, 1948) is a study of the rights of women within marriage, again with a strong female character, Alessandra, who fails to find marriage the source of passionate commitment patriarchal ideology had led her to expect. Later novels – *Quaderno proibito* (*The Secret*, 1952) or *Prima e dopo* (*Between Then and Now*, 1956) offer a clear-sighted vision of female autonomy. To look for happiness and fulfilment through love, the traditional occupation of women, is to be doomed to disappointment. But escape in post-war Italy is too difficult for Valeria, the housewife-drudge in *The Secret,* who confides her shocking realization of the emptiness of her life to her diaries. De Céspedes's characters are not heroic Shirley Valentines, nor is this the Doll's House; it is for the generation of Valeria's daughter once more to make the break. De Céspedes, like Cialente, reflects a critical moment both in women's writing and in the history of Italian women. Her characters do not manage to break the chains that bind them to traditional beliefs, but they certainly rattle them, reflecting the real achievements of the post-war women's movement and anticipating in large measure the resurgent feminist consciousness which was to challenge the social and cultural ideologies against which their protagonists chafed. Like Cialente, De Céspedes's contribution to post-war Italian literature, with narratives which express the quintessential dilemmas of modern women and their struggle for individual fulfilment, is yet to be fully acknowledged.

The heroines of Milena Milani are sensual non-conformists,

seeking gratification and pleasure outside traditional roles. Anna Drei's search for freedom in *Story of Anna Drei* (1947) and the refusal of prescribed sexual roles or demure femininity in the later novel *A Girl Named Jules* (1964) led to an obscenity trial, which finally vindicated Milani. Her characters' demand for freedom and sexual autonomy, their conscious refusal of orthodox bourgeois customs, clearly prefigure the upheaval in sexual mores and expectations which was about to overtake Italy.

The four writers discussed in this Part – Anna Banti, Natalia Ginzburg, Elsa Morante and Anna Maria Ortese – sketch out a female response to a specific set of social and political imperatives. They come from widely different backgrounds and cultures, from middle-class urban Jewish, to Roman proletariat, to upper-middle-class Florentine. All four come to maturity during the Fascist period; all four are acutely concerned to offer a closely observed perspective on the fast-changing social conditions of post-war Italy.

Each of these four writers offers a different aesthetic and philosophical vision of 'reality', and each keeps her distance from the orthodoxies of Neorealism. In *Artemisia*, Banti's harrowing experience of wartime destruction is filtered through the largely invented biography of the Renaissance painter Artemisia Gentileschi, while her subtle conception of history is an enormous advance on the sentimental historical fiction of Gina Algranati, or Maria Bellonci's elegant but traditional biographies of Renaissance women. Ginzburg's fictions continually expose the flux of emotion and experience which lie beneath the surface touched by political ideologies; Morante's massive and impassioned novels deal not with orthodox history but with the dialectic between official history and the myriad small stories which that history suppresses, between dominant and marginal cultural forms; Ortese refuses to name what she sees around her as 'reality' at all, aiming in her increasingly fantastic and suggestive works at a literature which takes us to the heart of our metaphysical and phenomenological experience of the world. In accordance with a political ideology of inclusiveness, Neorealism sought to draw the nation together once more, to represent all parts to all other parts in the mirror of literature. The engagement of these writers is more ethical than party-political, more encompassing in its humanitarian aims, more ambitious in its goals and its effects.

7
Portraits of a Writer: Anna Banti (1895–1985)

> Underlying the question about women as artists, we find the whole myth of the Great Artist – subject of a hundred monographs, unique, god-like, bearing within his person since birth a mysterious essence, rather like the golden nugget in Mrs Grass's chicken soup, called Genius.
>
> (Linda Nochlin, 'Why have there been no great women artists?', in *Women, Art and Power and Other Essays*)

When Anna Banti died in 1985 at the age of ninety, the headline run by the Florentine daily *La Nazione*, 'Addio, Artemisia!', revealed the extent to which the writer had merged in the popular cultural imagination with the figure of the seventeenth0century painter, Artemisia Gentileschi, whose life she recounted in the novel published almost half a century before. In a writing career which spanned almost sixty years, from the 1930s until shortly before her death, Banti published novels, several volumes of short stories and essays, two volumes of autobiography and a study of the Neapolitan writer Matilde Serao as well as translations (including Virginia Woolf), and art-historical studies of Lorenzo Lotto, Fra Angelico and Giovanni da San Giovanni. *Artemisia* (1947), the most dense and suggestive of her many achievements, is aptly described by Cesare Garboli as 'confession half true and half invented, biography and autobiography, one of the strangest and most dense works in the whole of twentieth-century Italian literature'.[1]

Artemisia is an imaginative evocation of the life and work of Artemisia Gentileschi, uncompromisingly affirmed by the art critic Mary Garrard as the greatest woman painter of all time.[2] The novel interweaves the narrative voices of the author/narrator and the character/historical figure, offering a multiple perspective which reflects simultaneously on the dramatic successes and failures of Artemisia and the destruction and devastation in the principal narrator's own life, for the context of the writing is the devastation of Florence as the Nazis retreat before the advancing Allies in 1944. The text of *Artemisia* defies all neat categories of historical novel, imaginative fiction or biography. What it offers above all is a meditation on the woman artist: the text hinges around Artemisia's own paintings, and Banti's startlingly fresh interpretations leave them, and her own text, as a complex metaphor for female creativity, for the split, fragmented self of the female artist, for the intricate dialectic of the public and private in a woman's life.

Banti's double focus on her subject matter – history and its reinvention, art and its iconoclastic reinterpretation, the substance and imagining of a woman's life – can be traced to the struggle between public and private, work and marriage, which she felt so acutely in her own life. Marisa Volpi, herself both writer and art critic, comments of Banti and Artemisia: 'they are both women who renounced their own femininity in order to affirm themselves: Artemisia Gentileschi in a world which had wounded her, Banti in the face of a husband with an overpowering personality. It is this struggle which unites them.'[3] Banti is a pseudonym for Lucia Lopresti, who was born in 1895 and studied art history with the influential writer and critic Roberto Longhi. Following a short spell as museum curator in the Abruzzi, Banti married her teacher, after which she gave up her own career as art historian, if not her passionate interest in the subject. It was a renunciation which, though never overtly regretted or condemned, was to haunt her for the rest of her days, and which she recounts in *Un grido lacerante* (A Piercing Cry, 1981) under the name of Agnese Lanzi. Living side by side with the great Master, Agnese barely dares name her own unhappiness: 'leaning on the arm of the man who had so miraculously become her husband, she drank in, so to speak, his daily lesson. Every day a new artist to discover, a problem to unravel, the pleasure of unexpected praise: how could she have dared ask for more?'[4] Banti is simultaneously enriched and cancelled out by her more illustrious husband; what she has renounced is her public persona expressed through 'autonomous, fulfilling and concrete work' *(A Piercing Cry*, p. 37): writing is very much second-best, 'the tombstone of her youthful hopes' *(A*

Piercing Cry, p. 43), a 'vice'.[5] Her invented name as writer of fiction offers the lonely refuge of independent identity, for 'she had won it by herself, with bitterness and boldness, refusing both her birth and her marital status . . . that name, clumsy and graceless though it was, remained the only thing that was truly hers' (*A Piercing Cry*, p. 50), but it is an identity which has constantly to be reasserted and reclaimed.

Banti's most powerful stories and novels are historical fictions of passionate intensity, dealing with women artists and female creativity and rooted in the author's own sense of fissured identity. Two of her short stories, 'Lavinia fuggita' ('Lavinia Has Fled') and 'Le donne muoiono' ('Women Die'),[6] express the clash between female ambition and the dominant ethos which excludes women from the role of creator and originator of culture. The atmospheric and evocative 'Lavinia fuggita', first published in 1937, is an account of a gifted young musician who lives in an orphanage renowned for its music, among a community of women devoted to art. Lavinia is encouraged to perform to the highest of standards, but may perform only the works of others; her desire to compose – to be the creator, the artist – is disallowed by the conventions of her day. While music offers some of her talented fellow orphans an escape from the constraints of their daily lives through marriage, Lavinia seeks not just to escape the orphanage but to transgress the prescribed role of woman and performer/executor of art. The only route open to her creativity – which takes on the characteristics of a vice in its compulsion – is through subterfuge: she alters the music given to her, and substitutes one of her own works for a new work by the master, Vivaldi: 'They would never take me seriously, they'll never let me write music. Other people's music seems like words addressed to me, I have to answer and hear the sound of my own voice. And the more I hear the more I know that my song and my sound are different' ('Lavinia', p. 32). Her ruse discovered, she is punished and her music is destroyed. Banti cannot bring herself to destroy the creator too; unwilling to compromise, to conform to the mediocrity expected of her, Lavinia runs away in the pursuit of a wild romantic dream; and another artist is lost.

Banti's views would seem at first sight to overlap with those of the emancipationists with whom she grew up in the early decades of the twentieth century, although she also hints at a substantive 'difference' ('my song and my sound are different') which anticipates some of the theoretical positions to emerge in the 1960s and 1970s. Yet Banti never regarded herself as a feminist: indeed, she professed a deep distaste for the term. Banti's 'feminism' would appear to be yet another contradiction, another dilemma which was to follow her into old age, as she looked back on the writing of 'Lavinia fuggita':

> The facts recounted were probable, if not exactly authentic, but thinking over them again Agnese felt herself caught up in a *parti pris*, in a suffocated rage which she had known in her youth in the behaviour of her peers: she who had always wished to abstract herself from the present. So they were right to accuse her of feminism, a word she hated. No, she had demanded nothing other than equality of mind and liberty of work, something which tormented her even now, in her protesting old age. She had loved few men, in fact only one, but even fewer women, and always the same: the myth of the exception against the norm of conformism. And since the exception was out of reach, she had invented it herself, attributing it to a faceless girl from other times who wanted to play her own music and was not allowed to. (*A Piercing Cry*, p. 112)

The aloof, 'difficult' Banti resists making common political cause with other women. She is not interested in feminism as an extension and reaffirmation of the democratic body politic; like Natalia Ginzburg she distrusts a movement which she believes will further divide the sexes. To attempt to rescue or 'reclaim' Banti for 'feminism' would be as simplistic as the all too frequent and rather glib assertion that women writers must necessarily be 'feminist', and therefore regarded benignly; a critical position which forbids women's writing to inhabit the spaces between and beyond theoretical precepts and prescriptions excludes as effectively and as efficiently as Lavinia's orphanage. This is not just to say that women have the right to write badly, but it is to maintain that women's writing should not be made to serve as handmaiden to the literary theory of feminist criticism, which has its own cultural and political agenda.

Banti's is a case where practice might inform theory rather than the other way round. She takes an intellectual — even elitist —

position, concerned to stress the androgynous nature of artistic talent and to expose the social and institutional practices which prevent women from achieving their potential. Her underlying preoccupation is less with frustrated Genius, with recovering and displaying a series of past heroines for us to admire like a string of pearls, than with a dichotomy between public and private which forever means that women's creativity is marked by a sense of loss, division and fracture. Banti stands apart from any specifically feminist ideology, but her texts are paradigmatic, transhistorical metaphors for the woman writer or painter, for the female artist.

'Le donne muoiono' ('Women Die', 1952) is set in the twenty-first century and recounts the gradual discovery by men that they can recall their previous lives. The claim to previous existence and the guarantee of future presence is a strictly male privilege, for women have no access to the immortality granted by reincarnation. Once again women are, like Lavinia, disinherited and orphaned, their condition recalling the 'dark fate of woman in centuries gone by, which they thought was gone for ever', and which 'had returned once more under the sign of a fundamental exclusion'. Denied this 'second memory', women are once more condemned to die, irrevocably, 'obscure and ephemeral as night butterflies' ('Women Die', p. 145).

The discovery of the 'second memory' – which Banti recounts with a sober humour worthy of the best science fiction – inevitably signifies the end of hard-won equality between the sexes. Men's attention becomes refocused on the past and future tenses; with the passing of the years, their previous intense attention to the present is displaced by a carelessness and callousness which are the products of certain rebirth. As the mutual responsibilities of humanity retreat, men are, ironically, diminished by their own certain immortality. Women, on the other hand, freeing themselves largely from matrimonial and family ties, become artists, poets, musicians and painters. Preferring to live in female communities strongly reminiscent of the cloister, they achieve the exquisitely successful sublimation of the libido which is the prerequisite for their art. If another life is not theirs by birthright, Banti's women, doomed to die, will make it for themselves, seeking immortality not in their bodies but in their art:

Knowing themselves to be abandoned and shipwrecked in eternity, closing their eyes to invent another life, had been first tragedy then discovery. . . . Fervently in love with their brief stay on earth, they treasured every moment, stretching each and every instant into echoes as profound as they were parsimonious. ('Women Die', p. 154)

Banti anticipates Elaine Showalter's fundamental point that women's cultural history is subject to disruption and discontinuity, their own tradition fractured and fragmented. When one day a gifted young musician, Agnese Grasti (and Agnese is the name given to Banti's autobiographical *alter ego* in *A Piercing Cry*), finds herself playing an unknown sonata from centuries before, she realizes that she is the first woman to experience the stirrings of the much-desired 'second memory'. But the different experience of men and women has suggested that memory, tradition and access to the past are not in themselves sufficient; any humanity worth having is not given but must be struggled for, is granted not by inalienable immortality (or gender) but by the achievements of the individual's highest gifts through art. Agnese does not divulge her discovery, and her secret dies with her. Women will be the artists of the future, but at the price of their own death.

Banti's interest in the past, despite her undoubted scholarship, is finally that of the artist rather than the academic. While the story of Lavinia's frustrated gifts could as easily have been applied to young women of Banti's own generation, the story of Agnese Grasti demonstrates a more complex and symbiotic relationship between past and present, between tradition and art. It is this complexity which lies at the heart of *Artemisia*.

The established and recorded facts of the life of Artemisia Gentileschi are so few as to make any reconstruction of her life inevitably largely fictitious. She was born in the last decade of the sixteenth century (Banti suggests 1598; more recent scholarship prefers 1593), daughter of the great painter and follower of Caravaggio, Orazio Gentileschi. With false promises of marriage she was seduced by Agostino Tassi, friend of her father and himself a painter. Her father denounced Tassi for rape: although Artemisia was herself the plaintiff, she was routinely subjected to torture at the trial. Banti quotes Artemisia's bitter wit, recorded by still extant trial documents, as she holds out her hands with the thumbscrews to Tassi and comments: 'This is the ring you gave me, these are the promises!'[7]

The trial inevitably tarnished Artemisia's reputation and made her the object of idle and malicious gossip. With more socially acceptable feminine roles no longer available to her, she concentrated on her painting, becoming one of the most accomplished artists of the day. Artemisia's achievements as an artist were paradoxically and intricately bound up with the unavailability to her of more orthodox roles, as Germaine Greer comments: 'the abortive trial had left Artemisia nothing but her talent. She could no longer live a life of matronly seclusion: she was notorious and had no chance but to take advantage of the fact.'[8]

A marriage of convenience to a certain Pietro Antonio Stiattesi followed soon after the trial. They do not appear to have lived together long, as Artemisia is recorded as being in Florence soon afterwards. She bore one or perhaps two daughters, one of whom became a painter in her turn. Apart from these meagre facts, little more information about Artemisia's life has survived. She lived in Rome, Florence and Naples, and travelled to England to visit her father Orazio, who was employed at the English court. Where and when she died is unknown.

Artemisia is recorded as being a successful and sought-after painter of portraits, but few of these works survive. Her best-known extant works, apart from her self-portraits, are probably her depictions of scenes from the Old Testament, in particular the decapitation of Holofernes by Judith, of which there are several versions. Her paintings, and her female characters, evince a violence and voluptuous strength which scandalized the more demure tastes of some of her viewers. In the nineteenth century the English art historian Mrs Jameson recognized but refused the challenge of Artemisia's work. Faced with one of the *Judith* paintings, a study of calm and steadfast female heroism in the face of the oppressive and overbearing male, she remarked, rather peevishly: 'This dreadful picture is a proof of her genius and, let me add, of its atrocious misdirection.'[9]

The decapitation of Holofernes was not an unusual subject for painting – Caravaggio, as well as Orazio, had already produced works on this theme. Artemisia's treatment of the subject is marked out by a distinctive female vision not only of women's bodies but of their potential, their power of feeling and their sense of purpose. Orazio had also painted versions of *Giuditta e la fantesca* (Judith and the Maidservant), a theme which was to provide Artemisia with the material for one of her best works. Artemisia's representation of the communion between women – whether as accomplices in murder, as in the decapitation of Holofernes, or in the more lofty theme of the Annunciation – consistently demonstrates a moral and spiritual dimension to female relationships lacking in the work of her male peers.

In writing the story of Artemisia Gentileschi, Banti clearly faces a complex series of aesthetic and ideological issues in that she is mingling history, biography and art history, stitching together objective 'facts' and subjective 'interpretation'. Banti's notion of biography approximates most closely to the views expressed by her beloved Virginia Woolf in *Orlando*: while the first duty of the biographer may be to plod methodically along 'till we fall plump into the grave and write "finis" on the tombstone above our heads' (*Orlando*, p. 41), she has well learned Woolf's lesson that history is not the seamless, readable text which would make the biographer's task an easy one but is, rather, full of holes, tears, gaps and fissures, like an old cloth to be darned. History is given coherence, as the life of Artemisia herself is given form, by the act of memory, by the will of the writer: 'Memory is the seamstress, and a capricious one at that. Memory runs her needle in and out, up and down, hither and thither' (*Orlando*, p. 49). Even more problematic is the fact that she is writing about a woman who breaks all the rules: for in this most conventional of genres, how is one to write of a woman who behaves in the most unwomanly fashion, who flouts all social convention? Woolf is deliciously ironic in describing the woman who refuses to adopt conventional thoughts, roles and habits as a woman who *cannot* exist within the parameters of literary biography, a woman who literally *cannot* be written about: 'If, then, the subject of one's biography will neither love nor kill, but will only think and imagine, we may conclude that he or she is no better than a corpse and so leave her' (*Orlando*, p. 168).

Artemisia has habitually been labelled a 'historical novel', and we might pause over this term and its implications for Banti's work. The fact that Banti re-creates Artemisia amid the ruin and rubble of a bombed Florence suggests a divergence from Georg Lukács, whose admiration for the historical novel was rooted in an artistic purpose dressed in the livery of utopia and engaging in battle with the dragons of the past: for Lukács, 'the principal front of struggle in the artistic sphere . . . is the conquest of harmful legacies'.[10] Clearly, given the degree to which she is compelled to invent, to conjure up Artemisia out of a few extant documents and a paucity of real information, Banti's novel is more 'art' than 'history', no matter how accurate her portrayal of seventeenth-century life and customs. While she eschews ahistoricism and rejects a facile, if tempting, identification of human – or female - experience across the centuries, Banti is less convinced of human progress than the Hungarian Socialist critic. She is unimpressed by and customarily dismissive of the resurgence of the historical novel which Lukács found so encouraging – for Banti, literature that poses as documentary is little more than a sham: 'The historical novel does a Proustian operation on history, reinvents it. . . . It's not enough to write factually on the basis of documents: literature has to be able to say something more than that.'[11]

Banti would concur with another contemporary Italian writer, Vincenzo Consolo, that the writing of historical fiction as genre has nothing to do with escapism or nostalgia, nor does it defer to utopia. Rather, like Agnese Grasti's refusal to shift from the present into either past or future, it is an ideological choice, a move which is both critical and ethical. Consolo, like Banti, Sir Walter Scott and Alessandro Manzoni before him in *I promessi sposi* (*The Betrothed*, 1827), refuses to countenance the separation of the historical and the contemporary; both 'real' and 'invented' characters in such fiction reflect both their own time and ours; the lesson to be drawn from the best writers of historical fiction is that it serves as a metaphor, a double image, a reflection on both the time written about and the time of writing. Banti prefers to call her own work not a historical novel but a 'hypothetical interpretation of history' (*A Piercing Cry*, p. 120).

Under the rubble that was Anna Banti's house lies the original manuscript of the original novel *Artemisia*, of which not a single page will be recovered. The novel we now have, a reconstruction (of a reconstruction) of the life of Artemisia, is placed firmly within the most dramatic and turbulent moments of Banti's own life. As

she sits disconsolately in the Boboli Gardens after a night of shelling
and bombing, she hears Artemisia's voice returning to her, begging
her not to cry. The grief of the artist and of the writer become
merged into one: 'I can feel her, with a young girl's despair,
gripping my knees. I have still not got up onto my feet and now
my sobs are for myself and her alone; for her born in 1598, old in
death, the death that is all around us, and now buried in my fragile
memory.'[12]

The narrator of *Artemisia* thus opens her narrative with an
account of a double loss. This evocation of the past seeps through
the fissures of the present, as 'hordes of swirling images pour out
from hidden wounds in my mind' (*Artemisia*, p. 4). The early pages
of the novel present a shifting narrative which skilfully intertwines
present and past, 'fact' and fiction, in a narrative strategy which
explicitly rejects realism as the dominant aesthetic: 'I am shocked
by the impetus with which I am carried beyond the limits my
memory allows me, beyond the bounds of history,' comments
the narrator (*Artemisia*, p. 12). With its shifts in narrative voice
and kaleidoscopic temporal structure, *Artemisia* is a novel which
constantly overflows its own self-imposed limits. The aesthetic
of the work is all the more extraordinary for its distance from
the dominant Neorealist mode – which produced some works
Banti admired, even though she distrusted its aggressive popu-
lism and disregard for 'style' – which was similarly attempting
to come to terms with the disaster of war. As the stones of
Florence crumble, as ceilings and floors cave in, the act of
remembrance, of creating a relationship across the ages which
is itself creative, takes on a critical significance. The account
of Artemisia's rape and trial, the removal from her of both her
virginity and her status, becomes a metaphor for the loss of all
liberties:

> Our paltry freedom is linked to the humble freedom of a virgin
> who, in the year sixteen hundred and eleven, has only the
> freedom of her own intact body, the eternal loss of which
> she can never come to terms with. For the rest of her
> life she endeavoured to replace it with another, higher and
> stronger, but the regret for that unique freedom never left her.
> (*Artemisia*, p. 18)

Refusing to succumb, outcast from the normal roles and expectations of young girls, Artemisia transforms her situation into legitimation of her position as artist. Denied the meagre consolations of femininity, the role of wife or even daughter to a largely indifferent Orazio, condemned by her scandalous fame to 'an unruly, besieged solitude' (*Artemisia*, p. 26), she claims the right to live, and to work, as a man. With her move to Florence after a hasty arranged marriage, Artemisia becomes established as a painter, one of her most important early commissions being to paint *L'inclinazione* (widely regarded as a self-portrait) for the Casa Buonarroti, where it can still be seen. Banti's narrative prefers to concentrate on the extraordinary painting of *Judith Decapitating Holofernes*, an act of sensual violence envisaged by the text as a displaced castration and, as such, a consummate and definitive act of vengeance wreaked on the male body. Two versions of this painting exist, one in the Capodimonte Museum in Naples, the other in the Uffizi Galleries in Florence. The two paintings are almost identical in composition: the foreshortening leaves the face of Holofernes turned out in desperation to the viewer, and the unnecessarily long sword centre stage; blood spills thickly on to the white pillow. The servant girl Abra pushes Holofernes down on to the bed, while Judith calmly and inexorably plies her sword.[13] For the first time the apocryphal Jewish heroine is depicted as a cold-blooded killer: any sense of pity or outrage is overwhelmed by sheer violence and hatred.[14]

Even more than on the painting itself, Banti's narrative focuses on the process of its composition as iconographic representation of Artemisia's anger and desire for revenge. As she paints, the artist is watched by a group of women whose views and confessions about sexual relations take an increasingly virulent and aggressive turn. When the flash of a knife incites the women to enact on the docile Greek model the example of Judith, the painting's symbolic status as representation of female rage is confirmed. Artemisia's own sense of revenge feeds on the savage anger of these women; the act of applying paint is born of a murderous impulse, the brush is wielded as though it were a knife. '"I painted it, and it's as if I killed a tyrant"' (*Artemisia* p. 61). Excluded from the social order as defined by patriarchy, Artemisia enters – temporarily – a wild zone reminiscent of the island in William Golding's *Lord of the Flies* (1954) in its violence, its inversion of habitual social rules.

Painting functions as revenge, therapy, exorcism, an affirmation of the (creative) self, of womanhood, where her womanhood has been trampled on.

But Artemisia is not a prophet for the simplistic platitudes and fecklessness of such as Lorena Bobbitt, who notoriously castrated her husband in 1993 and got away with it. With *Judith Decapitating Holofernes* she achieves identity, but the identity of a woman artist is a complex, lonely one. While she feels a sense of victory, she also feels a deep sense of shame; for in order to express her own sense of violation, she has violated in her turn. Art is not to be turned to the base purpose of unsubtle revenge, and should transcend the purely vindictive.

With her rape by Agostino Tassi exorcized, Artemisia discovers a deeper communion not with women thrown together by the sense of otherness – for common gender is insufficient to broach existential solitude – but with fellow women artists. Simply to bemoan one's fate as a woman is to succumb to the most insidious of violations, to accept the mantle of otherness, and thus eternally to be marginalized. Artemisia's is a harder path, as the artist refuses the crumbs of consolation offered by masochistic victimhood, and feels a returning compassion for men: 'Poor men, too, tormented by arrogance and authority' (*Artemisia*, p. 51).

Artemisia returns to Rome and, for a short time, enjoys an unexpected conjugal intimacy with her shy, tender, husband Antonio Stiattesi, marked off from his rowdy, grasping and vulgar family by a generous and utterly seductive delicacy for which she is unprepared. Taking up the role of wife means setting aside the hard and bitter struggle to establish her own identity: '"How lovely it is," she thinks, enraptured, forgetful, as she drifts off into sleep once more, "how lovely it is to belong to someone, to lose one's identity, to become different, unrecognizable. How lovely is it?"' (*Artemisia*, p. 73). The question mark reveals the dilemma: forced to choose between living with Antonio and taking up a position as respected and independent artist, she barely hesitates. If Banti gave up her work for her love, Artemisia makes the opposite choice. Neither woman ever found peace: *Artemisia* is a deeper work than wish-fulfilment, or an elaborate construction with which Banti rearranges the pieces of her own life. Artemisia cannot have both love and art. Pregnancy, and the wisdom and solidarity of the working-class women who attend her, almost induce her to renounce her virile ambition, to suppress 'the burning pain of that "if only I were not a woman," that futile lament' (*Artemisia*, p. 88).

The irreconcilable choice between head and heart, between her art and the more comfortable intimacies of family ties, is one which is continually before her. Artemisia – like Banti? – counts no women among her friends. As one who has renounced tenderness and given up the role of wife, who has opened an art school and drawing academy, who has to compete on an equal footing with men, she cannot allow herself to indulge her sometimes overwhelming passion for her daughter, Porziella. As she embraces her child, she is aware of an unbridled emotion 'that catches in her throat with a taste of blood. Is it permissible to love a daughter in this voracious, greedy manner, the manner of female animals and of destitute women in their hovels?' (*Artemisia*, p. 93).

Artemisia's dedication to the 'higher' pursuits of artistic and intellectual life, which she claims as her absolute right, is clearly in conflict with a desire to immerse herself in her own biology. Artemisia – and Banti – have no way of resolving the dilemma, of healing the split. Her guilty snatches at the pleasures both of marriage and of motherhood underline the tragedy of the woman artist: that her self-affirmation in the public domain is achieved only by radical surgery on her private life, by exercising the strictest economy of libidinal energy.

The central scenes of the novel outline a complex web of relations between the author-narrator Anna, Artemisia, and the woman she hoped to befriend, Annella de Rosa. While they speak of the desire for communion and understanding between women, even across the centuries, the narrative suggests somewhat forlornly that it is a vain hope. Banti's gift is to write a text which is at once a compelling narrative and a complex metaphor which peels away layers of ideological platitudes. Giving a reception, Artemisia wishes the world to see that she is not threatened by the younger, immensely beautiful and talented painter Annella. The very urgency of her feeling betrays her need to convince herself as well as her guests, as well as her own desire. Annella, whose husband beats her, publicly rejects the offer of friendship and abandons Artemisia to her solitude:

No one can hurt her as much as another woman: this is what she ought to have explained to those men who were perhaps amused at the conflict between the two painters. 'Look at these two women,' she should have said, 'two of the best, the strangest, two who most resemble exemplary men. See how they have been driven to being false and disloyal to one another in the world that you have created for your own use and pleasure. We are so few and so besieged that we can no longer recognize or understand or even respect each other as you men do. You set us loose, for fun, in an arena of poisonous weapons. And so we suffer.' (*Artemisia*, p. 107)

There is no communion between Artemisia and Annella in a patriarchal world which would set them at odds. Anna the narrator-author has made Artemisia into an imperfect, proud woman who would rather be a man, and has failed to construct for her a desirable ideal freedom. There is no chance of a 'joint collaboration, active and shared, the convulsive game of two shipwrecked women who do not want to abandon the hope of being saved on a barrel' (*Artemisia*, p. 109). Neither can there be any real understanding between protagonist and narrator, between Artemisia and Anna: the desolation of the present, the continuing cycle of ruins and despair, suggest that few lessons have been learned. The historical novel becomes a clear metaphor for the present, as the narrator declares that she will 'limit myself to the short span of my own memory, condemning my presumptuous idea of trying to share the terrors of my own epoch with a woman who has been dead for three centuries' (*Artemisia*, p. 111).

Artemisia visits her beloved father Orazio in England. The one work from this stay which Banti discusses in detail is the *The Allegory of Painting,* still to be seen at Hampton Court. It is normally viewed as a self-portrait, but Banti gives a very different reading of the work as a portrait of Annella de Rosa, the painter of genius who died young, stabbed by a jealous lover. If the earlier account of her meeting with Annella had emphasized the difficulties of two women artists being anything other than mortal enemies in the competitive artistic economy of patriarchy which will recognize a female artist only as an odd exception, then this painting is a gesture towards a different hope – of real communion, generosity and even love between women, no longer set up one against the other:

> Artemisia feels compelled to take her brush and caress that painted hand slightly more than is necessary. She crosses herself. But the Hail Mary that rises to her lips is not for the repose of a soul but for the eternal image of a passionate love, for the realization of an arcane, selfless hope. And the painting lay uncovered on the easel the whole night long. (*Artemisia*, p. 197)

The painting of Annella takes place within the context of Artemisia's reunion with Orazio, the beloved father who, like his daughter, has sacrificed all other affections to his art. The analysis Banti gives of Artemisia's paintings would seem to be crucially connected to Artemisia's relationship with her father and with the male tradition of art which he represents. Orazio has consistently refused the role of father; in order to win him over and gain for herself his 'difficult love', she must become an artist herself, seduce him with her talent. In painting *Judith Decapitating Holofernes*, Artemisia's sense of vengeance and shame is matched by pride that she has won her place within the male tradition of art, that she has proved herself as good a painter as any man, that here is a painting which would win her father's recognition: hers is 'the awful pride of a woman who has been avenged, in whom, despite her shame, there is also room for the satisfaction of the artist who has overcome all the problems of her art and speaks the language of her father, of the pure, of the chosen' (*Artemisia*, p. 46).

Judith Decapitating Holofernes, act of revenge for the ultimate violation of the female body, is itself an embodiment of the aesthetic forms of male tradition. It is almost ironic that the painting should be so good; Artemisia has learnt her lessons well. Yet the painting inscribes itself not only within a male aesthetic but within a male vision of the world. With the later painting, on the contrary, Artemisia has been acknowledged as an equal; no longer a pupil, she has become her own master. Banti is not here making a case for a painterly equivalent to *écriture féminine*; Artemisia does not become an artistic revolutionary, and her author is too much of a historian to distort or disregard the role and function of tradition in any artistic enterprise. But she imagines for Artemisia equality on the highest possible level, that of the creative imagination which, as in Woolf, is androgynous: 'One noble and secret language was spoken in an exchange of glances. . . . Two minds, not a man and a woman, not a father and daughter' (*Artemisia* p. 183).

This is a utopia rarely available to women, built on denial and loss. Banti makes a passionate claim for the quality of art by women, and a powerful plea for an end to their seclusion and exclusion. At stake for society is a renewed humanism after the cataclysm of war; at stake for women is an end to the solitude of Lavinia, exiled and condemned to wander for ever in strange, wild lands.

8
Memory and Melancholy
in Natalia Ginzburg (1916–91)

Oh yes, I've known quite a different world in a sense – in a
sense, but I don't think it's as different as people say. I think that
a good many of the differences are aeroplanes and motor cars and
things on the top. I don't think that human relationships are very
different.

(Ivy Compton-Burnett,
in *Ivy and Stevie: Conversations and Reflections*)

In 1984 Natalia Ginzburg wrote: 'when I write novels I always
feel as though I am holding broken mirrors in my hands; I always
used to hope that one day I could finally put a whole mirror back
together again but it has never happened, and as I went on writing
the hope faded away.' It was a hope which, after almost half a
century of literary production, had faded completely: 'this time I
had no hope right from the start, the mirror was broken and I knew
I would not be able to put the pieces together. I would never have
the pleasure of having a whole mirror in front of me.'[1]

Ginzburg's narratives hold up a fragmented mirror to a fragmented society. Her novels, stories and plays offer a minute,
painful and ironic analysis of almost half a century of Italian
life, charting the minimal flurries and currents of personal and
family sentiment from the alienation and dissociation of Italian
society under Mussolini's regime to the tawdry brashness of the
1980s. Ginzburg's work is an oblique representation of history
in the lower case; her characters are never the protagonists of
textbooks but drift on the eddies of larger events being played
out elsewhere; they do not make history but risk being unmade by
it, and have only a partial vision of the circumstances which control
and organize their lives. The tragic oppression of Fascism resonates

in the claustrophobia of personal relationships lived in the key of solitude and despair, leavened by the ironic wit and compassionate humour of the writer; the tone of Ginzburg's best work is one of simultaneous humour and compassion, a lightness of touch which exposes, yet will not judge too harshly, the foibles of humanity.

Despite the beguiling simplicity of Ginzburg's writing, she addresses the world from a position which is oblique and complex. She refuses any *parti pris*, any formalized ideological position. Educated to politics by a family with a strong Socialist and anti-Fascist tradition, she finally became a deputy to Parliament as an independent voice on the Left. Her Jewish roots (her family name is Levi) lead her to understand alienation and marginalization, but not to beat any religious or sectarian drum, and there are few Jewish characters in her work. She exposes the humiliation and degradation of women's lives, but will take issue with many of the assumptions and conclusions of neo-feminism; she will not adopt radical feminist positions which proclaim the plight of oppressed women. As a writer she shares the Neorealist compulsion to direct representation unmediated by any concern for *belles lettres*, but she rejects their preoccupation with the class struggle, with heroic resistance or with the heroic poor. She focuses on relationships within families, between friends and lovers, life in small towns, the rituals of everyday experience, the problems of human relationships which lie at the heart of all our lives.

The fascinating accumulation of detailed lives and interwoven stories to be found in Ginzburg has been compared to the work of Isaac Bashevis Singer; Ginzburg, too, takes risks with the everyday, weaving stories and novels out of the stuff of the minutiae of human experience. Her prose style, sober and unrhetorical, with both lexis and syntax indicating a move away from the Italian obsession with 'high' culture, is pared of complex clauses or elaborate metaphor. She writes with a rhythmic tension, a tight and sober use of adjectives, a spare but evocative style that recalls in particular the work of American writers such as Ernest Hemingway, Gertrude Stein and William Faulkner. She was later to be influenced by Marcel Proust, whose work she translated into Italian, but the greatest influence from an early age was Chekhov, who similarly sought the hidden and subtle dynamics of personal and family life as a reflection of wider social tensions.

Ginzburg's own social and family position falls between classifications or categories of experience. Her mother was Catholic and her father Jewish, although the family was not orthodox. She was born in Palermo in 1916 but grew up in Turin, and it is this city in Piedmont, with its strong intellectual Socialist and Communist traditions, which has provided the backcloth to the greater part of her work. The lack of glamour available to an aspiring middle-class Jewish writer in industrial Turin led to initial despair: 'We were, alas, bourgeois. Not only that, we were Jewish, and both these things seemed to me a million miles away from the world of poetry.'[2] Ginzburg had limited access to the working-class traditions of culture and language which were the heritage of novelists such as James Kelman or Jeff Torrington in Turin's twin city, Glasgow. Her aesthetic emerged from her acknowledgement that poetry lies not in the exotic but precisely in the familiar, that art is a matter less of the imagination than of intimate knowledge, of memory.

Ginzburg's early fears of dullness and irrelevance proved unfounded. A child under Fascism, she witnessed the persecution and harassment of her family both as Jews and as political activists. Still a young woman, she married Leone Ginzburg (1909–44), a Russian-born intellectual and active anti-Fascist who worked with the publishers Einaudi in Turin. Within two years of their marriage he was banished by the Fascist authorities to the Abruzzi in indefinite *confino*, or internal exile. Natalia accompanied him, together with their two small children, and the experience of being uprooted from Turin to live in a small Southern village was to leave a profound mark on her. She wrote under an assumed name – the racial laws passed in 1938 forbade Jews to publish or, indeed, to hold any professional position. In 1943, with the fall of Mussolini's government, Leone Ginzburg left exile to return to Turin and Rome to run a clandestine newspaper. He was arrested soon after, and Natalia never saw him again; he died in prison in February 1944 at the hands of the Nazis. Ginzburg experienced at first hand the dramatic, tragic turmoil of modern Italy, her life a miniature mirror-image of the devastation and painful reconstruction of a nation.

Ginzburg's first short novel, inspired by the experience of living in a small Southern village, was *La strada che va in città* (*The Road to the City*), written in 1941 and published the following year under the assumed name of Alessandra Tornimparte. In this novel the young village girl Delia aspires to live, like her sister Azalea, in the city, with its paved streets, shop windows and perceived glamour: to this end, and out of a childish desire to arouse her friends' envy, she starts seeing the doctor's son, who is well placed to advance her socially and economically. The wretchedness and poverty of village life contribute in no small way to Delia's disastrous family life in which the father beats his children and the bitter, overworked mother, confined to the family home by a jealous husband, curses her own offspring. This catastrophic family life is symbolized by the frequently repeated imprecation 'maledetta la madre che t'ha fatto', 'a curse on the mother who bore you'. The stoicism with which the mother receives the news of her daughter's unwanted pregnancy, attempting to divert the worst of her husband's rage, suggests resignation rather than compassion, and hers is an attitude which brings no intimacy and little comfort. The mother's fleeting solidarity springs from a common female destiny of subservience and double standards, and there is clear anger at the social injustice by which Delia is kept hidden until she gives birth, while her heartless seducer is free to continue both his studies and his other affairs in the city.

Delia's pregnancy leads to an unwanted, enforced marriage and the tardy realization of her love for her cousin, Nini. It is too late: Nini dies, and the lost opportunity for happiness is melodramatically underlined. Delia is left with little choice but to go on with her apathetic marriage and tread the same dubious path as her sister before her. Mother–daughter relationships come under further scrutiny at the house of Delia's aunt, where the girl is sent – after harsh squabbles over money for her keep – out of public view, until her marriage and the birth of her child. Her aunt's account of the life which awaits her properly engaged daughter Santa holds out little promise of happiness: 'when a woman marries, that's when the trouble starts. There are the kids who cry, the husband who has to be served, your in-laws who make your life hard' (*The Road to the City*, I.54). Here, too, there is little solidarity or sympathy between the generations beyond a bitter recognition of a shared condition. Mother and daughter do not console but torment each other. Despite their much-trumpeted moral virtue, the superior position they take over Delia's condition is a false

one: Santa's future husband – should her mother ever finally
put her dowry together - is a peasant, and Santa envies Delia
her life of relative comfort and ease in the city; mother and
daughter harbour a grudging admiration for Delia's strategy in
evading Santa's own fate.

Yet the city is revealed to be neither the consumer paradise
of Delia's hopes nor the sinful hole of Santa's excited fantasy.
Relationships here fail just as easily. Nini and Delia's brother
Giovanni have an affair with the same woman, but both take
care to leave before demands of marriage are made. Her sister
Azalea, who has trodden the road into the city before her, has a
series of traumatic and hysterical affairs with younger men. Too
late, Delia regrets her rejection of Nini. She is briefly aware that
things might have been different, but 'bit by bit I began to live like
Azalea. I spent the day in bed and towards evening I would get up,
paint my face and go out, my fox fur flung over my shoulder. As
I walked along I would look around me and smile impertinently,
like Azalea always did' (*The Road to the CIty*, I.89).

The failure of women in Ginzburg's early stories to realize
themselves, or even to comprehend their own feelings, is matched
by the failure of their men to offer relationships which are anything
more than superficial or casual. *E' stato così* (*The Dry Heart*, 1947)
again verges on melodrama, for the narrator has just murdered her
husband: 'I went into the kitchen and made the tea, I added milk
and sugar and poured it into the thermos, screwed the lid on tightly
and went back into the study. Then . . . I took the revolver from
the drawer and shot him right in the eyes' (I.89). In these opening
lines banality is a mask for despair, the narration of the everyday a
fragile covering for that which cannot be recounted. The dramatic
pistol shot (itself reminiscent of Chekhov's *Uncle Vanya* and *The
Seagull*) erupts into the cracked, brittle surface of the story, with its
concentration on ordinary actions and objects – the thermos, the
tea, the flask. It mirrors the protagonist's own fractured perception,
which is finally and brutally clarified not through language, but by
her husband's casual drawing, compelling her both to a recognize
her own degraded subservience and to reflect back to him a
gratifying image of his careless power.[3] Alberto is irredeemably
superficial and inconstant, like 'a cork floating on the sea water
and waves rock him gently but he will never know what is at the

bottom of the sea' (*The Dry Heart*, I.92).

Ginzburg probes the narrator's conviction that she is in love with him, a conviction based largely on fantasy, lack of experience and loneliness. The narrator – unnamed, like so many of Ginzburg's women – succumbs to a degenerate Bovaryism, falling prey to the most banal and clichéd of romantic fantasies and illusions. Alberto's drawings are a pictorial representation of the truth which she fails to uncover. Once they are married: 'I told him he should do a cat with his face and a mouse with mine. He laughed and asked me why. . . . The mouse looked terrified and humiliated and was knitting, the cat was black and fierce and was sketching in a notebook' (*The Dry Heart*, I.107). The narrator's unreasoning despair is again represented in this *mise en abîme* of powerlessness in the face of unthinking and unconscious cruelty. Like many of Ginzburg's early characters, she accepts the part of victim; there is no solution to her unhappiness other than death and self-destruction – no sublimation, no work (she has given up her teaching job on marrying), no friendship. The world these women inhabit is totally closed and forever dark. Life is more complex than her dreams, and her murder of Alberto will, the text suggests, be swiftly followed by her own suicide.

Even while her early female characters can be seen as passive victims, Ginzburg's stance is never that of an essentialist feminism which would posit an unbridgeable gulf between the sexes and consider all human exchange in terms of oppressive sexual relationships. Ginzburg calls for greater sophistication, and greater complexity, in our view of human intercourse. While it is true that women have been exploited and humiliated for centuries, this is only one aspect of the female condition and one perspective on it:

> It is wrong to think that the humiliations suffered by women are the single essence of the relationships between women and men. It is a crude, impoverished, reductive and limiting vision of the world. It is a vision of the world which does not reflect reality. The world is complicated and multiform: particularly complicated, multiform and dramatic are the relationships between men and women.[4]

Ginzburg pleads for complexity rather than conformity. While she supports all the practical demands for emancipation, she shuns what she sees as the reductive dogmatism of ideological feminism, with its assumption of women's oppression as the common denominator of the female condition.

If our material lives are marked but not, finally, determined by the fact of gender, the same can be said of art. As a young writer Ginzburg, working in a literary culture which deemed art an almost exclusively male activity, sought to disguise her sex, eschewing styles and techniques such as autobiography which she considered – and dismissed – as 'feminine' and experimenting with a male narrator as alibi. In her writing as in her life, Ginzburg attempts to put sexuality in its place – as a significant but not categorical imperative in our lives and in social organization:

> In our best moments our thought is neither that of man or of woman. It is, however, equally true that on everything we think or do lies the imprint of our separate physiognomy, and if we are women, the female signs of our temperament are stamped on our actions and words. But our ultimate goal is to reach that domain where men and women alike can recognize themselves in us and our physical presence is forgotten. ('La condizione femminile', p. 653)

The short story 'La madre' ('The Mother', 1948) shows the dangerously tragic limitations of women's lives in the immediate post-war period. It is a remarkable sketch of a young woman, widowed, living in a single room in her parents' house with her two small sons. The comment made in Luigi Pirandello's play *Six Characters in Search of an Author* that the similarly unnamed mother 'non è una donna, è una madre' ('is not a woman, she's a mother')[5] is equally pertinent here, where a rigid, traditional social code denies the woman sexual and emotional independence. Her vitality and sexuality earn her the disapproval not only of her parents but also of her children: she no longer represents the clarity and natural authority which they seek and which lends order to their world. This volatile mother, who stays out late, plucks her eyebrows, puts yellow powder on her face and smokes in bed, earns only their contempt and mistrust. Traditional life is represented by the more solid grandparents and the family servant, Diomora. The boys are captivated by the brief unorthodoxy in which they live when their grandparents are away for a few days, and their mother's friend visits the house bringing with him tales of Africa and new storybooks; yet still the return of customary order is welcomed with relief.

This sober, austere story offers no solution to the tension between woman as sexual being and woman as mother within a rigid family and social structure, and when the lover returns to Africa the mother commits suicide in a seedy hotel room. Yet the real tragedy begins after her death, as her sons gradually and inexorably forget her: she is erased from their memories, from a powerful patriarchal tradition, just as she has erased her own body with poison, and the crucial dilemma between a woman's desiring body and the social role imposed on her remains unresolved. Like the narrator of Sibilla Aleramo's *A Woman*, she rebels against her restrictive role as sacrificial mother, but this mother is no potential heroine for the feminist movement, and there are no alternative spaces for her outside the patriarchal home; the neighbours' whisperings about her failure to love her own children contain a harsh truth in a world where maternal love is itself poisoned by its enforced exclusivity, by the impossibility of loving elsewhere.

While definitions of Neorealism are as many as those who were supposed to have taken part in its enterprise, Ginzburg shares the Neorealist polemical urge to look squarely at reality, with all its defects and faults. In one of her most polemical pieces, she argues that there are still those who

> complain that writers adopt a bitter, violent language, that they tell harsh, sad stories. . . . We cannot lie in our books and we cannot lie in any of the things that we do. And perhaps this is the only good thing to have come out of the war. Not to lie and not to tolerate the lies of others. That's how young people are, that's how our generation is.[6]

She is resistant to novels which announce only their own difficulty, novels as dry and hard as sawdust or stones. She is hostile to wilful elaboration, to the perverse shuffling of space and time. Ginzburg, then, consistently advocated clarity and readability, but it is with *Tutti i nostri ieri* (*All Our Yesterdays*, 1952), her first long novel, that she engages most directly with the tenets of Neorealism. This work, an account of the impact of history on individual human destiny, is set in the period of anti-Fascist struggle and the fight for the liberation of Italy from the Nazis; the title, taken from the last act of Shakespeare's *Macbeth*, suggests the tragic destiny of a whole generation:

> Tomorrow, and tomorrow, and tomorrow
> Creeps in this petty pace from day to day
> To the last syllable of recorded time,
> And all our yesterdays have lighted fools
> The way to dusty death. (*Macbeth*, Act III)

All Our Yesterdays relates the intertwining destinies of two bourgeois professional and business families from the North. The father of one family is a lawyer engaged in a solitary, futile struggle against Fascism, writing memoirs which are little more than personal diatribes, and are eventually burnt. The other family is that of a wealthy industrialist with a dissatisfied wife. The novel weaves its way around the lives of the children of these two families. The lawyer's daughter, Anna, begins an affair with Giuma, who is narcissistically obsessed with hermetic poetry and his own doubtful talents; she falls pregnant and is effectively abandoned by him. She is gathered up by an old family friend, Cenzo Rena, who marries her and takes her to the South. The vibrant, warm Cenzo Rena is shot by the Germans as he attempts to save the lives of some of the local peasants. Anna returns to Turin to be reunited with family and friends who have survived.

While the structure of the novel takes the reader through different social and cultural contexts, Ginzburg never sets out to provide a sociological or historical survey of Fascism, war and resistance. The novel refuses the engaged political stance of Neorealism; its ambition is not to provide the 'national-popular' literature desired by Gramsci and hunted down in post-war fiction by eager critics. Like Elsa Morante in her later novel *La storia* (*History*, 1974), Ginzburg takes a worm's-eye view of history, eschewing the grand design, the all-encompassing flourish, the inclusive and definitive explanation. Anna is both protagonist and victim, caught up in events which are much bigger than her and which she barely comprehends. For the writer, human motivation and action never have the clarity attributed to them by politicians or ideologues. In the Northern city we see the three young bourgeois intellectuals, Danilo, Emmanuele and Ippolito, collaborating on anti-Fascist propaganda. Danilo, who had courted Anna's sister Concettina, is imprisoned for his activities, marries a Party comrade, and after the war cynically adapts himself to the political and ideological compromises of post-war Italian life. Emmanuele, who writes for a clandestine newspaper during the Resistance, returns to run his father's factory. The suicide of Anna's brother at the news that Italy is to enter the war is an act of despair rooted in his difficult and dramatic relationship with an unloving father rather than a gesture of political defeat.

The dubious motivation of the three self-proclaimed anti-Fascists is contrasted with the spontaneity and warmth of Cenzo Rena, one of the most positive characters in the whole of Ginzburg's work. From his first appearance, trailing suitcases full of tinned tuna fish and endless yards of rough material out of which he plans to make his underwear, to his tetchy attempts to cure the village children of chronic diarrhroea, to his selfishness in his long refusal to share his house with refugees from bombed cities, this is a portrait not of an idealized martyr but, like Thomas Keneally's portrait of Oscar Schindler, of a man whose faults and failings are redeemed by his generous and spontaneous courage. Other novels of the Resistance present us with the ritual self-sacrifice of one of the main characters in order to save others, presented in saintly, Christ-like terms: Berardo in Ignazio Silone's *Fontamara* (*Fontamara*, 1930); Maciste in Vasco Pratolini's *Cronache di poveri amanti* (*Chronicle of Poor Lovers*, 1947), whose murdered body lying in the street is splayed out as on a cross; or the torture of Manfredi in Rossellini's film *Roma, città aperta* (*Rome, Open City*, 1945). Rena, on the contrary, does not act out of political or ideological conviction; the hero's portrait is made human by whimsical irony.

Similarly the peasants, so frequently idealized in novels and films of the period, do not appear here as the future saviours of a corrupt Italy, or as the repository of moral values abandoned and suppressed during twenty years of Fascism; nor is there any attempt to reproduce dialect for greater authenticity. Instead, there is mutual incomprehension: Anna finds the peasants tedious, while they, for their part, cannot understand why Rena, whom they like and admire, married her.

All Our Yesterdays follows the minutiae of the lives of its characters as they come together, drift apart, and move towards each other or are lost. The whole is given consistency by the historical circumstances which form the stage on which they play out their lives. The shifting focus and choral nature of the novel leads to a fragmentation of the representation of history, no longer allied to an abstract narrating voice. History is woven into the lives of ordinary men and women: 'the seamstress used to tell the story of when she hid the red flag in her baby's cot, the baby who was twenty now and had been taken prisoner in Somalia, but perhaps he still remembered that flag stuck one night into the straw of his cot while the fascists let off shots all round the house' (*All Our Yesterdays*, I.510). Ginzburg is doubtful that the experience of war, fear and hunger leads to greater wisdom or understanding. Seen by Cenzo Rena as a little insect hanging forlornly on a leaf, after her dramatic experience of maternity, loss and death Anna is now hanging on to only a slightly bigger leaf. The novel emphasizes not heroic knowledge achieved through suffering, but our partial perception and understanding of our own lives.

Le voci della sera (*Voices in the Evening*, 1961) was written during a stay in London when Natalia Ginzburg's second husband, Gabriele Baldini, was Director of the Italian Cultural Institute. In England Ginzburg discovered the work of Ivy Compton-Burnett, an influence she readily acknowledges.[7] In Ginzburg's work, however, dialogue does not function as a social mask or disguise but, in its tone of almost incantatory melancholy, gestures towards a 'haemorrhage of sentiments lost and unexpressed' (Sanvitale, p. 32).

Voices in the Evening shows further stylistic development as Ginzburg sheds her revulsion towards autobiographical writing and draws, if indirectly, on her own experience. While she professed her enormous admiration for writers such as Annie Vivanti and Elsa Morante, her early equivocation about being identified or labelled as a 'woman writer' led to conscious stylistic choices, including early experiments with male narrators. Autobiography had, for Ginzburg, been associated with the narcissistic sentimentalism which she found all too often in women writers, and was desperate to avoid:

I had an overwhelming horror of autobiography; I was terrified, petrified by it: because I felt a strong pull towards autobiography, as I know many women have . . . I had a terrible fear of being 'sticky and sentimental', even though I had a strong inclination to sentimentalism, a defect which seemed to me hateful because it was feminine; and my desire was to write like a man. ('Nota', I.1121)

Written during the economic boom, *Voices in the Evening* explores personal and family relationships in a time of crisis and the fragmenting of old certainties, of traditional moral and political values. Shifting social structures are obliquely mirrored in Ginzburg's evolving style; the melodrama has all but disappeared, in an epistemological and aesthetic rupture with the past. In the novel the narrator, Elsa, has a fragile relationship with Tommasino Balotta, youngest son of a wealthy industrialist. Elsa and Tommasino meet secretly: when their affair becomes public it splinters, a fragile thing crushed by the pressure of conformity. They break off the relationship, and Elsa returns to her previous monotonous existence.

Elsa's own story is dispersed, emerging only gradually through her memories of the Balotta family. Vincenzino, the eldest son, returns to the village after a period spent in America, but the indifference which soon creeps into his marriage to the beautiful Cate causes them both unhappiness; Vincenzino dies in a car crash, and Cate goes to Rome to begin a life as woman of the world to which she is manifestly ill-suited. At the moment of their final parting, she asks: 'but why, why have we ruined everything?' (*Voices in the Evening*, I.725). It is a question echoed by Elsa herself later in the novel as her engagement to Tommasino collapses: 'So, everything is ruined . . . but why have we ruined everything?' (*Voices in the Evening*, I.760). Mario marries an eccentric Russian exile whom he met in France; his happiness is a lazy, undemanding contentment. The younger sister, Raffaella, finds some sort of freedom in fighting with the partisans; but after the war she joins ever smaller political splinter groups and ends up marrying Il Purillo, an ex-Fascist.

Attention gradually focuses on the youngest brother, Tommasino. The affair and subsequent engagement fail: this is no longer the time, it seems, for great or consuming passions. 'It wasn't a great passionate, romantic love. But it was something, something intimate and delicate with its own kind of fullness, its own kind of liberty. You and I, with no plans for the future, with nothing, we were happy, in some way of our own' (*Voices in the Evening*, I.768). Tommasino is incapable of love, as he is incapable of engagement with the world, and there is a chasm between the experience of his generation and that of those who grew up under Fascism and lived through the war. The inability of the older generation to comprehend the 'subtle, complicated psychological problems' (*Voices in the Evening*, I.773) of their offspring is matched by the fragility of youthful love, the precariousness of feeling, the inability to speak words which are not simply protective or defensive. Moments of intimacy have the quality of a prayer. With their failure, Tommasino and Elsa are left to rue what they have lost – and loss of memory, of the past, is the greatest loss of all.

Repeated patterns of almost incantatory dialogue between Elsa and her mother, recalling the work of writers such as Marguerite Duras or even Harold Pinter and Samuel Beckett, both structure the narrative and offer an interpretative key. As the novel opens Elsa is taking her mother home after a visit to the doctor. The dominant verb, 'disse', 'she said', both gives the mother a voice and underlines the daughter's silence:

> My mother said: – I can feel something like a walnut in my throat. If I swallow, it hurts.
> She said: – Good evening, General.
> My mother said: – What a lovely head of hair, even at his age.
> She said: Did you notice how ugly the dog has got?
> – Now I've got a taste of vinegar in my throat. And still that knot, all the time, which hurts. (*Voices in the Evening*, I.667)

Two pages of the mother's comments on people they meet eddy round her comments on her daughter: 'She said: – Is it not possible just once in a while for a miracle to happen and for you to open your mouth?' (*Voices in the Evening*, I.670). The dominant form 'disse' is displaced in the centre of the novel by 'diceva', the past continuous tense effectively slowing down time, undermining the linear progression of the story; the tightening circles of what is possible for Elsa and Tommasino become an iconic representation of the desperate aimlessness of their generation, adrift on a sea of changing moral and social values:

> He used to say: – What is it you want?
> He would say: – You wanted me to marry you, and I'm marrying you. What more do you want?
> I would say: – I don't know.
> He would say: – You're so complicated! Women are so difficult, so complicated!
> He would say: – I suppose we can look forward to a nice evening in your sitting room with aunt Ottavia? . . .
> He would say: – If only you were at least happy! (*Voices in the Evening*, I.765)

Elsa's silence, her suppression of her own narrative, are echoed at the end of the novel. The novel, too, is circular: there are no more goals, nowhere else to go. Again, it is autumn. Again, mother and daughter are returning to the village. The change to the present tense suggests the end of change, of progression. Elsa's minimal speaking voice is now completely silenced:

> My mother says: – I've got a stiff neck, I wonder why. . . .
> She says: – Tommasino is weak, he's feeble. All in all it's just as well you didn't marry him. . . .
> She says: – Being so weak Tommasino will have heeded Purillo's advice. Purillo must have told him to look for a richer girl, one with no socialists in the family. . . . (*Voices in the Evening*, I.777)

With *Lessico famigliare* (*Family Sayings*, 1963), her best-known novel, Ginzburg completes her journey from the third to the first person, from a desired 'masculine' objectivity to 'feminine' autobiography, from description or free indirect discourse to dialogue. In this re-creation of her family through language, snatches of rhyme, family stories, idiosyncratic expressions, language becomes the connective tissue which unites the members of this very modern Jewish family, scattered in a new kind of diaspora:

We are five brothers and sisters. We live in different cities, some of us are abroad, and we rarely write to each other. When we meet we can be distracted and distant with each other. But all it takes between us is a word. Just a word, a single sentence, one of those old old sentences heard and repeated any number of times when we were children. (*Family Sayings*, I.825)

Family Sayings is a humorous, affectionate, nostalgic portrait of Ginzburg's family, traced from the early years of Fascism through to the years after World War Two, and remains her most consistently popular novel. Eccentricities are lovingly depicted: her father, university professor, anti-Fascist, passionate, intolerant, despotic, temperamental, given to loud rages interspersed by moments of clumsy tenderness and disarming innocence; his wife Lydia, with her snatches of opera and her sudden enthusiasms just as soon forgotten; Natalia's sister and brothers, with their childish pranks and chatter, later to become actively involved in anti-Fascism – some of the leading opponents of Mussolini's regime were friends of the family. It is this environment of convinced public political positions and chaotic private relationships which is evoked through recollections of fragments of language, 'sayings', a mixture of mispronunciations, childish rhymes, incorrect usages or dialect words. The sayings are humorous, idiosyncratic, frequently without referential meaning, and their function is less to give information than to reinforce and confirm an almost tribal sense of community. The characters depicted in *Family Sayings* have everything in common because they have language in common, however far apart and dispersed they were. By one of those intuitions which occur in a state of grace, Ginzburg connected the reciprocal recognition of different members of a Jewish family to a poetic perception of life, to a sense of 'belonging'.[8] Language is totalizing: public and family figures alike are seen from this perspective – the inclusive, all-absorbing family lexis results in a demystifying levelling of conventional hierarchies. Monumental events of recent Italian history are undercut by the family lexis, thus avoiding both private sentimentality and public melodrama.

The one character largely missing from the text is Natalia herself. She tells us only elliptically of her marriage to Leone Ginzburg, the Communist intellectual avoided by the bourgeoisie of Turin as a dangerous conspirator: 'He didn't care about that one bit, he seemed to have forgotten all those houses which once he had been in. We married, Leone and I' (*Family Sayings*, I.1026). Ginzburg's venture into pure autobiography could not be more stripped of the sentimentalism she so despised, but is none the less poignant for its reserve, as when she describes the fatal return to Rome and Leone's death in prison. Ginzburg achieves dramatic effect by dramatic understatement: as in Primo Levi's accounts of Nazi prison camps, horror is conveyed not through hyperbole but through restraint, through what remains unsaid: 'When I reached Rome I drew my breath and believed that a happy time was starting for us. . . . Leone was running a clandestine newspaper and was always out. They arrested him, twenty days after our arrival. I never saw him again' (I.1061).

Ginzburg's nostalgic sense of family as community finds itself repeatedly tested over the course of the 1960s and 1970s, as the culture and values of youth protest against the bourgeois culture in which she believes so firmly. Crisis in social value has become crisis in representation, and her analysis of the rapid disintegration of family life shifts from fiction to the theatre: in a series of plays such as *L'inserzione* (*The Advert*, 1965, performed at the National Theatre London, with Joan Plowright), *Fragole e panna* (Strawberries and Cream, 1966), *Paese di mare* (Seaside Town, 1968) and *La porta sbagliata* (The Wrong Door, 1968) Ginzburg explores the dramatic changes in social organization which even today have yet to be fully assimilated. She accommodates herself to the modern world, offering us in her plays seedy seaside towns, powerful cars, psychoanalysis, mismatched couples with no real motivation or purpose. Their parents, remnants of a previous generation, offer useless, irrelevant advice. The women are no longer passive victims, no longer the centre of home and family, but neurotic, disordered and aimless: 'They talk, and talk. They talk about themselves, continually, monstrously, while their husbands and lovers serve them, betray them, abandon them. And hit them – out of virile weakness' (Sanvitale, p. 35).

The novel *Caro Michele* (*Dear Michael*, 1973) is an attempt to come to terms with the society which produces terrorism: the eponymous Michael has had to leave Italy for England as a consequence of his dabbling on the fringes of violent, revolutionary extra-parliamentary groups. Yet once again Ginzburg is less interested in the workings and failings of the state, after the manner of Leonardo Sciascia's novels or Francesco Rosi's films, than in the shifting, porous membrane which separates the private from the public, the personal from the political. In Michael's absence the novel takes the form of letters, an exchange between those of his family, friends and associates most compelled by his disappearance to renegotiate their own lives and relationships – his mother, his impoverished lover, the child who may be his. The few superficial, short lines which Michael scribbles from England, where he makes an unhappy marriage to a university lecturer, only deepen the crisis of alienation. With the shifting, insubstantial story of Michael and his family scattered across a series of letters and notes, there is no one coherent point of view, no central story, no dominant character. Where *Family Sayings* posited language as poeticizing, totalizing metaphor for human contact, the heart of *Dear Michael* is silence. With *Dear Michael* – as with Ginzburg's last stories, *Family* (1977) and *The City and the House* (1984) – we see the social fabric torn, the mirror of both life and art in pieces; the 'family lexicon' which held the Levis together no longer exists.

9
The Deforming Mirror: Histories and Fictions in Elsa Morante (1912–85)

A lived event is finite, concluded at least on the level of experience. But a remembered event is infinite, a possible key to everything that preceded it and to everything that will follow it.

(Walter Benjamin,
quoted in G. Lukács, *The Meaning of Contemporary Realism*)

In Elsa Morante's controversial novel *La storia: romanzo* (*History: A Novel*, 1974), the narrator speaks almost despairingly of the condition of Italian Jews who have survived the Holocaust and returned to Rome. Marked out by their skeletal frames, their sunken, toothless cheeks, their shaven heads and haunted eyes, they swiftly learn that tales from the death camps are not welcome in post-war Rome. Theirs are not the romantic tales of sea captains or travellers to distant lands. The Jews are 'spectral figures, like negative numbers', no longer entitled to a hearing or to common sympathy; like the mad or the dead, they are to be swept out of sight:

Nobody wanted to listen to their stories: some people's attention wandered straight away, while others would interrupt them soon enough on some pretext or another. Some went so far as to push them aside with a laugh, as if to say 'Brother, I'm sorry for you, but can't you see I'm busy?'[1]

While the novels and stories of Elsa Morante address themselves to some of the most dramatic social, historical and psychological events and conditions of the twentieth century, they offer a voice to those who, like the returning Jews, have been silenced, who are marginalized, sidelined or disquietingly alienated by official politics and culture.

Morante was a permanent political and cultural dissident, an exile from successive factions and conformist fashions. She was always reluctant to identify the 'oppressed' with categories as defined by political or, later, feminist theories; her consistently anti-ideological stance, her refusal to be co-opted into any of the socio-political movements and 'isms' which have dominated post-war Italian cultural life – Neorealism, Marxism, Catholicism or feminism – spring from a deep distrust of totalizing systems and inevitably led her to clash with the dominant philosophies of her day. With the publication of *Menzogna e sortilegio* (*The House of Lies*, 1948) at the peak of the Neorealist enterprise, she was accused of indulging in bourgeois escapism; the publication of *History* in 1974 led to claims that she was what in our times might be called 'politically incorrect' in her rejection of history and class struggle as a means of defining and understanding human relations. More recently, some feminists have objected to what they perceive as her identification of women with the natural world, seeing her strategy, and her failure to offer portraits of women more consonant with their ambitions for woman in a modern age, as a diminution of their own claim to a full stake in humanity.

Morante's is no orthodox historicism, but a passionate interest in the workings of time in the lives of individual men and women. She is acutely modern in her awareness of the fragility of the human ego, and her texts exhibit a painful familiarity with the dramas of the desiring, fragmented psyche. She is concerned with the intrusion of the unconscious into our lives, with the legacy of past trauma, with the banal daily dramas of love, power, humiliation and rejection as ripples from earlier experience, where psychic damage can be as destructive to people's lives as anything wrought in Auschwitz. Her novels explore the messages from underground, from the unconscious, which are normally as welcome in our daily lives as the Jews' dark tales.

Morante paints a wide canvas in her works, but her deepest sympathies lie with the small, the oppressed, that which is unvalued by our social structures, the detail which is disregarded. Her anarchic view of art – and humanity – distanced her from specific programmes or theories of social or cultural reform, and led her to an aesthetic which aims not to contain reality, to pin it to the page, but to turn the raw data of individual experience into the shared, communicable meanings which constitute the metaphysical and the poetic.[2] At the same time she is a committed teller of stories, clinging stubbornly to narrative modes and forms which movements such as the French *nouveau roman*, or the experimental and avant-garde Italian Gruppo '63, attempted to dismiss as inadequate and inauthentic vehicles for a more complex and refracted contemporary consciousness. Yet she deploys the strategies of classical Realist texts with a considerable degree of irony, parody even: her 'realism' is closer to the subjective relativism of Pirandello than the all-encompassing omniscience of Balzac or Dickens. While she may be a 'Scheherezade of our times, writing stories to console the sad night of an alienated, mechanical and desperate civilization',[3] she is much more than a spinner of comforting tales or lonely minstrel to the world's demise.

Morante's work is deeply rooted in European cultural history, and can usefully be seen as embodying a tension between the strands of thought represented by Nietzsche and Rousseau, between the will to power in all its brutal consequences and the need for an imaginative locus of uncorrupted innocence; she exemplifies a conflict over the need for citizenship and the aspiration towards pure liberty beyond the framework of human society. Morante's is a mythologizing instinct; her appeal to myth – in particular the myth of nature – and her idealized view of childhood draw on a tradition of European consciousness which is sceptical about the achievements of the Enlightenment. The world of nature, away from the city of humanity, represents innocence before the Fall, while the world of animals and children (as well as – more problematically for recent critics – peasant women) offers an alternative to the doubtful imperatives of civilization and the social order. The very title of one of her works, *Il mondo salvato dai ragazzini* (*The World Saved by Little Children*, 1968), essay-poem-document, suggests the seriousness of her purpose, which is not a flight from history but an attempt to lead us out of the heart of our civilized darkness. Morante's exaltation of nature and childhood, the space and time of innocence, is never sentimental, but a gesture towards an alternative vision to that which has led only to the gas chamber.

The House of Lies (1948), Morante's first full-length novel, is set in Sicily, although every historical and geographical notation has been attenuated to produce an atmosphere which is legendary and mythical, remote in both time and space to the point where Sicily becomes 'a distant, fairy-tale land, alive only in the memory' (Sgorlon, p. 50). This is not the Sicily of Leonardo Sciascia (1921–89) or Vitaliano Brancati (1907–54), with its precise social and historical contours; Palermo is indicated by the cursory capital letter 'P'. While the novel would appear to be set around the turn of the century, there is no mention or memory of Garibaldi's 1860 landings in Sicily, no hint of a wider political struggle.

The characters in *The House of Lies*, which follows the experience of three generations, are all pinned to the same tragic fate of misrecognition, of living in the dimension not of reality but of delusion. Cesira, grandmother of Elisa, the narrator, an educated, poor and socially aspiring governess, marries the aristocratic, degenerate Teodoro Massia in the mistaken hope of social advancement. Once his real destitution is fully revealed to her, Cesira lapses into bitterness and hatred. Their daughter Anna falls prey to a similar delusion in her infatuation with her wealthy, handsome but ultimately fickle cousin Edoardo Cerentano, son of Teodoro's sister Concetta; abandoned by him, she marries his friend Francesco, poor student and self-styled Baron whose Socialist rhetoric thinly conceals a parallel desire to usurp the privileges he professes to despise. Francesco's adoration of the distant, aloof Anna remains unreciprocated, while he in his turn is the object of passion for the warm, foolish Rosaria. Francesco is finally killed in a railway accident and Anna dies shortly after, blaming herself for chasing phantasms and destroying her husband's life. In Morante's hands the *topoi* of popular fiction and romantic sagas – unrequited passion, divided families, love across the social classes – become the stuff of dark tragedy, and the *petit-bourgeois* drama of frustrated ambition is knowingly transformed into a drama of the desiring psyche flawed by obsession. To love is inevitably to lose, and the tragedy of Morante's characters is the endless compulsion to repeat and re-enact a primary loss. This is not a historical novel, or a revelation of history, but its exorcism. Already in this first novel, history is unorthodox, unsequential; Morante's anti-historicism is already in evidence as her characters endlessly repeat the same disastrous error.

The family history which Elisa – and the similarity of her name to that of the author cannot be missed – begins to recall at the start of the novel is immediately collapsed from within as a series of *menzogne*, or lies, its status as 'history' denied. The novel is prefaced by a poem to the main character, Anna, and in this poem the writer reveals herself as a Homeric, Circe-like figure, the witch who enchants Ulysses but fails to keep him, who weaves her stories at her loom, enveloping herself with her own fictions. Morante is ambiguous in her use of genre: if she adopts the conventions of the traditional realist novel, it is at once to exploit and explode them. She undermines the genre of love story from within; while this novel has the syntactic organization of nineteenth-century fiction from Balzac to Dickens, the style is one almost of ironic parody. The text is riddled with asides to the reader which proclaim the failure of omniscience and underline the ambiguous position of the narrator in relation to her text. The narrator apologizes to the reader for lingering over the trivia of Anna and Edoardo's affair: his jealousies and demands for proof of her affections, his whims, her naive hopes that she can prove her innocence, their childish games and the ceremonial, ritual cruelties of courtship.

With the arrival of Elisa, daughter to Anna and Francesco, the psychological mainspring of the tale is wound even more tightly. The abjection of the adoring child, the 'carnal devotion which tied me to my mother',[4] prefaces the abjection of the lover and becomes the pattern for future experience of unachievable desire. The childish murmurings of Francesco and Edoardo, their desire to 'marry' their own mothers, are just a prelude to Elisa's painful, masochistic desire for recognition from her beloved Anna. Elisa is bewitched, as were her parents before her:

> My love for my mother was something sacred and vile at the same time, not far removed from the feelings of a savage in the presence of a dazzling idol. Her harsh, arid severity held me in a perpetual state of trepidation and submission. [My] deep yearning to win her esteem was always disappointed. She was the only one whose applause I begged. (*House of Lies*, p. 442)

While Morante's work is contemporaneous with that of De Sica's film *Bicycle Thieves* and Sartre's *Les Mains sales*, she adopts no orthodox political historicism. The core of the novel and centre of the narrative is a lengthy flashback to Francesco's own childhood in the countryside, as a beautiful and intelligent boy before being struck with the smallpox that marks not just his face but his whole life. Morante anticipates writers like Anna Maria Ortese, Pier Paolo Pasolini, Carlo Levi and Vincenzo Consolo in her rejection of the post-war rush to modernity, the abandonment of the 'civiltà contadina', the peasant and rural civilization threatened by industrialization and mass emigration. While the heart of this novel is nature, it is nature as a metaphor for a way of life which is threatened with destruction. Morante here recalls Rousseau, while the mother–son relationship in this context is seen to be the perfect idyll, in sharp contrast to the despotic rule and servitude which the young Edoardo imposes on his own mother and sister.

Strict social divisions are echoed in an unquestioned hierarchy of the sexes. Edoardo's hold over Anna is rooted in an almost parodistic male supremacy, as he outlines his idea of marriage – male rights and female obligations, male freedom and female enclosure, male beauty and female degeneration through repeated pregnancy. Francesco, too, cannot resist a thrill of pleasure when Anna, defeated, offers herself to him as wife, as the object of his will. Endless miniatures (Nicola Monaco's affair with the compliant Alessandra, or Morante's unsentimental account of village life) underline the prevailing codes of domination and obedience between the sexes. But this is not a novel of social manners, and cannot easily be co-opted by either the Socialist or the feminist camp. The lies and fictions by which people live are here less a matter of morality than of metaphysics, closer in spirit to the masks of Pirandello than to Balzac or Zola.

While Morante plays with the traditional conventions of the genre, her philosophy is one which could recognize itself in modernism and in the literature of psychoanalysis. Morante's unique gift is to stand between tradition and the avant-garde, to gesture to the limits of conventional narrative forms even as she refuses to adopt narrative strategies which might cost her her readership and comprehensibility, to examine the deepest recesses of psychic desire in texts which are at once profoundly social and acutely personal. Her characters retain an independence and an impenetrability which distance them from both the omniscient narrator of classical realism and the ideological schema of much post-war fiction. The ambiguity and opaqueness which she admires in her characters are features of her own narrative, which is double-edged, an endless travelling over the surface and a simultaneous gesture to the void beneath. The line between 'reality' and 'fiction', or the 'lies' of the title, blur within the novel as each character lives out his or her life according to a misrecognition and distortion of reality.

With the death of the adored Edoardo, the first of many sun-god figures in Morante's fiction, his mother Concetta, driven mad by grief, demands that Anna produce the letters purportedly written to her – a demand with which Anna is only too eager to comply. The lies and fictions of the title are turned another notch tighter as the women play out, more or less consciously, their own delusions and fantasies. Edoardo emerges as a figure evoked by the desire of three women – the mother, the lover and the writer – but as impossible to describe, as inaccessible to language, as a scent, a musical phrase. Anna shares in Concetta's madness, her belief in the willing fiction. The *mise en abîme* of the 'letters', which Elisa describes but refuses to transcribe, is a consolatory fiction which would magically ward off the ugliness and pain of real life. Elisa's purpose is to resist the same temptation, to expose the letters as 'lies': with the end of her own narrative she will burn them in an attempt to separate herself from her mother, to break out of the vicious circle which holds them captive. But the ambiguity which characterizes Morante's characters is mirrored in the fiction itself. The end of the novel brings us back to the originating moment of the text, and there is no guarantee that through her narrative Elisa will achieve her own liberation. In the text, as in people's lives, there is no forward motion, only an endlessly repeated circularity.

Morante's second full-length novel, *L'isola di Arturo* (*Arthur's Island*, 1957), again has overtones of myth. The narrative is related by the now adult Arturo, and deals with his emergence from blissful childhood on the wild island of Procida, fuelled by his reading of legends and chivalric stories and his passion for his father Wilhelm, through an uneasy adolescence as his father brings home a new child-bride, to early adulthood as he retreats from his own sexual-psychological confusion and leaves the island, never to return. The narrative moves from the monumental, mythical time of childhood, with its certainties, its heroes and its marvellous deeds, to the linear time of history and society, with its inevitable disappointments and its more tentative ambiguities. Arturo's feelings for his new stepmother, who is barely older than himself, are increasingly unsettled as his initial childish, macho and straightforward contempt gives way to a complex desire for her approval and finally for her affections. The capricious god Wilhelm, whose love and approval are sought all the more for being erratic and unpredictable, is revealed to be not the heroic stuff of legend but an unhappy homosexual derided by his lovers.

The title of the novel is itself ambiguous, and holds within it the many-faceted experience which is to be described. Arturo's island is clearly a time, a space, a state of mind, a formative trauma, a compulsive memory. Like the city of 'P' in *The House of Lies*, it is cut off from the instance of narration just as the geographical island is cut off from the mainland, distanced in both time and space. It symbolizes the moment of plenitude when the child is master of all he surveys, and carries within it the loss of this same state of bliss. The island is the repository of the static condition of certainty, the Garden of Eden before the child is ejected into linear history: 'cursive time', as Nietzsche called it. The hero of this mythic, heroic age is the god-like, mysterious father, Wilhelm, blond, tyrannical, whose fascination lies in his unknowability, his capriciousness, the areas of his life from which Arturo is excluded. Wilhelm, like Edoardo, is the blond sun-god figure worshipped by his dark-skinned son; he embodies a dichotomy, or binary opposition, to be found in much of Morante's fiction from *The House of Lies* to *Aracoeli* (1982) – between light and dark, North and South, male and female.

But life cannot remain on the level of a myth. To experience time is to experience pain, doubts, the end of all certainty: the conscious, recollecting mind is inevitably a suffering one. The story of *Arthur's Island* re-enacts the story of the Fall, where the entry into time and history is marked by loss and death. As a boy, Arturo is haunted by the death of his own mother in childbirth, an anxiety underlined by the death of his dog Immacolatella in birthing. Death, the ultimate reminder of history and time, is the only stain on the otherwise sunlit landscape of his childhood, and one which he refuses to accept.

The rejection of women by Wilhelm, and the young Arturo after him, is a rejection of the power over life and death which women are seen to represent. Wilhelm articulates this fear of women, who are held responsible for the ejection of humanity from Eden:

> 'The love of women is the OPPOSITE of love. What women want is to degrade life. If it weren't for women it wouldn't be our destiny to be born and to die like beasts. The female race hates what is superfluous and unmerited, and is an enemy to everything which has no limits. They want drama and sacrifice, the ugly things, they want time, decay, massacre, hope. . . . They want death! If it weren't for women, existence would be an eternal youth; a garden.'[5]

Over the course of the novel Arturo moves from a 'masculine' to a 'feminine' model of existence, from the singular and heroic to the double, the multiple and the ambiguous. The god-like Wilhelm is deposed from his throne, and Arturo's almost religious awe of him gives way to the far more human and painful sense of compassion. The naming of Wilhelm as 'Parodia', 'Parody', indicates the inauthenticity of Arturo's own model of life based on the image of Father as Hero. Yet at the same time, while Wilhelm is a mystery which crumbles and disintegrates over the course of the novel, the perception of the female by the adolescent Arturo, increasingly aware of his own sexuality, becomes more ambiguous, less clear, more susceptible to interpretation. The figure of Nunziata, Wilhelm's second wife, is the double one of mother and object of desire, and it is this state of sexual confusion which dominates much of the book.

Nunziata, the teenager from the slums of Naples, whose ignorance is matched only by a trusting faith in the Madonna whose images soon litter her room, is clearly attractive to Morante, although she has proved less so to a generation of feminist critics. Nunziata, with her thick ankles and stocky legs, her credulity, her unquestioning obedience to her domineering husband and her maternal rapture at the birth of her son, encounters little sympathy in an ideology which would cut the umbilical cord of woman and nature, and claim a place for the female sex as subjects as well as the object of cultural production. For Morante, Nunziata epitomizes instinctive, all-embracing compassion, the female gift of maternal love, which, like the innocence of children, is humanity's best feature. This is curiously close to the claims of some radical feminists that only women — against the violence, greed and domination which characterize 'male' culture - can save the world; and if Morante cannot have it both ways, then neither can feminism.[6]

The drama of the desiring psyche, the experience of love as heaven and hell in equal measure, was a theme to which Morante returned in *Aracoeli*[7] (*Aracoeli*; 'Aracoeli' means 'altar of heaven'). Aracoeli, distant cousin to Nunziata, is a poor peasant Andalusian girl, uneducated and primitive, who falls in love with a handsome Northern Italian stationed in Spain. The narrator is their son, Manuele, now in his forties, a restlessly masochistic, self-hating homosexual tied to his mother's memory by simultaneous adoration and loathing. His narrative recounts a journey to Andalusia in order both to rediscover Aracoeli and to free himself of her. Once more a binary opposition is set up between the blond, Northern, refined but repressed male and the instinctual, enigmatic, dark and passionate female.

Manuele's period of childhood bliss with Aracoeli comes to a dramatic end with the death of the second child, a baby girl. Unable to grieve properly, Aracoeli turns from idyllic mother into the other side of the female stereotype in Western culture, the whore. Hysteria is followed by a hysterectomy, and she finally enters a brothel. Manuele's fragmented narrative represents both a painful search for the warm, nourishing Aracoeli of his earliest memories and the need to exorcize her from his failed life, in a double movement of compulsion and rejection which marks out the experience of love for so many of Morante's characters. *Aracoeli* differs from *Arthur's Island* in that motherhood, too, is fraught with pain, anguish and loss, as nature is compressed and confined by the requirements of bourgeois culture and seemliness.

Morante's most controversial achievement remains *History: A Novel*, the publication of which in 1974 caused a furore in Italian intellectual and cultural circles, particularly on the Left. The novel was and has remained an enormous success with the reading public; it soon achieved the status of bestseller, a new phenomenon in a country where the cultured, even literate elite was still very restricted - and it has to be said that initially, at least. the fuss was as much about the marketing strategy of the publisher, Einaudi, who brought it out immediately in an economical, paperback edition, as about its 'ideology' or significance. In conflating genres, fact and fiction, 'history' and 'literature', Morante flouted the unspoken conventions of an ideological decade which preferred political theory to narrative, and revolutionary rhetoric to the distractions of such a 'bourgeois' form as the novel.

Morante's work tells the story of Ida Ramundo, lower-middle-class schoolteacher, caught up in the terrible machinations of the Second World War. Ida Ramundo is neither brave nor victorious; she does not come through the war with a deeper knowledge of herself or of the world and its ways. A sufferer from intermittent epilepsy, widowed, raped and made pregnant by a German soldier passing through Italy on his way to die in Africa, left homeless by a bombing raid and struggling to find enough food for her newborn child, Ida is a far cry from the women of Renata Viganò, who join the partisan brigades, or those of Fausta Cialente, who turn an unorthodox social situation to their own advantage. Ida, with the shameful secrets of her epilepsy, her Jewish blood and her illegitimate child to keep hidden from the world, is no gender or class militant. She seeks not subjectivity but invisibility, not dynamic change but the enveloping protection of stasis; she is not history's protagonist but its victim.

Morante's is a dialectic between versions of history which elides the distinction between objective record and subjective memory, between the social and the individual. The novel covers the war and its immediate aftermath, 1940–47, and takes what initially appears to be a rigidly chronological form. Each year in the life of Ida Ramundo and her continuing struggle for existence is prefaced by an objective, if slightly idiosyncratic, summary of events on the national and world stages, recognizable from any number of more orthodox historical texts. Her own story – the desperate fight for survival, her eldest child Nino, who becomes first Fascist then partisan, the odds which are stacked too heavily against the survival of the bastard child Useppe – is encircled and compressed by this 'official' history.

Morante sides openly with the 'little' people, as yet uninfected by the drive to power which increasingly technological capacity could only exacerbate: 'The world's technological-bureaucratic organization was still in a primitive phase: that is, it had not yet irremediably contaminated the popular consciousness. Most people, in a sense, still lived in pre-history' (*History*, p. 79). The history to which she objects is one in which the human is cancelled out, and her critique is of History as understood by Hegel and Marx, especially Marxist historical materialism. While the work of writers such as Bertolt Brecht continually sacrifices the individual to the forces which create History, Morante overturns that order and restores pride of place to the individual: paradoxically, to be human is to be outside of History. Humanity and History are almost incompatible terms, as humanity resides in a way of living which is marked by being rather than becoming, closer to the cyclical rhythms of nature than to teleological theories of History.

History is an urban tale; none the less, the role played by the natural, animal world is perhaps even more significant here than it is in *Arthur's Island*. The differences between the human and animal worlds are elided: Ida is frequently referred to as a small, frightened animal, a cat with her ears flat against her head; Davide Segre grabs food offered to him like a starving puppy; the photograph of the murdered prostitute Santina shows her eyes like those of an animal resigned to slaughter. Meanwhile the dog Blitz shares Useppe's love of life, while Bella takes over Ida's maternal role of protecting Useppe. Again we might say that where people are most like animals, there they are most 'human'.

In *History* the weight and might of 'History' are ranged against one small defenceless boy, Ida Ramundo's bastard son Useppe, in a modern version of David and Goliath in which David is this time bound to lose. Morante explicitly places Useppe outside conventional social structures – he is illegitimate, to be hidden from the world for as long as possible – between cultures and between social classes. His mother is Italian, his father German; he is conceived through a rape at a historical moment in which Italy and Germany were notionally allies. While Ida is unquestionably raped – losing consciousness in a return of her long-dormant epilepsy – the portrait of Günther is far from unsympathetic. He is young, away from home and family for the first time, capable of tenderness as he makes love to Ida a second time and she responds with something approaching warmth, if not exactly pleasure. Morante has Günther die in the ill-conceived African campaign, less as punishment for his outrage than as a paradoxical prefiguring of Useppe's own death. History is a matter not of nationhood but of power, and Morante controversially mourns the loss of life of the small cogs in the power machine – German and Italian, Nazi and partisan alike.

Useppe's undernourished fragility is counterbalanced by an unfettered and unembarrassed joy and delight in life, the ability to take the world apart and see it afresh with the innocence and pleasure of childhood. Morante herself would like to take the world and make it anew as a world for children: 'He didn't see things only in their usual aspects, but as multiple images of other things . . . the colour of a rag, of a scrap of paper, suggesting to him the resonance of all prisms and scales of light, was enough to transport him to awed laughter' (*History*, p. 104). A line of cockroaches are observed as if they are wild horses on the plain; his underpants hanging out to dry become 'wallows' (swallows). Useppe's delight in language for its own sake disrupts the discourse of dominant power and aggression, and defies its power to kill and destroy: 'Even more than by music, perhaps, Useppe was bewitched by words. Obviously words, for him, had a sure value, as if they were one with objects. He had only casually to hear the word *dog*, to laugh heartily, as if suddenly the familiar and comical presence of Blitz were there, before him' (*History*, p. 112). Useppe is enamoured with a world where love and recognition are the natural state, where hostile aggression for its own sake – a specifically human capacity - has to be learned. The room which he and his mother share with other families after the destruction of their house is a source of untold pleasures, and even SS patrols hold no fear for him.

Useppe's progressive awareness of humanity's barbarous potential is marked by moments which, in this story of one small boy's calvary, recall the Stations of the Cross in their liturgical import. On one of his first excursions out of the house Useppe and Ida pass through Tiburtina station, where the sight of a tied-up calf casts the first shadow into the young boy's eyes. The sight of a dead horse and the death of the family's dog – ironically named Blitz - in a bombing raid impinge further. The dramatic *tour de force* of their return to Tiburtina station, to come across not a calf but hundreds of Jews from the Roman ghetto, piled aboard a cattle truck and ready for deportation to Germany and the death camps, is one of the most powerful moments in all of Morante's work in its understated sense of shock. Morante here recalls Primo Levi in her ability to let the seemingly insignificant, normal detail – a man telling his wife to leave lest she too be caught, the flurry of pencilled notes dropped out of the tiny gratings as those inside the cattle trucks desperately hope that someone is left to retrieve and deliver them, a lost shoe – carry the reader into the heart of an experience whose horror can only be hinted at or portrayed elliptically through images. Each moment of revelation – from the death of a dog to the magazine photographs showing hanged partisans – mark a step towards death for Useppe, not the destruction of his will to live but, on a symbolic level, the impossible survival of innocence in a deranged world.

Morante never shirks the violence of her material, and her almost compulsive need to follow her characters' stories leads her to recount their lives – and deaths – in the wheels of history. Of the partisans, active along with Nino, Mosca is tortured to death; Quattro is shot in the chest, then crushed by a German truck; Maria, Nino's girlfriend, is made drunk, raped and repeatedly slashed with a bayonet. Morante lingers awhile over the fate of Giovannino, a young man sent to the Russian front, where he dies of the cold, hallucinating of his home town and abandoned by his fellow soldiers who have no strength to help him.

Useppe is between cultures, his value for Morante lying precisely in the fact that he is of little value to anybody else, a poor scrap of humanity who is all the more human in his naked defenceless-ness. Neither will Morante take sides politically. Her stance is determinedly anti–ideological. In a post-war period which drew a sense of pride from the Resistance and in an intellectual climate dominated by left-wing theories of history and hopes of revolution, Morante deliberately lays herself open to the charge of masochism (her portrayal of Ida) and reaction (her portrayal of Davide Segre). She is almost unpatriotic in her presentation of the Resistance and the partisans, whose political ideals she exposes as utterly naive and whose motivations are largely suspect. The exuberant Nino joins the Resistance after an early flirtation with Fascism for contingent rather than ideological reasons, while the level of political and strategic awareness among Morante's partisans is minimal. Morante is not so much against politics as against obscurantism and cant, the rhetoric which leads people to forfeit their own lives. Worse, with the Allied victory Nino's wartime contacts and experience are put to the service of shady business dealings which lead eventually to his death in a motor accident in an attempt to avoid the police. Morante could not make a clearer comment on the failure of the Resistance – whatever the rhetoric of the Left – to live up to its own ideals.

Morante's final boot in the face of the ideological Left is perhaps the kicking to death of a German soldier by Davide Segre. Segre, a middle-class Jew from Bologna, first appears under the name of Carlo Vivaldi, on the run from just such a cattle truck as Ida and Useppe had seen at Tiburtina station. After his initial, misanthropic lethargy he joins Nino's partisans and wreaks his revenge on the enemy but, like Nino, his decline precipitates after the war. In his flirtation with Socialism he takes a job in a factory out of some misplaced sense of solidarity with the working class. The work makes him physically ill to the point of nausea, a symptom of his continuing alienation that the leftist discourse of class solidarity cannot overcome; talk of revolution and class consciousness while men work such sweated labour is so much empty, posturing rhetoric. Davide rejects the easy optimism of Remo, former partisan and now member of the Communist Party, who is convinced of the inevitability of revolution. For such as the prostitute Santina, injustices and inequalities cannot be articulated or even perceived; they are simple facts in a brutal life. Ida, too, wonders if in Remo's brave new world there will be space for small creatures like Useppe.

Davide turns to alcohol and drug abuse – morphine is plentiful and cheap – in an almost prophetic account of disaffected youth. Davide, like Useppe, has slipped outside the social forms which position us in society. While Useppe's optimism is countered by Davide's own black pessimism, he articulates most clearly Useppe's anomalous position in the world: "'You're too sweet for this world, you don't belong here. What is it they say: *Happiness is not of this world*'" (*History*, p. 441).

With Useppe's befriending of the recalcitrant Davide, the two opposites are brought together. Neither can survive – Useppe dies in an attack of the *grand mal*, while Davide overdoses on drugs. Davide's long speech to his fellow drinkers, while high on drugs, articulates the extent of the despair which is Morante's final exposition of the significance of 'History'. His exposition of the failure of class analysis, the functioning of the economy and the gravitational pull of power, always and everywhere, takes place not at a political rally but in a bar where others are more intent on their card games, the latest songs on the radio and the football results than the solipsistic rantings of a junkie. Davide has no power either to prevent his own decline or to get his message across. His speech – in some ways a summation of the brutal experiences described throughout *History* – labels 'History' a pornographic farce, an eternal repetition of the same drive to power and control, of which money is just an outward sign.

History is deliberately open in both its beginning and its end. While it deals principally with the war years and their aftermath, the first and last chapters deal with the unspecified, framing years 19. . . . 'History' goes on, and while 'these last years . . . have been the worst obscenity in all History, History has been an obscenity from the beginning' (*History*, p. 584). The belief that Fascism has been defeated is an illusion: behind the scenes the same people still hold the strings of power, the poor remain poor and desire only to displace the rich. Davide refuses the class analysis of Marxism, just as he refuses on an existential level easy notions of 'good' and 'evil'; we all have within us both Christ and the SS, the ability to recognize beauty and to grind it underfoot.

Morante lived in an era, and belonged to a generation, which had to make sense of some of the great evils of Nazism, Fascism, and genocide on an unprecedented scale, whose imagination was haunted by film and photographs from the hell of the death camps, the memoirs of the few survivors. The deathly legacy of the Holocaust, bitterly captured in film, photographs and narratives as well as personal accounts, and the brute revelations of barbarous cruelty and inhumanity at the very heart of the civilized world, had finally routed rationalist optimism and belief in scientific and social progress. After the refined tortures of the death camps, art could no longer be held up as natural ally to an ameliorating, improving humanism; the divorce of aesthetics from ethics was absolute and final. Morante draws on the structures of traditional classical realism, aiming for the clarity of plenitude in her exhaustive will to relate stories, to pursue to the last detail the facts of her characters' lives, unwilling to cast any of them off with a mere brush of the pen. And at the same time the reality which she presents so completely becomes almost a poetic myth, is transfigured by a poeticizing consciousness. Her texts explicitly present themselves as fictional constructs, as self-consciously literary, while rejecting alike the politicized aesthetic of post-war Neorealism and the easy seductions of a more abstruse avant-garde. The ambivalent tension of Morante's work springs from an implicit dialectic between an intellectual engagement with history in the modern world as a sequence of disastrous tyrannies, and a search for a dimension of time and space which holds out the hope of redemption, purity and salvation, and reconstructs – or mythologizes – the best of human imagination.

10
'Such stuff as dreams are made on':
Anna Maria Ortese (born 1914)
and the Art of the Real

> In its more modern form the dream is introduced there precisely
> as the *possibility* of a completely different life. The life seen
> in dreams makes ordinary life seem strange, forces one to
> understand and evaluate ordinary life in a new way.
>
> (Mikhail Bakhtin, *Problems of Dostoyevsky's Poetics*)

In 1844 Edgar Allan Poe published a short story called 'The Spectacles', in which the handsome and vain, but seriously short-sighted,
Napoleon Buonaparte Froissart falls in love with a French widow,
Eugénie Lalande. They marry, and on their wedding day Eugénie
has her ardent young lover don her spectacles and thus contemplate
her properly for the first time. His shock and horror are profoundly
comic as the glasses bring into focus a suspicion of rouge, a series
of wrinkles and an alarming lack of teeth.[1] Eugénie is, we learn,
eighty-two, and his great-great-grandmother at that: the marriage
is an elaborate hoax, a joke, and in this story Poe makes a mockery
of the romantic assertion of love at first sight. Froissart goes on to
marry more appropriately, and to view the world – and his wife –
with his glasses firmly on his nose.

Just over a century later Anna Maria Ortese published a collection of stories, *Il mare non bagna Napoli* (*The Bay is not Naples*,
1953) which remains one of her best-known works. In 'Un paio
di occhiali' ('A Pair of Glasses'), the young Eugenia, myopic to the
point of blindness, is to be given a pair of glasses, a reluctant gift
from her grudging, unmarried aunt, and some small compensation
for a life of unredeemed poverty. Eugenia's excited anticipation is
matched only by her optimism in the face of the humiliations of
poverty, her conviction that spring is on its way, and her disarming

conviction that beyond the cloud that constitutes her vision lies a world of beauty and joy.

With the eventual arrival of the spectacles the world revealed to Eugenia's weak eyes provides for a humour much blacker than in Poe's tale. Eugénie the perpetrator of an elaborate trick has become the beguilingly innocent victim Eugenia, whose gratitude when the family's grasping, sanctimonious landlady hands her a ragged, cast-off dress is touchingly misplaced. Amid the aunt's loud complaints about the high price she has had to pay, and the neighbour's grumbling about the fish bones littering the stairs, Eugenia puts on the glasses. The kindly, harmonious world of her imagination is dislodged by a harsher, more brutal reality. Images of light and spring vanish as swiftly as the radiance from Eugénie Lalande's eye. The heart of this story is the clash between utopian and dystopian vision; what is revealed is the courtyard strewn with rubbish and cabbage leaves, and the pockmarked faces of her ragged neighbours looking on in a mixed response of concern, amusement and derision. Eugenia, defeated, is overcome not by rage or rebelliousness, but by a wave of nausea.

The stories in *The Bay is not Naples* [2] constitute a collective denunciation of the old Bourbon city, plagued by seemingly endless poverty, where dehumanizing conditions are borne with resignation by a suffering people ill-served by politicians and a ruling class largely indifferent to their plight, and Ortese's exposure of dire conditions in the city is as powerful as the condemnation by Matilde Serao of government indifference and incompetence in *The Belly of Naples*. In 'Interno familiare' ('Familiar Interiors') the author analyses the feelings and hopes of Anastasia Finizio, a woman no longer young, who is resignedly compelled to maintain her whole family through her own work. A glimmer of hope brightens the static immutability of her life in the shape of an old suitor returned to the city, but her brief glimpse of a better life, as for Eugenia, is soon crushed. Anastasia, like Eugenia, exemplifies the condition of the whole Neapolitan people, condemned to unchanging resignation, whose momentary rebellions are swiftly eclipsed. The third story in the collection, 'La città involontaria' ('The Involuntary City'), a guided tour of the city's worst slums, is a kind of *voyage en enfer*, whose protagonists are not the carefree, big-hearted folk of Neapolitan popular culture but people reduced to a level less than human by a precarious life of privation, poverty and disease. The final – and most controversial – section of the book, 'Il silenzio della ragione' ('The Silence of Reason'), exposes the failure of writers and intellectuals in that city to stand by the reforming ideals of their youth, and their catastrophic slide into abstraction and self-absorption.

Ortese lived mostly in Naples between 1928 and 1950, and together with other writers such as Domenico Rea she rejected standard cultural and literary representations which focus on Naples as the land of song and passion, a touristic façade of noisy sentiment. Theirs was a rejection of Southern self-representation (such as Rea's criticism of Matilde Serao, and more recently Sebastiano Vassalli's hostility to Leonardo Sciascia) which brushed off social disasters such as organized crime in its wish to present the best face possible to the nation; national literature and culture – echoing repeated political failures – were only too glad to be able to ignore the problems altogether.

In post-war Italy, Ortese was witness to a reconstruction fuelled by rapid economic and industrial development, which dramatically changed the face of the land. Her rejection of the catastrophic consequences for individuals of modern economic and industrial power had much in common with thinkers on the ideological Left such as Herbert Marcuse. She felt instinctive sympathy with the PCI, the Italian Communist Party, and in 1954 she travelled to Russia under the aegis of the UDI, the women's organization backed by the PCI, a journey recounted in *Il treno russo* (*The Russian Train*, 1982). Despite the experiences of Orwell, Koestler and Gide she maintained a pronounced optimism about the possibility of social and political progress, writing with enthusiasm of a country which she believed – until the invasion of Hungary, at least – to herald the utopia still only dreamed of in capitalist societies. Ortese stands as an intermediary figure, coming from the West but looking to the East for a regeneration which was more optimistic than practicable and which, as for many others, was to end in bitter disappointment and disillusion with orthodox politics.

Ortese came to maturity as a writer at a time when the emphasis of cultural politics fell not on imagination or fantasy but on a reaffirmation of realism as the goal and expression of intellectual effort. *The Bay is not Naples* was written at the height of the

Neorealist literary movement, and shared the avant-garde urge to moral as well as urban renewal. 'Realism', however, is just one side of Ortese's extraordinary output, and is a term which she gradually contests as her fictions come closer to fairy-tale and fable. Like Pasolini and Consolo, she abhors what is lost with rapidly growing consumerism: her texts consistently, if obliquely, reject the headlong rush to technological progress and advanced industrialization as the path to the greatest happiness for all. Political alienation is reflected in stylistic dissidence, and Ortese remains doubtful as to whether the Neorealist project of the post-war period, with its claims to dispassionate objectivity, can go beyond a superficial materialism. Her first collection of short stories, *Angelici dolori* (*Angelic Sorrows*, 1936), an evocation of the imagination of a young child, was published with the support and backing of Massimo Bontempelli, the writer who coined the term 'magic realism' which has such currency today. Her latest work to date, *Il cardillo addolorato* (*The Sorrowing Goldfinch*, 1993), is a large, fantastic narrative, an epic fairy-tale. While Ortese never flinches from exposing oppression and injustice, the realist style and technique of *The Bay is not Naples* is dismissed as inadequate, a tool too blunt to capture the psychological and metaphysical complexities of modern life.

The stories and novels of E.A.Poe deal with the fantastic, the strange, the fine borderline between the natural and the supernatural, and while Ortese writes within a different intellectual and cultural context, her narratives similarly challenge the notion of the 'real' which is so undermined by writers from Hoffmann, Gogol and Maupassant in the nineteenth century to Nabokov, Borges and Kafka in the twentieth. Texts which unsettle and disturb become an index of man's discomfiture and disquiet in the modern world. If the work of Poe, Algernon Blackwood, M.R. James and Ambrose Bierce can be seen as a response to the increasingly positivist, scientific, rationalist novel of the nineteenth century (as indeed are some stories by renowned 'realists' such as Balzac and Zola in France, Dickens, Mrs Gaskell and Mrs Oliphant in Britain and Matilde Serao and Giovanni Verga in Italy), an equally strong case can be made for some writers of the twentieth century. The rather prim realism of the traditional English novel in the twentieth century has been nudged by the generous imagination of narratives emerging from South America, and post-modernism has given a wider context to the elaborate fictions of writers like A.S. Byatt, Julian Barnes and Michel Tournier. In Italy, too, writers are once more drawing on literature of fantasy and the imagination as the old political and cultural certainties are toppled, and younger writers are engaging with a tradition sparsely, if brilliantly, represented by the evocative landscapes of Dino Buzzati, the intellectual concoctions of Italo Calvino and the more intensely erotic fictions of Tommaso Landolfi.[3] It is in this climate that Anna Maria Ortese is finally achieving the recognition and status she deserves.

Poveri e semplici (*Poor and Simple*, 1967) explicitly exposes the inability of Neorealism to do anything more than skim the surface of our perceptions. A young, struggling writer of 'stories in the Neorealist style, as they used to say', is confronted with the gulf between 'realism' and 'reality' alluded to by T.S. Eliot.[4] This is where Ortese differs so drastically from the politicized aesthetic of Neorealism, which sought moral regeneration for Italy through direct representation of the material and physical world; the reality which Neorealism takes for granted is rendered problematical and opaque in her work.

Ortese's protest against 'realism' is more than stylistic and expressive dissent. In refusing the dominant literary orthodoxies of Neorealism, she represents a dramatic ethical and cultural alternative grounded in the 'marvelling innocence' of childhood, which attempts to heal the split between mankind and the natural-phenomenal world. Her stories and novels consistently challenge elements of conventional narrative structure such as plot and character, dealing instead with the ebb and flow of experience, emotion, thought and dream which escape the constraints of logical reasoning.

In rejecting Neorealism and the transforming power of economic development, Ortese also rejects party politics as too narrow to encompass her ambitious hope for the world. Instead, the existential alienation of Pirandello or Kafka is echoed in her work, as mankind drifts in an incomprehensible world, fettered by mental activity which would seek to seize and constrain 'reality' for its own purposes. If for Pirandello we are cut off from the world precisely by our attempt to make it the cognitive object of our reason, that 'infernal little machine', for Ortese mankind is the only creature whose ridiculous efforts to understand the world estrange him from it and exclude him for ever from the 'real' world, which is content for ever to renew and repeat itself in a kind of 'divine sleep'[5] to which man can never return. The role of literature is to remind us of what we have lost, to repair the alienation in which we all live: 'Literature, when it is real, is nothing other than the memory of our lost lands, nothing other than the recognition and the melancholy of exile.'[6]

L'iguana (*The Iguana*, 1965), one of the strangest and most icono-clastic novels to come out of the post-war period in Italy, belongs to the genre of fantasy fiction. The Milanese Count Aleardo, trav-elling on behalf of his mother in search of land suitable for purchase and development, arrives on a mysterious, haunted island off the coast of Portugal inhabited by an aspiring poet and his two uncouth brothers, and falls in love with their servant-girl, an iguana. The appearance of the iguana is already an echo, or perhaps a realization, or even a dream, of a conversation between the Count, known as Daddo, and a Milanese publisher before his departure: the two had speculated on the literary (and marketing) potential of a man falling in love with, precisely, an iguana. The iguana, formerly beloved of her young master Don Ilario, has been pushed aside: no longer is she going to Paradise but, on the contrary, has been cast in the role of the embodiment of evil. Into this atmosphere of degeneracy and crushed hopes comes the American Hopins family, whose daughter is to marry Don Ilario and thus revive the family fortunes: Estrellita, the iguana, is to be sent to Cole's circus.

In this novel, identities shift and metamorphose one into the other. The young poet on the island is now the eager, literate, lonely Don Ilario, now the powerful, self-confident hidalgo Jimenez. The iguana herself is now an innocent girl, now a truculent creature avidly counting out the stones which she is given in mock payment. The arrival of the Hopins, together with their obsequious prelate, signifies the financial rescue of the young Don Ilario's fortunes through marriage, but simultaneously points to a more sinister regime for Estrellita herself as the last remaining vestige of an old way of life which must be cleansed and purged. There is an intensely comic scene in which the prelate attempts to exorcize the spirit of evil from the iguana's room, to the consternation of Mrs Hopins, whose double chins have to be revived with salts. Reality and unreality, dreams, desires and fears begin to pursue each other, and dream states are barely distinguishable from more conscious ones as the narrative slides in and out of the Count's conscious and unconscious mind; he finally lapses into a hallucination of the trial of God's murderer, and God's tender corpse, a white butterfly, is brought in as evidence. The novel ends with the death of the Count and the transformation of the island into a windswept holiday resort which none the less fails to find favour with the demanding Milanese bourgeoisie.

The Iguana is at once poetic myth, fairy story, romance and moral tale, shot through with the blackest of humour and the lightest of despair, its exploration of the divided psyche reminiscent of Ortese's beloved Robert Louis Stevenson. The text has a density which offers a multitude of interpretations and ways of reading, demonstrating the 'startling clarity that could only continue to grow and never possibly diminish, while nonetheless remaining an absolute mystery'[7] which so disorientates the Count.

On the island of Ocaña, conventions of time and space are put aside. It appears on no maps; internal and external space become increasingly difficult to calculate; Ocaña has two moons, and dates correspond to no standard calendar. In so far as Ortese is unafraid to tackle the larger questions which most writers of our secular age eschew as unsolvable - the problem of good and evil, the relationship of man to nature - the island of Ocaña can be seen as a Garden of Eden after the Fall, abandoned by God and any credible higher authority, a place of former bliss now run-down and degenerate. On this tattered land, with its fragmented memories and its gaudy rags of former happiness and harmony, ideas of economic power, social relations, democracy and literature, are played out in miniature: 'And what is time, the time in which such thoughts and actions find articulation? And what is space, if not ingenuous convention? And what is an island, or a city, the world itself with its multitudinous capitals, if not simply a theater where the heart, stricken by remorse, can pose its ardent questionings?' (*The Iguana*, p. 171).

Together with the Count, the reader gradually learns that Estrellita, now spurned and scorned, formerly enjoyed her master's affections as Perdita, whose name indeed underlines what both Don Ilario and the object of his love have lost. The image of the iguana herself is a complex one, more than a metaphor, never overburdened with too specific a meaning. She stands for the inarticulate and helpless oppressed whose only strategy is to oppress in her turn, for there is no dignity in suffering; she is nature, once beloved by man but now abandoned in the industrial age, left to fend for herself. It is also tempting to see her as an image for the woman writer herself, cast out and vilified for daring to write, for daring to believe Don Ilario might love her.

Daddo's journey, too, can bear the most diverse interpretations: the pressing need to redress man's unbalanced relationship with nature, caustic comments on Milanese economic imperialism and an acerbic account of the pretensions of the cultural and publishing industry. *The Iguana* clearly represents Ortese's humanitarian and political concerns about man's relationship to nature, which she sees as fundamental to our continued existence on the planet, and with the absurd oppression of power. Her literary polemic is synonymous with her political dissent from orthodox Marxism, and Daddo wryly admits the taste of the new reading public for stories about barbarism and oppression, anxious for novelty on which to squander its new-found wealth. Yet for Ortese, both a degenerate reading public and political theorists fundamentally misunderstand the nature of oppression in assuming that the oppressed have a voice at all, are able to speak, defend and redeem themselves:

> Not even feelings survive – neither feelings nor any desire to express them – when people have no money (given the world's time-honoured conventions), or where money can buy everything, or where penury cohabits with great ignorance. Briefly put, the Milanese were persuaded that some world of oppression had something to say, whereas the oppressed don't even exist, or can't, at least, have any awareness of being oppressed. . . . The only thing left is the oppressor, who likewise has no knowledge of what he is, even while sometimes, out of habit, aping the stances and behavior that would legitimately befit his victim, if any such victim had escaped extinction. But these of course are sophistries that could never have assuaged the publishers' hunger for things with which to whet the public's languid appetite. Such arguments slow the rhythm of production. (*The Iguana*, p. 4)

Ortese will have nothing to do with the romanticism of political theories which see in the oppressed a redeeming dignity or a sense of moral purpose: oppression is always brutalizing, always dehumanizing and diminishing. Neorealism's attention to the peasants and workers as the source of moral regeneration after two decades of Fascism seems to her fundamentally to misunderstand the nature of oppression, whose iron grip destroys completely. Cast out of Don Ilario's sight, Perdita/Estrellita turns dull and spiteful, muttering ugly words under her breath, breaking dishes, attempting to frighten the Guzman brothers by leaping out at them or emitting strange howls from beneath the table.

The iguana calls to mind Shakespeare's romance *The Tempest* (indeed, the second part of the novel bears the same name as the English dramatist's play), where another spirit has been similarly enslaved and brutalized. Caliban, once the favourite of Prospero and Miranda, has been rejected, and his rejection is all the more bitter for the love formerly shown him. Prospero remains unrepentant about his harsh treatment of Caliban, and it required a change of political culture for Ernest Renan to be able to write *Caliban*, a rebuttal of Prospero's automatic right to rule. For Ortese the distinction between master and ruled is even less clear, just as the distinction between mankind and nature or the animal world is an arbitrary, imposed one whose purpose is to sanction power and abuse. She offers an alternative mark of humanity as that which lends a voice to the suffering of others:

> Only the greatest philosophers and most elevated scholars can begin (perhaps) to tell us where the animal ends and where the true human being commences . . . the human consists of everything that can voice a lament, whereas subhumanity (or animal life) comprises everything that refuses to assuage that lament, not to mention the things that provoke it. (*The Iguana*, p. 112)

The oppressor, too, is oppressed by his own actions, removing freedom from himself as well as his victim. Don Ilario's rejection of Estrellita has led not to the liberty and prosperity which he sought, but to his own unhappiness and despair; the Count remarks on his 'vandalized smile as proof of the damages which a freedom unchecked by any knowledge of the rights of others had wreaked on Ilario's soul, driving it to an otherwise incomprehensible desperation' (*The Iguana*, p. 119). Ortese has no doubts that the snake in the Garden of Eden is the pursuit not of sexual happiness but of economic status; in a social order based exclusively on wealth, money corrupts both those with and those without it, 'bringing about the downfall of gentle souls like Ilario and consigning them to perversion. As a result of this power accorded to money, crimes heaped up torture and loneliness as the only lot of anyone who had none of it' (*The Iguana*, p. 181).

The *Iguana* also states the dilemma for literature and art, faced with the constraints of publishers eager to maximize sales and a reading public hungry for exotica that will provide grist to the mill of the chattering classes. The post-war period saw, for the first time in Italy, the consequences of higher levels of literacy and a wider reading public. Ortese's writing has itself never been 'popular', even though it has been much admired, for while she draws on traditional forms and genres, she makes few concessions to contemporary taste and a new audience. She is scathing about the lack of engagement and challenge which ensures success in a complacent and self-satisfied industry, subservient to a complacent social order content with its sudden and dramatic, if precarious, wealth. Don Ilario's derivative and unoriginal work, which, 'perfectly incomprehensible, might have been purposely designed to excite precisely those feelings of perplexity and boredom that were a sure guarantee of good sales' (*The Iguana*, p. 44), would be sure to find favour with a new reading public unsure of its own taste. Even on his island, Don Ilario has caught a straw in the wind about the new 'realism' in vogue – a clear reference to the intellectual and cultural dominance of Neorealism. What is realism? he asks the embarrassed Count:

> 'What it ought to be,' replied the Count, feeling slightly clumsy, 'is an art of illuminating the real. But people, unfortunately, don't always affirm the awareness that reality exists on many levels, and that the whole of creation, once you analyze the deepest level of reality, isn't real at all, and simply the purest and profoundest imagination.'
>
> 'I've had exactly that feeling, living here in my solitude,' the young man exclaimed with an expression of joy that strangely affected the Count – an effect, though he understood the boy's

emotion, almost of compassion. 'You'll correct me, Daddo, if I'm wrong, but all of this could finally free us from the ancient conceptions of nature and spirit, and the real and the imaginary. That's what it all leads up to, now isn't it?' (*The Iguana*, p. 52)

The Iguana is a clear refusal to legitimize either the platitudes of Neorealism or the othodoxies of post-war, left-wing politics, but the novel is reducible neither to metaphor nor to allegory. It does not reproduce the complete pattern, a narrative of equivalents, which marks allegory. It would be possible to regard the novel as the account of a Fall: of the Segovia Guzman family, of the iguana-nature, of the island-world, of the relationship between man and nature or, indeed, man and reality, but a multilayered and dense text fortunately dissuades us from settling on one meaning to the exclusion of others.

Ortese constructs increasingly large, fantastic tales where the transformations and metamorphoses of classical myth resonate against a continuous undercurrent of metaphysics. It is almost impossible to place her within any coherent group of writers, or to identify her work within a specific trend: hers is very much a solitary voice, whose surreal humanity occasionally rises to the surface of an Italian cultural scene which she sees to be largely abandoning its task to reveal 'reality', to strip the mask off the face. Her most recent work, *The Sorrowing Goldfinch*, is a dense, complex tale which reworks the structures and conventions of the traditional fairy story to such a point that even a brief summary is of necessity a distortion. The novel is set at the end of the eighteenth century, and all eyes are on France at a time when, the narrator comments acerbically, 'the Revolution had only taken its first steps on the path of the cult of the economy' (*Goldfinch*, p. 122), when ideals are already beginning to be corrupted, when political philosophy gives ground to economic expediency. Three young Belgians – the wealthy prince Neville, the merchant Nodier, and the struggling artist Dupré – travel to Naples to visit the noted glovemaker Don Mariano Civile, and his beautiful, blonde daughters. Dupré falls in love with the silent Elmina who, disinherited and with no dowry of her own, accepts his offer of marriage. On Dupré's untimely death Nodier offers his hand; Neville's initial aversion to Elmina also turns out to be the beginning of passion.

Elmina is silent and cold, but this is not a modern version of Turandot. Beneath surface appearances in 'this tale which is a continual saying and unsaying' (*Goldfinch*, p. 353) lies a story which unravels to ever greater complexity and suggestiveness. Ortese gives us a complex narrative, but not to satisfy the reader's thirst for story lines, for clarification or for explanation. The initial story of Elmina's disinheritance is taken up, fragmented, multiplied, and scattered across the generations in a disconcerting game of mirrors – and in the Spanish language 'cardillo' ('goldfinch' in Italian) is also a game of mirrors used to entertain children – leaving fleeting shadows and images rather than a firm sense of 'real' events. While the first impression is one of a love story, the 'complicated and ridiculous facts which weave the stellar plot of those wonderful human passions' (*Goldfinch*, p. 120), the tone of light opera gradually becomes a counterpoint to deeper and darker mysteries: the dead who speak – crossly – to the living; portraits which appear and then fade away again; names on a tombstone which similarly appear and disappear; Elmina's neglected daughter Paumella, who flies when no one is watching; the Duke whose eyeglass gives him access to the lives and hearts of men; visions and hallucinations; allusions to Elmina's beloved brother, Hieronymus Käppchen, a three-hundred-year-old spirit, malicious and frail in turn, who must be adopted if he is not to die, and whose salvation is her only concern: 'an elfin sprite . . . perhaps the last . . . a soul lost in this world after the Declaration of the Rights of Man' (*Goldfinch*, p. 328).

The narrative is punctuated with references to the 'cardillo', the goldfinch, 'that bird which wasn't a bird but a sort of destiny' (*Goldfinch*, p. 192). The goldfinch first appears as the innocent victim of childhood neglect, or childhood jealousies and rivalries, the most harmless and defenceless of victims. Over the course of the narrative the 'cardillo' takes on other resonances as an image of what has been carelessly lost or destroyed, a part of our past from which we are permanently cut off, but which still calls us; as 'the lament of sorrowing love' (*Goldfinch*, p. 304) the 'cardillo' 'reminded everyone of *something* barely glimpsed, instantly lost and loved for ever' (*Goldfinch*, p. 137). The 'cardillo' is also the voice of reason which re-emerges only to be silenced again by other and more powerful forces. As the narrative progresses the 'Cardillo' acquires a capital 'c', and is rumoured to be French, pursued by the Bourbon police on suspicion of being a Jacobin, an expression of the discontent of the people. Above all the 'Cardillo' expresses the suffering of innocence in 'this infernal dwelling-place which we call the world (simply because we have no other name to give a place which is so little known and which is so melancholic)' (*Goldfinch*, p. 405). The cry of the 'cardillo' is the painful memory of what we have glimpsed and lost, a happiness and joy beyond the reach of social and economic orders based on competition and power. Ortese's view of children is far from sentimental, but like Elsa Morante she sees in childhood an innocence lost in a world of greed and violence:

> 'This pain (or joy? or yearning? or simple desire for joy?) which the famous bird expresses does not, if you think about it, have much to do with the world of adults whether they be intellectuals or noblemen, but only with the world of small children and of all those who even if they get to be twenty or thirty or a hundred years old, remain "children". There is a pain', he said, 'experienced by children, in the world of Naples or elsewhere (perhaps even as far away as Germany) which is bigger and deeper than the pain of intellectuals, of those in love with reforms and even those who are anxious about the Constitution – a pain which is *not* that of adults, which is the one we always hear about and which people generally refer to when they pronounce the magic word: pain. Because pain is a desert . . . a desert of love.' (*Goldfinch*, p. 267)

Prince Neville echoes Ortese's own position when he comments: 'I consider consent to the suffering of others – though they be enemies or sinners – but especially of the birds and the flowers, to be the saddest of sins' (*Goldfinch*, p. 301). Behind Reason lies Nature, which, like the 'cardillo', is victim of human greed, jealousy and oppression sanctified by our social and political structures. The great 'Masters of Change' (Voltaire, Rousseau and the Encyclopaedists) have, for Prince Neville, brought about very little positive change at all, and Ortese remains deeply hostile to an idea of progress which widens the gulf between man and nature, and eliminates compassion:

> [Prince Neville] felt that this was exactly what was missing, in the old and new reshaping of the world: respect for the dawn, for the cry of the Goldfinch; respect for his demand that we remain faithful . . . to compassion for those who are abandoned, that we have the utmost regard for every Hieronymus Käppchen. (*Goldfinch*, p. 394)

Ortese's work is a protest against the smallness of political as well as cultural vision, against the dehumanizing power of industrial civilization, of our rush to modernity and our all-consuming belief in Progress. Reality for Ortese resists observation, compels us to look beneath the surface of things. Less than a series of observable objects and actions, it is a moral, ethical relationship between individuals, between humankind and the natural world. The purpose of writing is a highly moral one: to restore a sense of belonging, to minister to an irremediable sense of loss.

Ortese may deal in metaphysics, but she has precise ideas about the need for a social order based on civil rights and obligations rather than simple prerogative, as the 'cat-man' who haunts Milan Central Station in an early story makes clear:

> 'If I am hungry, in Italy, it's part of the scenery. If I lose my wife, in Italy, it's a matter for the tourist board. If I walk along roads that are stifling, in Italy, wishing for the sea, if my room is suffocating, if noises kill me, if, in a word, I die, it concerns only the Board for the Conservation of Artistic Heritage. Your rights, in Italy, are a laughing matter, if they are not pushed aside by economic power. Indeed, the only rights are those of economic power. So thought fades away, words die in confusion in your throat, and madness remains the only proper way for a gentleman to express himself.'[8]

Current political and social practice alienates and disinherits the vast majority of the population – just as Elmina has been disinherited – and so diminishes mankind, condemned to drift in non-humanity and non-reality:

The fundamental reality, in order for a man to become a man, is the civic one, bringing with it obligations, which we all have, but also rights, which on the contrary belong to just two or three people. And it is from our failure to understand this that is born the constant sensation of being carried off, whisked away as on a magic carpet, which is the will of the few.[9]

While Ortese's best hope lies in the radical politics and ethics of the Left, she remains independent from political *parti pris* and from the social and political assumptions which underpinned Neorealism and were endorsed by the cultural politics of the Communist Party. Profoundly hostile to the facile dogmatism that equated progress with industrialization and the economic development that bred the consumer society, Ortese resists the siren call of 'explainability within this world of inscrutable phenomena within which you too make your home' (*The Iguana,* p. 170). Her fictions of fantasy and the imagination, with their mixture of humour and despair, their eroding of narrative conventions in search of a deeper truth, their refusal to be blinded by the dazzle of surfaces, leave us, like the myopic Eugenia, with intimations of a different way of perceiving reality and the world around us: 'the voice, or the cry of the Goldfinch, is never silenced' (*Goldfinch,* p. 258).

Ortese's is a quest for light in darkness, for reality in a world of sham and illusions, and her fantastic fictions lightly mask a seriousness of purpose rarely to be matched in modern Italian fiction. Her polemic is with 'realism' understood not simply as stylistic technique, as a mode of cognition, but as the literary outpost of an economic and social order rooted in the distorted and corrupted ideals of the Enlightenment. Ortese points to what she sees as the vast error of Western industrial and political civilizations based on dehumanizing capitalism, on the power of wealth and financial advantage which gives the lie to rhetoric about democracy and equal rights, where reason has been obscured and dimmed by the imperatives of economics. For this writer the achievements of the Enlightenment and 'Voltaire's bastards' are hollow; trapped by notions of reason and progress, chained to a scientific technocracy whose goal is profit rather than human happiness, mankind has succeeded only in alienating itself from the 'real' world.

PART III
1964–94

11
Revolution and Reaction

With the 'economic miracle', Italy was swiftly transformed into one of the leading industrial countries of the West. Technical innovation, entrepreneurial skill and an expanding foreign market, particularly within the Common Market, combined with cheap labour costs and limited trade-union power to transform the face of Italy. Heavily industrialized areas spread beyond the golden triangle of Milan, Genoa and Turin down the Po valley and east to the new steel town of Ravenna.

Standards of living rose to unprecedented levels. However, there was an increasingly conspicuous gulf between individual wealth and public poverty as the development of infrastructure and social amenities lagged behind individual consumption. The possession of durable goods such as televisions, washing machines, fridges and cars rose dramatically; the image of black-garbed women rapidly began to disappear from urban Italy as clothes and shoes were mass-produced for a mass market. Yet public planning to deal with the social consequences of change, reform in working practices, education and public services was almost non-existent. The 'miracle' was 'an exquisitely private affair, which reinforced the historic tendency of each family to fend for itself',[1] while the failure of politicians to stimulate social reform which would keep pace with economic progress was a significant factor in the widespread unrest and struggles of the late 1960s.

Industrial development and economic advancement had a price. The gap widened still further between the North, enjoying ever-increasing levels of private wealth, and an impoverished South. Immigration into Northern cities in search of work created enormous social tensions in the struggle for adequate housing and schooling, tensions dramatically represented in films such as Luchino Visconti's epic *Rocco and his Brothers* (1960). In a country where the majority of people still spoke their own dialect, the culture clash which inevitably followed large-scale internal immigration was exacerbated by mutual incomprehension even on a linguistic level.

THE STUDENT MOVEMENT OF 1968

The education system was much expanded in the 1960s, as for the first time the population benefited from mass education beyond primary levels. With the abolition of *numerus clausus* in 1965, the number of university students spiralled, but an archaic, inefficient and inadequate university system could cope neither with vastly increasing numbers nor with students' demands for radical educational reform. No new universities were created to absorb the new students, and the old ones continued to churn out excessive numbers of unemployable graduates in traditional subjects such as law and philosophy. Many more women now went to university, but in 1968 they still formed less than a third of the new intake. The supposed widening of access to students from the working classes was countered in practice by the sheer financial struggle faced by those with neither state grants nor obliging parents.

Over the course of the 1960s, students increasingly rejected what they perceived as the materialist values, the inward-looking and self-serving creed of their parents' generation, and sought both a widening of personal freedoms and a recognition of a greater social responsibility than the 'economic miracle' had yet elicited. In the 1960s they rebelled, battling with the police in Rome in March 1968, two months before the more famous outbreak in Paris. The class bias of the university system was deplored, as was the rampant individualism which the universities as institutions were seen to uphold.

Other factors clearly influenced the revolts of the late sixties, which had a strong ideological component as well as being a protest about more immediate material conditions. The Civil Rights marches in America and the widely reported events at the Berkeley campus, together with newsreels showing the devastation of Vietnam, the appalling bombing and napalming of defenceless villages in the name of greater political virtue, resonated strongly in an increasingly restless Italy. Young Italians finally woke from the Great American Dream which had drawn generations of their forebears; protest against a quickening Cold War compounded a crisis of authority in which all institutions – education, the family, the Church, unions and politics – were all called into question. 'I want to be an orphan', ran one extreme slogan, suggesting exasperation with the traditional Italian preference for the individual and family unit over a wider collective sense of identity. Yet it is perhaps paradoxical that the manner and means of dissent was itself – initially, at least – an imitation of the American model.

The student rebellions failed to act as a focus for the established Left, however. The students derided the institutionalized status and cautious policies of the PCI and stood against the 'state capitalism' of the USSR. Their ideological Marxism was tinged with anarchism, as their attachment to a 'communist' ideal, which found its gurus in Marcuse and the Frankfurt School, went hand in hand with profound distaste for the parties and states which claimed to represent that ideal. In Italy they were attacked by the PCI for being irrational and infantile. Following the 'Battle of Valle Giulia' in Rome between students and police, the writer Pier Paolo Pasolini wrote a controversial piece which accused middle-class students of taking up arms against their working-class brothers – the majority of policemen at lower levels were drawn from poor immigrant families from the South.[2] Yet, for all its naiveté, the movement drew large sections of the middle classes to the Left for the first time, as they aspired to a society which envisaged individual freedoms barely conceivable just a few years before.

THE WORKERS' MOVEMENT

While the student revolt – exhilarating and formative on a personal level but with more limited long-term consequences – declined, the focus for revolt spilled over from the universities to the unions and extra-parliamentary political parties well beyond the control of the official Communist Party. Students stopped going to classes and began picketing outside factory gates. A whole array of small groups sprang up, such as 'Potere Operaio' (Worker Power), 'Lotta Continua' (Unceasing Struggle) and 'Il Manifesto', a small group of intellectuals who were to found a successful and still-running newspaper. These groups were widely criticized for their obsession with ideological correctness, and above all for the startling ease with which some of them accepted violence as an alternative to the institutionalized processes of democracy.

After twenty years of reasonably successful labour relations, Italian industry was hit in 1968 and 1969 by a long series of demonstrations, wildcat strikes and factory occupations. The Centre–Left coalitions in place since 1963 (Christian Democrat and Socialist) had done little to better the conditions and wages of workers; the wretched conditions of some Southern immigrants and the continuing inadequacy of public services and housing outside the factory also fuelled unrest and dissatisfaction. Workers elected Factory Councils, demanded control over factory conditions, and denounced not only management but official unions and parties for manifestly failing in their obligation to the workers. Groups like 'Lotta Continua', however, overestimated the revolutionary potential of the situation and underestimated remaining loyalty to traditional parties and representatives of the workers on the Left.

Labour agitation over the next two to three years spread outwards from the factories to the railways, building and chemical workers. Some areas of the labour force, such as shop and hotel workers (mainly women), took part in protests for the first time. There were real gains for workers, such as the right to 150 hours' annual paid education or training, and the end to regional variations in pay levels. In 1975 the 'scala mobile' was introduced, index-linking all pay to inflation. While in some ways workers made real gains, sharply rising wages led to spiralling industrial costs, and to unemployment as many firms were priced out of the market. High inflation and low investment spelled serious trouble for the official economy, a situation only worsened by the escalating price of oil and a flourishing black economy. Added to Italy's generous social benefits, pensions and allowances, this scenario laid the foundations for the later notoriously uncontrollable budget deficit. Economic disaster was coupled with a series of financial scandals involving the ruling parties, the full implications of which were to emerge only with the political upheavals of the 1990s. Lockheed was only the biggest of these scandals; others involved the oil and major construction industries, where the 'little envelope' had become a way of life.

TERRORISM

The attempts to transform all aspects of Italian life – work, education, politics and culture – did not quickly fade away, as in many other countries. The most striking consequence of the social upheavals of these years was the rapid growth of organized crime and of terrorism, both 'red' and 'black'. Neo-Fascist groups, armed with considerable funding and obscure connections within the police force and security services as well as sophisticated weaponry, responded to the 'Hot Autumn' on behalf of a beleaguered and alarmed bourgeoisie in a manner even more vicious than the Fascist squads of half a century before. Fascists were later proven to have been responsible for the massacres of the late 1960s and early 1970s. The first act of the modern terrorist campaign was the bombing of a bank in Milan's Piazza Fontana in December 1969, killing sixteen and injuring ninety; other outrages included the derailing of the Rome–Munich express in August 1974 and, in August 1980, the bomb at Bologna railway station which left eighty-four dead and more than two hundred wounded. Nobody has ever been found guilty of any of these outrages. Dario Fo's bitterly satirical play *Accidental Death of an Anarchist* expresses by its farcical form the absurdity of the authorities' attempt to inculpate a supposed anarchist cell for the bombing in Milan; the play deals with the 'accidental' defenestration of Giuseppe Pinelli, one of two anarchists hastily rounded up by police and claimed to be implicated in the bombing.[3] According to initial reports Pinelli committed suicide, a claim systematically demolished by the writer and journalist Camilla Cederna, veteran of many Socialist and feminist campaigns.

What was becoming increasingly apparent was that murkier forces on the Right, with the collusion of some parts of the secret services, were engaging in a so-called 'strategy of tension', an attempt not to calm the social and political situation but to exacerbate it, to create panic, and to pave the way for a return to authoritarianism. The workings of this strategy, already tried and tested in Greece, were tellingly portrayed in Leonardo Sciascia's *Il contesto* (*Equal Danger*, 1971) and Francesco Rosi's subsequent film of 1975, *Cadaveri eccellenti* (Illustrious Corpses).

Left-wing terrorism, too, was a complex phenomenon, a response to neo-Fascism. A multitude of small terrorist groups sprang up. These groups chose largely 'symbolic' targets such as judges, high-ranking officials and Fiat managers; while they were violent and ruthless, their attacks did not have the indiscriminate randomness of right-wing terror. The majority of terrorists were male, but women, too, played an important role: the joint founders of the Red Brigades were Renato Curcio and Mara Cagol, who was later killed in a shoot-out with the police.

Official figures suggest that by the late 1970s about two thousand acts of terrorism, including murders, bombings and kidnappings, were perpetrated annually. With the military efficiency of their kidnapping of the senior Christian Democrat politician Aldo Moro in 1978, the Red Brigades seemed to have the state on its knees. The ruling parties wrung their hands for two months, but refused to negotiate: Moro was murdered, exposing both the incompetence of the Italian police forces and the self-interest of the political parties. However, this apparent success was in fact the beginning of the end as the groups, no longer able to attract wide support, began to fall apart, leaving behind them an enfeebled and debilitated Left.

THE EMERGENCE OF FEMINISM IN ITALY

By the late 1960s and early 1970s rapid urbanization, economic development and increased educational opportunities for girls had led to a startling transformation in the expectations and self-image of Italian women. A survey in 1972 showed up these changes: where two decades before most would have wanted a traditional family role, they now wanted education, paid work, prosperity, and freedom (Clark, *Modern Italy*, p. 380). Women had achieved parity in access to education and the labour market, while changes in family law finally gave them equal formal rights over their children.

Women were at the forefront of trade-union agitation in the factories, yet despite its egalitarian rhetoric, political activism in the 1960s was a specifically male province. Women struggled to be seen as equals, despite parity of class, education and culture; they were more often sent off to hand out leaflets at factory gates, where they could be guaranteed attention from the workers. At the same time, the new sexual freedoms all too frequently turned into sexual obligations as women's right to refuse was undermined by changing ethical codes as well as advances in contraception. Within the workers' movement, politics was deemed to be for men. In a famous cartoon of the time, a young woman, her hair uncombed, a broom in one hand, a baby up against her shoulder and another small child she is attempting to keep away from the washing machine with her foot, is speaking into a telephone which she holds between her shoulder and her ear: 'No, my husband's not in,' she is saying, 'he's out fighting for the oppressed.'

The early 1970s saw a remarkably rapid growth in women's collective consciousness, even while the degree of participation varied considerably according to region, age and class. From 1970 onwards feminist groups began to appear in the major cities, with women practising their own form of consciousness-raising, or 'autocoscienza', seen as 'a radical break with the moderate and conciliatory aspects of emancipationism, the tough-minded demand for the movement's autonomy, an antagonistic relationship to all institutions, the exposure of the man–woman contradiction in all moments of our lives together'.[4]

Many soon came to the conclusion that real freedom for women – liberation rather than the mechanistic economic and juridical equality proposed by emancipation – was not to be found within revolutionary or left-wing groups which insisted on the primacy of class analysis, where excursions into the personal, an individual's experience of her own life, let alone questions of sexual difference, were postponed until after the revolution.

Carla Lonzi, one of the most influential feminist thinkers of the early years of neo-feminism in Italy, wrote powerfully of the Marxist call to revolution that it held no promise within it of an end to patriarchy, and argued that the oppression of women needed to be understood and theorized outside the specificity of class. For Lonzi, the whole tradition of Western philosophy was predicated on an *a priori* misogynistic premiss which confined women to their separate spheres, to the passive and the negative, the private rather than the public, body rather than spirit. From the Greeks to Hegel the cornerstone of philosophical thought had been the drive to define women's 'essence' in such a way as to provide a theoretical justification for a regressive social practice, and she argued passionately against using the tools of orthodox Marxism to analyse the female condition. For Lonzi, 'subsuming the feminine problem to the classist conception of the master–slave struggle is an historical mistake', for 'Woman is oppressed as a woman, at all social levels; not as a class, but as a sex.'[5]

The diversities of women's experience in the Italian context were movingly and passionately underlined by writer, critic and anthropologist Armanda Guiducci (b. 1923). Arguing that feminism is a predominantly urban, middle-class or proletarian movement marking the confluence of precise historical forces, Guiducci went in search of the women marginalized from social and political discourse by poverty, those 'women deprived of any voice by a series of subtractions – from history, from the proletariat itself, from female emancipation – which reduces them to the zero point of femininity'.[6] In the descriptions of their lives by two women, the chaste housewife and the whore, the two sides of the feminine myth, Guiducci shows both to be pawns in a patriarchal structure designed to accommodate men's social and sexual needs.[7] Her discussions with women from Sardinia, Sicily, Campania, but also the poorer parts of the central and Northern regions, define feminism as a luxury of the hegemonic culture, while the women who remain tied to the land by centuries of tradition and continuing hardship are mystified by modern civilization's iconic view of nature as an instance of a lost, and better, world. This is popular culture – or the culture of misery – where the feminist concern with female subjectivity is undermined by the absence of personalized, individual culture; where all understanding and experience are based on tradition and collective memory; where Marxist dialectics are lost amid a welter of different dialects and standard Italian is the language of the oppressor; where customs and habits are the remnants of past traditions from which the ruling class has long moved on. These women describe the rituals and 'primitive' beliefs which hedge female experience – remedies for illness, charms, the burial of the placenta after childbirth to ward off harm to the newborn, sexual precociousness coupled with utter ignorance, as well as their back-breaking labour, dozens of childbirths and their continuous experience of death. Guiducci emphasizes that these women are part not of some exotic, primitive, 'other' culture, but of our own: her exposure of the limitations of feminism points simultaneously to a society radically and eternally divided from itself.

LEGISLATION: DIVORCE AND ABORTION LAWS

Following the practice of 'autocoscienza' in the early 1970s, women rapidly organized into a widespread movement which began to press for a number of specific social and political changes, and the question of divorce provided the first focus for feminist intervention in the public political arena. Church marriages could be annulled on limited grounds. Similarly, state tribunals could grant 'legal separation': custody of children was usually given to the father in these cases. Legislation passed in the 1970s included, finally, a divorce law (passed in 1970 and upheld overwhelmingly by referendum[8] in 1974), the lifting of the ban on advertising contraception (1971), a reform of family law to give equal rights to both parents (1975), a national plan for nurseries (1971; nursery provision in Italy to this day far outstrips the limited options available in the UK) and family planning clinics. In 1977 women were granted improved rights in the workplace, including equal pay for equal work. That same year women's pensionable age was raised to sixty-five, while paternity leave was introduced along with a comparatively generous five-month statutory maternity leave provision for women.

Other legal reforms spoke of long-overdue changes in the status of women in Italy. The beginning of the 1980s finally saw repealed the law limiting sentences for murder in the cases of discovered adultery, a crime of honour, to between three and seven years. At the same time the law decreed that rape, which previously could be pursued through the courts only if the plaintiff so willed, was to be regarded as an offence against the person rather than against morality, and the article of the Code which expressly envisaged cancellation of the crime by a marriage of 'reparation' was struck out.[9]

Party-political preoccupation with the changing role and composition of the family was paralleled by the dramatic growth in feminism with its debates on contraception, abortion, women's health, and women as mothers, while policies of the Communist Party in particular were influenced by feminists within its ranks. The struggle for legalized abortion was perhaps the one issue which united the various strands of Italian feminist opinion and perspective, and was something of a watershed for the movement, which never again managed to mobilize on such a scale. Illegal abortions had blighted the lives of countless Italian women (both women and abortionists risked five years' imprisonment), while those with more resources could go abroad. While the women's movement encompassed a wide range of opinion, the campaign for legalized abortion mobilized women in their hundreds of thousands. A referendum organized by the Radical Party and the Movimento per la Liberazione della Donna (MLD, the Movement for the Liberation of Women) forced the matter before Parliament, and after a protracted struggle abortion was finally legalized in 1978. There were, however, limits to access to abortion: young girls under eighteen were required to seek parental consent, and abortions could take place only in authorized hospitals. More problematically, perhaps, the predominance of male Catholic doctors, who could object on grounds of conscience, meant that in practice abortion could still be difficult to obtain, while Italian women relate tales of insensitivity on the part of doctors and even the mournful tolling of bells in nearby churches when abortions were carried out in local hospitals. None the less, the law met with wide approval among both women and parties of the Left (the Radicals and, a little more reluctantly, the Communists), and a further referendum three years later in 1981 to overthrow 'Law 194' was defeated.

THE DIFFERENCE OF ITALIAN FEMINISM

The continuing strong regional basis of Italian cultural life was reflected in the establishment of influential local women's groups with their own specific identities and interests, brought together in a loose federal structure. Groups such as the Libreria delle donne di Milano (Milan's Women's Bookshop), Rivolta Femminile (Female Revolt, Milan), the Movimento Femminista Romano (Roman Feminist Movement) and Diotima (Verona), published – and continue to publish – variously on questions of philosophy, ethics, history and politics. The creation of autonomous spaces outside the institutions in which women could meet, discuss strategy and evolve theory was also in accord with the separatism which marked Italian feminism, its increasing emphasis on locating and understanding female subjectivity in relation not to institutions or to men, but to other women.

Issues raised by Italian feminists included a hard-fought campaign for paid housework, as once more the precarious status of bourgeois women was brought into view. The issue of housework was another aspect of the Italians' assault on the patriarchal family and women's prescribed roles within it. A number of women-only health centres were set up, a policy designed to restore control of their bodies to women themselves. There were concerted protests, sit-ins and demonstrations against male violence, and an attempt to change the status of rape and sexual violence as a crime of violence against a specific individual rather than as a crime against morality. Women entered the debate on military service, with a wide range of views on conscription for women as for men as a denotation of equality. The involvement of women in terrorist cells provoked heated debate. While there were few persistent calls for a women's party, parliamentary representation and gender was put firmly on the agenda, particularly by women in the PCI.

Every area of social, political and cultural life in Italy was challenged, to be rethought through the new dimension of gender. Women's Cultural Centres were set up, and the feminist press in Italy flourished. Journals such as *Sottosopra* (Upside Down), *Effe* (F) and *Donnawomanfemme* were established between 1973 and 1975; bookshops were set up in Milan, Rome and Bologna; feminist publishing houses were founded; Radio Donna began transmitting in 1976 and continued for many years despite appalling and repeated physical aggression, culminating in 1979 when four women were shot and wounded; in 1973 the women's theatre 'La Maddalena', set up by Dacia Maraini, opened its doors.

Feminism in Italy was an eclectic movement, borrowing widely from American as well as other European feminisms and adapting a multiplicity of models to the specific – and dramatic – situation in which Italians found themselves in the late 1960s and 1970s. Given the strength of the Italian philosophical tradition, feminists in Italy did not share the Anglo-American distrust of theory, and drew on a number of diverse traditions to come up with a very particular mix of theory informed by political practice. As well as the practice of consciousness-raising, American feminism contributed substantially to the debate on lesbianism. Italian feminists were much influenced by the work of French philosophical and psychoanalytical writing, that of Luce Irigaray in particular, and they have produced a large body of work on the vexed topic of sexual equality and sexual difference.

The most significant and original theoretical contributions of Italian feminism are its elaboration of theories of sexual difference and its continuing preoccupation with relationships between women. Sexual difference, as it is understood in Italian theory, is to be equated neither with the determinism of biology nor with the social construction of gender. This is not the British and American concern with the sexism which inscribes women's social inferiority in language (equating humanity with maleness, for example, or referring to God the Father), nor is it the French preoccupation with elaborating the subversive potential of *écriture féminine* (not to be equated with writing by women). For the Italians, social recognition of equality is a poisoned chalice which would eliminate women's difference by assimilating them to the historically dominant male modes of understanding and interpreting the world. The philosopher Adriana Cavarero and the group Diotima continue to explore ways of thinking about sexual difference through a system of thought which itself expressly suppresses that difference. Cavarero calls for a dualistic philosophy, the recognition that 'being a man or being a woman is something originary which requires a dual conceptualization, an absolute duality, a kind of paradox for the logic of the one–many'.[10] This dualism – similar in spirit, perhaps, to the 'due soli', the twin suns of Empire and Papacy, which Dante longed for as a just distribution of power and influence in the world – would require a fundamental shift not only in philosophical discourse but in the organization of the institutions.

Over the course of the 1970s and early 1980s Italian feminism, in its theoretical inflections, became less concerned with relations between women and men or institutions than with relations between and among women themselves. The practice of 'affidamento' ('entrustment') clearly came out of the practice of 'autocoscienza', and was an attempt to acknowledge the social, intellectual and power differences, the tensions and inequalities between women in their public as well as their private lives. Through the notion of 'affidamento' Italians reached for what they termed a 'dynamic separatism'.[11] 'Entrustment' implies supportive networking, the focusing on another woman as reference point in the effort to achieve one's ambitions and desires.

While it is difficult to assess the success of this endeavour, it is interesting to speculate on the Italian emphasis on relations between women as a reaction to traditional cultural values. In their acknowledgement of the disparities between women, the Italians follow Irigaray in her belief in the need to prioritize the relationship with the mother as model for other personal and social relationships. One observer speaks of 'the persistence in Italy of powerful common cultural accounts of mothers',[12] their role – together with the pre-eminence of the male child – underlined by the dominant ideology of Catholicism and reinforced in modern times through Fascism. In this sense 'entrustment' sent a challenge to the dominant cultural and political representations of the relationship between women, for which the mother–daughter relationship served as a paradigm.

Italian feminism, abstract and abstruse as it can appear – and it has been accused by Italian women themselves of obscurantism – has always retained its links to political activism and a continuing commitment to social change and intervention in the public arena. The stormy social and political situation in Italy has always been crucial to the development there of feminist thought, which offers a bridge between the preponderance of French theory and the pragmatism of the Anglo-American tradition.

FEMINIST LITERATURE AND CRITICISM: POETRY

In 1976 Lidia Ravera (b. 1946) published *Porci con le ali* (*Pigs with Wings*), an ironic pastiche of the traditional boy-meets-girl theme set within the context of a revolutionary political movement clearly modelled on one of the many extra-parliamentary groups of the late sixties and early seventies. Ravera ruthlessly satirizes the pretentious ambition of the new cultural and political discourses, as her character Antonia listens to an earnest – and incomprehensible – analysis of pop music as 'metalanguage':

> Having fulfilled its associative function of collective – and collectivizing - discharge of erotic energy repressed by civilization which 'kills Eros in the name of the reality principle' (Oh my!), 'pop music today is reduced to a mere consumer product, sucked right into the obscene market of the superfluous' ('Induced needs', he adds, with the air of someone who wants to make everything clear).[13]

Confronted with the alienating and gender-blind discourse of Marxism and other leftist ideologies, many women on the radical

Left in the late 1960s and 1970s sought to define their own cultural and critical space. The Centro Culturale Virginia Woolf was set up in Rome; women began to write their own syllabuses and set up their own small but successful publishing houses. The organization of the women's movement in Italy was distinctive in that it resisted becoming absorbed within the institutions – and particularly the universities – as happened in Britain, France and the United States. Italian universities are notoriously hostile to change, and the development of degree-awarding courses in Women's Studies, for example, was almost inconceivable. Neither has Italian feminism been as dominated by literary and textual studies as feminism in other Western countries.

Women challenged the critical tenet that art, and quality in art, is neutral, untainted and unprejudiced by the conditions of its production. Dacia Maraini's emblematic poem 'Poesie delle donne', 'Poems by women', dismisses the notion that 'poetic results', like 'holes in donuts', can be achieved equally by men and women; she speaks cogently of women's access to poetry and relationship to poetic form, and of women's voices as emerging painfully from darkness and silence. Forms of women's poetry will be unsophisticated, because sophistication is a product of power. Like Virgil when he first appears to Dante, the woman poet's voice is hoarse from disuse:

> Her voice will perhaps be harsh and earthen
> but it's the voice of a lioness who has been
> taken for a sheep for too much prudent time.
> It is a feeble voice, crude and mutilated
> that comes from a long way off, from beyond
> history, from the hell of the exploited.
> A hell which does not improve people
> as is believed, but makes them lazy,
> sick, and enemies of themselves.[14]

In 1974 Mariella Gramaglia, discussing Anglo-American feminist poetry which had appeared over the previous decade, drew a clear distinction between 'literary' poetry and 'cultural' poetry, remarking of much feminist output: 'it is not literary poetry, then, but "cultural" poetry in the anthropological sense of the word, poetry which defines you and expresses you. And these poems are without doubt the fruit of a new woman.'[15] The new self-consciously feminist writers in Italy similarly had as their primary objective a renewed investigation of female subjectivity and sexual identity, and their dramatic expansion of what poetry could be deemed to discuss indicates the degree to which they tapped into international intellectual debates on feminist aesthetics. Poetry, the most prestigious of art forms in Italy, was to be reappropriated, reshaped and remade by women. To write, to grasp the 'phallic pen', was to challenge the marginalization of women and female culture, for 'a woman who writes is, potentially, revolution, that impossible and worn–out word'.[16] This was poetry of rage, a deliberate jolt to the platitudes of feminine gentility and delicacy in art. Marta Fabiani's poem 'The Poetess' rails against the limitations of women's lives, and simultaneously suggests women's own experience as the basis of a new aesthetic:

> The poetess has paragraphs of words
> threads she unravels as phrases
> unusual comparisons
> among the gleams
> of a kitchen stove.
> She reaches the eternal
> by little
> unveilings,
> the infinite is the leaking
> tap, the row
> of empties to return.[17]

Feminist poets rejected the formal syntactic and linguistic experimentalism of the neo–avant–garde and the Gruppo '63, in favour of forms which were more immediately communicable and comprehensible. Collections of contemporary poetry tended to focus on representations of the female body, with poems grouped around themes of maternity,[18] lesbianism (Marianna Fiore, b. 1948), menstruation as symbol,[19] and the relationship of women to language and poetry itself, for 'in the general masquerade the part of the body has fallen to the woman – she has not been able to be the word. Only its limit, if anything: rim and vaginal space which contains and embraces the erupting, phallic, male, penis-word.'[20]

What women wrote, and how they wrote it, the assumption of

a subjective speaking voice and the introduction of feminist issues
– and feminist anger – into aesthetic debates was initially perceived
as a matter of politics. The poet and critic Biancamaria Frabotta was
to comment a few years later:

> 'Taking the floor' was considered the end and means of libera-
> tion. In the majority of instances, the type of language adopted
> was coldly pre-constituted for communication, exhortation and
> propaganda. This at least holds true for the flyers, documents,
> songs of struggle and, later on, for the poetry and novels that
> were defined as 'feminist realism'.[21]

Beyond a brief and heady historical moment, many women
none the less resisted – and continue to resist – being thought
of as 'women writers', fearful of new and insidious forms of
discrimination and marginalization. When Biancamaria Frabotta
published her anthology *Donne in poesia* (Women in Poetry,
1976) a questionnaire answered by contributing poets revealed
the level of distrust and apprehension at such a move in a culture
where difference was only too swiftly converted into hierarchy.
Other writers looked forward to a time when Virginia Woolf's
androgynous ideal would become the norm, when 'woman writer'
would no longer be a term accepted reluctantly out of the need
to indicate that art and poetry were still in the grip of a powerful
masculinist culture unwilling to make space for female experience
or for the female imaginary.

THE NOVEL

The 1970s in Italy were not dedicated to literature as aesthetic
enterprise; the struggle for form was largely subservient to the
struggle for the political contextualization of all cultural activity.
The novel was regarded with suspicion as a withered, worm-eaten
bloom of bourgeois culture, rooted in capitalist economics, which
could speak neither to the radical revolutionary nor to the new
feminist consciousness. Novels were written none the less, and
if literary and textual criticism did not mushroom in Italy as it
did in the States or in Britain, a certain amount of attention was
paid to issues of women's writing and discursive representations
of gender.

Italian critics found themselves on something of a cleft stick.

Some complained that feminism had made little or no impact on what or how women wrote novels; that women's fiction continued to be regressive, infantile and conciliatory.[22] Those influenced by Anglo-American models of women's writing and history, usually professors of English or American literature, wrote books on Jane Austen, the Brontës and Emily Dickinson. Others, influenced by the theories of Hélène Cixous and Julia Kristeva, who are considerably more hostile to women's writing as lacking any radical and subversive edge, similarly declined to look to the production of their own countrywomen. As a result, it was some years before the rediscovery and reprinting of writers such as Neera, Contessa Lara and Maria Messina got under way, and little was written about Italian women's own substantial literary history.

Closely tied into the theoretical formulations of the women's movement, Italian feminist novels of the 1970s reflect the ideological shift in neo-feminism beyond the struggle for emancipation and equality to the larger task of challenging the economic and political bases of contemporary society. The demand for emancipation, for the right to education and work, which marked *fin-de-siècle* feminist literature was displaced by the demand for a new sexual ethical code, for a recognition of the 'political' at the heart of the 'personal', the assertion of women's rights and needs in their private as well as their public lives, and an analysis of the family as the most intransigent locus of patriarchal power. Giuliana Ferri broaches the complex and guilt-ridden terrain of maternity in *Un quarto di donna* (A Quarter of a Woman; Marsilio, Padua 1973); the novel's very title outlines the fragmented nature of women's lives at a time of social transition, torn between the demands of the intelligence and the desire for emtional fulfilment as mother as well as partner. In Chiara Saraceno's *Dalla parte della donna* (On the Side of Woman, 1971) it is no longer the vamp or the mistress but the professional woman who is socially stigmatized as destroyer of the family; while in Marina Jarre's *Negli occhi di una ragazza* (In a Girl's Eyes, 1971) a woman's destiny is still equated by family expectations with her reproductive anatomy. In *Lunga giovinezza* (Long Childhood, 1976) Gabriella Magrini explores the sexual misery and joylesness – as well as continual fear of pregnancy and feelings of violence – within bourgeois marriage.[23]

The works of these writers expressed no utopian solutions:

rather, they formalized the issues explored in consciousness-raising groups and debates within the women's movement about sexuality, autonomy, female subjectivity, the family, maternity, and the dislocation between public and private. It is perhaps a comment less on politics than on literature that so many feminist novels of the 1970s appear dated, tied to the theoretical formulations of a specific moment, the representation of a political position covered with a thin veneer of fiction. Dacia Maraini's challenge to poetical lyricism was echoed in fiction, where a style overtly antagonistic to any tradition of prosody or *belles-lettres* verged on the sloganistic, and the aesthetic position was a consciously politicized anti-aestheticism. Any pretence of 'objectivity' was exploded, the gap between author and character was elided as writers adopted semi-autobiographical styles, reappropriating and politicizing traditionally 'feminine' forms such as letters and diaries, offering a fragmented text as an iconic image of women's fragmented lives.

There were, obviously, exceptions to these generalizations about specifically feminist writing in the wake of the emergence of the women's movement. Maria Letizia Cravetta's ironic pastiche *Tutti sanno* (Everyone Knows, 1976) satirizes the publishing industry itself, interweaving the fictitious correspondence of two editors setting up a new journal (entitled *Flourishing Oedipus*), with the tale of Donata, whose failure to achieve fulfilment either in writing or in heterosexual relationships leads her to abandon both. The editors' declared intention, to present revolutionary, subversive (and feminist) material to a new public, is undermined by a more powerful impulse to rewrite, to suppress, to turn the real despair of people's lives – such as that of Donata herself – into consumable fiction. Donata resists this transformation, determined to continue the struggle to make make her way as (feminist) writer.

While Cravetta plays with the conventions of the novel even as she exposes its normalizing and homogenizing function, Silvia Castelli's experimental novel *Pitonessa* (The Female Python, 1978) recalls Monique Wittig's *Le corps lesbien* (1973). Written in unpunctuated paragraphs arbitrarily spaced across the page, it is a textual gesture towards a language of the body outside social and political constructions, just as the narratives adumbrated within the text are disrupted by mysterious *bambine*, little girls, who point to a habitable space outside the rigid social categories into which they are expected to fit as they reach adulthood.

THEATRE

'Italy, ever as poor in drama as she is rich in theatricality',[24] has in the past few decades been notoriously unable to foster new writing or to create a vital atmosphere of innovation and change; despite producing widely acclaimed directors such as Giorgio Strehler and Luca Ronconi, theatre in Italy, dependent on state subsidy awarded for political allegiance rather than artistic merit, has tended to feed the public a safe diet of Luigi Pirandello, Carlo Goldoni and Shakespeare rather than new work. Among those who did write for the theatre, the predominance of already established novelists led to a work based on linguistic text rather than exploiting the multiple possibilities of dramatic form offered by the theatrical space.

Granted these limitations, women in the 1970s began to involve themselves in theatrical activity at all levels, as writers, producers and theatre managers as well as performers, looking back to women such as Isabella Andreini and others involved in the *commedia dell'arte* tradition who ran companies and produced their own material. Dacia Maraini's women-only theatre 'La Maddalena', set up in 1972, will be discussed in more detail in the next chapter. In Turin the 'Teatro Settimo' (Settimo is a district in Turin) opened its doors in 1975, and is still performing and travelling abroad, including performances at the Edinburgh Festival in 1990 and 1993. Members of 'Teatro Settimo' devise their own texts, drawing as freely from South American 'magical realism' as from Italian sources, and perform in unconventional spaces, including people's homes.

The most successful performer whose work has been deeply influenced by the women's movement in Italy, both nationally and internationally, is Franca Rame, long-time companion and partner to Dario Fo. Fo and Rame established their own theatre co-operative, 'La Comune', which was to dispense with traditional hierarchical working practices and make decision-making and planning collective while playing to an alternative circuit. Like Maraini, they discovered that this project was a utopian one, but they shared with the radical intellectual Left the need to break with traditional forms and traditional spaces. Also like Maraini, Fo and Rame identified with the non-sectarian Left, critical of the Communist Party which was perceived as too rigidly authoritarian, hierarchical as well as patriarchal, too locked in rigid ideology, too inimical to culture as well as too timid for revolution.

The attribution of authorship to Rame, even of her feminist monologues from the mid-seventies, *Tutta casa, letto e chiesa* (*Female Parts*),[25] is problematic, given her close working relationship with Fo and the finalization of texts on the stage, in rehearsal and in performance, rather than on the page. From 1977 onwards Rame gave over three thousand performances in Italy, Britain and the Americas. Yvonne Bryceland performed *Female Parts* at the National Theatre in London in June 1981, and Rame herself appeared at the Riverside Studio the following year. Proceeds from the shows were donated to the women's movement, to finance factory occupations and counselling centres.

Rame's dramatic and multivoiced monologues require both enormous skill from the actress, with their swift and dramatic changes of tone, voice and pace, and a complex audience response: in the manner of Brecht's epic theatre the spectator is stimulated to anger, sympathy and shock, to intellectual analysis as well as laughter. Rame's women produce a stream of consciousness, a densely layered 'take' on the common complexities of women's lives: 'mingling actual events and psychological insights [Rame] alternates between descriptions of what's happening on stage, and comments, explanations, political analyses, memories relived with the same immediacy as present events, and associations of ideas'.[26] The monologues range over issues of rape, terrorism, the deadening routine of work, housework and childcare, as well as the Church, drugs and the female body as manipulated by the fashion industry. *The Rape* is a powerful, direct account of an all too common experience of physical violence, as the woman, beaten and burned with cigarettes as well as raped, is unable to bring herself to report a crime for which an unsympathetic legal system will only victimize her twice over. *Rise and Shine* uses elements of frantic mime to highlight an attack on the drudgery and pressures of family life. A woman factory worker struggles to prepare herself and her child for a working day, unsuccessfully negotiating baby, housekey, breakfast and irate husband. In the tradition of farce, radiator paint is mistaken for deodorant, grated cheese for the baby's talcum powder, and in an elaborate effort to locate the housekey she re-creates a succession of rapid scenes from an impoverished married life – only to realize that it is, after all, a Sunday. *A Woman Alone* combines the dramatic features of monologue and farce as the woman on stage relates her tale, an increasingly grotesque and manic parody of male oppression – her husband on the end of the phone, the Peeping Tom opposite, the heavy breather who also phones, the sexual maniac brother-in-law encased in plaster and confined to his wheelchair, leaving only his hand free.

Like Dacia Maraini, Rame has also turned to the classics, and in her interpretation of *Medea* she condemns a culture which equates feminine desirability with youthful good looks. While Pier Paolo Pasolini's 1973 cinematic interpretation of the story has Medea suggest the primitive, the rawly emotional, the rural, the unruly unconscious, confronting and defeated by the thrusting, urban and ambitious Jason, Rame's Medea posits the more banal and thus more tragically familiar situation of the woman who, in ageing, loses her claim on society and on her man: 'Everyone's embarrassed by a woman who's surplus to requirements'.[27] The murder of her children becomes for Medea a conscious act not of revenge but of breaking the patriarchal law which demands that women sacrifice themselves to their children.

Rame's feminism is, however, by no means separatist or antagonistic to men. Dario Fo's *Coppia aperta* (*Open Couple*, 1983) based on his (frequently very public) extra-marital experiences, turns out to be an impassioned defence of monogamous marriage. Rame is critical of what she calls brutal, hard-line feminism, commenting with typical nonchalance and panache: 'I am in complete agreement with those women who are struggling for liberation, once and for all, from those senseless inhibitions which have been inculcated into us over the years. But I would always, even when dropping my knickers, like to achieve that with a minimum of style.'[28] In performance, Rame refuses the underlying puritanism of much British and American feminism and exploits her own glamorous sexuality on stage, appearing in a series of elaborate costumes including a much-commented-upon see-through nightie. Euphemisms of dress or language are equally spurned. The question of gendered use of language in particular is addressed head on, to both shocking and hilarious effect. In one notable passage Rame compares the ludic, grandiloquent, evocative names men give to their male organs to the deadly, terrifying and alarming terms granted to women's anatomy:

> 'Vagina'! The best you could do with a vagina is slip on it. . . . But the first prize must go to another term, one that I can hardly bring myself to utter – orgasm! It is a word addressed almost exclusively to women. Men experience pleasure, but women orgasm. The very sound is enough to make the hairs stand up on the back of your neck. It summons up monsters. . . . Can you see the headlines in the morning paper: 'Giant orgasm escapes from city zoo!' 'Nun assaulted by mad orgasm on run from American circus.' (*Tricks of the Trade*, p. 105)

Humour and satire are the essential elements of Fo and Rame's style of theatre. As long as satire exists there remains the possibility of democratic politics, and it is satire which becomes the great debunker of the phallocratic myth.

DOPOFEMMINISMO: THE END OF FEMINISM AND ITALY TODAY
In 1980 Maria Antonietta Macciocchi declared that feminism was finished: 'The great drinking bout is over. The confrontation feminist is going home. She can sit down, put her banners and placards away.' Macciocchi's irony springs less from dissent than from disappointment. She looks forward to a resurgence of feminism after the coming years of reaction, anticipating 'a molecular reorganization, invisible from the outside, of behaviour, of sensuality, of contact with one's own body, of words themselves. . . . Nothing will be forgotten.'[29]

Observers generally agree that with the achievement of legalized abortion, feminism lost its mass appeal and its ability to mobilize large numbers of women from all areas and classes of Italian society. Other factors, too, were at play in marking the end of militant activism in what was one of the most dramatic and dynamic feminist movements in the Western world. 1977 saw the Italian Communist Party's policy shift from ousting the ruling Christian Democrats to a so-called 'historic compromise', in reaching an understanding with the Centre Right. The great era of collective action – whether feminist, socialist or Marxist – appeared to have had its day as Italy festered in the grip of terrorism, shallow political rhetoric and a largely obeisant press. A general weariness with systems, struggles and ideologies brought the Right to power elsewhere, while the monolithic and stagnant nature of Italian politics led instead to the 'riflusso' – to reaction and the retreat from the public arena into the personal.

Macciocchi underestimates, however, the success of Italian feminism and the movements of the sixties and seventies in changing women's perceptions of themselves and paving the way for a remarkable expansion of opportunities in the professions, management, journalism and the academies, and women have entered massively into the labour market. While the Vatican maintains a rigid stance on contraception and abortion, the thinking of the Church, too, has shifted with regard to the role women can play in society. There has been a massive increase in 'unorthodox' households, with couples living together rather than marrying, women begin families later, or not at all (the birth rate has fallen sharply from 2.7 in 1964 to barely 1.1 in 1991); and there is good childcare provision. All this has dramatically altered life for the vast majority of women, even in the South and in more remote areas.

The repercussions of the fall of the Berlin Wall and the end of the Cold War were instantly felt in Italy with the collapse of the PCI, the most powerful Communist Party in Western Europe, and the narrowing of the ideological divide. The Italian 'revolution' led in a very few short years to the end of the old, seemingly immutable parties of the Socialists and Christian Democrats and the rise of new forces such as Umberto Bossi's Northern League. Italian magistrates under the indefatigable Antonio Di Pietro began the mammoth task of detailing the corruption which had dominated Italian political and public life, and even such previously untouchable and impervious figures as the Socialist Bettino Craxi and Giulio Andreotti, five times Christian Democrat Prime Minister, stood accused on numerous accounts of corruption, graft, and even association with the Mafia.

Italy's Second Republic was ushered in with the meteoric political success of the business and media magnate Silvio Berlusconi, in alliance with Bossi's League and with the neo-Fascist Alleanza

Nazionale (National Alliance). While some observers abhor the masculinist rhetoric of political movements such as Umberto Bossi's 'Lega Nord' or Northern League (with unrepentant slogans such as the almost untranslatable 'La Lega ce l'ha duro', 'The League's hard'),[30] it is an uncomfortable fact that the League had a massive appeal to women, just as Berlusconi's alliance drew in numerous voters from the traditional Left. There are still very few women in positions of political power: despite changing roles and expectations, their representation in political life remains stuck between seven and ten per cent. Feminists who grew up in the sixties and seventies have been provoked, however, by the new women who have achieved prominence. Alessandra Mussolini, granddaughter of Benito, moved from being a film star of dubious quality to become the darling of the Fascist party in Naples; Tiziana Parenti, an ex-magistrate in Di Pietro's 'Clean Hands' campaign against political and industrial corruption, became a member of Berlusconi's 'Forza Italia' movement and Chair of the Anti-Mafia Commission; the 'leghista' Irene Pivetti, barely into her thirties, was made equivalent of Leader of the House and stirred debate by using masculine linguistic forms to refer to herself. Pivetti denounced the revolutionary cultures of the 1960s and 1970s, picking out feminism for particular criticism and claiming that as a movement it was now dead in the water. While Dacia Maraini comments that, for the first time in Italy, women are seen to have 'both brains and beauty – and balls',[31] such overt hostility from the centres of power, together with the beginnings of an attempt to overturn the law regulating abortion, suggest that Macciocchi's 'molecular reorganization' has a long way to travel, as leading feminist thinkers acknowledge the difficulty of defining political objectives for women in the 1990s and beyond.[32] Women's lives have been revolutionized, but feminism needs new battles to fight if it is to renew itself and its appeal to the mass of Italian women.

CONTEMPORARY WRITING

Writing by women, on the other hand, and narrative in particular, has become hugely successful in recent years. There has been an explosion of interest in writing by women as they have scooped up numerous literary prizes, vital in Italian cultural life as both guarantee of sales and unique indicator of prestige. Some of those whose lives and imaginations were formed with feminism and the turbulent movements of the 1960s and 1970s continue, however obliquely, to explore sexual difference, while many younger writers have refused the close meshing of ideological formulation with linguistic strategy, of political conviction with artistic form, reserving the right to produce work which was precisely 'literary' rather than 'cultural'. Even while some observers wonder if, like Donata in Maria Letizia Cravetta's *Everyone Knows*, women have become victims of their own success and fallen into the hands of an exploitative cultural industry, 'caught between a patriarchal publishing market that threatens to neutralize them and definitions of feminine discourse that exclude them',[33] the prominence of contemporary women writers points to more than successful marketing strategies, for women have taken up influential positions within cultural, publishing, academic and media institutions. It is surely a matter for celebration rather than anxiety that, for the first time, women are at the centre of literary and cultural activity and no longer consigned to the margins, respected but largely unread, and in this context the work of older writers such as Lalla Romano (b. 1909) is receiving more, and better-informed, critical attention. Romano's work is consistently autobiographical, based on her own experience: but it is, at the same time, elliptical, enigmatic and poetic. The author of such remarkable texts as *Le parole fra noi leggere* (Words Light Between Us, 1969) and the more recent *Le lune di Hvar* (The Moons of Hvar, 1992) is yet another writer who deserves more serious attention and translation.

Women continue to make a significant contribution to poetry. Maria Luisa Spaziani (b. 1924), lends a female voice to the poetic avant-garde, as her work engages with the tradition of Rilke, Montale and Dylan Thomas. While in a recent collection of Italian poetry in English, 'Fourteen Italian Poets for the Twenty-First Century',[34] only four are women, they continue the work of Mariella Bettarini (b. 1942) and particularly Amelia Rosselli (b. 1930) in rejecting abstract experimentalism. Anna Cascella (b. 1941) and Bianca Tarozzi (b. 1941) employ an easy, conversational style, almost prose poems, with a specifically female perspective.[35] The sensual, ironic poems of Patrizia Cavalli[36] focus on the grim realities of daily existence, while Patrizia Valduga (b. 1952) ignores current poetic fashions altogether and returns to the closed forms of an older tradition. Italian dramatists, too, have achieved international success. Patrizia Monaco's work has been performed in New York and Quebec (*Summer at Casa Magli*, about Mary Shelley, and *The True and False O'Brien*).

It is in narrative prose, however, that women writers have had the greatest impact, both in Italy and abroad. While Maraini may have had the biggest commercial and international success with *The Silent Duchess* (1990), other writers have imposed themselves on public attention with the depth and complexity of their work. Fantasy has become a popular short-story genre.[37] Some persevere in a realistic mode which earns the disapproval of critics who deplore the gap between the theoretical insights of feminism and post-structuralism, and more traditional narrative forms. The female protagonists of Gina Lagorio have a strength and courage in the face of a bleak and solitary existence which recalls the short stories of Anna Banti. *Tosca dei gatti* (Tosca of the Cats, 1983) delineates the everyday words and gestures of an ageing and lonely woman determined to maintain contact with the world, if only through a love of animals. Gina Lagorio has also written for the theatre, plays which similarly explore female emotion in a realist manner.

Works such as Marisa Volpi's *Maestro della betulla* (The Birch Tree Painter, 1986), Marta Morazzoni's *Ragazza col turbante* (Girl with Turban, 1986) and Elena Belotti's *Il fiore dell'ibisco* (The Hibiscus Flower, 1984) work to deconstruct a social and symbolic order which empowers the male gaze. Volpi's historical tales, like Virginia Woolf's evocation of Shakespeare's sister, privilege the voices suppressed by a dominant culture – Mozart's wife, or, in an overturning of Pushkin's better-known story, Da Ponte's humiliation at the hands of the resident court musician, Salieri. The title 'Girl with Turban' is taken from a portrait by the Dutch painter Vermeer; the book explores a male gaze oblivious to the real woman but rapt in contemplation of her representation. Humour is a further strategy for dismantling the patriarchal gaze.

Marina Mizzau, Ginevra Bompiani, Laura Mancinelli and Maria Corti are part of a new group of writers/academics who, in their fiction, bring to bear the theoretical insights of linguistics, post-structuralism and literary theory, but whose touch is sure and light for all that. Mancinelli's first novel, *I dodici abati di Challant* (The Twelve Abbots of Challant, 1981), uncannily echoed the medieval setting and something of the whodunnit plot of Umberto Eco's contemporaneous *The Name of the Rose* (1980); while her second novel, *Il fantasma di Mozart* (Mozart's Ghost, 1986) is similarly an ironic, witty thriller. The female protagonist receives anonymous phone calls where she hears not words but snatches of Mozart's Haffner sumphony and later a duet from *Don Giovanni*. The search to unmask the ghost, set against a magical, disturbing and occasionally surreal Turin, leads her – and again the parallel with Eco is striking – to a monastery which houses Plato's last dialogue.[38]

Mizzau's academic and theoretical work deals with the gaps and silences which disrupt discourse, and considers them in the context of sexual difference and economic power. Her fictional work depicts, to frequently humorous ironic effect, the confusions and conflicts which lie beneath the surface of our most banal and trivial daily actions. *Come i delfini* (Like the Dolphins, 1988) comprises the lightest of dilemmas – how to make a proper Martini, at what point to salt the water for the spaghetti, how to decide who should water the plants.[39] Mizzau's minimalism amplifies and dramatizes the minute hesitations and doubts, the complex motivations which fracture the automatism of surface language, action and thought. Ginevra Bompiani similarly refuses an outmoded realism; her tales – whether of an ordinary Sunday recounted in extraordinary prose (*Vecchio cielo nuova terra* [Old Sky New Earth], 1988), the allegorical and surreal tales of emerging consciousness in *L'incantato* (Enchanted, 1987) or a short story of fantasy such as 'Il ladro',[40] articulate a very post-modern displacement of consciousness and subjectivity as they explore the paradoxes of time and language. Elisabetta Rasy, founding member of the publishing house Edizioni delle donne, follows Kristeva in her exploration of language as a process of repression and the site of potential subversion. Her first novel, *La prima estasi* (The First Ecstasy, 1985) was a psychoanalytical account of Saint Teresa di Lisieux; *Mezzi di trasporto* (Means of Transport, 1993) again shows a post-modern sensibility; in narratives which mimic the flux of sensations, these surreal stories explore the fragmented desires, anxieties and solitude which are the tramlines of modern consciousness.[41]

If a core theme of writing by women has been marriage, the family and maternity, recent novels and stories underline how far women have moved. Lara Cardella's provocative autobiographical novel *Volevo i pantaloni* (I Wanted to Wear Trousers, 1989) – half in Sicilian dialect, half in Italian – can be seen as the product of a new ethos in Italy, where young, and female, authors had suddenly become marketable. However, the novel's clamorous success was an echo of contemporary concerns in Italy and Britain, with its open denunciation of incest and child abuse as common practice within the family. Two years later Susanna Tamaro published a series of more restrained but deeply shocking short stories, *Per voce sola* (*For Solo Voice*), which explore the social and psychological dynamics within the family – and her characters are principally bourgeois, from the same middle classes who have traditionally propounded the ideology of the family unit – which lead to neglect, abuse and even murder, to hysterical pregnancy, to psychosis and schizophrenia.

Tamaro's subsequent best-seller, *Va dove ti porta il cuore* (*Follow Your Heart*, 1993), takes the form of a diary written by an ageing grandmother for her granddaughter who has left for America. The grandmother is ill – she has had a stroke – and as death approaches she records the daily, ordinary gestures of her failing body, a record interspersed with snatches of her own personal history: her bourgeois marriage, her lover, her daughter who was caught up in the 1968 movement, underwent brutal psychoanalysis and died in an accident. The novel speaks of the difficult love, the unresolvable conflict between generations of women, the illusions of feminism and psychoanalysis, the solitude of the everyday. In this novel Tamaro speaks for a younger generation of women no longer within the ambit of feminist or political ideologies, once more coming to grips with their own personal history and the puzzling complexities of a genealogy of women.

The following chapters trace the move in contemporary writing by women from feminism as social and political movement to the current fragmentation of a constellation of writers who no longer align themselves to ideologies or party politics. Dacia

Maraini makes the condition of women the thematic focus of her work, her feminist politics informing both the subject and style of her vast output. Chapter 13, on 'Renegotiating Motherhood', considers Italian responses to a relationship much discussed both in feminist theory and among a generation of women coming to terms with their own history, with changing family structures, and new relations between women themselves. Finally, Chapter 14, on 'post-modernism', looks at some of the most vibrant and innovative contemporary work which, in its intellectual reach, once more opens up new areas for women's writing.

12
The Silencing of Women: The Political Aesthetic of Dacia Maraini (born 1936)

The opening pages of *Bagheria* (1993), Dacia Maraini's only overtly autobiographical work to date, recount her return as a young girl from Japan to the Sicilian town of Bagheria, near the capital Palermo, in the aftermath of the Second World War; her family, who since 1938 had been in Japan, where Maraini's father was a Professor of Oriental Studies, was interned following the fall of Mussolini, and the family suffered acute hardship in the Japanese concentration camps of Nagoya and Kobe. Maraini's narrative begins with a description of a photograph of herself as a young girl, with her blonde, sun-bleached hair, her blue eyes and red tennis shoes, her hand held by an American Marine. In her, she writes, the Marines could imagine their own daughters. One officer shows her photographs of his own little girl, and begins to touch her: 'It was then I learned something about a father's love, at the same time so tender and so lascivious, so overbearing and and so gentle.'[1]

Bagheria ends as Maraini encounters another image: a painting of one of her Sicilian ancestors, Marianna Valguarnera Gravina Palagonia. The eighteenth-century noblewoman was deaf and dumb, and she is depicted holding the pen and small block of paper with which she communicated with the world. The painting inspired Maraini's most successful novel to date, *La lunga vita di Marianna Ucrìa* (*The Silent Duchess*, 1990), which recounts the story of Marianna, raped by her uncle when she is just five years old, with the complicity of her adored father. Maraini's work, which from the beginning addresses the silencing of women, the cancelling out of their subjectivity, of their desires, their history and finally their language, engages with a patriarchal culture which is both violent and seductive, infinitely powerful and infinitely dangerous. *The Silent Duchess* is a reconsideration of the fascination of the father, a renegotiation of terms, as women emerge from silence and create their own cultural spaces within the dominant patriarchy.

Maraini began writing and publishing in the early 1960s, and in recent years she has become one of Italy's most prominent authors. Her work has been widely translated, and her plays have been performed on international stages from Japan to Britain (by Monstrous Regiment, London 1977) and America. Closely involved with both political and feminist movements in Italy, Maraini has lived and experienced at first hand the extraordinary turmoil of social, cultural and political life in Italy, the dramatic changes which have fundamentally altered the fabric of contemporary Italian society. While her works from the early 1960s predate the rise of neo-feminism in Italy, they express to a remarkable degree those feelings of alienation and loss of subjectivity – what one critic has called the 'degree zero of being a woman'[2] – which the practice of 'autocoscienza' or consciousness-raising was to explore within a few short years. In America Betty Friedan was publishing *The Feminine Mystique* (1963) and exposing the myth of the happy housewife which conspired with identifiable interest groups to keep women safely within the confines of the home. Maraini's novels are similarly a vivid representation of the annihilation of the self and suppression of individual identity which Friedan analysed in her work.

The adolescent female characters of Maraini's early novels, *La vacanza* (*The Holiday*, 1962) and *L'età del malessere* (*The Age of Malaise*, 1963), inhabit a world which insists on reducing them to the specifically physical and sexual; their engagement with this world is less that of conscious, political militancy than that of a passive, almost autistic paralysis. These are not characters who have achieved control over their own bodies, or have been empowered by contact with a vigorous body of thought, the comfort of female solidarity, or the certainties of political practice. These works constitute an Italianized, feminized version of Flaubert's *éducation sentimentale*, reflecting an inchoate complex of unease and oppression which has not yet been analysed or named, clearly prefiguring a consciousness and a perspective which were to be given a focus by feminist activism and thought.

The protagonist of *The Holiday*, Anna, spends a summer vacation away from her boarding school, with her father and younger brother. Here she becomes the object of the sexual attentions of the men around her, from a shy and awkward teenager to a middle-aged businessman. The final days of Fascism form the background to this series of encounters, with Allied aeroplanes crossing the beaches on their way to Rome, and young men disappearing to fight for the newly established Republic of Salò. Anna emerges into adulthood against this background of social and political crisis, which she registers not so much with objectivity as with a passive, mute indifference.

Anna is reduced to the margins of the lives of men, a fetishistic commodity to be picked up, used and discarded, a way of passing the time. Hers is the 'diminished voice of the dispossessed',[3] and the attenuation of the speaking voice echoes the identification of a minimal sense of self with the erotic fantasies of others. *The Holiday* is less a rewriting of Nabokov's *Lolita* than a restatement of the existential crisis expressed in Pirandello's *Come tu mi vuoi (As You Desire Me*, 1930) in a feminist key. The contrasting figures of the physically exuberant Nina, the father's mistress, and the rather smug Signora Mary, the neighbour's wife, gesture to the restrictive codified and antithetical roles available to women, where both physical and social identities, that of Madonna or that of whore, are conferred by relationships to men.

Most striking, however, is Maraini's narrative technique, which refuses both the confessional subjectivity of much feminist writing and the invasiveness of traditional omniscient narration. At the same time, the failure of the first-person narrative to take the reader beyond surfaces, beneath the skin, only increases the prevailing sense of isolation and solitude. We have no privileged access to Anna's thoughts or emotions: as narrator, she offers not omniscience but an expressive, enigmatic silence.

In Maraini's second novel, *L'età del malessere (The Age of Malaise*), the consciousness of the protagonist, Enrica, begins to shift from passive submission to something approaching rebellion and self-awareness, exercising a new determination to take control of her own life and to move out of the role of sexual object whose existence is defined as a function of men's sexual need. At seventeen, three years older than Anna, Enrica has moved beyond the point of initiation into the adult sexual world, and has now to deal with sexuality, family and work. As in *The Holiday*, the first-person narrating voice registers the absence of any cognitive or emotional psychic dimension, denoting an existence experienced in the immediacy and physicality of the present tense. Set in Rome rather than Sicily, at the beginning of the 1960s, over winter and spring, the novel suggests a symbolic awakening, and an incipient reappropriation of individual subjectivity.

Enrica's acquiescence to the sexual demands of Cesare is less a foretaste of the 'permissive' society to come than a continuation of an age-old submissiveness to the dominant and demanding male, while her mother's pale hopes that Enrica's life will be better than her own reveal little more than a resigned despair; men and women alike are finally crushed by social and family structures which organize sexual relations in terms of possession and control. The birdcages constructed by Enrica's father, beautiful but finally useless, become a poor substitute for human contact, a final seductive refuge for despair and neurosis, as Enrica dreams of being shut inside. She begins to reject the sexual demands made of her, and resolves to find work: her small victory at the end of the novel is a determination to achieve economic independence and sexual autonomy. The long stasis of winter is over; summer is on the way.

By the late 1960s Maraini's level of production – theatre and poetry as well as prose fiction and an intense journalistic activity – was extraordinarily high. She became closely involved with the burgeoning feminist movement as writer, commentator and political activist, joining first 'Rivolta femminile' and then the 'Movimento femminista romano'. She was a vigorous campaigner in the struggles for a divorce law and for the legalization of abortion in Italy. She challenged what she perceived as a narrowly bourgeois, *bien-pensant* categorization and regulation of sexuality as serving the interests of rhythms of production and reproduction in a capitalist society, and her unrepentant declaration that bisexuality, as opposed to heterosexuality, was the norm was deeply shocking to a profoundly conservative political establishment which was already being shaken to the core.

Aesthetics had clearly become a branch of politics. *Memorie di una ladra* (*Memoirs of a Female Thief*, 1972), later filmed with Monica Vitti, was the direct result of a widely felt resistance on the Left to the notion of literature as an essentially bourgeois act of voyeurism and exploitation. Maraini's effort was to challenge cultural representations of women, searching for a way to give voice to those who had been silenced by literary, social and political discourse.

The author met Teresa Numa while researching the conditions of women in Italian prisons in the 1960s. This was a neglected, taboo subject, addressed also in Giuliana Morandini's . . . *E allora mi hanno rinchiusa* (. . . And then they locked me up).[4] Both writers provide a poignant account of women imprisoned not simply for theft or violence, but for failing to fulfil the prescribed role for their sex with due decorum and propriety: difference, especially sexual difference, Maraini and Morandini assert, is swiftly criminalized.

Born into a large working-class family in Anzio, Teresa Numa was semi-illiterate, condemned by both gender and class to a life of hardship and destitution. Maraini was drawn to Teresa's robust account of her own alienation and marginalization. Health problems - peritonitis, kidney trouble and fainting fits – were exacerbated by being sent to a hospital for the criminally insane for uncooperative behaviour. Maraini underlines a fundamental discrimination before the law, a system of jurisprudence shot through with the same gendered assumptions as all other social structures. Men are punished for what they do, women for what they are: male prisons, lay institutions, exact retribution for illegal acts, while women's prisons, in the hands of nuns, punish those who step outside prescribed roles (particularly sexual roles), and whose very bodies constitute an infraction of – and offence against – patriarchal law. The nuns 'tend to re-educate rather than punish, but they impose on their inmates complete conformity to a specific model, seeing them as poor irresponsible girls without any personality, hapless minors who have gone off the rails and must be reformed into good wives and good mothers after the Catholic model' (*Memoirs*, p. v).

Teresa related her life to the author, who transcribed and rewrote in an attempt to fuse her own voice with the authentic voice of the other woman (with whom she subsequently shared royalties from the published work). Maraini gives shape and form to the material of Teresa's life, even while refraining from authorial comment and allowing the facts to speak for themselves. Teresa recounts the appalling and punishing conditions meted out to those who fail to fit into the system, including beatings, solitude, the withdrawal of food, water and blankets, and scraps and soup liberally laced with bromide as a tranquillizing agent. She also tells the story of her own marginalized, unprivileged life, from her birth in 1917 to the end of the 1960s. As with Anna and Enrica before her, there is minimal reflection or analysis, and here too there is no concession to sentiment or a pitying compassion. Where *Teresa* marks a new departure is in her spontaneous, robust, popular speech, reminiscent of picaresque novels such as *Lazarillo de Tormes* or, indeed, *Moll Flanders*, a model Maraini readily acknowledges. The exuberance with which Teresa relates her precarious existence, as well as her distance from the material values of the bourgeoisie Maraini was so eager to shock, makes the facts of her life in the gutters all the more startling.

Teresa recounts the inauspicious beginning of her life, a dramatic image of her future relegation to the realm of the unwanted and undesired; believing her to be dead, her father prepares to throw her out with the rubbish. Her schooling consists of copying out inane phrases such as 'L'Italia è bella' ('Italy is beautiful) or 'L'Italia è la mia patria' ('Italy is my country'), ironic assertions – of beauty and a sense of belonging – of what will, on the contrary, be denied to her. Women's lives are seen as unremitting drudgery, enslavement and imprisonment of one kind or another. Her mother dies, unable to take to her bed to recover from influenza for fear of her husband; Teresa's husband encourages her to accept the sexual attentions of her employer, forcing her into prostitution. Things are no better for women in the countryside, where even small boys wield a brutal power over their mothers, nor does the entrapment and gilded enclosure of a bourgeois marriage offer any solution preferable to the cages constructed by Enrica's father. Teresa enjoys little solidarity from her peers: every time she is sent to prison her home is robbed and her meagre possessions are stolen. She finds herself marginalized, manipulated, her sense of her self and of her own body fundamentally and purposefully damaged as in fact her body is literally deprived of its primary reproductive capacity in a move which smacks of eugenics. When she was suffering from peritonitis, she recounts, 'they also froze my ovaries, and stopped me from having any children. After that in fact I was sterile. My liver's in a bit of a bad way, too. I've got a tooth missing. All in all I'm not what I was' (*Memoirs,* pp. 183–4).

Maraini describes *Donna in guerra* (*Woman at War*, 1975) as her most consciously feminist novel in its move from the singular and private to the public and political. While her previous work had spoken about women on an individual, existential level, 'a feminist consciousness consists in recognizing the common wrongs which women suffer and in understanding the political nature of relations between women and men, women and culture, women and institutions'.[5]

Woman at War picks up and complements Aleramo's *A Woman*, placing personal awareness within a clear historical context, while Maraini's character will achieve a similar but rather more assertive liberation at the end of the book. In its adoption of a feminist ideology which separates itself from more orthodox left-wing political positions, the novel also mirrors the development of the feminist movement in Italy, growing out of, but then away from, the extra-parliamentary Left.

The novel, written in the diary form so closely associated with women's writing, presents itself as not simply a record of external events but a reflection of a woman's developing consciousness. The diary covers one summer in the life of Vanna Magro, a schoolteacher in the suburbs of Rome. Her experiences, as well as people she meets – on an island in the Bay of Naples, away from the structures and rhythms of normal life – challenge the premisses of her relationship with Giacinto, exposing the closed, narcissistic and demeaning assumptions of bourgeois marriage. Vanna rebels against the expectation that she will service Giacinto's needs, from the domestic and material to the emotional and sexual. She finally articulates what Anna and Enrica could not express: the refusal to obliterate the self in favour of the other, the demand for identity and subjectivity, the right to pleasure.

Woman at War repeatedly highlights the physical and sexual, less in a move towards biologism than in acknowledgement of sexuality as privileged site of an individual's self-understanding, of human relations and power: Elaine Showalter, commenting on physical imagery, observes that 'factors other than anatomy are involved in it. Ideas about the body are fundamental to understanding how women conceptualize their situations in society.'[6] Acquiescence to

Giacinto's sexual demands, his appeals to Vanna's 'kindness', are symptomatic of her acquiescence to his dominance, her acceptance of the primacy of his pleasure. Yet *Woman at War* is hostile less to men than to the system which guarantees their dominance and thus corrupts them; Giacinto, too, is belittled and diminished by the system which is designed to work in his favour; lying asleep, he curls himself into a foetal position, defensive and fearful of loss.

Anna's entry into adolescence in *The Holiday* took place against the backdrop of Italy's emergence from the long sleep of Fascism and the need to take on the responsibilities of a modern democratic society. Vanna's existential crisis similarly reflects a wider social malaise, taking place against a background of persistent poverty and violence, in an Italy struggling to come to terms with rapid changes in the economy and shifting patterns of power both within the family and within an increasingly urbanized society. In this context of failed hopes and ideals, in which the optimism of the post-war period has given way to a stale despair, Vanna encounters a number of catalysts for change. Suna, a militant feminist, states the case for understanding gender roles as a product of socialization and political conditioning rather than a biological necessity, whereby centuries of domination have left men and women as subject and predicate in the grammar of power. Suna is closely involved with one of the many revolutionary groups which sprang up all over Italy in the 1970s, and Maraini ruthlessly reveals the ideological blindness to the question of gender which led to women's dis-illusion with orthodox politics, and the establishment of separate and autonomous women's groups. For all his revolutionary airs, Vittorio, the political activist, likes his women young, pretty and preferably virgin; Suna's involvement is tolerated, as she provides substantial funds.

The novel is punctuated by an encroaching violence as Vanna begins to deviate from her allotted role. The gang rape of an Englishwoman is approved as an act of manly courage; the molestation of a girl with Down's syndrome reveals that she is fully sexually aware, and clearly suggests that she has been initiated by members of her own family. Vanna is pursued by two men, taken for a prostitute, assaulted and robbed. Her husband commits conjugal rape; the resulting pregnancy is unwanted, and she has an illegal abortion. None the less, despite the evidence piled up to the contrary, she remains optimistic that satisfactory relationships with men are possible, as her brief affair with Orio, too young yet to have assumed the dominant, overbearing assertiveness of older males, makes clear. Suna, on the other hand, makes a positive case for bisexuality. Like her author, Vanna rejects the straitjacket of sexual orthodoxy, servant to a culture of dependency which disinherits women. She finally leaves her husband – she has won a battle, but the war has only just begun.

Maraini's theatre attempted to take account of both her feminism and her left-wing politics. In 1968 she set up 'La compagnia blu' and, later, Teatroggi, under the aegis of the Communist Party. This was an attempt to bypass traditional theatrical and cultural spaces run by and for the ruling elite, and to take theatre to those on the margins of bourgeois culture. The attempt to establish a theatre in the Roman suburb of Centocelle met with limited success, as a genuinely popular culture proved almost impossible to uncover among a shifting urban population. Also, relations between innovatory theatre practitioners and the PCI were never smooth, and Dario Fo, too, was accusing the PCI of failure of nerve: the Party appeared to take fright once its theoretical pronouncements on the need for self-management, alternative touring circuits and 'decentramento', a decentring of cultural activity, began to be put into practice.[7]

Maraini's most significant intervention in the cultural sphere was her establishment of the Teatro della Maddalena in Rome, in 1973. This was the first theatre in Italy to be run by and for women, and the initiative survived for almost twenty years, finally closing its doors in 1990. The cultural ambition of the radically new theatre was to establish a new feminist aesthetic, to place women's lives and experience at the centre rather than the margins of political thought, to challenge conceptual categories of thought seen as exclusively male, and to revitalize a 'female' culture in Italy. Maraini denounced the 'almost non-existent feminist consciousness of women working in the sphere of culture, who are still trapped within the ideological schemas of patriarchal society', and asserted the need to 'discover an autonomous language created by women to speak about women'.[8]

With regard to artistic practice, Maraini was close to Pasolini's contention that theatre should find a way forward which was neither traditional and academic nor the worst excesses of the avant-garde, but a 'debate, an exchange of ideas, literary and political struggle'.[9] Maraini, too, wanted a form of theatre different both from the empty, meaningless exchange of traditional theatre and the extreme forms of experimentalism which avoided engagement with language at all. Maraini never doubted the primacy of the word in theatre: anything else was a rejection of thought and intellect, a refusal of politics and a narcissistic pandering to the unconscious mind.[10]

Maraini blamed the failure to foster new writing for the excessive formalism and abstraction of much Italian theatre, which had distanced itself from the real debates and struggles that absorbed so many in the 1970s. She attempted to put into practice the manifesto of the Maddalena, to provide a forum for women writers and actors, and in her own plays she addresses the sociological and cultural marginalization of women by a patriarchal culture. She draws on a wide variety of sources, and in her effort to see women through new eyes she revisits some of the classic texts of Western drama.

I sogni di Clitennestra (*The Dreams of Clytemnestra*, 1973) is a reinterpretation of Aeschylus, an intertwining of the classical tale with a modern version of the same events. Clytemnestra is both the character from Greek drama and a housewife from a small town north of Florence whose husband has emigrated to America in search of work; Aegisthus is a good-for-nothing incapable of holding down a job, living off his lover; Orestes is the avenging, tormented son, a *Gastarbeiter* in Germany, a homosexual who, in a new production, would probably be suffering from AIDS; Iphigenia is both killed as propitiatory sacrifice and married off to settle a debt, subsequently dying in childbirth.

This is not simply tragedy turned into soap opera; the superimposition of characters on another version of themselves, their performance of a role within a role, allows for a critical examination of relationships between men and women, and between women themselves. The startling - and often moving - juxtapositions of the classical text with a more modern idiom constitute a dramatic dialectic: Agamemnon dies as he lies in bed with his American mistress Cassandra; she believes the murder is a terrible dream, and sings him a lullaby to soothe him. In the modern version of the story, Clytemnestra's belief that she has murdered her faithless man reveals itself to be a delusion, as she is threatened with electric shock treatment in the asylum. Clytemnestra's 'madness', her unconscious, her dreams, her sexuality which she refuses to suppress during the long absence of her husband, represent a challenge to the patriarchal order for which she must be punished. Clytemnestra dies at the hands of her son, her throat cut at a family dinner while all the other characters calmly proceed with their meal.[11]

The central conflict and dilemma in the play, however, is not marital infidelity, the traumas of an ageing woman left for a younger one (the interpretation Franca Rame was to give in her version of *Medea*), nor even the question of violence and matricide which informs the Greek tragedies. In keeping with the discussions within the Italian feminist movement about the relationships between women, the main clash and focus of the play is the relationship between Clytemnestra and her daughter Electra, the contradictory loyalties and ties experienced by women. Maraini was not the only writer to adopt the story of Clytemnestra in order to expore relations between women, and between mother and daughter. In 1976 the Women's Experimental Theatre in America produced 'The Daughter's Cycle Trilogy', consisting of three parts, 'Daughters', 'Sister/Sister' and 'Electra speaks'. The Experimental Theatre rejected the classical and bloody conclusion to the tale in the name of enlightened and restored relations between women. In the American version, Electra 'does not collude in the murder of her mother' but, rather, 'attempts to sever her ties with the House of Atreus. Separation leads to survival for Electra, the daughter born under a feminist sun.' Electra becomes focus for the 'commonality of all women as daughters, and the reclaiming of all our matrilineage'.[12]

Maraini's play concentrates on the mother figure, as Clytemnestra, too, makes a plea for an alternative allegiance, for a shattering of the patriarchal hall of mirrors, but like her fellow writers and theorists in Italy, she is considerably less idealistic and more pragmatic about the possibilities for change. The rich density of her lines evokes women's powerful psychological and erotic investment in patriarchy:

You and me, face to face. I'm the same as you. A woman who stinks of onions and the washing. Just like you. But you don't look at me. You don't see me. You think of him, over the sea. Your eyes are heavy with black light. You, my daughter, a woman like me, instead of being on my side you live only for him, you lick the ground where he walks, you keep his bed warm, you are his spy, his guard-dog.[13]

The invasion, control and eventual destruction of the female body by a dominant patriarchy is carried to its logical extreme in the novel *Isolina* (*Isolina*, 1985), where the body of the young girl Isolina is violated, and finally dismembered, in the reconstruction from newspaper accounts and from trial documents of chilling events in Verona at the turn of the century.

The story of Isolina is dramatic enough. In January 1900 the bloody remains of a dismembered, pregnant woman were washed up on the banks of the River Adige in Verona. The head was discovered a year later. The butchered remains were, it seemed, those of the young Isolina Canuti: suspected of her murder was her lover, Lieutenant Carlo Trivulzio, who was lodging in the Canuti household. A member of the prestigious Alpine Corps, from a wealthy family with a long military tradition and with the backing of his army superiors, Trivulzio denied the murder, despite much incriminating evidence that he had encouraged Isolina to have an abortion. Public opinion was split between those who were convinced of the young lieutenant's guilt and those who suspected an unpatriotic Socialist plot against the army.

The case, which was soon openly discussed as the Italian Dreyfus affair, became a focus of national and political interests which, Maraini clearly suggests, shuffled aside more fundamental questions of truth or justice. Trivulzio was given a conditional release, and the speed with which the case was subsequently dropped so enraged the Socialist paper *Verona del popolo* and its editor, Todeschini, that a series of provocative articles was published in order to flush out Trivulzio, and force him to take proceedings against the newspaper in order to defend his good name.

The tactic was successful. Evidence new and old was heard at the trial, which strongly suggested that Isolina's murder was the unintended consequence of a botched abortion: spending an evening with officers in the private room of a restaurant, Isolina had apparently been the object of a drunkenly gruesome attempt to induce abortion by inserting a fork inside her. Further evidence, never fully investigated, came to light to suggest that a friend of Isolina's who knew the truth of that evening's dreadful events had been poisoned while in hospital, with the connivance of the same doctor who changed his assessment of Isolina's stage of pregnancy in order to exculpate the young lieutenant. Witnesses for Todeschini were all declared alcoholics, pathologically neurotic or even mad; Trivulzio claimed that Isolina herself was a whore; Todeschini himself was attacked for being against the military. Todeschini lost his case, and was sentenced to imprisonment and a heavy fine for libel: 'but what, finally, did the life of a girl from a poor, obscure family count for, when opposed to the honour of the army? And it was that which finally triumphed, with all the strength of an ideology that gives expression to a country's ideal.'[14]

With *The Silent Duchess*, Maraini returns to the question of silence and women's culture. The story of an eighteenth-century Sicilian woman, deaf and dumb after being raped at the age of five by her uncle,[15] begins two years after the first traumatic experience: the young girl is taken by her adored father to see a public execution in the hope that a second shock will displace the trauma of the first and restore Marianna to speech. This attempt fails, and is repressed in its turn. Aged thirteen, Marianna is married to the very uncle who caused her condition, and she bears him a number of children over the years.

The novel is far from being an illustration of Andrea Dworkin's thesis that all men are – potentially, at least – rapists; nor is it a representation of all women as passive, sexual victims. Marianna is unable to speak, but unlike most of her peers, she learns to read and write in order to be able to communicate with her family. Her husband Pietro has a substantial library, and Marianna becomes a great reader, the written word making possible a dialogue not only with her family and with classical culture, but also with contemporary freethinkers and sceptics: with the French Enlightenment (Voltaire) and the Scottish philosopher David Hume. After the death of her elderly husband, Marianna risks her family's wrath and social condemnation by having an affair with a young servant. Having rediscovered her own body, her own sexuality, she defies all restrictions placed on her by her class and her gender, leaving her home and her family and taking to the road with nobody but a young female servant for travelling companion.

A number of readers in Italy understood this work as a classically feminist novel which vindicates the historic silence of women, their absence from discourse and culture, and restores them to their rightful place as subjects rather than objects of the cultural order. The fact that numerous books on women as authors have on their dustjackets pictures of women writing suggests the powerful urge to retrace a tradition of women as producers of culture rather than its objects or its consumers. *The Silent Duchess*, from 1990 rather than 1970, suggests a considerable step forward from the logic of woman as oppressed victim propounded by some sections of the feminist movement. Marianna Ucrìa does not become a radical feminist, nor does she become a writer, despite her voracious reading: if this is not a novel of the seventies, nor is it a novel of the eighties, when new life was breathed into the pickings of women's cultural history. This novel emphasizes not the text, the word, but the body itself as the primary expression of female identity and self. Perhaps even more vital than tracing a course for women through cultural history is the need to reconnect with other women's bodies. Marianna's discovery of her own sensuality is paralleled by the rediscovery of the mother, erased and cancelled in favour of the father. Her growing awareness of her own body as source of pleasure, her reinvention of a body that has been 'mutilated', is closely bound up with the return to the conscious mind of both the initial trauma and the physical presence of her mother.

Rape as legitimate, sanctioned act is the signature of a family and social code which is dangerous to and negates women. Yet over the course of the novel silence as traumatic, hysterical response gives way to silence as a sign, an expression and affirmation of the body as subject. Maraini employs an image of mutism whose meaning shifts over the course of the narrative from pathological symptom in response to trauma to an affirmation of individuality and identity, challenging the repression of the female body and female desire. The initial violence of rape deprives Marianna of her voice, but the social context she inhabits steals her whole body. The social order which dispenses with the bodies of others is vividly imagined in the opening scene of the novel: the men who stand in judgement over the young boy about to be hanged, who wear the solemn garments of high office, have the same power over their women. The word used to suggest Marianna's brutal sexual encounters is 'inforcare', and here there is a clear play on words: 'inforcare', a surprising word in this context, has 'to bestride' as one of its standard meanings, but 'forca' is a clear reference to the gallows of the opening scene.

Patriarchy exacts a price of unhappiness for men, too. Pietro, too, lives dutifully within the constraints of the social order which have the rigidity suggested by his own name: patriarchy can signify petrification for the oppressor as well as the oppressed, and as such these terms need to be redefined. Pietro is unable to conceive of gentler, more loving forms of sex than those neither he nor Marianna enjoys; he too is deprived of pleasure by an ideology which names the bodies of women as objects of his pleasure, not subjects of their own. *The Silent Duchess* is not a radical feminist text denouncing men, but a complex attempt to forge a female identity within a social and cultural system which would suppress it, to express female desire in a society which would deny it.

Maraini's character recalls the 'io', the first-person narrator of Sibilla Aleramo's *A Woman*, in her early passion for her father, her refusal to countenance the maternal role or figure, and points forward to Maraini's own father-worship as revealed in *Bagheria*. The description of sensual characteristics which repel rather than draw in show her writing at its most suggestive:

> The child stops still a moment, overcome by the honey-sweet scent of the snuff mingled with all the other odours that accompany her mother's awakening: attar of roses, coagulated sweat, stale urine and lozenges flavoured with orris root. . . . For a moment the child fixes her gaze on her mother the Duchess's plump chin, on her beautiful mouth with its pure outline, on her soft pink cheeks, on her eyes with their look of innocence, yielding and far away. I shall never be like her, she says to herself. Never. Not even when I am dead. (*The Silent Duchess*, p. 10)

Marianna, like Aleramo before her, rejects the image of motherhood as sacrifice, based on negation and loss of self. She gives us an image of institutionalized maternity as immolation of the self, moving past the bedrooms of her children as though they were the Stations of the Cross. The tie between mother and daughter is renegotiated, rediscovered, over the course of the novel, as Marianna discovers that her mother's somnolence and lethargy were the result not of indifference towards her children but of an attempt at obliteration of the self through laudanum. Censure and blame are displaced by desiring, sensual nostalgia, as Marianna is haunted by memories of her mother 'as if she were seeing them for the first time: how she used to dangle her white swollen feet from the side of the bed, her big toes like two puff-balls, twitching as if she were playing an imaginary spinet with her feet' (*The Silent Duchess*, p. 53).

Marianna finally recalls the initial trauma which has led to her silence. But silence shifts from being simply a passive response to take on positive connotations, becoming less an 'illness' than a 'vocation' (*The Silent Duchess*, p. 14). The mute body of Marianna 'speaks pain, desire, speaks a force divided and contained',[16] of past trauma; but it also speaks positively, in that her body is now outside the symbolic order, unbound by the social laws of class and gender as she leaves family and obligations to begin travelling. The restoration of her 'atrophied' memory does not lead her, as in classical Freudian analysis, to be reinserted into social discourse, but to real scandal, which is less the original complicitous outrage than for a woman to disregard conventions, to refuse her position of invisibility and inaudibility and to assert her own self, freely and joyfully. Marianna is still marked, still 'mutilated', but it is a mutilation which now signifies not her suppression by but her distance from the family, social and cultural codes which sought to silence her.

The Silent Duchess is the culmination of a writing career that in fiction, theatre, poetry and essays has consistently attempted to recover and create cultural spaces from within which women might speak, and from where they might challenge the hegemony of patriarchy. Maraini firmly refuses a masochistic vision of woman as victim: such a move would only further the reification of women and increase their alienation from their own subjective will. If she begins with a feminist politics which identifies the social and political practices which silence and marginalize women, she ends with a female aesthetic which asserts women as the subjects of both language and culture.

13
Clytemnestra or Electra:
Renegotiating Motherhood

There must be an attentiveness to these beings who are so
close, so feminine-familiar that they are forgotten, that is
just as powerfully thoughtful, alert and open, if there is to
come a time that the women who have always been there
will finally appear.

(Hélène Cixous, 'L'approche de Clarice Lispector')

I am guilty.
I was burning with desperate rage against her;
Yet she was my mother, I her daughter.

(Euripides, *Electra*)

NARRATING MOTHERS AND DAUGHTERS

In one of the many recent narratives which address the complex,
tangled relationship between mothers and daughters, a young
woman is asked to visit her half-sisters in China and speak to
them of her mother's life since emigrating to the United States.
The request leaves her bemused: '"See my sisters, tell them about
my mother," I say, nodding. "What will I say? What can I tell
them about my mother? I don't know anything. She was my
mother"'[1]

The narrator's doubtful uncertainty as to how she is to articulate
this relationship, so close and yet so so opaque, mirrors the
hesitation experienced by writers and feminist thinkers with
regard to mothers and daughters. Italian narratives suggest not just
a multiplicity of perspective but a divergence between theory and
practice: a political agenda, which would take the mother–daughter
bond as the primary model for relations between all women, is
challenged by narratives which instead explore tensions, conflicts,
murderous impulses even, and which, in their intensity, recall

the fierce dramas of the Electra cycle addressed by Euripides and Aeschylus.

While Freudian psychoanalysis and the Oedipus theory focus on mother–son relationships, and to a lesser extent the daughter's view of the father, they have little to say of the mother–daughter bond and its significance for female psychological development. Freud speaks almost admiringly of a little girl's seductive, 'affectionate attachment to her father, a need to get rid of her mother as superfluous and to take her place, a coquetry which already employs the methods of later womanhood'.[2]

It was for later thinkers to offer alternative accounts to that presented by Freud. Simone de Beauvoir argues persuasively that the relationship between mother and daughter is much more dramatic than that between mother and son: from her son the mother expects difference; from her daughter, sameness, an image of her own fragmented self in an endless hall of mirrors. In her daughter, for de Beauvoir, the mother 'does not hail a member of the superior caste; in her she seeks a double. She projects upon her daughter all the ambiguity of her relation with herself; and when the otherness of this alter ego manifests itself, the mother feels herself betrayed'.[3]

Melanie Klein similarly emphasizes the contradictory, painful nature of the relationship, suggesting that 'identification with the father is less charged with anxiety than that with the mother; moreover, the sense of guilt towards her impels to over-compensation through a fresh love relation with her'.[4]

Italian feminists would see the mother–daughter bond as a model for relations between women and across the generations.[5] Much influenced by the work of Luce Irigaray, they follow her call for renewed and revitalized relations between mother and daughter in order to pave the way for new modes of women being together, sharing her conviction that 'woman must ceaselessly measure herself against her beginning and her sexuate determination, beget anew the maternal within her, give birth within herself to mother and daughter in a never-completed progression'.[6] Irigaray calls for women to think back through the mother rather than the father – not simply in order to shift emotional and political allegiance, but to discover ways of establishing separate identities which do not simultaneously destroy the other. For Irigaray, it is vital to acknowledge and assert the genealogy of women which we are frequently persuaded to forget or to deny in 'our exile in the land of the father-husband' (Irigaray, p. 44).

If, as psychoanalytical and sociological theory suggests, male identity is formed in opposition to the mother and in identification with the father, then female identity, fused with that of the mother, struggles to find autonomy and separate subjectivity.[7] The danger is that the daughter 'will eat the mother alive, as it were, use her insides, her body, her mucus, her membranes, to form her own outer, protective skin; in the process the mother, devoured and sacrificed, disappears'.[8] Or, as Orestes and Electra state the case as they plan to murder their mother Clytemnestra, 'We are her children, and we have wolfish fangs.'

In the 1970s, the American poet Adrienne Rich's perception was that the mother–daughter bond encounters only silence in our cultural representations.[9] In Italian writing, the rediscovery of the mother has been a recurrent motif from Sibilla Aleramo onwards. The move is never a simplistic celebration of female solidarity across the generations, however, or a joyous reconnection with a female tradition and lineage, and in recent years the focus has shifted from the plight of Clytemnestra to the dilemma of Electra. The ideology of the mother–child bond as the overriding datum of a woman's life is questioned by Oriana Fallaci's poignant *Lettera a un bambino mai nato* (*Letter to an Unborn Child*, 1975), while the gulf between ideology and experience is revealed in Rosetta Loy's compelling and underrated *La porta dell'acqua* (Gate in the Water, 1974),[10] which focuses on the relationship from the child's point of view. These works by Fallaci and Loy date from the 1970s, when the issue of maternity was opening out into a matter of political as well as ethical debate, and the presiding iconic image of the mother bending over the cradle was challenged as women called for choice and began to explore the emotional, social complexities and dilemmas of the mother–child bond.

The mother–daughter bond is also the central motif of Francesca Sanvitale's *Madre e figlia* (Mother and Daughter) and Fabrizia Ramondino's *Althénopis* (Althénopis), both of which appeared in 1981. These novels take the debate a stage further, considering the mother–daughter relationship in its symbolic as well as purely personal dimension. For the narrators of both texts, the drive to relate – and to remake – the relationship with the mother springs from her death, her absence. While the two novels share a refusal to idealize the mother–daughter bond, they are markedly different in tone and in their conclusions. The intense, closed and dramatic circularity of Sanvitale's text gives way to a more extensive female genealogy in Ramondino's work. In Sanvitale the act of writing functions almost as necromancy, a bringing back of the dead. Reconciliation with the mother, a fragile hope at best, is given a greater chance by Ramondino's feminine erotics, where the narrating voice emerges from a recognition of the mother as sexual, autonomous subject.

ORIANA FALLACI AND ROSETTA LOY

In *Letter to an Unborn Child*, the unexpected pregnancy of Fallaci's narrator becomes the focus for a poetic and deeply philosophical work which subjects the woman/mother divide to intense scrutiny. The narrative explores the reasons and motivations behind maternity, and the place of maternity in the life of an independent woman who resists being defined in terms of her incidental reproductive powers:

> I'm not interested in bringing you into the world for my sake and that's that. All the more because I have not the slightest need of you. . . . I can't see myself walking down the street with a huge stomach, I can't see myself feeding you and washing you and teaching you to talk. I'm a woman who works and I have a lot of other things to do, other things that interest me.[11]

The novel is not propaganda for abortion, an option from which the narrator recoils, refusing the comforting notion that during its early days the foetus is something less than human. The joyful recognition that 'there is something marvellous about enclosing another life inside your own body, knowing that instead of one you are two' (*Unborn Child*, p. 12) conflicts with the guilt and fear that a woman's identity as well as her body is co-opted against her will. The dramatic intensity of the work lies in the superimposition of lyrical evocations and descriptions of the growing child, granted understanding, intelligence and humanity as the nominal addressee of the text, with the traumatic disintegration of the woman's own life. Her study of photographs of foetuses at different stages of development, the enlargements which she hangs on her wall, are juxtaposed with increasingly pressing decisions about career, work, finally even movement, for there are medical complications and her only hope of saving the child is to keep to her bed for the next six months. She refuses, and the unborn child dies. The text culminates in a hallucinated imaginary trial as she stands accused of infanticide. The woman risks death and annihilation, both from her precarious medical condition and as object of conflicting beliefs represented by a changing and gradually less paternalistic medical profession, her parents, her boss, her feminist friends. Their contradictory and mutually accusing voices, claiming variously the child's right to life, the mother's right to her own life, maternity as choice rather than inevitable consequence of biology, are refocused at the end of the text in a moving moment of unavoidable grief for the dead child and recognition of a complexity which evades the nets of ideological dogma.

In Rosetta Loy's *Gate in the Water* childhood is viewed neither elegiacally nor nostalgically, but as a moment of trauma and loss which sets the pattern for our whole lives: it is, for Loy, the 'bitter root' which lies at the heart of female experience, an inevitable and incurable sense of pain. The scenario is one of privilege, but privilege is seen to produce its own kind of cruelties and alienation. The rituals of piano lessons, convent education, servants and governess conceal a more subtle agenda of repression; ironically humorous accounts of music lessons and the nuns' conspicuous grieving for poor Jewish children denied the benefits of a Catholic education deftly unpick an almost invisible drive to ideological conformity.

Gate in the Water, however, more than an account of a repressive, class-based education, is a contemplation of the devastating effect of early experience, a re-creation of the calamity of childhood. The child experiences a gratifying sense of bliss with her beloved Anne Marie, the German governess (for in this social circle the mother herself is largely absent), a sense of plenitude close to the pre-linguistic, undifferentiated bliss posited by Jacques Lacan: the time of perfect happiness, the moment before entry into the symbolic order and the schism between self and other. The child's sense of reality is intimately bound up with the physical sensation of oneness with this mother figure, and Loy's concentrated narrative intensifies this sensory, physical tie: 'I saw her and felt her in one single sensation; dry as mercury, but soft and clinging. She is immense, I am small, she is weightless. She came towards me in a crescendo which had something of the sublime. She covered me, enclosed me, leaving no spaces or cracks' (*Gate in the Water*, p. 3).

The beloved image of Anne Marie stands as a miraculous guarantee against the threat of loss and emptiness; her embrace offers completion and plenitude. The child's desire is, however, disrupted by the symbolic code. Anne Marie reads the story of Paulinchen, who disobeys her mother, plays with matches and is burnt to death. The small girl draws from this story not a lesson in moral order but a deep, outrageous sense of injustice about the differentiated fate of girls, or Jews, or those without power. Again the political or even philosophical point is all the more cutting for being experienced for the first time, and for instantly revealing the false premisses of distinction and privilege: 'How could you bear the idea of such an atrocious punishment for the little curiosity of a girl left alone at home? . . . Every possible logic was shattered in the anguish of her irremediable fate. I thrashed furiously on the floor, Paulinchen's fate was unacceptable, it made you sick and giddy' (*Gate in the Water*, p. 11).

The narrator is betrayed by the story, the logic of her world smashed; soon afterwards she experiences a second betrayal as the unpredictable, volatile Anne Marie deserts her without warning at the end of the narrative. With her compulsive demand to hear the story of Paulinchen over and over again, the small child rehearses and internalizes the mechanism whereby mothers and daughter are irredeemably and irretrievably doomed to separation and schism, where the daughter will be cast off and abandoned by the person she loves most. The sense of plenitude and completeness is lost; the charmed circle is broken.

FRANCESCA SANVITALE: *MOTHER AND DAUGHTER*

Adrienne Rich comments that 'we are, none of us, "either" mothers or daughters; to our amazement, confusion, and greater complexity, we are both'.[12] *Mother and Daughter* is a text beset by this same ambiguity, exhibiting and analysing the complexities of the relationship; the dyad of mother and daughter in the title suggests both multiplicity (a mother and her daughter) and an internal split (the character Sonia, figure for Sanvitale herself, as both mother and daughter). The emotional nexus is one of simultaneous hatred, envy and desire for the mother's body; the daughter experiences a conflicting urge both to destroy the mother and to beg her forgiveness, to absolve and to be absolved of guilt. While it is loosely based on Sanvitale's own experience, the novel is closer to fiction than to traditional autobiography. Sanvitale is herself the daughter of an unmarried woman of an impoverished and decadent aristocratic family; like her character, she lived in Florence, Milan and Rome; she, too, worked to support her mother, eventually married and had a son. At the same time, the narrative is an account of a family in decline, a story of disintegration, fragmentation and decadence which echoes the history of a nation's struggles to find its own identity.

The novel structures itself as a labyrinth, its numerous stories within stories offering a rococo, kaleidoscopic glimpse not just of Fascism and war but also of the Italians in Ethiopia, the war against French colonization of Algieria, the disastrous flood in Florence, the shell-shock victims of the First World War. Yet Sanvitale's is not a claim to mimesis or to an accurate reflection of details of her own life. Like writers before her such as Ortese, Banti and Morante, she picks her own way between the dominant aesthetic orthodoxies of her day, refusing both realism and the experimentalism of the 1960s, accepting 'psychology and narcissism, which constitute, for better or for worse, the ambiguity of my condition'.[13] With its intermingling of autobiographical details and fictive elements, real and invented events, this novel lends itself to a more modernist reading as simultaneous self-discovery and self-creation, as itself a piece of fiction.

Mother and Daughter begins with a glimpse of Marianna, the mother's, own childhood, a time of almost mythical bliss: the youngest of eight children − and the first and only girl − is the exclusive love object of an adoring father who writes her impassioned letters, a pouting little Countess who holds absolute sway over all the men who surround her, while of her mother there is barely a mention. Her fairy-tale existence, and her illusion of feminine power, is soon revealed to have as little substance as a dream: her intended husband, who had announced his intention to give up his lover when he took a wife, breaks off the engagement when his lover kills herself, and Marianna is sacrificed to moral double-dealing. She responds by running away with a handsome (married) army officer on a white horse, and before long falls pregnant. He then abandons her and her daughter to a life of wandering poverty, keeping them on the margins of his existence with the false threat of his vengeful wife who, he claims, will pursue and murder them. The story which frames the life of mother and daughter together locates itself in the realm of mythical fantasy: the magical garden created by her father for his 'adorata poesia', his 'adored poem', the dramatic elopement with the dashing uniformed man are like the stage set of a theatrical melodrama or opera, the dramatic backdrop and painted scenery to the more intense drama of the relationship between the two women. It is the stuff of myth and legend, told and retold, transformed into some kind of apotheosis by Marianna as she lies dying of cancer in her old age.

The novel begins when most of its main characters are already dead. The act of imagination summons up only half-truths, and the relationship between narrator and character echoes some of the trauma of the mother–daughter bond:

> As my thoughts of war sweep over her, the little Countess Marianna puts her hands up to her face and cries. Her little apron is crumpled, her plait trembles, her eyes are full of fear. She doesn't see me any more. She slips out of the reality I have given her. The war has still to arrive but she runs away in a rush of wind. I chase after her through nocturnal, silent streets with remorse and desperation, in a nightmare. I am the war which is looking for her to kill her. I can't speak, but I feel my heart thudding. I ask her to forgive me from far away, without a voice.[14]

Sonia – daughter and narrator – justifies her evocation and re-creation of her mother through writing, by reference to her own desire, which is the primary desire of the child for the mother: 'I love her body even old, even dead, even decomposed. Only the body of my mother is for me a body of love . . . I run my mind over what I wouldn't do, what I would stop at, to have her restored to me, but I can find no limits, not even that of crime' (*Mother and Daughter*, p. 5). From the outset, however, the desire for the primary love object is already mingled not with tender nostalgia but with a deeper, fiercer, homicidal emotion: writing is seen both as conjuring act and as moment of propitiation for her murderous impulses.

The mother is spirited up by the miracle of fiction: 'I have invented this open door, the Baroque arch, the Corinthian columns on either side blackened over the centuries, the low inner gate. In this arch I have painted pots and plants in grey. My mother is luminous in this half light' (*Mother and Daughter*, p. 3). Sonia's necromancy recalls the development of a photograph, colour gradually emerging from darkness, risking disintegration like a fleeting dream which recedes from us as we approach it. Images superimpose themselves one upon the other. She protects Marianna from a horde of angry villagers who would attack her; she sees her mother's lace dress, her kid shoes, slender leg, fur coat, black coat of mourning, gown of apricot satin, the white scar across her chest where her breast should be, the gaping, bleeding wound being cleaned, her delicate coquetry as the Colonel takes her photograph, her paralysed, staring eye.

The shocking insertion into the list of elegant trifles of the missing breast, a bleeding wound, which recurs throughout the text, suggests a key to the complex and contradictory nature of Sonia's feelings for her mother. Melanie Klein similarly endorses an anti-romantic view of 'love', characterized by a multilayered complexity and barely conscious. The ego's love, formed in the relation of the infant to the mother's breast, is accompanied by guilt:

> Full identification with the object based on the libidinal attachment, first to the breast, then to the whole person, goes hand in hand with anxiety for it (of its disintegration), with guilt and remorse, with a sense of responsibility for preserving it intact against persecutors and the id, and with sadness relating to expectation of the impending loss of it. These emotions, whether conscious or unconscious, are in my view among the essential and fundamental elements of the feelings we call love.[15]

The potentially murderous nature of the relationship is brought out clearly in Clytemnestra's foreboding dream that her breast will be bitten by a snake, and Orestes' pitiless lines: 'Then, as she gave suck to a devilish thing, / She dies in her blood; and I am dragon-fanged / To kill her as the dream would have me do (Aeschylus, *Oresteia*).

In the accumulation of memories of the mother at the beginning of Sanvitale's text, the mother is seen primarily not as a whole, but in parts: her eye, her breast (or lack of it), her hand, her slim ankles. According to Kleinian theory, at six months the baby, who up to now has perceived the mother only in parts, such as the breast, begins to see her whole. The crisis of the manic-depressive state, which is as important to Kleinian theory as the Oedipus complex is to Freud, is to negotiate the arising conflicting feelings towards the newly internalized 'good' mother which must displace previous destructive urges towards the 'bad' mother, who withdraws the breast: the baby must overcome its sadistic feelings towards her. It would be possible to read Sanvitale's text as a Kleinian renegotiation of the ego as it forms itself in its relationship with the mother figure, an attempt to recapture and reorder the fragments of Sonia's own existence, and thus enable her to go on living.

The relationship between mother and daughter is outlined not as a continuous narrative flux but as a series of snapshot memories. The narrator describes in vivid detail their poor living conditions, the refusal of the aristocratic Marianna to do anything to improve their lot, the excitement generated by the Colonel's letters announcing a rare visit, the seedy hotel they live in for a while, their encounter there with other relics of a bygone age who spend their evenings playing cards, dancing to old gramophone records and pretending the old social order has not been challenged. Moments of closeness between mother and daughter are expressed through a shared delight at Shirley Temple's latest film or in window-shopping, the two behaving at the seaside as though they were Esther Williams. But if Marianna can act as companion, the good mother, she also acts as the bad, failing to protect her daughter. She stands condemned of indifference and even of complicity in Signor Andrea's less than chivalrous attentions to Sonia as they spend the evening in the hotel dancing, or in Uncle Paris's obsession with his teasing young niece, whose naked body is a surprise to herself as much as it is to the man who glimpses it through the open doorway.

Sublimation is one solution to Sonia's social predicament – the nuns uncharitably refuse to educate an illegitimate child – as she achieves success and praise in melodramatic school productions deemed morally edifying for young minds. Mother and daughter exist in a theatrical fantasy, a series of alibis and falsehoods. Sonia's success in the school plays, an evening concert at the Castello Sforzesco in Milan given by Beniamino Gigli, Marianna's magical garden, the landscape which is painted like a stage set, all point only to a deeper sense of unreality. The absent father figure, the nameless officer, has imposed upon them a peripatetic existence, the 'theatre of delirium' in which they play out their parts, fleeing from the madwoman in the wings brandishing a revolver. Each emotion is refracted through a theatrical or cinematic image, reinterpreted by the melodramatic, larger-than-life conventions of pre-war movie culture. Driven to murderous exasperation with Marianna, Sonia puts her hands around her mother's throat:'"Kill me!" the mother exclaims unexpectedly and fearlessly, with the melodramatic tone of the cinema, full of aristocratic anger and disdain. "Kill your mother, if you've got the guts!"' (*Mother and Daughter*, p. 131). Sonia's disgust is as much at this false note as at the horror of her own actions.

Sonia's relationship with her father is one of mutual hostility. As a young woman the one gift she receives from him is an over-large, red, flashy fox-fur jacket, apparently cast off by one of his lovers. Here, too, there is paradox. Sonia takes over his role as provider for Marianna, impelled by a sense of rivalry with the father for exclusive possession of the mother – 'her mother was hers, had always been hers alone' (*Mother and Daughter*, p. 206). Her desperate attempts to extract them from poverty are consistently frustrated by Marianna, who recklessly incurs huge debts behind her daughter's back. Verging first on suicide, then on murder, Sonia leaves, unable to resolve the conflict between Marianna's need for care, and her own hatred and resentment.

The abandonment of the mother is followed in the text by the death of Sonia's baby in her womb and the return of Marianna. Mother and daughter are inextricably linked by a sequence of physical disasters and loss, by the fatalities of female biology, which weave their lives more tightly together: the reconnection with the maternal body here has the startling dramatic overtones of the womb as bearer of life and death. The account of Sonia's miscarriage is followed by the episode of Marianna's operation for breast cancer, and the full drama of the mother–daughter relationship, where each is a plague visited upon the other, is revealed. Sonia is horrified at the devastation of her mother's body: 'she herself was a festering wound which snaked across her mother's slender chest in place of the small breast which had suckled her' (*Mother and Daughter*, p. 151). Her sense of guilt towards her mother compels her to relate the appearance of the tumour to her own recent marriage. When secondary cancer appears in the mother's throat and lungs she once more displaces all else in Sonia's life, becomes her *raison d'être*: 'was time not full of circularity and was it not her mother herself who was calling Sonia to her with this illness? Was she not defrauding her out of everything yet again, to force Sonia to live only for her?' (*Mother and Daughter*, p. 196).

Mother and daughter find themselves in each other's power in a closed circle which recalls Sartre's vision of Hell in *Huis clos*, a world in which humans can never escape each other; neither can they avoid inflicting pain on each other. The relationship between mother and daughter acquires almost mythical status, and in its torment and mutual infliction of pain is close to Greek tragedy. Erotic fantasies about the neurologist who is treating her dying mother reveal not sexual desire but rivalry with the mother, whose sickness has first claim on him. If Marianna's illness is resented as blocking for her daughter other ways of living, then Sonia is more than half aware of her position as her mother's 'carnefice', her persecutor or executioner. She is horrified when she is told that she is clearly happiest when her mother is sick; further analysis suggests that Marianna does not have the tumour which Sonia is convinced she has. The moment of Marianna's death vividly recalls that of Zeno Cosini's father in Italo Svevo's novel *The Confessions of Zeno*, both in its ambiguity and in the profound sense of guilt experienced by the child.[16] Marianna and Sonia are left alone: Marianna stops breathing, and Sonia removes the oxygen respirator from her nostrils:

> With a violent shudder the mother, fully awake, her whole body shaken by a mute scream within her, the first and last in life, as if coming from another world, raised her head, opened her eyes wide and opened her mouth in a spasm, gasping for the air her daughter refused her. (*Mother and Daughter*, p. 224)

The depersonalization of the mother at this point, no longer referred to even by her name, underlines the violence of the moment and its abstract, mythical quality, and the scene recalls the passion of Electra's revenge.

Sanvitale's novel is an impassioned search for freedom – from the past, from guilt, from 'sickness which becomes a way of living' (*Mother and Daughter*, p. 200), from the detritus of past memories, dreams and fantasies which continue to haunt her narrator. Memories are discrete shards of experience, snapshots, paintings, snatches of film sometimes spun off the reel, reflecting an uncontrollable kaleidoscope of images and colours. The struggle for freedom of the libido, of desire, is a simultaneous struggle for style and form. Omniscient plenitude is discarded; if to write is to impose an uneasy harmony on the fragments of our lives, the novel reaches for a narrative process that will allow Sonia to escape the cloying, restrictive conventions of melodrama, romantic novels and Hollywood films. How to write about this mutually devastating relationship is a central problem of the text. While the narrative concentrates on Sonia's position, it is intersected by a multiplicity of combating, warring voices which mirror the complexity of women's lives and their psychological development. The ambiguous narrating voice drifts in and out of Sonia's perspective to the point where first- and third-person narrative can become interchangeable. The flowing, dreamlike style is reinforced by the lack of standard chapter divisions, the manipulation of the narrative into juxtaposed blocks of memories, the disruption of normal time sequences and chronological order. Sanvitale confronts us with the seemingly irreconcilable dichotomy of public event and private experience: writing hovers between the restrictions of linear, historical narrative, with its need for times, dates, befores and afters, and the more fluid structures of dream.

If writing is, for Sonia, exorcism, the route to freedom and autonomy, it is simultaneously a redressing of the balance of power.

Power is, throughout the related events of the novel, asymmetrical: the daughter is dependent, expectant, suffragan, while the mother is carelessly indifferent. The power of the writer is here wielded to restore equality. Marianna's death is framed between two dreams. In the first, Sonia returns to the castle of her aristocratic forebears, passing through corridors and tunnels to reach the central, circular camera obscura: 'She reaches the room conceived by the monsters of her nightmares where she seeks shelter from men even at the price of being walled in alive. . . . Sonia enters the circular room as a chamber torture' (*Mother and Daughter*, p. 218). Sonia flees the castle, with its terrifying reflected images and its grotesque womb. The final vision, on the contrary, offers the hope of serenity, but it is a fragile one, subject to disintegration. The castle is transformed into an ancient, Rococo palace which emerges from the rocky cliff just as Marianna emerged from the void at the beginning of the narrative; Marianna herself appears as a venerable, aged queen against the background of the palace, eternal place of rest for the elderly. While the dream is of a calm the narrator has yet to achieve, it holds out an ambivalent vision of hope: that the ghosts of the past can finally be laid to rest, that the narrator will finally be free.

FABRIZIA RAMONDINO: *ALTHÉNOPIS*

In the opening pages of Fabrizia Ramondino's *Althénopis* (1981) the narrator is confronted with the signs of a specifically female sexual condition, with objects which map out her own physiological destiny. The grandmother's creams and ointments, never referred to in more than hushed tones and hidden away in a drawer, are whispered to be treatments for venereal disease; her skirts are impregnated with the smell of these mysterious unguents, mute indicators of an unhappy marriage and marital infidelity, as well as with the pungent smell of menstrual blood. In the bathroom are to be found at regular intervals buckets of soapy water with bloodied towels from her mother, which are a source of puzzlement to a callow child whose own blood flows only from scraped elbows and knees; the cerebral, incorporeal and ascetic mother, smelling only of soap, lying with a vinegar-soaked cloth pressed to her forehead to allay her migraine, has no obvious bodily connection with the mysterious pails in the bathroom. Liquids, blood and creams stand in for the female physical and sexual body, and establish the parameters within which the young girl must develop and understand her own sexual identity.

The narrator comments: 'it happens in the life of many women that the death of their mother signals a moment of reflection, of weighing up their own existence, of secret anguish and anxieties which up until now they had managed to contain'.[17] At the end of the novel the narrator, now adult and independent, returns home as her mother is dying. The fastidious, scientifically minded, aloof and distracted mother scandalizes her relatives in her final delirium as she shockingly begins to masturbate; her hand is removed by chiding elderly female cousins who tell her, as if speaking to a child, that it 'isn't done'.

The recollections of childhood which constitute the main body of the text are decisively framed by the unseemly and scandalous intrusion of the hidden recesses and functions of the female body into the public sphere. With the death of the narrator's mother the text reverses itself, inviting a retrospective reading as an excavation of the narrator's psychological development, formed and framed in relation not to the men in her family but – *pace* Freud – exquisitely and painfully to the maternal lineage and the many women – grandmother, mother, aunts, great-aunts, cousins – who pass through the pages of the novel. While the grandmother and the mother in particular are portrayed in all their singularly bizarre and quirky eccentricity, what emerges over the course of the narrative is a profound link to a maternal genealogy, a reaffirmation of the mother–daughter bond which, far from constraining women within their sexual physiology, is the source of new creative energies.

Althénopis is an account of the rarely named first-person narrator's peripatetic life in Naples and the Campania countryside in the immediate post-war years, as her extensive family struggle to come to terms with a new economic structure and social order which has seen much of their former wealth and status dissipated; she stays first with her grandmother, then with a series of more or less hospitable relatives while she waits for the father's fortunes to change once more. While the text shapes itself around the principal events of these early years – the period with the grandmother, her mother's arrival, the removal to the city, her own departure, the death of her mother – there is little plot as such; the narrative tissue is a gradual reappropriation through memory of the colours, the sounds, and especially the places of childhood. The text as archaeology, as a mapping-out, leads to a metonymic structural narrative of detailed vignettes, fragments of stories and snatches of history combining into a kaleidoscopic, multiple vision which resists linearity and closure.

'Every place I looked at reminded me of an incident, a story' (*Althénopis*, p. 92): in the first section the narrator turns her gaze from the grandmother to the square, the house, the nearby paths and villas, the marina and the rooftops in an exploration which is at once material and psychological, with an acute attention to sensory detail. Luce Irigaray's hypothesis of women's writing aptly describes some of Ramondino's effects, which depend on the senses of smell and touch at least as much as sight: 'This "style", or "writing", of women tends to put the torch to fetish words, proper terms, well-constructed forms. This "style" does not privilege sight; instead, it takes each figure back to its source, which is among other things tactile.'[18] The grandmother is the first significant figure in the memory and consciousness of the child, sweeping into the narrative on the opening page of the novel, moving across the square of Santa Maria del Mare as across a floodlit stage, with colours glinting and darting around her, the 'flashing lights of Hell, of luxury and lust around the poor woman' (*Althénopis*, p. 5). She represents a mythical time of long gone family splendours and glory, brought into the present by talismanic objects – laces, pieces of jewellery – which magically conjure up the past, 'traces of the family stories and legends which my grandmother told me' (*Althénopis*, p. 7). It is through the grandmother's stories and narratives that the small girl is introduced to the wretched, teeming life of the sidestreets and alleys of the city. These stories invoke specifically Neapolitan forms of literary representation, gesturing towards the uncompromising style of a Matilde Serao. But the poor are deserving only as long as they make no claims to be anything more than that, and the realism of her tales is tempered by the 'heavenly, shining aura' (*Althénopis*, p. 9) with which she surrounds her characters, obviating the need both for naturalism and for a more profound sense of social justice. She claims direct descent from Saint Clare herself, founder of the religious order of the Poor Clares, perversely regarding the numbers of the poor in the city as a blessing in disguise, as consoling evidence that the rich and powerful do not hold complete sway.

The grandmother's wildly extravagant cooking takes no account of financial exigencies or balanced nutritional requirements, nor of the bad temper of the servant whose task it is to clear up after her. Modelled on fantasy and imagination rather than necessity or even recipe books, her elaborate, frothy concoctions – which flout the diktats both of hygienists and of the household economy – are loved by the children, disdained by other women, and in men arouse a response almost of fear. Ramondino does not hesitate to poke fun at these men from the South, 'who suspect a fly in every little parsley leaf, who in a quivering jelly fear the quicksands of sex and prattle on the whole of their lives about their mother's cooking, how from her hands alone would come creams and parsley leaves which could be trusted' (*Althénopis*, p. 15). The grandmother's cooking, on the contrary, is an act of transgression, a profanity, as are her ill-executed card tricks, her love for dialect poems in a household dedicated to the purity of the Italian language, and her faith in herbal medicine in an increasingly scientific age. She gives unwarranted credence to the grasping peasants who cheat her at every turn and whose every hard-luck story moves her to a misplaced generosity with the family fortune. When her brother returned home late one night from an assignation and fell asleep on the toilet, she covered up for him, sending him off to bed after telling him to wipe himself clean, and such unseemly behaviour could be mentioned only in the most hushed of scandalized tones.

With the arrival of the mother this guilty profligacy and transgressive excess are displaced by a stricter regime based on Swiss manuals of nutritional hygiene and puericulture. Fantasy and fairy stories are displaced by the mother's 'pitiless sense of reality' (*Althénopis*, p. 36) and by her refusal of prayers and tears, the consolations and illusions of superstition and indulgent emotion. Economic hardship and the vicissitudes of life have left her 'prosaic to the point where she no longer believed in fairy stories nor in death nor in love' (*Althénopis*, p. 41). The mother, whose early life was spent in the depths of the countryside, who loves the bare forests of winter and prizes reason and rationality above superstition, religion or emotion, who was a reader of the German poets, married when she was already in her mid-thirties, and found herself thrust into the sticky fluidity which marks feminine sexual identity:

> From that mineral and vegetable nature she suddenly entered into the blood, humours and sweats of sexual intercourse, of childbirth, of milk. Born of vegetal ascendants, with flowers curling round her ear, her legs like reeds, her eyes reflecting the blue of flowers, the subtle grey of moss and at times even the icy emerald of the sea, she was plunged into the third realm: the zoological realm. And along came the blood, the milk, the humours, the sweats. And, above all else, her 'troubles'. (*Althénopis*, p. 38)

The portrait of the mother offered by the now-adult narrator can clearly be reread as a series of signals about her discontent not only with her fortunes but also with her own sexual destiny, which manifests itself as a desire to cancel and obliterate her own body. On their rare picnics the mother demonstrates an almost obsessive concern to leave no traces of their presence, to bury any remaining scraps, not simply to distance herself from the dirty commoners but also because 'it seemed she wanted to swiftly remove from around her all edible traces, as if those remains held within them a presage of decadence, a mysterious and disturbing warning' (*Althénopis*, p. 45).

The fluidity which marks the female body is repeated in images throughout the text of water, blood, or the sticky, melting nougat mother and daughter buy at the fair, which presages the warm torpor of the maternal body. The mother of Mariarosa, the narrator's friend, wants no more children after the birth of a malformed boy, and the reader is left to piece together her abortions, regularly induced by infusions of parsley and passed off to her daughter as colic and diarrhoea. Menstrual blood threads its way in and out of the narrative as the sign of femininity, of womanhood, the substratum of life. Demure girls on the beach are envied because they have already begun to menstruate; the second part of the novel opens with an image of blood as the narrator's friend Vittoria pulls up her skirt to show the red trail emerging beneath.

Althénopis traces the ties of blood and sweat which link generations of women, a tie far deeper than the almost casual bond between father and daughter. When the narrator herself begins to menstruate, it is to her grandmother that she returns in her imagination as she washes dishes in the greasy, slippery water:

> In that grey, smelly water I thought I could glimpse the turbid secrets of life. That was a way I had of interpreting the resurrection of the dead, for through the steam, sweat and sharp smells of the kitchen I could see the outlines of my grandmother taking shape, and as I began to menstruate with the onset of adolescence, I missed her desperately. Indeed, when my first period came I dreamt of the resurrection of my grandmother in my blood while I experienced the loss of my father as a social fact . . . or as a tragic abstraction: as a misfortune or ill-luck or being an orphan. (*Althénopis*, p. 177)

The liquid flow of femininity – whether feared, desired or resented – is counterpoised to the sparser evidence of the presence of men, marked by the drops of urine on the toilet seat or the damp magazines strewn on the bathroom floor, leaving behind them a smell not of bodily odours but of stale cigarette smoke. Uncle Chinchino appeals to a childish fascination with excrement, as his plastic miniatures and images of shit echo the travelling gypsies' offer of a cream which will produce a satisfyingly gigantic turd. In *Althénopis* men make temporary incursions into the life of the family, but always turn out to be a disappointment. With the return of Achille from India after the war, his doting grandmother, who has spent the intervening years embroidering elaborate knick-knacks for him, is as excited as a young lover as they fly into each other's arms and whisper tenderly. But Achille soon drifts away, irritated by the old woman's attentions. Husbands are inimical to female intellectual activity: Aunt Anita, one of the first five women to take a degree in the post-Unification period, was thereby destined to linger in the twilight of spinsterhood. The occasional appearances of the father are marked notably, once again, in relation to food: in the presence of her husband, the mother feels obliged to produce meals worthy of the social status to which they aspire. Men who marry into the family 'tried, at least in the early years of marriage, to loosen the ties between all those women, perhaps because they could not separate the features of their loved one from those of all the others and they felt as though they were being swallowed up by that promiscuous confusion' (*Althénopis*, p. 110). The husbands feel an inglorious sense of triumph when the phalanx of women is breached, as if each moment of dissent and difference among the women constituted an implicit acknowledgement that they belonged primarily not to the female collective tribe but to their respective men.

Between childhood and adolescence, wealth and poverty, country and city, mother and grandmother, denied the clarity of fixed identity and social status, the narrator hovers between her sunburned tomboy friends and the delicate blond children from the villas who wear sunglasses to protect their eyes, sandals to protect their feet; whose mothers – so unlike her own – solicitously smear cream over their pubescent daughters' shoulders and meticulously count the hours after eating before a swim can be risked. It is this lack of determinacy, this unwillingness to submit to the tyranny of a single point of view, which lends the text its multiple perspective, its evocation of the fluid interstices between a more 'masculine' account of history. As a young girl the narrator attempts to catch a glimpse of herself from behind in order to resolve the enigma of the face which stares at her out of the mirror. She bemoans her lot at having Virgo as her zodiac sign; most desired is the double sign of Gemini: 'not to be just myself, always to be accompanied by another!' (*Althénopis*, p. 96). Duality marks both the text and her relationship with her mother, which is the fruit of the uncertain circumstances of her life but which is also the unavoidable destiny of mothers and daughters. Just as the text requires us to read it in reverse, or to reread after the final section of painful epiphany in which the mother–daughter bond is exposed to the marrow, so it also suggests that female sexual identity can be traced back through a line of blood to the mothers and not, as Freud and classical psychoanalysis would have it, to the fathers.

Just as the daughter is contained within the mother, so the mother is contained within, given birth to by, the daughter in a reciprocal movement which defies linearity and hierarchy. There are early intimations of this reciprocity when the mother, presented with a pine nut to burn on the fire, with a handful of herbs or an oddly shaped potato, or with a brief revival of her fortunes, temporarily forgets her 'troubles': 'at those times a child–mother was revealed to us, companion in our games, far removed from the other one with her Swiss manuals, her fights with our grandmother and her never-ending headaches. . . . At that time I felt like a mother to her, seeing her so happy' (*Althénopis*, pp. 39, 160).

As the narrator approaches puberty and menstruation, she feels within her a simultaneous dying and rebirth which links her to her female progenitors, the 'weak and insistent call of that thing which was shrinking and dying, to which I could not give a name' (*Althénopis*, p. 216). This experience which has no name is simultaneously the end and the beginning, death and birth: imagined in the form of a cat, it is covered with damp fur, from amniotic fluid or the sweat of death. The conflict experienced by the adolescent girl is here made clear: to separate herself from the mother is to deny her physical self, while to identify with the mother is to risk being unable to form any identity of her own at all. This is the dilemma confronted by the final section of the novel, which recounts the narrator's traumatic homecoming to witness her mother's death.

Ramondino does not give us any account of the narrator between her departure for the North, as she cut the umbilical cord for the second time, and this return home. It is possible to discern the outlines of a well-worn narrative filial rejection of the maternal, the daughter's desire for a room of her own, the reduction of all contact to 'signs' or 'hieroglyphics', the banal commonplaces that mark failed communication. With the separation of daughter from mother: 'the Daughter found her destiny, but the Mother disappeared' (*Althénopis*, p. 236). As in Sanvitale's novel, the depersonalizing refusal of names suggests that there is more at stake here than a single relationship, and intimates a deeper psychic structure.

With the mother's illness she is returned to the condition of the child: her gestures are similarly uncontrolled, while the catheters, feeding cups and stained sheets recall the dependence of the baby. '"I'm a little girl! I'm a little girl!"' she cries in her delirium. This is the epiphany of the final moments of the text, the revelation not of separation but of a profound and indestructible bond between mother and daughter that transcends emotional, intellectual and experiential ties: just as the daughter had experienced the maternal within herself, so the mother contains the child within her, and the little girl in the mother is resurrected in her last few days. The woman is mother and daughter simultaneously: 'The messy baby with its frail and trembling gestures, its uncertain little laughs, its milk already clouded in the mystery of blood, was born without lace or frills from the womb of the dying Mother and stammered on the stomach of the decayed body of the old woman' (*Althénopis*, p. 261).

The reaffirmation of the relationship with the mother and her insertion into a specifically female genealogy offers a symbolic and psychic structure from within which the narrator can reshape her own sexual identity. The daughter mirrors the mother in her reproductive capacity, while the formation of a separate sexual identity which does not exclude, constrain or abandon the other leaves open the possibility of a speaking voice which is not univocal but multiple in its effects: through the separation of mother and woman, the narrator creates a space from within which she can write.

14

From Feminism to Post-modernism: Duranti (born 1938), Petrignani (born 1952) and Capriolo (born 1961)

> Roland thought, partly with precise post-modern pleasure, and partly with a real element of superstitious dread, that he and Maud were being driven by a plot or fate that seemed, at least possibly, to be not their plot or fate but that of those others. And it is possible that there is an element of superstitious dread in any self-referring, self-reflexive, inturned post-modernist mirror-game or plot-coil that recognizes that it has got out of hand.
>
> (A.S. Byatt, *Possession*)

The 1970s were years of dramatic gains for women in Italy, where the women's movement was characterized by a militancy which united women of diverse class and experience in the pursuit of common goals and objectives. With the 1980s, however, the denunciation of oppressive social and cultural structures gave way to a more abstract – and many would argue more abstruse – theorizing of sexual difference, the elaboration of alternative spaces for women within the discourses of philosophy, historiography and psychoanalysis. Political certainties of the 1970s, unquestioned in the quest for radical social change, have modulated, fragmented, and feminists find themselves searching for a new agenda which would fire the imagination and provoke argument – such as Camille Paglia clearly found recently with her goading statements on date rape and her attacks on atrophied forms of feminism itself.

With the increasing philosophical and critical dominance of Deconstructionist theories and their Italian inflection, 'weak thought' [*il pensiero debole*], propounded in particular by Gianni Vattimo and Pier Aldo Rovatti, the strategic risks of essentialism as basis for feminist theory were increasingly counterbalanced by the perception that it gave women not only a platform, but a position from which to speak and to assert their subjectivity.

Aldo Rovatti and Gianni Vattimo launch an attack on theory 'understood as power, capacity to control, implication and totalization'.[1] Proponents mark their distance from Marx, Nietzsche and Heidegger, who are still seen to be in search of the transcendental, engaged in uncovering what lies behind the world of appearances. 'Weak thought', on the contrary, takes a more conciliatory look at the world of appearances, but without the perceived idealizing tendencies of Deleuze or Beaudrillard; thought must 'articulate itself in the half-light' (Vattimo and Rovatti, p. 9) and Vattimo reaches for a new ontology which will not underpin but undermine notions of being. In his preference for aesthetic intuition over logical demonstration 'truth' becomes not a dominant but an interpretative category. 'Weak thought' asserts the need to focus on the local rather than the global, to limit thought to ordinary experience and material context.

While 'weak thought' shares many discursive positions with feminist theory, it has been justly criticized for ignoring the fundamental site of difference, that of the body. It proclaims the superiority of difference to dialectics but simultaneously ignores feminism's revolutionary uncovering of sexual difference in the realms of the discursive and the symbolic as well as in material oppression. Other feminists are uneasy about the unseemly haste with which academics and theoreticians seek to dispel the subject: Rosi Braidotti comments that 'one can never deconstruct a subjectivity one has never been fully granted',[2] pointing up the paradox of a discourse which liquidates the subject and the power of the word just at a point when disadvantaged and oppressed groups are asserting that subjectivity for the first time. The arguments about feminism and post-modernism rage on in Italy as elsewhere. Cultural critics have been accused of naiveté in believing women to be free-willed subjects, while followers of Deconstructionist theories have been accused of ahistoricism, and of portraying woman as helpless victim of social and linguistic forces which always originate elsewhere.

Despite the strong influence of French feminism in Italy, the Marxist underpinning of Italian feminism has led to a considerable scepticism as to the value of privileging discourse over the eradication of oppression as the site of struggle. Although Italian feminists are receptive to post-modern theories which undermine humanism and capitalism and posit writing as a potentially revolutionary and subversive space, they are less convinced of the usefulness of uncovering a 'repressed feminine' in poetic discourse. Poet and critic Biancamaria Frabotta refutes the strategies of Elisabetta Rasy, Julia Kristeva's most significant follower in Italy, arguing that to privilege a pre-symbolic maternal state is to invite rather than forestall nostalgic regression. Other Italian thinkers demurred over Kristeva's view of the loss of identity and the self as potentially liberating, arguing that this position would keep women permanently locked into uncreative oppression. Like Kristeva, Frabotta is unconvinced that the solutions to women's problems are political, but she is wary that Kristeva's semiotic politics would return women from collective action and struggle to individual, ethical isolation.

Teresa de Lauretis, in *Alice Doesn't*, argues for a redefinition of notions of the subject and experience in order to combat theoretical discourses which deprive the interpretant of subjectivity and simultaneously objectify women, making of them 'a negative semantic space of the [male] imaginary fantasy of coherence'.[3] De Lauretis argues the need to theorize this exclusion, 'an experience to which sexuality must be seen as central in that it determines through gender identification, the social dimension of female subjectivity, one's personal experience of femaleness' (de Lauretis, p. 184). Otherwise we are left with the unresolvable paradox articulated by Rosi Braidotti: since fragmentation of subjectivity and consciousness has been the historical condition of women, 'we are left with the option of theorizing a general becoming woman for both sexes, or else of flatly stating that women have been post-modern since the beginning of time' (Braidotti, 'Envy', p. 237).

The intricate relationship between feminism and post-modernism in the work of Italian writers mirrors the hesitations of feminist theory when confronted with an epistemology which would radically decentre subjectivity and deny transhistorical essence. Some feminists welcome post-modernism as belated validation of feminism's unsettling of the individual – assumed, but methodologically unstated, to be the white heterosexual male. Others deplore a strategic move which would deny women – as well as other social and geographical 'minority' groups – a perspective sufficiently stable to support a political platform from which they can speak, and raise the possibility that 'Since men have had their Enlightenment, they can afford a sense of decentred self and a humbleness regarding the coherence and truth of their claims [while] for women to take on such a position is to weaken what is not yet strong.'[4] Women's writing in Italy embodies the impassioned search for a balance between autonomy and difference on the one hand, equality and emancipation on the other. Of the three writers considered here, Francesca Duranti's early work bears traces of a feminist demand for equality, but she rejects the notion of writing as an engendered act and claims 'neutrality' as a writer; Sandra Petrignani was closely involved with the feminist movement in the 1970s and 1980s, but her sexual politics have evolved away from the markedly separatist tendencies of Italian theory; for Paola Capriolo, born in 1962 and the youngest of the three, feminism appears to be ancient history and gender an irrelevance in both her life and her work, while her frame of reference from Romanticism to Modernism makes of her an ideally 'post-modern' writer. The fragmentation of feminism in Italy has led to a proliferation of ideological positions in theory and, more especially, in practice. But the personal, practical and political gains made for women have been real ones. Perhaps, as with all revolutionary movements, feminism is paying the price of its own success.

FRANCESCA DURANTI

Francesca Duranti's most successful work to date has been *La casa sul lago della luna* (*The House on Moon Lake*, 1984). Her earlier novels, *La bambina* (The Young Girl, 1975) and *Piazza mia bella piazza* (Round and Round the Garden, 1977) draw largely on autobiographical material.[5] The first describes Duranti's early childhood at the end of the Second World War; the second, the break-up of her marriage following her insistence on writing despite her husband's opposition, and the final achievement of autonomy, independence and success. It is perhaps significant for Duranti's ambivalent attitude to feminism that she will not allow this second novel – a feminist *Bildungsroman*, or education to writing – to be reprinted.

With *The House on Moon Lake* Duranti turns from autobiography to explore new territory. Like other novels to appear at this time, *The House on Moon Lake* refuses to linger over the social and political condition of women in contemporary Italy, or to indulge in writing as denunciation or as aggressive affirmation of self. Duranti shares the post-modern refusal of fiction as documentation of external reality or inner interrogation of the psyche, as well as its fascination with intertextuality and the possibilities offered to the creative imagination by pastiche, rewriting, and a self-conscious encounter with other texts and different genres.

In *The House on Moon Lake*, Fabrizio, an insecure intellectual and impoverished aristocrat, makes a precarious living as a badly paid translator, while aspiring to the status of 'Germanist'. Fabrizio resolves to rescue himself from obscurity by hunting down and translating the forgotten masterpiece of one Fritz Oberhofer. The Austrian's novel is entitled – of course – *The House on Moon Lake*. Finally tracking down a single copy of Oberhofer's last great work, apparently written in the context of a mysterious love affair, Fabrizio returns from Mondsee (Moon Lake) with a photocopy. The ease and rapidity with which he translates the novel spring from 'a kind of affinity . . . I know how I must translate because I am already familiar with the formless images' (*Moon Lake*, p. 77).

His own preface to the hugely successful translation is rejected on the grounds that it is redolent of an author's false humility in speaking of his own work, and Fabrizio writes instead a biography of the Austrian writer. The work proceeds almost to its conclusion with Fritz seemingly hovering at his elbow, as if 'it was he himself telling his own story' (*Moon Lake*, p. 105). The last three years of Fritz's life, however, before his death at the age of thirty-eight (Fabrizio's own age), when the great novel was written, stubbornly resist his attentions. In desperation, pressed by his publisher to meet a deadline, Fabrizio decides to invent, and fabricates the last great love who inspired *The House on Moon Lake*.

Fabrizio's creation of Maria Lettner is ambivalent. With Maria giving her name to the second part of the novel as his lover Fulvia gave hers to the first, Fabrizio turns from the warm, sunny Fulvia to the abstract world of phantoms and conjured images, 'identifying with a dead man in order to live out a love affair with a woman who had never existed' (*Moon Lake*, p. 119). Maria Lettner is created as a lover less for Fritz than for himself, to establish 'the perfect closed circle in which Fabrizio was creator and worshipper, Maria creature and goddess' (*Moon Lake*, p. 123). The reciprocity Fabrizio fails to achieve in his earthly life becomes irrelevant in the regressive, narcissistic fantasy which he creates for himself: Maria was, after all, created by combining the characteristics not of real women but of flowers, including the *Narcissus poeticus*. Duranti herself has commented: 'Maria is an ideal woman precisely because she doesn't exist. It's not that she doesn't exist because she is ideal: she is ideal because she doesn't exist'.[6]

Delirium for Fabrizio begins at the point when translation becomes interpretation, when the linear transfer of form becomes a narcissistic appropriation of the imaginary. Language, detached from its object, conjures up not reality but the world of ghosts.[7] The abstract exclusiveness of the perfect circle is ruptured as the imaginary slips over into the real and the boundary between them is blurred for both Fabrizio and the reader; the Other, deemed to be an extension and a property of the Self, refuses the position of mirror to the ego. Maria the ethereal ideal becomes all too real as readers of Oberhofer begin to supplement Fabrizio's faked biography with memories of her from the past. Photographs are produced of her as a young woman; clippings of her hair are discovered. It is not long before an upwardly mobile academic Germanist demonstrates that *The House on Moon Lake* was not written by Fritz Oberhofer at all, but by Maria Lettner. In escaping the control of her creator Maria has, for Fabrizio, violated the terms of her existence, run off with 'the Others: architects, magistrates, living-room radicals, snobs, women, students, structuralists, sociologists, communists . . .' (*Moon Lake*, p. 149). Maria's adulterous failure to remain within her allotted role – not unlike that of Frankenstein's creature before her – means that she must be destroyed.

The image of Maria resurfaces in the person of her supposed granddaughter, Petra Ebner, who lives in Moon Lake. Letters are produced from Fritz to Maria; Fabrizio is given copies. Petra is herself an image, a simulacrum almost, as the warm brightness of Fulvia is again displaced by the neutral, colourless cold of this woman whose smooth, featureless body is dematerialized or dehumanized to the point of being a 'celluloid doll'. The would-be Germanist has fallen into his own Romantic trap, forgetting the lessons of Goethe's *Faust* and Chamisso's *Peter Schlemihl's Remarkable Story*.

The House on Moon Lake subsumes the genres of Gothic thriller and psychological drama into a very post-modern staging of writing itself as the means of evoking the past, the philosopher's stone which transmutes the past into the present. Fabrizio is himself a relic, operating with a *démodé* model of culture, out of step with the thrusting aggressiveness of the modern cultural industry. As a translator, he occupies an intermediary position not only between two cultures and two languages but between reader and writer, between the living and the dead.[8] Notions of textual authority and authorship are put into play with the disappearance of the one surviving copy of Oberhofer's original book: all that remains is an image – the photocopies – which themselves function as intermediary between the 'original' and translations. The loss of the original novel, as of Fritz's own letters, erases boundaries between the Austrian and the Italian; in the absence of any 'original', authorship cannot be guaranteed, and the relative status of original, sham, imitation and fake is thrown into doubt.

The figure of Maria Lettner, evoked to give value to Fabrizio's own neurotic life, also occupies an intermediary position between artistic creation and 'real' person. There is no external authority to establish hierarchies or to patrol the borders of the real and the imaginary, while conflicting, antithetical images of Maria as idealized product of the desiring imagination or as independent being remain unresolved. As she emerges only too vividly into the sphere of the real, Fabrizio's project – to turn the real into the imaginary, the present into the past, life into art – is itself overturned. The closed circle of writing implodes, perilously out of control of its own product: language takes on its own life, its own revenge. In the creation of Maria we also see not just an image of writing but a metaphor for reading, one which would be less likely to take reality as a form of writing than writing as a form of the real.

With its destabilizing of authority and control, its transmutation of representation into nothing but fleeting images, fakes and shams, *The House on Moon Lake* suggests the anxiety produced by proliferating images in a cracked mirror, by the loss of ultimate meaning. Suspended in his final intermediacy between the living and the dead, Fabrizio is held as if enchanted; as in magic tales, Petra as priestess is endowed with the power to speak the words which will release him from the spell, but the words are never spoken. Fabrizio's neurotic obsession and gradual detachment from the world and human relations are paralleled by a progressive erasure of language to the point where Petra, in her chilly, smooth whiteness, suggests the delirium of the blank page, the page made flesh. Fabrizio has come full circle. As the book opens he has a completed manuscript, a finished translation; now he has only blankness, a drift into silence.

SANDRA PETRIGNANI

Sandra Petrignani's first novel, *Le navigazioni di Circe* (The Navigations of Circe, 1987), offers a reinterpretation of the dramatic encounter in Homer's *Odyssey* between the hero Ulysses and the witch Circe, the 'formidable goddess with a mortal woman's voice'.[9] The new tale is related by the woman herself, now turned into a writer who is harassed, bothered and frustrated to a point that fans of Claire Brétécher's cartoon characters would recognize.

In Homer, Circe drugs Ulysses' advance party, turns them into pigs from the shoulders up, and leads them weeping into her sty. Hermes protects Ulysses himself from the transforming, castrating power of Circe, and the witch becomes herself bewitched; she bathes the great hero, frees his men and enslaves herself to his will. Circe, who 'robs men of their courage and their manhood', is in her turn tamed, conquered by a greater sexual power than her own. In Petrignani's witty and elegant novel the action is moved from a marble palace in a wooded clearing to an untidy, ramshackle hut beside the shore. Here there are no willing maidens on hand to do the housework; the tamed wolves and lions of legend become two large dogs and a rather spiteful, ill-tempered cat. Circe is not loftily controlled but disordered, sensual and humorous; for Petrignani she is 'femaleness, woman in her natural state before the gains of feminism',[10] an amalgam of Mother Earth figure and female counterpoint to the male myth of Don Juan. Circe is as much entrapped by her own seductions as are the lovers who prostrate themselves as slaves to her sexual will and eager inhabitants of her cage. Unlike Homer's creature, the modern Circe herself falls hopelessly and repeatedly in love. Indeed, passionate love is for her a state of sickness, the enclosure of her lovers the only cure; the cage becomes a form not of sexual aggression but of self-defence against neurosis.

Petrignani comments: 'Circe is an artist – she writes. She has an almost neurotic relationship with the banality of the everyday - she's part of a separate world, the world of neurosis, the world of art.'[11] Circe relates her own story, for she has become a writer, filling in the spaces between the visits of the errant Ulysses by narrating her conquests, her struggles with the spying 'pilgrims', the malicious gossip of the hostile crowd on the shore, the jealousies and quarrels between her lovers, the revolt of her prisoners. Lending themselves to Rimbaud's theory of synaesthesia, each sheet of paper is shaded a different colour through which the events of this very unspiritual witch are perceived – red for passion, yellow for struggle, pink for the exquisite pleasure of anticipation, green for waiting, brown for despair. The result is a chromatic scale of emotional and narrative response in which Circe recounts simultaneously her affair with the elusive Ulysses and her encounter with the paper which mediates her relationship with the world. Ancient Circe, seducer of all men, is herself conquered at the beginning of her narrative, not by Ulysses but by a brand-new pile of paper: 'I realized that there was a silent challenge in that whiteness – no paper in the world can calmly bear the fate of remaining white – and that I would end up accepting the insidious invitation.'[12] After Calvino's privileging of the reader in the narrative process in works such as *If on a winter's night a traveller*, in Petrignani's account it is not Ulysses nor even Circe but the paper itself which sets the parameters of the tale as it resists, refuses to be ordered, demands to be written on, gets torn, dirty and lost.

Writing, for Circe, is 'an alibi for doing nothing, it is an activity which does and undoes itself' (*Circe*, p. 10). While Homer's Circe 'went to and fro at her great and everlasting loom, on which she was weaving one of those delicate, graceful and dazzling fabrics that goddesses make', the more earthy Circe weaves only snatches of impressions, the briefest of tales, on her coloured sheets of paper. Writing can never tell a complete story, nor the whole story; the sheets which get lost, destroyed or simply put in the wrong order (for Circe never remembers to date them) tell their own tale about the impossibility of closure, of a narrative which denies the foreclosure of the 'real'.

Circe airily refers to the empty centuries of her existence, where nothing happens because nothing is written. The process of writing, however, leads to Circe becoming a mere mortal. Her prisoners stage a revolt; although this is not a new event, the telling of it changes its significance:

> Writing is a process of fission, it causes all sorts of splits, it breaks up unity. It's a faithless repetition, the beginning of an inexhaustible chain of doubts. Since I started writing I'm not the same; a fracture has gradually appeared between me and my heroic past, my legend no longer protects me and Ulysses allows himself to resist me. (*Circe*, p. 103)

Petrignani's Circe sees writing as a contradictory activity which simultaneously imagines the real as past and cancels it out as present, reflecting Susan Sontag's description of writing as 'an ideally complex form of consciousness: a way of being both passive and active, social and asocial, present and absent in one's own life'.[13] Circe is horrified when she becomes a reader of her own work:

> What was all this stuff which presented itself as a brazen duplication of life? Even if it was full of holes, the result of a casual selection due to the gusts of wind, flames and other natural factors which we already know about, it was still a shameless duplication. But if I've spent my time writing down my life in such minute detail, how much have I managed to live it? (*Circe*, p. 75)

This is Circe's sense of writing which 'does and undoes' simultaneously. As a means of deferral, of displacement, writing becomes the embodiment of sexual desire, its extension and intensification, where the exquisite frustration of anticipation outweighs the briefness of satiety and satisfaction. Narrative as a means of deferral, of anticipation, is interwoven with desire in a text whose aim is itself to seduce, which acts as a figure not for sexual bliss but for the erotic pleasure described by Roland Barthes in *Le Plaisir du texte*. In a typically anarchic dislocation of time and space, Circe crosses the sea in search of Ulysses, who is resident at the Hotel Radiant. She lingers, an object of curiosity with her wild hair and bare feet, 'as if the delay contained in itself desire and satisfaction' (*Circe*, p. 77). Later, deliciously dallying with two equally attractive cousins, Circe comments: 'I love to prolong the enchantment of these nights, wrapping my arms round my knees in anticipation of wrapping them round a new man. Which of the two cousins will it be? The fire lights up on their faces the ancient beauty of idols, the air is burning with desires. To defer is the secret of a more intense pleasure' (*Circe*, p. 44).

Circe as figure of legend finds herself entrapped by her own myth of compulsive seduction, condemned to a solitude peopled only by the evidence of her own failures. The *femme fatale* who uses sexuality as a trap is herself entrapped; only in Ulysses, the one man who resists her, can she find the equality, the specularity, which she seeks, the perfect reflection. The satisfaction of desire, the totalizing power of reciprocal love, displaces the need for narrative; when Ulysses is present, Circe does not write, the pages remain blank and uncoloured: 'The presence of Ulysses, filling up every instant of space or time, has eliminated distinctions and abolished colours. The triumph of white has meant the defeat of the pages, has denied stories and words' (*Circe*, pp. 110–11).

The totalizing, circular power of specularity is swiftly fragmented, as seduction turns into rupture, unable to resist the intrusion of narcissism, the desiring ego's refusal of duality. Ulysses' one gift to Circe is a bunch of narcissi; once on his island Circe discovers to her horror that he, too, possesses a cage just like her own, enormous and shiny, filled with the women he has conquered and who still desire him. Mutual attraction conceals a power game of mutual entrapment, and Circe's startled indignation cannot disguise her own identical strategy.

This is one novel of love in which there are no winners and no losers. Circe renounces her fetishistic dream of love as possession and appropriation of the other, for Ulysses will always remain stubbornly separate. Our material bodies, desiring and objects of desire, guarantee our isolation; the only mediation between individuals is through the illusion of physical unity in lovemaking, or else through narrative, through story-telling. The keeping of a cage, like writing, is an alibi, a sham.

In freeing her prisoners, Circe renounces her power and becomes a mere mortal. She takes to the seas, blurring distinctions between herself and Ulysses in her adoption of his role. The final pages of the novel, however, take us firmly in the direction not of appropriation or of a homogeneity which would abolish difference under the sign of the Same. Androgyny is toyed with[14] and rejected in favour of a celebration of difference: looking at her own image in a bucket of water on deck, for a moment Circe sees not her own face but that of Ulysses. She blinks, looks again, and sees her own image:

> His image reappears now in the pail of water, it coincides perfectly with mine. Tricks of the light. I close my eyes, reopen them, and look again. There, I see only Circe, her hair messed up by the wind, the tan which never fades, her healthy teeth, her beautiful arms. (*Circe*, p. 133).

Circe's aim is neither to produce a narrative of revenge nor to appropriate the male role; rather, she fulfils the 'need to realize her own hidden masculine side, without as a result losing or belittling the female/feminine side of her conscious life'.[15] The feminism of this novel has gone beyond the sociopolitical themes of the first wave of neo-feminism, and the radically separatist inflections which it took on in Italy, to a recuperation of the specifically female, a revaluation of the female body. Petrignani, along with much recent thinking in Italy, relocates identity firmly in the body. The risk of essentialism is worth running when at stake is a difference which can evade the trap, the cage, of hierarchy. Circe shares much of the philosopher Adriana Cavarero's 'desire to break the universalizing codes, to flee homologization', and Cavarero's concept of ensnarement is surprisingly close to Petrignani's image of a cage:

> To think oneself starting from oneself and no longer as thought by the other. But escape is not easy; I cannot simply skip out of all those conceptual grids which, even if they are the experience of otherness, are none the less the conceptual grids of my thought which is not mine. . . . The operation of thinking myself as subject is not then a simple exit from that thought which, precisely as subject, denies me; rather, it is its internal deconstruction as threshold to a word which is really mine.[16]

Petrignani's novel weaves a very modern self-irony into the

acceptance of sexual difference in a text in which the imperatives of feminism in the eighties and nineties might recognize themselves; post-modernism and feminism here merge in a text in which aesthetics and ethics find themselves allied. If we agree that 'the woman who produces culture finds herself caught in the dilemma of making her imaginary pass through the grating of a symbolic order preconstructed for her exclusion',[17] then the relationship between feminism and post-modernism is one implicitly confronted by all women writers of the contemporary avant-garde. Circe and Ulysses both renounce the attempt to ensnare the other, acknowledging sexual difference as a basis not for hierarchy but for equality: 'the concept of sexual difference, recognizing dual origin as an insuperable presupposition, excludes the logic of assimilation to the other'.[18]

An end is brought to Circe's story simply because the paper runs out; in a manner reminiscent of the closing paragraphs of *One Hundred Years of Solitude* by the South American writer Gabriel García Márquez, a wind whips up; with the disappearance of the pages the story itself ends. The tautological last line of Petrignani's novel ('and this is the last line'), while it underlines the convergence of the story with the very process of story-telling, also brings us to the end of a tale in which the navigations are no longer those of the 'homosexual Odyssey'[19] of philosophical discourse, but the navigations of the female subject around itself.

PAOLA CAPRIOLO

Paola Capriolo is one of the most successful of the young writers who have come out of Italy in recent years, although her work has yet to be translated into English. Born in 1962, she works as writer, journalist and translator from German (translating Thomas Mann among others), and indeed, her work is imbued with German literature and philosophy, from Schopenhauer and Goethe to Rilke and Heine. The rhythms and cadences of music, too, play a vital role in her work, and not just in her latest novel, *Vissi d'amore* (I lived for love, 1992), a reinterpretation of Puccini's *Tosca*, from which the title is taken. Capriolo's work is self-consciously literary, and has no qualms about engaging with the mainstream of Western literary and philosophical tradition. Like other writers who came to maturity in the late 1970s and 1980s, Capriolo turns aside from the direct political engagement of the previous decade and its preference for realism, its attempt to dissolve style as a belletristic diversion from what was widely seen as the fundamental purpose of literature, which was to inform and to persuade.

Yet while Capriolo's works make more or less explicit reference to Central European traditions of thought and culture, they align themselves within a very modern and post-modern drive to push at the limits of realism, to test the boundaries between reality and fantasy. While she does not have the bawdy earthiness of Angela Carter in works such as *Nights at the Circus* (1986), she shares the English writer's preoccupation with the borders between mythical structures and everyday life, between our individual existences and the stories we tell about them; she has been compared to Kafka in her evocation of atmospheres of uncomfortable alienation, to Borges and Calvino in her use of fantasy to illuminate the real; she approaches Dino Buzzati in the relentless excavation of psychological dislocation in a prose of immaculate clarity, and more recently Angela Carter as she begins to explore the territory of the mind in its psychosexual as well as its metaphysical dimension. In her tales and fables of love as metaphysics, of the extraneousness of romance and art, of the flux of pain and life redeemed by the fixities and certainties of form or labyrinths willingly embraced, of a torture chamber as the location of the apotheosis of sexual experience, Capriolo never loses sight of the writer as the one who pulls the strings, of fiction as yet another illusion in the mirror.

Paola Capriolo's first collection of four short stories, *La grande Eulalia* (The Great Eulalia), appeared to considerable acclaim in 1988.[20] While the stories follow a narrative logic which recalls that of the fairy-tale or fable, they share a common preoccupation, rooted in Romanticism, with art as bearer of both beauty and death. In Capriolo's early stories, everyday normality and tranquillity is ruptured and fragmented by the appearance of a beautiful ghost in the mirror, the glimpse of a woman's arm closing the shutters, a half-heard melody emerging from the cell of a prisoner serving a life sentence of isolation and solitude. In a clear echo of Edgar Allan Poe, tantalizing intimations of perfection act as Pied Piper to these characters, who are swept up in the morbid – and inevitably fatal - desire to imitate this beauty, to transcend themselves and mirror themselves in art. But art, the perfection of form, can have only a tangential role in life, can only be glimpsed in the mirror: to succumb to the seductions of art, to mirror the self in a desired perfection of form, leads inevitably to the fate suffered by Narcissus, and is to embrace death.

In the title story, 'The Great Eulalia', a young peasant girl is so entranced by the dramatic spectacle conjured up by a group of travelling players that she leaves her family and home to be with them, working as servant to the actress who decides to protect her, and who narrates the tale. To pay for the girl's keep, the actress sells a jewel, which is anyway too precious to be worn by day and without the sheen of fake jewels by night on stage: already illusion and image begin to take on a life which is more substantial and of more consequence than that which is 'real'. Their caravan is destroyed in a fire (the combustion of puberty and awakening sexuality, perhaps), and the one which replaces it has the magical properties necessary to fable: pulled by six black horses, it is decorated with gold stucco, exquisitely appointed and with limitless inner space. Eulalia's room has a wall of glass, where 'the girl's gaze lost itself ecstatically in that labyrinth of images' (*The Great Eulalia*, p. 17).

The stage thus set, Capriolo's sheer imaginative power, combined with a precise, measured prose style, draws the reader in. In her wall of mirrors the girl begins to see a marvellously handsome young man who appears only for her: 'all the earth's magnificence was no more than the faded echo of what appeared there, in the mirror' (*Eulalia*, p. 21). The young man's distant, indifferent and melancholy beauty renders his image inviolable: to break the glass would be a sacrilege. But her joy is tempered by the subsequent appearance in the glass of a princess even more perfect than her prince. Stung by the comparison with her own features, the girl begins her miraculous metamorphosis. The symbolic burning of her peasant's dress and adoption of a cast-off theatrical costume is followed by her complete transformation as she turns into the princess in the mirror: her skin is whiter, her lips are redder, her hair is more golden, her features are more delicate. Inevitably, she begins to appear on stage, swiftly becoming the renowned and adored Eulalia. But she is oblivious to the passions she arouses: 'she lived for those few hours on the stage, when by the light of the torches she was held up by the mirage which she herself had created and she wandered in the labyrinth of her fiction as in an unknown land' (*Eulalia*, p. 27).

Eulalia builds her own stage and her own home, three castles linked by crystal bridges, which show 'her taste for the most subtle of games between reality and fiction, for the infinite interweaving of likenesses, for the sublime deception of mirrors which capture the eye and bend it to the laws of perspective of an imaginary space' (*Eulalia*, p. 30). She appears to her guests in an infinite sequence of mirror-images, gradually approaching through a multiplicity of reflections and refractions. Each night, a flickering light in the surrounding forest comes closer to the castle, across the lines of rafts on the lake, to the crystal bridge. Eulalia, who has watched the approach of her beloved, moves to meet him. The next night the grandeur of the annual festival at her castle is suddenly halted, as she breaks down without a word: the man she went to meet, she confesses, was not the man in the mirror. Eulalia retreats into art and into the symbolic, shutting herself in the caravan which it is beyond anybody's power to open, refusing any further contact with life, preferring communion with the illusory, the ideal, the dead. She is never seen again.

The experience of the young artist in the second story, 'The Woman of Stone', is similarly chastening. Apprentice to a master carver in the magnificent subterranean realm of the dead, Mur sees the world as an inferior copy to the model, a rebellious, contorted and distorting shadow, while 'his art was the mirror which straightened up images, which restored to them their authentic form' (*Eulalia*, p. 47). Walking through the town to buy pigments, he glimpses a woman's arm closing a shutter. Mur becomes entranced by the fleeting, mutable beauty of the world above ground; taking his chisel, he breaks his vow of fidelity to the dead and sculpts the woman's arm on a stone wall. Abandoning his master, he catches a glimpse of the woman's face, and sculpts that; he hears that his master has died, and returns to the realm beneath the ground to take two black diamonds from the eyes of the white stag, his master's last work, to serve as the eyes for his creation. Capriolo here rewrites the story of Pygmalion, for in her fictions, as in those of Luigi Pirandello, life refuses to be imprisoned by art.

Mur is convinced that with his sculpting the woman he is tying her to him, possessing her, to the point where it is the work of art rather than the thought of the real woman which compels his spellbound attention. With the stolen diamonds in place, 'the eyes of the effigy shone like two black stars, and he looked at them, fascinated, and was lost in their dazzling brightness as in a secret garden which nobody else could enter' (*Eulalia*, p. 61). As the carving displaces the real woman in his imagination, he sculpts a companion figure for her, a projection of his own desire to possess. Returning to his stone wall one morning, he finds that the two touching hands, like those of Michelangelo's God and his creature Adam, have been destroyed: cast adrift into solitude, Mur returns to the world below ground.

Capriolo is not making a consciously feminist point here; indeed, in conversation she states that issues of gender, sexual control and ownership did not inform her writing of the story at all;[21] the ground she covers here is that of aesthetics and metaphysics rather than the construction of gender roles. Structurally, her stories recall Luigi Pirandello's 'theatre within theatre' plays (*Six Characters in Search of an Author, Tonight We Improvise*) as they hold out the temptation and seductive perfection of form within the fleeting mutability of daily life, and demonstrate only too clearly that the siren call of aesthetic perfection is inimical to life itself.

Perhaps the most haunting story of this early collection is 'The Giant'. A new commanding officer and his wife take up residence in a prison, the spatial dislocation of which recalls Dino Buzzati's fortress in *The Tartar Steppe*, whose geographical remoteness similarly reinforces the different order of logic and reason which prevail there. The prison has been built to house a single prisoner, unnamed and of unknown crimes, whose sentence of lifelong isolation has left him unseen, invisible. Like the fortress in Buzzati's novel, the prison - which will be destroyed on the death of its lone inmate – exercises a strange, compelling power over the soldiers garrisoned there. The only visible sign of the prisoner is a shadow he casts, which appears to the child Ottavio like that of a giant with a monkey on his shoulder. The monkey turns out to be a violin, the melancholy, compelling tones of which float across the courtyard. Adele, already a lover of music, becomes entranced, has new scores brought to her, neglects her household tasks and her son in favour of obsessive music-making, as violinist and pianist – both prisoners in their own way – weave their melancholy sonatas each evening.

But, in accordance with the insights of Romanticism, perfection of form exacts its own vampirish toll: Adele makes extraordinary progress as a musician, but becomes hollow and gaunt. The sonata is finished, she is consumed by a fever and dies before the eyes of her helpless husband and equally helpless doctor.

The collapse of conventional barriers between the internal and the external is shifted from aestheticism to metaphysics in Capriolo's most successful novel to date, *Il doppio regno* (The Double Kingdom, 1991).[22] As in 'The Giant', introspection is underlined by topography. In the prison all rooms, the prisoner's and Adele's alike, looked inwards to the courtyard; in the hotel in which the nameless protagonist of *The Double Kingdom* finds herself, not only are there no outside windows, there appears to be no way out at all. Like a Borgesian labyrinth or a Kafkaesque burrow, distinctions - between inside and outside, night and day, male and female - become muffled and blurred.

It is possible for the reader of *The Double Kingdom* to reconstruct, from the given fragments of the novel, a linear narrative of trauma and mental breakdown. The protagonist appears to have undergone a crisis - caused, perhaps, by a child drowning - which reaches a climax in the nightmare vision of a freak wave which threatens to engulf the out-of-season resort where she is staying. She flees inland and finds herself in a crumbling, faded hotel where she is the solitary guest. She begins a diary, where she writes the fragments of memory remaining to her and notes her gradual assimilation to the bizarre, if not hostile, routines of the hotel. She slowly loses signs of separate and singular identity, conforming to the hidden rhythms around her. She has no luggage; she is given a waiter's uniform to wear; her hair is cut after the manner of the waiters around her. Alarmingly, the door of her room is removed.

The hotel possesses a substantial library which is ordered according to no system accessible to ordinary logic. Its books contain not signs, referential meaning, gestures to the world outside, but symbols, signifiers with no signified, marks which point only to themselves, to their own aesthetic structure, gigantic palindromes or shapes which create their own rhythms of harmony and variations. This is not like the library in Umberto Eco's *The Name of the Rose*, repository of some dark secret which must be hidden at all costs if traditional power is to remain intact. In Capriolo's fantasy world there is only surface, over which we scramble as best we can.

Books with meaning, changes of clothes, rooms overlooking the sea, all suggest an openness to change alien to the hotel, the seductiveness of which lies in its very placid immutability, its unfailing adherence to its own inner logical system. Fragments of memories – a lover, a tabby cat under a lamp, the unseen face of a man – are like pointed shards, and to this extent we can see *The Double Kingdom* as the study of a mind which seeks retreat from pain in the deadening quietude to be found in this hotel, or in prisons, in Buzzati's fortress in *The Tartar Steppe*, or the convent in Matilde Serao's *Sister Joan of the Cross*. Immutable routine and unchanging practice ally themselves to a fixed aesthetic form which offers shelter at the price of total capitulation of will: 'I am nothing, or if I am anything I am the hotel', concludes the narrator (*The Double Kingdom*, p. 168).

The narrator contemplates the meanings which could be given to the surface events of her life. One interpretation would be to see the hotel – the fixity and reassurance of unchangeable form – as sanctuary from the outside world, and her increasing assimilation to – and absorption into – it as less a separation than a liberation. In this interpretation of events the fragmentation and dissociation of the 'I' becomes not an eternal punishment, with the hotel a modern hell, but a state of bliss. The day will soon come when she will be totally extraneous to herself, when 'inner' and 'outer', 'past' and 'present', 'I' and 'you' as terms of differentiation will be as meaningless as the books in the library; then she will be able to place her notebook in the library along with the others she has found, which are equally indecipherable.

A characteristic feature of the post-modern is its obsession with space. Replying to a note from the new commanding officer, the prisoner of 'The Giant' expresses his surprise that a world still exists 'out there' at all. In the hotel, the terms 'internal' and 'external' are similarly a matter of convention describing not radically different states but degrees, distance from a central point. A second interpretation of the hotel is put forward – as not outer but inner space, as a projection of her own will: 'sometimes I imagine that if I were to leave without a backward glance the whole hotel would instantly crumble and turn into a pile of dust, like the enchanted palaces in fairy-tales' (*The Double Kingdom*, p. 101).

The narrator hovers between two worlds, between different ways of understanding what is happening to her, between a desire to remember and an equally strong desire to cancel the past as an unwelcome intrusion into the present, between being seen as an elegant young woman and as a boyish waiter, between being enclosed, imprisoned, by the hotel and seeing the hotel as a projection of her own psychic will. Her theories are put to the test with the arrival at the hotel of three other guests. These apparent visitors from the outside would seem to confirm the initial hypothesis of trauma; they attempt to persuade her to leave with them, and hope to 'cure' her. It is their presence which reveals the extent to which her memories and thoughts, like the books in the libraries, have become a series of symbols with no referential equivalent in her own life, the 'symmetrical relationship which binds a figure to its specular image' (*The Double Kingdom*, p. 148); the poem she claims to have written is by Heinrich Heine, and gives the novel its title.

At the same time, however, the second hypothetical interpretation is given weight; the young man Bruno, whose desire to save her is fuelled by a growing emotional attachment, overlaps with a fragment of memory about another lover. The narrator strongly suspects that the others have been conjured up as incarnations of shreds of memory – lover, mother, friend – or as the objects of her creative fantasy: 'my creatures, incapable of deciding for themselves. Perhaps the hotel itself is only the cage which I have constructed, a way of creating a space for an unknown obsession. . . . They stand there on the margins, forgotten, puppets whose strings I have let go' (*The Double Kingdom*, p. 153).

Outer and inner become dissolved into a single consciousness fragmented and scattered across a number of different masks, male and female, present and past; the solitude of the consciousness which creates at will and destroys by the merest lapse of attention suggests a final solution to the enigma. The 'double kingdom' is not the fragmented world the schizophrenic, nor is this novel literature as psychology, even less literature as privileged excursion into the human condition, a reflection or an image of life. The mind described in almost pathological detail in *The Double Kingdom*, creating and destroying at will, unsure of the margins between flux and form, art and life, can best be understood as the mind of the writer, as 'I myself am the illusory image and the real one, I am the eye which sees, and I am the mirror' (*The Double Kingdom*, p. 162). Literature is a mirror which distorts rather than reflects. The mind in *The Double Kingdom*, at once creative, destructive, tormented and serene, is very close to the hapless, shambolic, distracted and forgetful creature described in a humorous short story by Capriolo, 'The Narrating God':

> He contemplates his creatures, hybrid fruits of tedium and distraction, and at times, if the actors are particularly gifted, he even lets himself be swept up by the spectacle of their destinies which he already knows. . . . And so he looks around here and there, and when he speaks he babbles, and muddles up before and after to the point where everything seems to be still, or he moves sideways like a crab.[23]

Omniscience, in its abolition of temporal process (for past and future are no longer mysteries) and its discrediting of causality (for there are connections between all things), no longer enables but hinders the act of narration. But if the post-modern writer is no longer an omniscient god, then paradoxically, as in *The Double Kingdom*, writing has expanded to fill the whole world.

An extract from Rainer Maria Rilke's *Duino Elegies*, much admired by Capriolo, might serve as a fitting conclusion to this discussion of inflections of post-modernism in some Italian women writers; Rilke eloquently expresses the fascination, the compulsion and the terrible danger of art, which is all we have with which to make sense of an uncertain world:

> For Beauty's nothing
> but beginning of Terror we're still just able to bear,
> and why we adore it so is because it serenely
> disdains to destroy us. Every angel is terrible.
> And so I repress myself, and swallow the call-note
> of depth-dark sobbing. Alas, who is there
> we can make use of? Not angels, not men;
> and even the noticing beasts are aware
> that we don't feel very securely at home
> in this interpreted world.

Conclusion

What, then, are the configurations of feminism, just a few decades after Carla Lonzi first introduced consciousness-raising, Italian-style, to a whole generation of women? Women's cultural politics in Italy finds itself in a a period of transition. The majority of legal, economic and social goals put forward by the emancipationists have now been achieved, and while there are still substantial regional variations, women have entered massively into the workplace and into the professions. However, despite women's dramatically changed opportunities and expectations, their representation in political life remains small, as in other countries with a longer history of stable democracy. Italian feminists continue to mobilize over issues such as the Chernobyl nuclear disaster, the Gulf War, and, more recently, the resurgence of the political Right, but less than ever can 'le italiane' be identified with a specific political programme.

Italian women have come a long way since the early post-Unification struggles for civil and legal rights, and for some degree of autonomy. In a country which barely existed as a coherent nation just one hundred years ago, which holds within its borders an enormous range of historical and cultural experience, the effort to achieve something approaching equality has been arduous. The social and political turmoils of Italy through two catastrophic world wars, civil war, twenty years of Fascism and belated modernization, have resulted in the fragmentation and frequently the suppression of women's claims over the course of the century. None the less, from its early fragile beginnings the women's movement has repeatedly resurfaced, and was given enormous impetus by the ideological ferments of the 1960s and 1970s.

Writing by women over this period has been closely interwoven with these larger public events. Earlier writers in particular address the problematic condition of maternity, the family, and in their work they offer revealing pictures of a society in slow and painful change. The writers who came to prominence after the Second

World War produced an extraordinary body of thematically radical and stylistically innovative work which challenged both the stereotypes of women's writing and the dominant cultural strategies of the day. If this work did not win the public recognition accorded that of some of their male colleagues, it nevertheless marked a new seriousness and a new ambition. In recent years women writers have suddenly found themselves at the forefront of Italian letters, internationally recognized, no longer marginalized and no longer ignored.

In this climate, readers and critics both in Italy and abroad have begun to take a new interest in the history of women's writing in Italy. This interest has been a long time coming, and in many cases information is all too scarce, but much work is now being done in republishing texts long out of print, and in reassessing women's enormous contribution to the cultural debates which have intersected one of the most dramatic and turbulent periods in Italian history. A tradition of women's writing is, finally, beginning to emerge. Much critical and historical work remains to be done in terms of recovering women's history and reprinting texts by women. Most of all, these writers demand to be read.

Notes

All translations from Italian in this volume are my own, unless otherwise stated.

PART I 1860–1922

CHAPTER 1 Making and Unmaking the Nation

1 See Denis Mack Smith, *Cavour*, p. 242.

2 See G.M. Trevelyan, *Garibaldi and the Thousand* (Constable, London, 1909).

3 G. Procacci, *History of the Italian People*, p. 349.

4 Camilla Ravera gives a detailed description of the hardships of life for the 'mondine', as they were known, the workers in the rice fields, in 'Le donne in risaia', in her column 'Tribuna della Donna', *Ordine Nuovo*, 5 May 1921.

5 Martin Clark, *Modern Italy 1871–1982*, p. 33, quoting from L. Carpi, *Delle colonie e dell'emigrazione all'estero* (Milan 1874), pp. 31–48.

6 Figures were approximately 170,000 women, 45,000 men and 80,000 children.

7 In Britain, for example, custody and maintenance rights had increased over the century. Women with the necessary property qualifications won the local franchise in 1882 and subsequently began taking up posts in provincial administration, sitting on school boards and even working as factory inspectors. They also gained much political experience from the prolonged campaign against the Contagious Diseases Act.

8 Quoted from the 1903 Court of Cassation by R. Canosa in *Il giudice e la donna* (The Judge and Woman), p. 90.

9 See Sandra Puccini, 'Condizione della donna e questione femminile 1892–1922' (Condition of Women and the Woman Question) in *La questione femminile in Italia dal '900 ad oggi* (The Woman Question in Italy from 1900 to Now), ed. G. Ascoli *et al.* (Franco Angeli Editore, Milan 1977).

10 See 'Le donne laureate in Italia' (Women Graduates in Italy), *Critica Sociale* XII, no. 9, May 1902.

11 Simone de Beauvoir, *The Second Sex*, pp. 139–69.

12 J.J. Howard, 'Patriot Mothers in the Post Risorgimento', in *Women, War and Revolution*, p. 239.

13 Camilla Ravera, *Breve storia del movimento femminile in Italia*, p. 69.

14 See Franca Pieroni Bortolotti in *Alle origini del movimento femminile in Italia, 1848–1892*.

15 R. Spagnoletti, *I movimenti femministi in Italia*, p. 79.

16 See 'Il lato femminile della criminalità' (The female side of criminality) in Valeria Barini *et al.*, *La donna nella scienza dell'uomo*, pp. 25–78.

17 Anna Maria Mozzoni, *La liberazione della donna* (The Liberation of Women), p. 35.

18 A.M. Mozzoni, 'La tutela della donna', *Avanti*, 7 March 1898.

19 Quoted in Gloria Chianese, *Storia sociale della donna in Italia (1800–1980)*, p. 54.

20 Anna Bravo, 'Peasant Women in Wartime', in *Our Common History: The Transformation of Europe* (pp. 163, 169).

21 Anna Kuliscioff, *Critica Sociale II*, no. 9, May 1892.

22 J.H. Whitfield, *A Short History of Italian Literature*, p. 245.

23 Luigi Capuana, *Letteratura al femminile*, p. 21.

24 George Eliot was to write scathingly of the absence of noted female novelists from Italy:

> We confess ourselves unacquainted with the productions of those awful women of Italy, who hold professional chairs, and were great in civil and canon law; we have made no researches into the catacombs of female literature, but we think we may safely conclude that they would yield no rivals to that which is still unburied. ('Silly Novels by Lady Novelists', in *Essays* [Routledge, London 1963], p. 64).

25 Antonio Gramsci, *Selections from Cultural Writings*, p. 273.

26 Jolanda De Blasi, *Antologia delle scrittrici italiane dalle origini al 1800*, p. 5.

27 Carlo Cattaneo, quoted in A. Seroni, 'L'impegno delle scrittrici dopo l'Unità' (The Task of Women Writers After Unification), *Rinascita* 1962.

28 Ada Negri, 'Sfida' ('Challenge'), printed with facing translation in *The Defiant Muse: Italian Feminist Poems from the Middle Ages to the Present*.

29 'Negri sacrifices to an imaginary duty, that of putting her verse to the service of the oppressed and the afflicted, a real duty, which is the one the artist has to his art; the "categorical imperative" to make a

beautiful work and nothing but a beautiful work.' Benedetto Croce, 'Ada Negri', in *Letteratura della nuova Italia*, vol. II, p. 359.

30 Annie Vivanti, *Vae victis!* (Quintieri, Milan 1918), p. 343. The theme of this novel was also dramatized in her play *L'invasore* (The Invader), staged in Milan in 1918. For a discussion of the play, see Anna Urbancic, 'L'invasore di Annie Vivanti', in *Donna: Women in Italian Culture*, pp. 121–30.

CHAPTER 2: *Neera*

1 Neera, *Una giovinezza del secolo XIX* (Growing up in the Nineteenth Century, La Tartaruga, Milan 1975), p. 16.

2 Carlo Cattaneo, 'Sul romanzo delle donne contemporanee' ('On Novels by Contemporary Women'), in *Opere edite e inedite di Carlo Cattaneo* (Published and Unpublished Works of Carlo Cattaneo), pp. 358–89.

3 Neera, *Le idee di una donna* (The Ideas of a Woman), ed. and introduced by Francesca Sanvitale (Vallecchi, Florence 1986), p. 51.

4 Olive Schreiner, *The Story of an African Farm*, 1883 (Penguin, London 1971).

5 See Sibilla Aleramo, *La donna e il femminismo (scritti 1897–1910)* (Editori Riuniti, Rome 1978), pp. 70–75; and Franca Pierangeli Bortolotti, *Alle origini del movimento femminista in Italia 1848–1892* (Einaudi, Turin 1963), p. 47.

6 Anna Santoro, *Narratrici italiane dell'Ottocento* (Federico e Ardia, Naples 1987), p. 18.

7 Neera, 'Un giorno di nozze', in *Monastero e altri racconti*, ed. A. Arslan and A. Folli (Monastery and Other Tales, Libri Scheiwiller, Milan 1987).

8 Neera, 'Paolina', in *Monastero e altri racconti*, p. 47.

9 Neera, *Teresa* (Teresa, Sellerio, Palermo 1986), pp. 82, 99.

10 Luigi Baldacci, Introductory Note to *Teresa*, p. vi.

11 Neera, *L'indomani* (The Next Day, Sellerio, Palermo), p. 12.

12 Neera, 'Nora' (1881), in *Monastero e altri racconti*, p. 71.

13 Neera, *Duello d'anime* (Battle of Souls, Treves, Milan 1911).

14 Giuliana Morandini, *La voce che è in lei*, p. 157.

15 Showalter, *A Literature of Their Own*, p. 21. A similar point has been made about nineteenth-century Russian writers:

> Women's writings about careers as writers face the difficulty that more often than not, their denial of ambitions toward such a career is a prerequisite for its very existence. Nearly all the Russian

women writers deny the writer's vocation, even as they practice it. They cite the urging of friends or editors, not their own ambitions, as the impetus for writing. (H. Heldt, *Terrible Perfection: Women and Russian Literature* [Indiana University Press, Bloomington and Indianapolis 1987], p. 1)

CHAPTER 3: Matilde Serao

1 Edith Wharton, *A Backward Glance* (Constable, London 1972), p. 276. The reference to Corinne is to Madame de Staël's novel *Corinne, ou l'Italie.*

2 Anna Banti, *Serao* , p. ix.

3 Edoardo Scarfoglio, 'Cronaca bizantina', *Domenica Letteraria*, autumn 1883.

4 Matilde Serao, letter to Mariani, 9 March 1882.

5 Carolina Invernizio (1858–1916) wrote over one hundred novels, which had a wide popular readership. Most of her work appeared in *La Gazzetta di Torino* and *L'Opinione Nazionale.* Francesco Mastriani was a prolific 'social' novelist, heavily influenced by Victor Hugo and by the philanthropic Socialism of Eugène Sue. His work – most notably *I misteri di Napoli* (The Mysteries of Naples, 1875) – was serialized in the Neapolitan press.

6 Antonio Gramsci, 'People, Nation and Culture', in *Selections from Cultural Writings*, pp. 208, 210.

7 Antonio Ghirelli, *Storia di Napoli*, p. 365.

8 In her lead article 'Suffragettes' dating from 7 November 1906, Serao writes of 'this human creature who can be physically weaker than man, but is often stronger than him psychologicaly or morally, this human creature who is not the same as man but different from him, but who sometimes in her difference is worth ten men'. At another moment she puts out a strictly Socialist line on feminism, declaring that 'feminism doesn't exist: only economic and moral questions exist, and these will fade away or will at least improve when mankind's general conditions are improved' (8 May 1908).

9 The first hydroelectric power station opened in Milan in 1883; Fiat began production in 1899. Umberto Eco comments on the relationship between the development of industry and the development of fiction:

Italian society is late with regard to national unity, industrial development, railways: and the novel. This is why the first examples of novels about the less privileged classes, capable of speaking directly to the hearts of ordinary people, appear after unification, when a busy and enterprising bourgeoisie spreads throughout the peninsula. (*Tre donne intorno al cor: Invernizio, Serao, Liala* [La Nuova Italia, Florence 1982]).

10 *Matilde Serao: tra giornalismo e letteratura*, p. 106.

11 The notorious 'legge per il risanamento della città di Napoli', the 'Law for the resanitation of Naples', was passed in 1885. Work did not start for at least another four years. In a second edition of *Il ventre di Napoli* published twenty years on, in 1904, Serao denounced the failure of the resanitation programme, the appalling use of public funds which had been either misspent or lost.

12 Renato Fucini, *Napoli a occhio nudo* (Einaudi, Turin 1976). This argument is put forward in Maryse Jeuland Meynaud, *La Ville de Naples après l'annexation (1860–1915)*, Editions de l'Université de Provence, 1973. Serao clearly has in mind also Emile Zola's *Le Ventre de Paris* (1873).

13 *Il ventre di Napoli* (The Belly of Naples, Treves, Milan 1884), p. 35.

14 *Il paese di cuccagna* (The Land of Cockayne, Treves, Milan 1891), p. 238.

15 The Neapolitan writers De Marchi, Scarpetta and De Filippo all give examples of charlatans who grew rich by virtue of their supposed magic powers to prophesy winning numbers.

16 M.G. Martin, *L'Œuvre romanesque de Matilde Serao*, p. 117.

17 Published in *All'erta sentinella!* (On Your Guard, Sentry!, Treves, Milan 1889), p. 240.

18 Domenico Rea, *Racconti* (Mondadori, Milan 1965), pp. 275, 277 and 281.

19 *Suor Giovanna della croce* (Treves, Milan 1901).

20 G.K. Chesterton, 'A Defence of Penny Dreadfuls', in *The Defendant* (J.M. Dent, London 1901), p. 21.

21 Q.D. Leavis, *Fiction and the Reading Public* (Chatto & Windus, London 1932), p. 138.

22 *Cuore infermo* (The Ailing Heart, Casanova, Turin 1881), p. 113.

23 Mario Praz, *Fiori freschi* (Garzanti, Milan 1982), pp. 136 and 137.

24 'A classically angelic female character is forced to recognise her other self, her passionate and potentially monstrous essence.' Ursula Fanning, 'Angel v. monster: Serao's Use of the Female Double', in *Women and Italy: Essays on Gender, Culture and History*, ed. Zygmunt G. Barański and Shirley W. Vinall (Macmillan, London 1991), pp. 263–92.

25 *Fantasia* (Fantasia, Casanova, Turin 1883), p. 78.

26 Krafft-Ebing's *Psychopathia Sexualis* appeared in 1882; Cesare

Lombroso's *La donna delinquente, la prostituta e la donna normale* in 1883; and Havelock Ellis's *Studies in the Psychology of Sex: Sexual Inversion* in 1897. As a friend of Lombroso, Serao was at least aware of the debates raging about homosexuality and 'deviant' behaviour. See also Ursula Fanning's 'Sentimental Subversion: Representations of Female Friendship in the Work of Matilde Serao', *Annali d'Italianistica*, vol.7 (1989), pp. 273–86.

CHAPTER 4: *Grazia Deledda*

1   See Pietro Frassica, *A Marta Abba per non morire: sull'epistolario inedito tra Pirandello e Marta Abba* (To Marta Abba not to die: The Unedited Correspondence between Pirandello and Marta Abba, Mursia, Milan 1991), p. 118.

2   *Cosima* (Cosima, in Deledda, *Romanzi e novelle*, ed. Natalino Sapegno, Mondadori, Milan 1971), p. 745.

3   Deledda, quoted in Attilio Momigliano, *Ultimi studi* (La Nuova Italia, Florence 1954), p. 87.

4   Deledda, letter to Stanis Mancam, 20 December 1893, quoted in *Metafora e biografia nell'opera di Grazia Deledda*, ed. Angelo Pellegrino (Tibergraph, Città di Castello 1990), p. 16.

5   R. Branca, *Bibliografia di Grazia Deledda* (L'eroica, Milan 1938), p. 7.

6   'I still write badly in Italian, because I was so used to the Sard dialect which is a very different language from Italian.' Momigliano, *Ultimi studi*, p. 89.

7   See Anna Dolfi, *Grazia Deledda*, for a full account of critical reaction to Deledda's work.

8   D.H. Lawrence, Preface to *The Mother*, reprinted in *Phoenix* in the *Complete Works* (London 1968), pp. 263–6. Lawrence speaks of Sardinia as 'An island of rigid convictions, the rigid conventions of barbarism, and at the same time the fierce violence of the instinctive passions. A savage tradition of chastity, with a savage lust of the flesh. A barbaric overlordship of the gentry, with a fierce indomitableness of the servile classes.'

9   For social conditions in nineteenth-century Sardinia see, for example, SVIMEZ, *Statistiche sul Mezzogiorno d'Italia 1861–1953* (Rome 1954); F. Nitti, *Scritti sulla questione meridionale* (Bari 1958); C. Cabitza, *Sardegna rivolta contro la colonizzazione* (Milan 1968); and C. Sole (ed.), *La Sardegna di Carlo Felice e il problema della terra* (Cagliari 1968).

10 Quoted in G.D. Rossi, 'I primi passi di Grazia Deledda', *La Tribuna*

(Rome, 2 September 1923).

11 Deledda's problem is essentially 'to make lack of value become value, without however damaging the acceptability of the image in the framework of centralizing and classless conformism; and without the reality of conditions in Sardinia which are the object of her reflections becoming an investigation of real causes and thereby becoming a real instrument of denunciation and struggle' Alberto Mario Cirese, *Intellettuali, folklore, istinto di classe* (Einaudi, Turin 1976), p. 41.

12 Duse gives her own interpretation of the book in a letter to her daughter Enrichetta:

> The Book is based on the necessity (no matter why) of a *separation* of a mother from her son. The mother – alone and poor – is brutalized by the death of her heart without love. But the son, sent – at the mother's wish – *among books*, undergoing a practical and poetic growth, becomes a Man, a true man – made of action, of dreams, and without sensual cruelty, but understanding *pity*. Something between the *Rolla* of de Musset, the *René* of Chateaubriand, and naturally something of the *thirst* for love (and sufferings) of Nietzsche. Then, when *Life*, his work, the moral development of his spirit, and the love of his heart *act* strongly on him (for he loves Margherita, a young girl). Then one must *act* in life. But his ideal of woman is so lofty that he wants: first of all to *find his mother again*, who abandoned him (for his good, his mother says, *but* abandoned); and then, he wants to establish, with his wife and his mother, a way of working and living. But the two forces abandon him. The *fiancée*, out of *shame* in sharing Life with a beggar like the young man's mother, and the *Mother*, who on her own recognizes herself as unworthy to share the Life of her son. (*Duse: A Biography* by William Weaver [Thames & Hudson, London 1984], p. 307)

Duse produced the film as well as starring in it, and Weaver gives a full account of its making and shooting.

13 *Romanzi sardi*, ed. Vittorio Spinazzola (Mondadori, Milan 1981), pp. 60–61.

14 *Canne al vento* (Reeds in the Wind), in *Romanzi e novelle*, p. 177).

15 *Romanzi sardi*, p. 801.

CHAPTER 5: Sibilla Aleramo

1 Maria Antonietta Macciocchi, preface to *Una donna* by Sibilla Aleramo (Feltrinelli, Milan 1973), p. 5. All references to *Una donna* are from this edition.

2 Paola Mattei Gentili, 'La donna nel romanzo di *Una donna*', *Corriere d'Italia*, 5 January 1907.

3 Laura Gropollo in *Caffaro*, 20 March 1907. Quoted in Matilde Angelone, *In difesa d'una donna*, p. 61.

4 Gina Lombroso, 'I diritti della maternità (a proposito di un romanzo)', *Avanti!*, 15 January 1907.

5 Dacia Maraini, *La lunga vita di Marianna Ucrìa* (Rizzoli, Milan 1990), transl. Dick Kitto and Elspeth Spottiswood as *The Silent Duchess* (Peter Owen, London 1992). See chapter on Dacia Maraini later in this volume.

6 Conti and Morino, *Sibilla Aleramo: vita raccontata e illustrata*, p. 59.

7 Sibilla Aleramo, *Andando e stando*, p. 126.

8 Adriana Cavarero, 'Per una teoria della differenza sessuale', 'Towards a Theory of Sexual Difference', in *The Lonely Mirror: Italian Perspectives on Theory*, ed. Sandra Kemp and Paola Bono, p. 197.

9 Hélène Cixous and Catherine Clément, *The Newly Born Woman*, p. 137.

10 Sibilla Aleramo, *Diario di una donna: Inediti 1945–1960*, p. 317.

11 Sibilla Aleramo, *Andando e stando*, p. 65.

12 Sibilla Aleramo, *Amo dunque sono*, p. 66.

13 Umberto Boccioni, letter to Aleramo dated October 1913.

14 Victoria De Grazia, *How Fascism Ruled Women: Italy 1922–1945*, p. 51.

PART II: 1922–64

CHAPTER 6: From Fascism to Reconstruction

1 For a full account, see David Forgacs, *Italian Culture in the Industrial Era, 1888–1980*.

2 For a description of the 'dopolavoro' schemes, see Victoria De Grazia, *The Culture of Consent: Mass Organization of Leisure in Fascist Italy*.

3 See Lesley Caldwell, 'Reproducers of the Nation: Women and the Family in Fascist policy', in David Forgacs (ed.), *Rethinking Italian Fascism*, pp. 110–41.

4 See Caldwell, p. 117, for details on financial incentives to marriage, including taxes and marriage loans.

5 The 'Giornata della Madre e del Fanciullo' (Mother and Child Day), held every 24 December, was established in 1933.

6 Maurizio Cesari, *La censura nel periodo fascista*, p. 36.

7 For a full survey of such work, see Perry R. Willson, 'Mussolini's Angels: Women in Fascist Italy', in *Fascism in Comparative Perspective*, ed. R. Bessel (Cambridge University Press, Cambridge 1994). Willson points out that while somewhat hagiographic accounts of women's lives, and particularly their participation in the Resistance, appeared from the early 1970s onwards, accounts of women and employment, health, abortion and the family and Fascist motherhood organizations are only just beginning to emerge.

8 Caldwell, 'Reproducers of the Nation', p. 111.

9 Maria Antonietta Macciocchi, *La donna 'nera'*, p. 6.

10 "It is true that deep down in woman you can find the stimulating aroma of the male vigour of the combatant which we feel you ready to pour freely over us, just as we have freely given our sons to our country." Ibid., pp. 36–7.

11 Elsa Emmy, *L'arte cambia sesso*, p. 67. D. Aringoli is quoted as saying in 1933: 'Two names, marvellously joined together in love and faith, are today on the lips of Italian youth: "Mamma!" "Duce!", quoted in P. Meldini, *Sposa e madre esemplare. Ideologia e politica della donna e della famiglia durante il fascismo* (Vallecchi, Florence 1975), p. 9.

12 Enzo Santarelli, 'Il fascismo e le ideologie antifemministe', in *La questione femminile in Italia dal '900 ad oggi* , pp. 75–106.

13 See Willson, 'Mussolini's Angels'.

14 Joyce Lussu, *Portrait: cose viste e vissute* (Transeuropa, Bologna 1988), p. 64.

15 Antonio Gramsci, 'People, Nation and Culture', in *Selections from Cultural Writings*, p. 211.

16 'If Italian intellectuals did not react more resolutely against Fascism, it was because they did not realize exactly what was at stake. It took twenty years of Fascism, a civil war and the Resistance to produce that change in Italian cultural life and begin to educate intellectuals in the values of freedom and democracy.' Lino Pertile, 'Fascism and Literature' in Forgacs (ed.), *Rethinking Italian Fascism* pp. 162–84 (p. 170).

17 Quoted in Giuliano Manacorda, *Montale* (Le Monnier, Florence 1969), pp. 1–2.

18 Daria Banfi Malaguzzi, 'Rassegna letteraria: Scrittrici d'Italia', in *Almanacco della donna italiana*, 1938, pp. 178–81. Quoted in Victoria De Grazia, *How Fascism Ruled Women*, p. 252.

19 Pietravalle's work includes *I racconti della terra* (Tales of the Earth,

1924), *Storie di paese* (Village Stories, 1930), *Le catene* (The Chains, 1930) and *Marcia nuziale* (Wedding March, 1932).

20 Anna Banti, 'Il "romanzo rosa"', in *Opinioni* (Il Saggiatore, Milan 1961).

21 'The Founding and Manifesto of Futurism' (1909), transl. in R.W. Flint (ed.), *Marinetti: Selected Writings*, p. 41.

22 Peter Nicholls, 'Futurism, Gender, and Theories of Postmodernity', *Textual Practice* 3.2, 1989, p. 18.

23 Rita Guerricchio, 'Il modello di donna futurista', *Donne e politica* IV, 1976, p. 35.

24 Lucia Re, 'Futurism and Feminism', *Annali d'Italianistica* (1989), p. 252.

25 Rosa Rosà, 'Le donne cambiano finalmente' (Women Are Changing At Last), *L'Italia Futurista*, 26 August 1917.

26 Valentine de Saint-Point, 'Il manifesto della donna futurista', 'Manifesto of the Futurist Woman' (25 March 1912), *I manifesti del futurismo*, p. 74.

27 Enif Robert, *Un ventre di donna*, Edizioni Futuriste di 'Poesia', Milan 1919, p. 4.

28 Much of this material is oral history, collected and examined in volumes such as Anna Maria Bruzzone and Rachele Farina, *La resistenza taciuta: Dodici vite di partigiane piemontesi* (The Silent Resistance: Twelve Lives of Women Partisans in Piedmont, La Pietra, Milan 1976); Bianca Guidetta Serra, *Compagne: Testimonianze di partecipazione femminile* (Companions: Stories of Female Participation, Einaudi, Turin 1977); Lidia Beccaria Rolfi and Anna Maria Bruzzone, *Le donne di Ravensbruck: Testimonianze di deportate politiche italiane* (The Women of Ravensbruck: Testimonies of Female Italian Political Deportees, Einaudi, Turin 1978). Other written accounts include Ada Gobetti's *Diario partigiano* (Partisan Diary, Einaudi, Turin 1972) and the fiction of Renata Viganò, particularly *L'Agnese va a morire* ([1949] Einaudi, Turin 1973).

29 Rossana Rossanda, *Le altre: conversazioni sulle parole della politica* (Other Women: Conversations on the Words of Politics, Feltrinelli, Milan 1989), p. 68.

30 Lucia Re, *Calvino and the Age of Neorealism: Fables of Estrangement*, p. 94.

31 Renata Viganò, *Donne della resistenza* (Editori Riuniti, Rome 1955); *Matrimonio in brigata* (Vangelista, Milan 1976).

32 Fausta Cialente, *Le quattro ragazze di Wieselberger* (Mondadori, Milan 1976), p. 73.

CHAPTER 7: *Anna Banti*

1 Cesare Garboli, Introduction to Anna Banti's *Artemisia* (Rizzoli, Milan 1947).

2 Mary Garrard, *Artemisia Gentileschi: The Image of the Female Hero in Italian Baroque Art* (Princeton University Press, Princeton 1989).

3 Marisa Volpi, interview with Ludovico Pratesi in *Panorama* for an article on Artemisia Gentileschi entitled 'Caravaggia', 9 July 1989, p. 101.

4 Anna Banti, *Un grido lacerante* (A Piercing Cry, Rizzoli, Milan 1981), p. 28. When this thinly disguised autobiography was first published, Banti found herself accused of asking for too much already, and was harshly censured by some for tarnishing the image of the legendary Roberto Longhi.

5 'Now and then I dedicate myself to my vice: writing'. Interview with Anna Banti by Sandra Petrignani in *Le signore della scrittura* (La Tartaruga, Milan 1984), p. 103.

6 Anna Banti, 'Lavinia fuggita', in *Il coraggio delle donne* (The Courage of Women', La Tartaruga, Milan 1983).

7 Quoted by Deborah Heller in 'History, Art and Fiction in Anna Banti's *Artemisia*', in *Contemporary Women Writers in Italy*, ed. Santo L. Aricò, p. 50.

8 Germaine Greer, *The Obstacle Race*, p. 193.

9 Elizabeth Ellet, *Women Artists in All Ages and Countries* (Harper & Co., New York 1859), p. 72. Quoted in Elsa Honig Fine, *Women and Art: A History of Women Painters and Sculptors from the Renaissance to the 20th Century* (Abner Schram, New Jersey 1978), p. 15.

10 Georg Lukács, *The Historical Novel* (Peregrine, London 1969), p. 422.

11 Interview with Banti by Sandra Petrignani, p. 104.

12 Anna Banti, *Artemisia*, transl. Shirley D'Ardia Caracciolo (University of Nebraska Press, Lincoln 1988), p. 6.

13 Gianni Papi gives the following account of the major differences in tone and mood between the two paintings:

> As far as the movement of the scene is concerned, there is an almost dancing rhythm about the Naples painting, a kind of stylized repulsion in the romboidal geometry of Judith's arms. In the Uffizi painting, on the other hand, the horror is stronger, any sense of composure disturbed by the forcible violence of the identical gesture, the longer sword, the spurts of blood, the tensed face of the heroine which in the Neapolitan canvas is much more relaxed, more attentive, as if intent on a surgical operation. (In exhibition catalogue to *Artemisia*, held in the Casa Buonarroti, Florence, 18

June to 4 November 1991, ed. Roberto Contini and Gianni Papi [Leonardo-De Luca Editori, Florence 1991], p. 116)

14 'The warm transparency of Artemisia's palette and her delicate chasing of linear effects, the rippling of the tufted hem of the bed-covering, the tinkle of blood against Judith's jewelled forearm, the sprouting of Holofernes' hair through her rosy fingers, are all expressions of callousness' (Greer, *The Obstacle Race* p. 191).

CHAPTER 8: Natalia Ginzburg

1 Natalia Ginzburg, *La città e la casa* (Einaudi, Turin 1984), p. v. Unless otherwise stated, all subsequent quotations from Ginzburg are taken from the two volumes of *Opere*, ed. Cesare Garboli, Mondadori, Milan 1986 and 1987.

2 Natalia Ginzburg, 'Nota', I.1120.

3 'The man's insignificant presence becomes positive only in the tormented relationship he establishes with his wife, in the way he makes her suffer, refraining from all communication with her and forcing her to mirror herself in her own ineptitude while she reflects back to him an image of absolute power.' Francesca Sanvitale, 'I temi della narrativa di Natalia Ginzburg: uno specchio della società italiana' 'The Narrative Themes of Natalia Ginzburg: A Mirror of Italian Society', in *Natalia Ginzburg: La narratrice e i suoi testi* (NG: The Narrator and Her Texts, La Nuova Italia Scientifica, Rome 1986), p. 28.

4 Natalia Ginzburg, 'La condizione femminile' in *Vita immaginaria*, II.652.

5 Luigi Pirandello, *Sei personaggi in cerca d'autore*, first performed in 1921, in *Maschere nude* (Mondadori, Milan 1977).

6 Natalia Ginzburg, 'Cent'anni di solitudine' ('One Hundred Years of Solitude'), II.51.

7 'They are novels made up almost entirely of dialogue; in the fog I heard the clicking of these dialogues, clear and precise as table tennis balls. I had not been writing for a long time, and all of a sudden I felt revive in me something which had been dead for some while; those exact, precise sounds had suddenly and imperiously put me back on a lost path.' Natalia Ginzburg, 'La grande signorina', in *Mai devi domandarmi* (II.95). Elsewhere Ginzburg comments on the public perception that 'it was not interesting to meet with [Compton-Burnett], because all she talked about was the weather or refrigerators. But I loved her books and would have liked, just once, to talk to her about refrigerators' ('Nota', p. 1131).

8 Cesare Garboli, Introduction to *Caro Michele* (Mondadori, Milan 1985).

CHAPTER 9: *Elsa Morante*

1 *La storia* (*History*, Einaudi, Turin 1974), p. 37.

2 The richness of reality . . . is inexhaustible: it is renewed and multiplied for every new living creature who sets out to explore it. The multiplicity of existences would have neither meaning nor reason were it not that each existence uncovers a different reality. . . . But contingent experience of his own adventure is not enough for the novelist, as it is not enough for any artist. His exploration must transform itself into a value for the world: corruptible reality must be transformed, by him, into an incorruptible poetic truth. This is the only reason for art. (Elsa Morante, 'Nove domande sul romanzo' ['Nine Questions on the Novel'] in *Nuovi Argomenti* no. 38–9, 1959, pp. 24–5.)

3 Carlo Sgorlon, *Invito alla lettura di Elsa Morante* (Invitation to Reading EM), p. 17.

4 *Menzogna e sortilegio* (*The House of Lies*, Einaudi, Turin 1948), p. 494.

5 *L'isola di Arturo* (Arthur's Island, Einaudi, Turin 1957), p. 146.

6 Morante is uncomprising in her view of women. She comments: 'Maybe I've just been unlucky, but I've never met a really intelligent woman. Women think only about themselves and their private affairs, they ape men, and wanting to be like men is just a sign of their stupidity. When they despise the great feminine qualities then they become despicable.' Quoted in Sandra Petrignani (ed.), *Le signore della scrittura*, p. 119.

7 Einaudi, Turin 1982.

CHAPTER 10: *Anna Maria Ortese*

1 Edgar Allan Poe, 'The Spectacles', in *The Complete Edgar Allan Poe Tales* (Crown Publishers, Suffolk 1981), p. 414.

2 *Il mare non bagna Napoli*, ([1953], Rizzoli, Milan 1972).

3 Other Italian writers who have produced stories which might be defined as 'fantastic' include Mario Soldati and Giuseppe Tomasi di Lampedusa, whose 'Lighea' again recalls a story by Poe, 'Ligeia'. For a study of the fantastic in Italian literature, see Neuro Bonifazi, *Teoria del fantastico i il racconto fantastico in Italia* (Theory of the Fantastic and the Fantastic Tale in Italy, Longo, Ravenna 1982).

4 The old Uncle asked us what we did, and when he heard that Sonia painted and Andrea and I were writers, that made him very happy. But since for years he had been far away from any centres of fashion, he did not know what 'realism' or rather 'Neorealism' was. Sonia explained it to him in her slightly childish way. With his blue, empty eyes, he seemed to be thinking. 'Yes, perhaps it's a good thing', he said then (referring to 'Neorealism'), but don't let all this make you forget our dear reality, children.' Anna Maria Ortese, *Poveri e semplici* (Vallecchi, Florence 1967), pp. 87–8.

5 *In sonno e in veglia* (Sleeping and Waking), Adelphi, Milan 1987, p. 99.

6 Interview with Anna Maria Ortese in *Le signore della scrittura* by Sandra Petrignani, p. 79.

7 *L'iguana* (Vallecchi, Florence 1965), transl. Henry Martin as *The Iguana* (Minerva, London 1987), p. 83.

8 Anna Maria Ortese, *Silenzio a Milano* ([1958], La Tartaruga, Milan 1984), p. 59.

9 Anna Maria Ortese, *La lente scura* (The Dark Lens, Marcos y Marcos, Milan 1991).

PART III 1964–94

CHAPTER II: Revolution and Reaction

1 Paul Ginsborg, *A History of Contemporary Italy 1943–1988* (Penguin, Harmondsworth 1990), p. 240.

2 'Now the journalists of all the world (including / those of the television) / are licking your arses (as one still says in student / slang). Not me, my dears. / You have the faces of spoilt rich brats. . . . / When, the other day, at Valle Giulia you fought / the police, / I can tell you I was on their side. / Because the police are the sons of the poor. / They come from subtopias, in the cities and countryside. . . .' *L'Espresso*, 16 June 1968.

3 Pietro Valpreda, a ballet dancer, was also arrested, imprisoned without trial for three years, and only finally cleared in 1985.

4 Lidia Menapace, 'Le cause strutturali del nuovo femminismo' ('Structural Causes of the New Feminism') in G. Ascoli *et al.*, *La questione femminile in Italia del '900 ad oggi*, p. 173.

5 Carla Lonzi, 'Sputiamo su Hegel' transl. Veronica Newman as 'Let's spit on Hegel', in Sandra Kemp and Paola Bono (eds), *Italian Feminist Thought*, p. 42. Carla Lonzi set up Rivolta Femminile, the group which denounced marriage and women's role in the

family as the source of male oppression. For a portrait of Lonzi, one of the most inspirational figures of Italian neo-feminism in its early days, see Grazia Livi, *Le Lettere del mio nome* (Letters of My Name), pp. 207–26.

6 Armanda Guiducci, *La donna non è gente* (Women Aren't People) (Rizzoli, Milan 1977), p. 3.

7 Armanda Guiducci, *Due donne da buttare* (Two Women to be Thrown Away) (Rizzoli, Milan 1976).

8 The Italian Constitution gives the option of a referendum if 500,000 signatures can first be collected. The referendum on divorce in 1974 was the first to be held since the one in 1946 which decided the fate of the Italian monarchy; the option has been widely taken up since.

9 Just one of many notable cases occurred in the 1960s when Franca Viola, a Sicilian, finally broke with tradition and denounced her aggressor, who was sentenced to prison. But Viola lost the support of her family and community when she refused the man's repeated offers of marriage, thus 'condemning' him to remain in jail.

10 *Italian Feminist Thought*, p. 191. See also Diotima's *Il pensiero della differenza sessuale* (The Thought of Sexual Difference), and P. Violi, *L'infinito singolare. Considerazioni sulle differenze sessuali nel linguaggio* (The Infinite Singular: Considerations on Sexual Difference in Language).

11 See the article 'Più donne che uomini', *Sottosopra* (January 1983), transl. Rosalind Delmar as 'More Women than Men' in *Italian Feminist Thought*, pp. 111–23.

12 Lesley Caldwell, 'Italian Feminism: Some Considerations', in *Women and Italy: Essays on Gender, Culture and History*, pp. 95–116 (p. 104).

13 Lidia Ravera, *Porci con le ali* (Savelli, Rome 1976), p. 64.

14 Dacia Maraini, 'Le poesie delle donne', transl. 'Poems by women' in *The Defiant Muse: Italian Feminist Poems from the Middle Ages to the Present*, pp. 94–9.

15 Mariella Gramaglia, 'Femminismo: tra denuncia e progettazione' ('Feminism: Between Denunciation and Project'), introduction to *La poesia femminista*, ed. Nadia Fusini and Mariella Gramaglia, p. 8.

16 Mariella Bettarini, *Poesia femminista italiana* (Italian Feminist Poetry), ed. Laura di Nola (Savelli, Rome 1978), p. 163.

17 Marta Fabiani, 'La poetessa', transl. 'The Poetess' in Beverley Allen (ed.), *The Defiant Muse*, pp. 132–3.

18 Margherita Guidacci (b. 1921), Anna Malfaiera (b. 1926) and Rosanna Guerrini (b. 1935) are just some of the writers who explored these themes.

19 *Inno all'utero* ('Hymn to the Uterus') and *Troppi morti* ('Too Many

Dead') by Livia Candiani (b. 1952); *Aspettiamo il sangue caldo* ('We'll Wait for the Warm Blood') by Dania Lupi (b. 1944) are just some examples, to be found in *Poesia femminista italiana*.

20 Nadia Fusini, 'Le donne e il loro poetare' (The poetizing [*sic*] of women), *Donnawomanfemme*, no. 5, 1977, p. 12.

21 Biancamaria Frabotta, 'Left Hand, White Poetry', in *Annali d'Italianistica: Women's Voices in Italian Literature*, ed. Rebecca West and Dino Cervigni, p. 342.

22 See, for example, Adele Cambria, 'Il neo-femminismo in letteratura: Dove sono le amazzoni?' ('Neo-feminism in Literature: Where are the Amazons?', in *Firmato donna: una donna un secolo* (*Signed Woman: A Woman a Century*, ed. Sandra Petrignani, 1986.

23 Chiara Saraceno, *Dalla parte della donna* (De Donato, Bari 1971); Marina Jarre, *Negli occhi di una ragazza* (Einaudi, Turin 1971); Gabriella Bagrini, *Lunga giovinezza* (Mondadori, Milan 1976).

24 Eric Bentley, *Thinking about the Playwright* (Macmillan, London 1986), p. 278.

25 *Tutto casa, letto e chiesa*, transl. *Female Parts*. The English title is rather unfortunate, given the sexist and specifically physiological overtones of the English phrase. The Italian title, which means literally 'All home, bed and church', is a wordplay on the expression 'All home, work and church', and is thus much more closely tied into the daily lives of women.

26 *La Repubblica*, 6 December 1977, quoted in David L. Hirst, *Dario Fo and Franca Rame* (Methuen, London 1989), p. 150.

27 Dario Fo and Franca Rame, *Medea* in *A Woman Alone and Other Plays*, ed. Stuart Hood (Methuen, London 1986), p. 64.

28 Franca Rame in *Dario Fo: Tricks of the Trade*, transl. Joseph Farrell (Methuen, London 1991), p. 182.

29 Maria Antonietta Macciocchi, 'Provaci ancora, donna' ('Play It Again, Woman'), *La Repubblica*, 30 May 1980, quoted in Susan Bassnett, *Feminist Experiences: The Women's Movement in Four Cultures*, p. 125.

30 See, for example, Rebecca West, 'The New Italian "Isms": Seismographic Soundings', *Romance Languages Annual*, vol. V, 1993, pp. 335–42.

31 Quoted in 'Ladies of the Right' by Dominique Jackson, *The Guardian*, 3 September 1994.

32 See the section on 'Le donne', 'Women', in *Stato dell'Italia* (The State of Italy), ed. Paul Ginsborg (Mondadori, Milan 1994), pp. 262–83. This section of the book is edited by Anna Rossi-Doria. See also Fosi Braidotti, 'Vedo nel tempo una bambina' ('I see a child

in time', *Donnawomanfemme*, 1986) for an early formulation of this sense of unease.

33 Carol Lazzaro-Weiss, 'From Margins to Mainstream', in Santo L. Aricò (ed.), *Contemporary Women Writers in Italy*, pp. 197–217 (p. 205).

34 'Fourteen Italian Poets for the Twenty-First Century', transl. Marco Fazzini and Christopher Whyte, *Lines Review* (ed. Tessa Ransford), 130, September 1994.

35 Anna Cascella's work includes *Le voglie* (Desires, 1980) and *Tesoro da nulla* (Tresure out of Nothing, 1990. Bianca Tarozzi has published *Nessuno vince il leone* (Nobody Wins the Lion, 1988).

36 Patrizia Cavalli has published *Le mie poesie non cambieranno il mondo* (My Poems Won't Change the World, 1974) and *Il cielo* (The Sky, 1981).

37 See *L'altro volto della luna: nuovo fantastico al femminile* (The Other Side of the Moon: New Female Fantasy Writing, ed. Gianfranco de Turris, M. Solfanelli, Chieti 1991). See also the work of Anna Maria Scaramuzzino, for example *Verde d'uomo* (The Green Man, La Luna, Palermo 1990).

38 Laura Mancinelli, *I dodici abati di Challant* (Einaudi, Turin 1981); *Il fantasma di Mozart* (Einaudi, Turin 1986).

39 Marina Mizzau, *Come il delfini* (Essedue edizioni, Verona 1988).

40 Ginevra Bompiani, *L'incantato* (Garzanti, Milan 1987); *Vecchio cielo nuova terra* (Garzanti, Milan 1988); 'Il ladro', in *Italian Women Writing*, ed. Sharon Wood (Manchester University Press, Manchester 1993).

41 Elisabetta Rasy, *La prima estasi* (Mondadori, Milan 1985); *Mezzi di trasporto* (Garzanti, Milan 1993).

CHAPTER 12: Dacia Maraini

1 Dacia Maraini, *Bagheria* (Rizzoli, Milan 1993), transl. Dick Kitto and Elspeth Spottiswood as *Bagheria* (Peter Owen, London 1994), p. 8.

2 M. Grazia Sumeli Weinberg, *Invito alla lettura di Dacia Maraini*, p. 38.

3 Bruce Merry, *Women in Modern Italian Literature*, p. 195.

4 Giuliana Morandini, *E allora mi hanno rinchiusa* (Bompiani, Milan 1977).

5 Paolo Ruffili, 'Tre domande a Dacia Maraini' ('Three Questions to Dacia Maraini'), *Il Resto del Carlino*, 18 November 1975.

6 Elaine Showalter, 'Feminist Criticism in the Wilderness', in *Writing and Sexual Difference*, ed. Elizabeth Abel (Harvester, Brighton

1982), p. 19.

7   Marco de Marinis, *Il nuovo teatro, 1947–1970* (The New Theatre, Rizzoli, Milan 1987), p. 245.

8   'La Maddalena-teatro', first published in *Effe*, no. 1, 1973, and reprinted in *La politica del femminismo*, ed. Biancamaria Frabotta (Savelli, Rome 1976), pp. 175–7.

9   Pier Paolo Pasolini, 'Manifesto per un nuovo teatro', *Nuovi Argomenti*, no. 7, 1968, p. 24.

10 'Theatre has lost the word. It has become deaf and dumb – an angelic, paralysing deafness. A devastating, violent muteness. Theatre now expresses itself through ever more sublime images which are abstract and diabolical: more and more suggestive, but less and less meaningful.' Dacia Maraini, *Fare teatro* (Making Theatre, Bompiani, Milan 1974), p. 66.

11 Luce Irigaray comments on the story of Clytemnestra:

Electra, the daughter, will remain mad. The matricidal son must be saved from madness to establish the patriarchal order. . . . This madness is, moreover, represented in the form of a troupe of enraged women who pursue him, haunt him wherever he goes, like the ghosts of his mother: the Furies. These women cry vengeance. They are women in revolt, rising up like revolutionary hysterics against the patriarchal power in the process of being established. . . . The murder of the mother results, then, in the non-punishment of the son, the burial of the madness of women – and the burial of women in madness. ('The Bodily Encounter with the Mother', in *The Irigaray Reader*, ed. Margaret Whitford [Basil Blackwell, Oxford, 1991], pp. 34–46 [p. 37].)

12 Sondra Segal and Roberta Sklar, 'The Women's Experimental Theatre', in Helen Crich Chinoy and Linda Walsh Jenkins (eds), *Women in American Theatre* (Theatre Communications Group, New York 1981), pp. 305–8 (p. 307).

13 *I sogni di Clitennestra e altre commedie* (Bompiani, Milan 1982), p. 37. Maraini further explores the fraught, complex but infinitely valuable relationship between women in several other plays such *Maria Stuarda*, published in *I sogni di Clitennestra*; and in both *Fede o della perversione matrimoniale* (Matrimonial Perversions) and *Mela* in *Lezioni d'amore* (Love Lessons, Bompiani, Milan 1982).

14 *Isolina* (Mondadori, Milan 1985), transl. Dick Kitto and Elspeth Spottiswood as *Isolina* (Peter Owen, London 1993), p. 153.

15 The inability to speak seems to have become something of a *topos* in recent Italian fiction: see, for example, Cristina Comencini's

The Missing Pages, transl. Gregory Dowling (Chatto & Windus, London 1993).

16 Hélène Cixous, *The Newly Born Woman*, p. 153.

CHAPTER 13: *Renegotiating Motherhood*

1 Amy Tan, *The Joy Luck Club* (Heinemann, London 1989). Other works dealing with this relationship include Simone de Beauvoir's *Une mort très douce* (Gallimard, Paris 1990), Christa Wolf's *Kindsheitmuster* (Luchterhand, Frankfurt 1976) and more recently *Mothers and Other Lovers* by Joanna Briscoe (Phoenix House, London 1994).

2 Sigmund Freud, *Introductory Lectures on Psychoanalysis*, The Pelican Freud Library, vol. 1 (Pelican, London 1973), p. 376.

3 De Beauvoir, *The Second Sex*, p. 532.

4 'Early Stages of the Oedipus Conflict' in *Selected Melanie Klein* , p. 78.

5 See Diotima, *Il cielo stellato dentro di noi: L'ordine simbolico della madre* (The Starry Sky Within Us: The Symbolic Order of the Mother) and Luisa Muraro, *L'ordine simbolico della madre* (La Tartaruga, Milan 1990).

6 Luce Irigaray, 'The Limits of the Transference', in *The Irigaray Reader*, p. 109.

7 See Nancy Chodorow, *The Reproduction of Mothering: Psychoanalysis and the Sociology of Gender* (University of California Press, Berkeley 1978).

8 Margaret Whitford, introduction to 'Psychoanalysis and Language' in *The Irigaray Reader*, p. 74.

9 Adrienne Rich, *Of Woman Born: Motherhood as Experience and Institution* (Virago, London 1977), p. 237. See also Nancy Friday, *My Mother, My Self* (HarperCollins, London 1979/1994) and *Mothering: Ideology, Experience, Agency* ed. Evelyn Nakano Glenn, Grace Chang and Linda Rennie Forcey (Routledge, London 1994).

10 Einaudi, Turin 1974.

11 Oriana Fallaci, *Lettera a un bambino mai nato* (Rizzoli, Milan 1975). Other novels by Fallaci draw on her wide experience as journalist. See, for example, the poignant *Un uomo* (*A Man*, Rizzoli, Milan 1979), a love story set amidst the turbulent politics of Greece; and *Insciallah* (Rizzoli, Milan 1990), which has a devastated Beirut as its backdrop.

12 A. Rich, *Of Woman Born*, p. 253.

13 Quoted from the dust-jacket of Sanvitale's novel *Il cuore borghese* (The Bourgeois Heart, Vallecchi, Florence 1972).

14 *Madre e figlia* (Einaudi, Turin 1980), p. 6. Other works include

L'uomo del parco (The Man in the Park, Mondadori, Milan 1984); *Il figlio dell'imperatore* (The Emperor's Son, Mondadori, Milan 1993, runner-up in the Strega prize); and a series of essays, *Mettendo a fuoco* (Focusing, Gremese, Rome 1988).

15 Melanie Klein, 'The Psychogenesis of Manic-Depressive States', in *Selected Melanie Klein*, pp. 116–45 (p. 125).

16 Italo Svevo, *La coscienza di Zeno* (Dall'Oglio, Milan 1923), transl. William Weaver as *The Confessions of Zeno*. In Svevo's novel, Zeno Cosini holds his father down on the bed, apparently in obedience to the doctor's orders that he should not move. The father raises his hand to his son's face. A final caress? Or perhaps a slap in the face of this son who seems to want to kill him?

17 *Althénopis* (Einaudi, Turin 1981), p. 174. Other works by Ramondino include *Storie di patio* (Patio Stories, Einaudi, Turin 1983); and *Un giorno e mezzo* (A Day and a Half, Einaudi, Turin 1988).

18 'The Power of Discourse', in *The Irigaray Reader*, p. 126.

CHAPTER 14: From Feminism to Post-Modernism

1 *Il pensiero debole*, ed. Gianni Vattimo and Aldo Rovatti (Feltrinelli, Milan 1983), p. 8.

2 Rosi Braidotti, 'Envy', in *Men in Feminism*, ed. Alice Jardine and Paul Smith (Methuen, New York, 1987), p. 237.

3 Teresa de Lauretis, *Alice Doesn't: Feminism, Semiotics, Cinema* (Indiana University Press, Bloomington 1984), p. 161.

4 Linda J. Nicholson (ed.), *Feminism/Postmodernism*, p. 6.

5 Francesca Duranti, *La bambina* (La Tartaruga, Milan 1975); *Piazza mia bella piazza* (La Tartaruga, Milan 1977); *La casa sul lago della luna* (Rizzoli, Milan 1984), transl. Stephen Sartarelli. Later works by Duranti include *Lieto fine* (Happy Ending, Rizzoli, Milan 1987); *Effetti personali* (Personal Effects, Rizzoli, Milan 1988) and *Ultima stesura* (Final Draft, Rizzoli, Milan 1991).

6 Interview with Francesca Duranti by the author, October 1990, published in *The Italianist*, no. 12, 1992, pp. 186–95.

7 Julia Kristeva comments pertinently:

Delirium is a discourse which has supposedly strayed from a presumed reality. The speaking subject is presumed to have known an object, a relationship, an experience that he is henceforth incapable of reconstituting accurately. Why? because the knowing subject is also a desiring subject, and the paths of desire snarl up the paths of knowledge. This dynamic of delirium recalls the constitution of the dream or the phantasm. ('Psychoanalysis and the Polis', reprinted in *The Kristeva Reader*, ed. Toril Moi [Blackwell, Oxford 1986], p. 306)

8 This clearly recalls Poe: 'The boundaries which divide Life from Death are at best shadowy and vague. Who shall say where the one ends, and where the other begins?': 'The Premature Burial'.

9 *The Odyssey*, transl. E.V. Rieu (Penguin, Harmondsworth 1991), Chapter 10.

10 Sandra Petrignani, in conversation with the author, January 1992.

11 Ibid.

12 *Le navigazioni di Circe* (The Navigations of Circe, Theoria, Rome/Naples 1987), p. 11. Other work includes *Il catalogo dei giocattoli* (The Toy Catalogue, Theoria, Rome 1988) and *Come i fulmini* (Like Lightning, Rizzoli, Milan 1991).

13 Susan Sontag, *A Susan Sontag Reader* (Penguin, Harmondsworth 1982), p. 433.

14 Biancamaria Frabotta comments on women's adoption of the ideal of androgyny: 'the *body* of literature as substitution and metastasis of corporality became for many feminists the privileged site of the androgynous dream, the paradise of delights': *Letteratura al femminile*, p. 12.

15 Silvia de Lorenzo, *La donna e la sua ombra* (Woman and Her Shadow, Edizioni delle donne, Rome 1982), p. 64.

16 Adriana Cavarero, 'L'elaborazione filosofica della differenza sessuale' ('The Philosophical Elaboration of Sexual Difference'), in *La ricerca delle donne: studi femministi in Italia* (Women's Research: Feminist Studies in Italy), ed. M.C. Marcuzzo and A. Rossi-Doria, pp. 173–87 (p. 178).

17 Silvia Veggetti Finzi, 'Alla ricerca di una soggettività femminile' ('In Search of a Female Subjectivity'), ibid., pp. 228–48 (p. 236).

18 Adriana Cavarero, *Diotima: il pensiero della differenza sessuale* (Diotima: Thinking Sexual Difference, La Tartaruga, Milan 1987), pp. 41–79 (p. 45).

19 Adriana Cavarero, 'Essere presso di sé: Noi che non fummo ad Ithaca' ('Being beside oneself: we who were not at Ithaca') in *Donnawomanfemme*, no. 4 (1987), pp. 11–16 (p. 13).

20 Feltrinelli, Milan 1988.

21 Unpublished interview by the author with Paola Capriolo, Milan, January 1992.

22 Bompiani, Milan 1991.

23 Paola Capriolo, 'Il dio narrante', in *Italian Women Writing* ed. Sharon Wood (Manchester University Press, Manchester 1993), pp. 129 and 131.

Bibliography

1. GENERAL

(a) HISTORY, SOCIOLOGY, POLITICS

Allen, Beverley *et al.* (eds), *Defiant Muse*. Feminist Press, New York 1989.

Bassnett, Susan: *Feminist Experiences: The Women's Movement in Four Cultures*. Allen & Unwin, London 1986.

de Beauvoir, Simone: *The Second Sex* (1949). Penguin, Harmondsworth 1953.

Cameron, Deborah: *Feminism and Linguistic Theory*. Macmillan, London 1985.

Cixous, Hélène and Catherine Clément: *The Newly Born Woman*, transl. Betsy Wing. Manchester University Press, Manchester 1986.

Freud, Sigmund: *The Standard Edition of the Complete Psychological Works of Sigmund Freud*, ed. James Strachey and Anna Freud. London 1955.

Glenn, Evelyn Nakano *et al.*: *Mothering: Ideology, Experience, Agency*. Routledge, London 1994.

Greer, Germaine: *The Obstacle Race: The Fortunes of Women Painters and Their Work*. Secker & Warburg, London 1979.

Irigaray, Luce: *Speculum of the Other Woman* (1974). Cornell University Press, New York 1985.

———: *This Sex Which Is Not One* (1977). Cornell University Press, New York 1985.

———: *The Irigaray Reader* (ed. Margaret Whitford). Blackwell, Oxford 1991.

Klein, Melanie: *Selected Melanie Klein*, ed. Juliet Mitchell. Peregrine, London 1986.

Kristeva, Julia: *Desire in Language*, ed. L.S. Roudiez. Blackwell, Oxford 1980.

———: *The Kristeva Reader*, ed. Toril Moi. Blackwell, Oxford 1986.

Lippard, Lucy: *Feminist Essays on Women's Art*. Dutton, New York 1976.

Nochlin, Linda: *Women, Art and Power and Other Essays*. Thames & Hudson, London 1989.

Rich, Adrienne: *Of Woman Born: Motherhood as Experience and Institution.* Virago, London 1977.

(b) GENERAL LITERATURE AND LITERARY THEORY

Bassnett, Susan: *Magdalena: International Women's Experimental Theatre.* Berg, Oxford 1989.

Braidotti, Rosi: *Patterns of Dissonance.* Polity Press, Cambridge 1991.

Chinoy, Helen Krich and Linda Walsh Jenkins: *Women in American Theatre.* Theatre Communications Group, New York 1981.

De Lauretis, Teresa: *Alice Doesn't: Feminism, Semiotics, Cinema.* Indiana University Press, Bloomington 1984.

———: 'The Essence of the Triangle or, Taking the Risk of Essentialism Seriously: Feminist Theory in Italy, the U.S., and Britain', *Differences,* 2, 1989 (pp. 1–37).

Felski, Rita: *Beyond Feminist Aesthetics.* Century Hutchinson, London 1989.

Flax, Jane: *Thinking Fragments: Psychoanalysis, Feminism and Postmodernism in the Contemporary West.* University of California Press, Berkeley 1990.

Forsås-Scott, Helena: *Textual Liberation: European Feminist Writing in the Twentieth Century.* Routledge, London 1991.

Greene, C. and C. Kahn (eds): *Making a Difference: Feminist Literary Criticism.* Methuen, London 1985.

Hutcheon, Linda: *A Poetics of Postmodernism. History, Theory, Fiction.* Routledge, London 1988.

Jacobus, Mary: *Reading Woman.* Methuen, London 1986.

Jardine, Alice and Paul Smith (eds): *Men in Feminism.* Methuen, London 1987.

Heilbrun, Carolyn G: *Writing a Woman's Life.* The Women's Press, London 1989.

Livi, Grazia: *Le lettere del mio nome.* La Tartaruga, Milan 1991.

Marks, Elaine and de Courtivron, Isabelle: *New French Feminisms.* Harvester Press, Brighton 1981.

Miller, Nancy: *Subject to Change.* Columbia University Press, New York 1988.

Moers, Ellen: *Literary Women* (1977). The Women's Press, London 1978.

Moi, Toril: *Sexual/Textual Politics.* Methuen, London 1985.

——— (ed.): *French Feminist Thought.* Blackwell, Oxford 1987.

Nicholson, Linda J. (ed.): *Feminism/Postmodernism.* Routledge, London 1990.

Olivier, Christiane: *Jocasta's Children* (transl. George Craig). Routledge, London 1989.

Showalter, Elaine: *A Literature of Their Own: British Women Novelists from Brontë to Lessing*. Virago, London 1978.

—— (ed.): *The New Feminist Criticism. Essays on Women, Literature and Theory*. Virago, London 1986.

Stubbs, Patricia: *Women and Fiction: Feminism and the Novel, 1880–1920*. Harvester, Brighton 1979.

Weedon, Chris: *Feminist Practice and Poststructuralist Theory*. Blackwell, Oxford 1987.

Woolf, Virginia: *A Woman's Essays* (ed. Rachel Bowlby). Penguin, Harmondsworth 1992.

2. ITALY

(a) HISTORY, SOCIOLOGY AND POLITICS

Acquaviva, S. and Santuccio, M: *Social Structure in Italy: Crisis of a System*. Macmillan, London 1976.

Allum, P.A.: *Italy – Republic without Government?* W.W.Norton, New York 1973.

Ascoli, G. *et al.*: *La questione femminile in Italia dal '900 ad oggi*. Franco Angeli, Milan 1977.

Babini, Valeria *et al. La donna nella scienza dell'uomo* (Woman in Man's Science). Franco Angeli, Milan 1956.

Balbo, Laura: *Stato di famiglia*. Garzanti, Milan 1976.

Barański, Z.G. and Lumley, R. (eds): *Culture and Conflict in Postwar Italy*. Macmillan, London 1990.

Bassnett, Susan: *Feminist Experiences: The Women's Movement in Four Cultures*. Allen & Unwin, London 1986.

Benussi, Cristina: *L'età del fascismo*. Palumbo, Palermo, 1978.

Birnbaum, L. Chiavola: *La liberazione della donna: Feminism in Italy*. Wesleyan University Press, Middletown, CT 1986.

Bortolotti, Franca Pieroni: *Alle origini del movimento femminile in Italia, 1848–1892*. Einaudi, Turin 1963.

——: *Socialismo e questione femminile in Italia, 1892–1922*. Mazzotta, Milan 1975.

Bravo, Anna: 'Peasant Women in Wartime', in Paul Thompson (ed.): *Our Common History: The Transformation of Europe*. Pluto, London 1982.

Buttafuoco, A.: 'Italy: The Feminist Challenge'. In C. Boggs and D. Plotke (eds): *The Politics of Eurocommunism*. Black Rose Press, Montreal

1980 (pp. 197–219).

Caldwell, Lesley: 'Reproducers of the Nation: Women and Family in Fascist Policy'. In Forgacs (ed.): *Rethinking Italian Fascism* (pp. 110–41).

———: 'Italian Feminism: Some Considerations'. In Barański and Vinall (eds): *Women and Italy: Essays on Gender, Culture and History* (pp. 95–116).

Canosa, R.: *Il giudice e la donna*. Rizzoli, Milan 1978.

Carocci, Giampiero: *Storia del fascismo*. Mondadori, Milan 1972.

Cesari, Maurizio: *La censura nel periodo fascista*. Lerici, Naples 1978.

Clark, Martin: *Modern Italy 1871–1982*. Longman, London 1984.

Cutrufelli, Maria Rosa: *L'invenzione della donna: miti e tecniche di uno sfruttamento*. SugarCo, Milan 1974.

De Giorgio, Michela: *Le italiane dall'unità ad oggi*. Laterza, Bari 1992.

De Grazia, Victoria: *The Culture of Consent: Mass Organization of Leisure in Fascist Italy*. Cambridge University Press, Cambridge 1981.

———: *How Fascism Ruled Women: Italy 1922–1945*. California University Press, Berkeley 1992.

Diotima: *Il pensiero della differenza sessuale*. La Tartaruga, Milan 1987.

———: *Il cielo stellato dentro di noi: L'ordine simbolico della madre*. La Tartaruga, Milan 1992.

Dobbs, D.: 'Extra-Parliamentary Feminism and Social Change in Italy, 1971–1980'. *International Journal of Women's Studies*, 5(2) (pp. 148–60).

Ergas, Yasmine: '1968–1979: Feminism and the Italian Party System: Women's Politics in a Decade of Turmoil'. *Comparative Politics*, 14, 1982 (pp. 253–79).

Flint, R.W. (ed.): *Marinetti: Selected Writings*. Secker & Warburg, London 1972.

Forgacs, David (ed.): *Rethinking Italian Fascism*. Lawrence & Wishart, London 1986.

———: *Italian Culture in the Industrial Era, 1880–1980*. Manchester University Press, Manchester 1990.

Frabotta, Biancamaria (ed.): *La politica del femminismo*. Savelli, Rome 1976.

———: *Letteratura al femminile*. Donato, Bari 1981.

Ghirelli, Antonio: *Storia di Napoli*. Einaudi, Turin 1992.

Ginsborg, Paul: *A History of Contemporary Italy: Society and Politics, 1943–1988*. Penguin, Harmondsworth 1990.

———: *Stato dell'Italia*. Mondadori, Milan 1994.

Gramsci, Antonio: *Opere*. Einaudi, Turin 1953.

———: *Selections from Cultural Writings*, ed. David Forgacs and Geoffrey

Nowell-Smith. Lawrence & Wishart, London 1985.

Hearder, Harry: *Italy in the Age of the Risorgimento 1790–1870*. Longman, London 1983.

Howard, J.J.: 'Patriot Mothers in the Post-Risorgimento'. In *Women, War and Revolution*. Routledge, London 1984.

Kemp, Sandra and Paola Bono (eds): *Italian Feminist Thought*. Blackwell, Oxford 1991.

—— (eds): *The Lonely Mirror: Italian Perspectives on Feminist Theory*. Routledge, London 1993.

Lange, P. and Tarrow S. (eds): *Italy in Transition: Conflict and Consensus*. Frank Cass, London 1980.

Lussu, Joyce: *Portrait: cose viste e vissute*. Transeuropa, Bologna 1988.

Macciocchi, M.A.: *La donna 'nera': consenso femminile e fascismo*. Feltrinelli, Milan 1976.

Mack Smith, Denis: *Italy, A Modern History*. University of Michigan Press, Ann Arbor 1959.

——: *Cavour*. Weidenfeld & Nicolson, London 1985.

Magli, Ida: *La donna: un problema aperto: guida alla ricerca antropologica*. Vallecchi, Florence 1974.

Marcuzzo, Maria Cristina and Anna Rossi-Doria: *La ricerca delle donne: studi femministi in Italia*. Rosenberg & Sellier, Turin 1987.

Morandi, Rodolfo: *Storia della grande industria in Italia*. Einaudi, Turin 1959.

Mozzoni, Anna Maria: *La liberazione della donna*, ed. Franca Pieroni Bortolotti. Mazzotta, Milan 1975.

Nicholls, Peter: 'Futurism, Gender and Theories of Postmodernity'. *Textual Practice*, 3.2, 1989 (pp. 18–36).

Nitti, F.: *Scritti sulla questione meridionale*. Laterza, Bari 1958.

Odorisio, Ginevra Conti: *Storia dell'idea femminista in Italia*. ERI, Turin 1980.

Olivieri, Mariarosa: *Tra libertà e solitudine: saggi su letteratura e giornalismo*. Edizioni dell'Ateneo, Pisa 1990.

Passerini, Luisa: 'Work Ideology and Fascism'. In Paul Thompson (ed.): *Our Common History: The Transformation of Europe*. Pluto, London 1982.

Procacci, G.: *History of the Italian People*. Weidenfeld & Nicolson, London 1970.

Rossanda, Rossana: *Le altre: conversazioni sulle parole della politica*. Feltrinelli, Milan 1989.

Salaris, Claudia: *Le futuriste: Donne e letteratura d'avanguardia in Italia (1909–1944)*. Edizioni delle donne, Milan 1982.

——: *Storia del futurismo*. Editori Riuniti, Rome 1985.

Serra, Bianca Guidetta: *Compagne: testimonianze di partecipazione femminile.* Einaudi, Turin 1977.

Spagnoletti, Rosalba (ed.): *Il movimento femminista in Italia.* Savelli, Rome 1978.

Spini, V.: 'The New Left in Italy'. *Journal of Contemporary History*, 7, 1972 (pp. 51–71).

Spotts, Frederic and Theodor Wieser: *Italy. A Difficult Democracy.* Cambridge University Press, Cambridge 1986.

Tannenbaum, Edward: *Modern Italy.* New York University Press, New York 1974.

Taricone, Fiorenza and Beatrice Pisa: *Operaie, borghesi, contadine, nel XIX secolo.* Carucci editore, Rome 1985.

Tessari, Roberto: *Il mito della macchina: letteratura e industria nel primo novecento.* Mursia, Milan 1973.

Trevelyan, G.M.: *Garibaldi and the Thousand.* Constable, London 1909.

Violi, P.: *L'infinito singulare. Considerazioni sulle differenze sessuali nel linguaggio.* Essedue, Verona 1987.

Willson, Perry: 'Mussolini's Angels: Women in Fascist Italy'. In R. Bessel (ed.): *Fascism in Comparative Perspective.* Cambridge University Press, Cambridge 1994 (pp. 46–58).

(b) ITALIAN LITERARY HISTORY AND THEORY

D'Alia, Fiorella: *La donna nel romanzo del settecento.* Fratelli Palombi, Rome 1990.

Aricò, Santo L. (ed.): *Contemporary Women Writers in Italy: A Modern Renaissance.* University of Massachusetts Press, Amherst 1990.

Barański, Zygmunt G. and L. Pertile (eds): *The New Italian Novel.* Edinburgh University Press, Edinburgh 1993.

Barański, Zygmunt G. and Shirley W. Vinall: *Women and Italy: Essays on Gender, Culture and History.* Macmillan, London 1991.

Bàrberi Squarotti, Giorgio: *La cultura e la poesia italiana del dopoguerra.* Cappelli, Rocca San Casciano 1972.

Bertacchini, Roberto: *Il romanzo italiano dell'ottocento.* Editrice Studium, Rome 1964.

Bonifazi, Neuro: *L'alibi del realismo.* La Nuova Italia, Florence 1972.

Capuana, Luigi: *Letteratura al femminile* (ed. Giovanna Finocchiaro Chimirri), C.U.E.M., Catania 1988.

Cara, Domenico: *Le donne della poesia: oltre il femminile.* Laboratorio delle arti, Ravenna 1991.

Cattaneo, Carlo: 'Sul romanzo delle contemporanee'. In *Opere edite e inedite*, ed. Agostino Bertani. Le Monnier, Florence 1882.

Caesar, M., and P. Hainsworth (eds): *Writers and Society in Contemporary Italy*. Berg, Oxford 1984.

Castelli, Silvia: 'Miti, forme e modelli della nuova narrativa emarginata'. In Walter Pedullà (ed.): *Letteratura emarginata*. Lerici, Rome 1978.

Chianesi, Gloria: *Storia sociale della donna in Italia (1800–1980)*. Guida, Naples 1980.

Cirese, A.M.: *Intellettuali, folklore, istinto di classe*. Einaudi, Turin 1986.

Corona, D. (ed.): *Donne e scrittura*. La Luna, Palermo 1990.

Croce, Benedetto: *Letteratura della nuova Italia* (3 vols). Laterza, Bari 1973.

Crocenzi, Lilia: *Narratrici d'oggi*. Gianni Mangiarotti, Cremona 1964.

D'Eramo, Luce and Gabriella Sobrino (eds): *Europa in versi: La poesia femminile del '900*. Edizioni Il ventaglio, Rome 1989.

Dolfi, Anna: *Del romanzesco e del romanzo: Modelli di narrativa italiana tra otto e novecento*. Bulzoni, Rome 1992.

Eco, Umberto *et al.*: *Tre donne intorno al cor: Carolina Invernizio, Matilde Serao, Liala*. La Nuova Italia, Florence 1982.

Fusini, Nadia: 'Sulle donne e il loro poetare'. *Donnawomanfemme*, no. 5, 1977 (pp. 5–21).

Livi, Grazia: *Le lettere del mio nome*. La Tartaruga, Milan 1991.

Lombardi, Olga: *Narratori italiani del secondo ottocento*. Longo Editore, Ravenna 1981.

Luti, Giorgio: *La letteratura del ventennio fascista*. La Nuova Italia, Florence 1972.

Madrignani, Carlo: *Ideologia e narrativa dopo l'Unificazione*. Savelli, Rome 1974.

—— and Franca Angelini: *Cultura, narrativa e teatro nell'età del positivismo*. Laterza, Bari 1975.

Manacorda, Giuliano: *Storia della letteratura contemporanea*. Editori Riuniti, Rome 1967.

——: *Storia della letteratura italiana tra le due guerre 1919–1943*. Editori Riuniti, Rome 1980.

Merry, Bruce: *Women in Modern Italian Literature*. Publication of the Department of Modern Languages, James Cook University, North Queensland 1990.

Momigliano, Attilio: *Ultimi studi*. La Nuova Italia, Florence 1954.

Morandini, Giuliana: *La voce che è in lei: antologia della narrativa femminile italiana tra '800 e '900*. Bompiani, Milan 1980.

Nozzoli, Anna: 'Sul romanzo femminista degli anni settanta'. *Donnawomanfemme*, no. 5, 1977 (pp. 55–74).

——: *Tabù e coscienza: la condizione femminile nella letteratura del Novecento*. La Nuova Italia, Florence 1978.

Petrignani, Sandra (ed.): *Le signore della scrittura*. La Tartaruga, Milan 1984.

——: *Firmato donna: una donna un secolo*. Il Ventaglio, Rome 1986.

Quartermaine, Luisa: 'Women's Viewpoint: Expectations and Experience in Twentieth-Century Italy'. In Helena Forsås-Scott (ed.): *Textual Liberation: European Feminist Writing in the Twentieth Century*. Routledge, London 1991.

Quintavalla, Maria Pia: *Donne in poesia*. Centro Azione Milano Donne, 1988.

Rasy, Elisabetta: *La lingua della nutrice*. Edizioni delle donne, Rome 1978.

——: *Le donne e la letteratura*. Editori Riuniti, Rome 1984.

——: *Ritratti di signora: Tre storie di fine secolo*, Rizzoli, Milan 1995.

Re, Lucia: 'Fururism and Feminism'. *Annali d'Italianistica*, vol. 7, 1989 (pp. 253–72).

——: *Calvino and the Age of Neorealism: Fables of Estrangement*. Stanford University Press, Stanford 1990.

Santoro, Anna: *Narratrici italiane dell'ottocento*. Federico & Ardia, Naples 1987.

Seroni, A.: 'L'impegno delle scrittrici dopo l'Unità'. *Rinascita* 1962.

Sozzi, Adelaide: *Neorealismo e neorealisti*. Cooperativa Libraria I.U.L.M., Milan 1980 (essay on Renata Viganò).

Whitfield, J.H.: *A Short History of Italian Literature*. Penguin, London 1960.

Wood, Sharon (ed.), *Italian Women Writing*. Manchester University Press, Manchester 1993.

(c) STUDIES OF INDIVIDUAL AUTHORS

Neera
Sanvitale, Francesca: Introduction to *Le idee di una donna*. Vallecchi, Florence 1977.

Serao, Matilde: *Ricordando Neera*. Treves, Milan 1920.

Matilde Serao
Banti, Anna: *Serao*. Utet, Turin 1965.

Fanning, Ursula: 'Sentimental Subversion: Representations of Female Friendship in the Work of Matilde Serao'. *Annali d'Italianistica*, vol. 7, 1989 (pp. 273–86).

Jeuland-Meynaud, Maryse: *La Ville de Naples après l'annexion (1860–1915)*. Editions de l'Université de Provence, Provence 1973.

——: *Immagini, linguaggio e modelli del corpo nell'opera narrativa di Matilde Serao*. Edizioni dell'Ateneo, Rome 1986.

Martin, M.G.: *L'Œuvre romanesque de Matilde Serao*. University of Grenoble, Grenoble 1973.

Pascale, Vittoria: *Sulla prosa narrativa di Matilde Serao*. Liguori, Naples 1989.

Tench, Derby: 'Gutting the Belly of Naples'. *Annali d'Italianistica*, vol. 7, 1989 (pp. 287–99).

Grazia Deledda

Branca, R.: *Bibliografia di Grazia Deledda*. L'eroica, Milan 1938.

Dolfi, Anna: *Grazia Deledda*. Mursia, Milan 1979.

Lawrence, D.H.: Preface to Deledda's *The Mother* in *The Complete Works of D.H. Lawrence*. London 1968, vol. VI (pp. 263–6).

Sibilla Aleramo

Angelone, Matilde: *In difesa della donna*. Fratelli Conti, Naples 1990.

Conti, Bruna and Alba Marino: *Sibilla Aleramo: Vita raccontata e illustrata*. Feltrinelli, Milan 1981.

Contorbia, Franco, Lea Melandri and Alba Morino (eds): *Sibilla Aleramo: coscienza e scrittura*. Feltrinelli, Milan 1986.

De Ceccatty, René: *Sibilla: vita artistica e amorosa di Sibilla Aleramo*. Mondadori, Milan 1992.

Forti-Lewis, Angelica: 'Scrittura auto/bio/grafica: teoria e pratica. Una proposta di lettura androgina per *Una donna* di Sibilla Aleramo' ('Auto/bio/graphical Writing: Theory and Practice. Towards an Androgynous Reading of Sibilla Aleramo's *Una donna*'). *Italica*, vol. 71, no. 3, 1994 (pp. 325–36).

Guerricchio, Rita: *Storia di Sibilla*. Nistri-Lischi, Pisa 1974.

Günsberg, M.: 'The Importance of Being Absent: Narrativity and Desire in Aleramo's *Amo dunque sono*'. *The Italianist*, no. 13, 1993 (pp. 139–59).

Macciocchi, M.A.: Preface to *Una donna*. Feltrinelli, Milan 1973.

Anna Banti

Biagini, Anna: *Anna Banti*. Mursia, Milan 1978.

Duncan, Derek: 'Reading the Past – Rewriting the Present: Anna Banti and Artemisia Gentileschi'. *Journal of Gender Studies*, vol. 1, no. 2, 1991 (pp. 152–67).

Heller, Deborah: 'History, Art and Fiction in Anna Banti's *Artemisia*'. In Santo L. Aricò (ed.): *Contemporary Women Writers in Italy*. University of Massachusetts Press, Amherst 1990 (pp. 44–60).

Natalia Ginzburg

Bullock, Alan: *Natalia Ginzburg: Human Relationships in a Changing World*. Berg, Oxford 1991.

Sanvitale, Francesca: 'I temi della narrativa di Natalia Ginzburg: uno specchio della società italiana'. In *Natalia Ginzburg: la narratrice e i suoi testi*. La Nuova Italia Scientifica, Rome 1986 (pp. 3–21).

Soave-Bowe, Clotilde: 'The Narrative Strategy of Natalia Ginzburg'. *Modern Language Review*, 68, 1973 (pp. 42–7).

Elsa Morante

Bernabò, Graziella: *Come leggere 'La storia' di Elsa Morante*. Mursia, Milan 1991.

Caesar, Michael: 'Morante'. In *Writers and Society in Contemporary Italy*. Berg, Leamington Spa 1984 (pp. 211–33).

Della Coletta, Cristina: 'Elsa Morante's *La storia*: Fiction and Women's History'. *Romance Languages Annual*, vol. V, 1993 (pp. 194–9).

Giorgio, Adalgisa: 'Nature vs Culture: Repression, Rebellion and Madness in Elsa Morante's *Aracoeli*'. *MLN*, 109, 1994 (pp. 93–116).

Lucente, Gregory: 'History and the Trial of Poetry: Everyday Life in Morante's *La storia*'. In *Beautiful Fables: Self-consciousness in Italian Narrative from Manzoni to Calvino*. Johns Hopkins University Press, Baltimore and London 1986.

Lugnini, L. *et al.*: *Per Elisa: Studi su 'Menzogna e sortilegio'*. Nistri-Lischi, Pisa 1990.

Mezzetti, Elena *et al.*: *Letture di Elsa Morante*. Rosenberg & Sellier, Turin 1987.

Pupino, Angelo Raffaele: *Struttura e stile della narrativa di Elsa Morante*. Longo, Ravenna 1968.

Ravanello, Donatella: *Scrittura e follia nei romanzi di Elsa Morante*. Marsilio, Venice 1980.

Re, Lucia: 'Utopian Longing and the Constraints of Racial and Sexual Difference in Elsa Morante's *La storia*'. *Italica*, vol. 70, no. 3, Autumn 1993 (pp. 361–75).

Sgorlon, Carlo: *Invito alla lettura di Elsa Morante*. Mursia, Milan 1972.

Venturi, G.: *Morante*. La Nuova Italia, Florence 1977.

Anna Maria Ortese

Falqui, Enrico: 'Anna Maria Ortese'. In *Ricerche di stile*. Vallecchi, Florence 1939.

Lombardi, Olga: 'Anna Maria Ortese'. In *La narrativa italiana nella crisi del novecento*. Sciascia, Caltanissetta/Rome 1971.

Wood, Sharon: 'Fantasy and Narrative in Anna Maria Ortese', *Italica* vol.71, no.3 1994 (pp. 354–68).

'Dodici domande ad Anna Maria Ortese' in *Nuovi Argomenti*, July/December 1976.

Dacia Maraini

Pallotta, Augustus: 'Dacia Maraini: From Alienation to Feminism'. *World Literature Today*, 58, 1984 (pp. 359–62).

Sumeli Weinberg, M Grazia: *Invito alla lettura di Dacia Maraini*. University of South Africa Press, Pretoria 1993.

Wood, Sharon: 'The Language of the Body and Dacia Maraini's *La lunga vita di Marianna Ucrìa*: A Psychoanalytical Approach'. *Journal of Gender Studies*, 1993 (pp. 47–59).

Francesca Sanvitale

Blelloch, Paola: 'Francesca Sanvitale's *Madre e figlia*'. In Santo L. Aricò (ed.): *Contemporary Women Writers in Italy* (pp. 125–37).

Caesar, Ann: 'Francesca Sanvitale: Investigating the Self and the World'. In Barański and Pertile (eds): *The New Italian Novel* (pp. 184–99).

Fabrizia Ramondino

Giorgio, Adalgisa: 'A Feminist Family Romance: Mother, Daughter and Female Genealogy in Fabrizia Ramondino's *Althénopis*'. *The Italianist*, no. 11, 1991 (pp. 128–50).

Usher, Jonathan: 'Fabrizia Ramondino: The Muse of Memory'. In Barański and Pertile (eds): *The New Italian Novel* (pp. 166–83).

Francesca Duranti

Vinall, Shirley: 'Francesca Duranti: Reflections and Inventions'. In Barański and Pertile (eds): *The New Italian Novel* (pp. 99–120).

'Writing in a Changing World': Interview with Francesca Duranti by Sharon Wood in *The Italianist*, no.13 1993 (pp. 186–95).

3. SELECT BIBLIOGRAPHY OF ENGLISH TRANSLATIONS OF WOMEN'S WRITING

Aleramo, Sibilla: *A Woman (Una donna)*, transl. Rosalind Delmar. Virago, London 1979.

Banti, Anna: *Artemisia (Artemisia)*, transl. Shirley D'Ardia Carracciolo. University of Nebraska Press, Omaha 1988.

Cialente, Fausta: *The Levantines (Ballata levantina)*, transl. Isabel Quigly. Houghton Mifflin, Boston 1963.

De Céspedes, Alba: *There's No Turning Back (Nessuno torna indietro)*, transl. Jan Nobel. Jarrolds, London 1941.

——: *The Best of Husbands (Dalla parte di lei)*, transl. Frances Frenaye. Macmillan, London 1952.

——: *The Secret (Quaderno proibito)*, transl. Isabel Quigly. Harvill Press, London 1957.

——: *Between Then and Now (Prima e dopo)*, transl. Isabel Quigly. Jonathan Cape, London 1959.

——: *Remorse (Rimorso)*, transl. William Weaver. Doubleday, Garden City New York 1967.

Deledda, Grazia: *After the Divorce (Dopo il divorzio)*, transl. Maria Lansdale. Holt, New York 1905.

——: *Ashes (Cenere)*, transl. Helen Colvill, John Lane, New York 1908.

——: *The Mother (La madre)*, transl. Mary Steegman. Berg, Leamington Spa 1974.

De Stefani, Livia: *Rosa (Rosa)*, transl. C. Barford and S. Hodges. Eyre & Spottiswoode, London 1963.

Duranti, Francesca: *The House on Moon Lake (La casa sul lago della luna)*, transl. Stephen Sartarelli. Collins, London 1987.

Fallaci, Oriana: *Penelope at War (Penelope alla guerra)*, transl. Pamela Swinglehurst. Michael Joseph, London 1966.

——: *If the Sun Dies (Se il sole muore)*, transl. Pamela Swinglehurst. Atheneum House, New York 1966.

——: *Interview with History (Intervista con la storia)*, transl. John Shepley. Liveright, New York 1976.

——: *Letter to an Unborn Child (Lettera a un bambino mai nato)*, transl. John Shepley. Simon & Schuster, New York 1976.

——: *A Man (Un uomo)*, transl. William Weaver. Simon & Schuster, New York 1980.

Ginzburg, Natalia: *The Road to the City (La strada che va in città)*, transl. Frances Frenaye. Doubleday, Garden City New York 1949.

——: *Voices in the Evening (Le voci della sera)*, transl. D.M. Low. Dutton, New York 1963.

——: *Family Sayings* (*Lessico famigliare*), transl. D.M. Low. Carcanet, Manchester 1984.

——: *Never Must You Ask Me* (*Mai devi domandarmi*), transl. Isabel Quigly. Michael Joseph, London 1973.

——: *Dear Michael* (*Caro Michele*), transl. S. Cudahy. Peter Owen, London 1975.

——: *The City and the House* (*La città e la casa*), transl. Dick Davis. Carcanet, Manchester 1986.

——: *Family* (*Famiglia*), transl. B. Stockman. Carcanet, Manchester 1988.

Loy, Rosetta: *The Dust Roads of Monferrato* (*Le strade di polvere*), transl. William Weaver. Paladin, London 1990.

Maraini, Dacia: *The Holiday* (*La vacanza*), transl. Stuart Hood. Weidenfeld & Nicolson, London 1966.

——: *The Age of Malaise* (*L'età del malessere*), transl. Frances Frenaye. Grove Press, New York 1963.

——: *Memoirs of a Female Thief* (*Memorie di una ladra*), transl. Nina Rootes. Transatlantic Arts, New York 1974.

——: *Woman at War* (*Donna in guerra*), transl. Mara Benetti and Elspeth Spottiswoode. Italia Press, New York 1989.

——: *Isolina* (*Isolina*), transl. S. Williams. Peter Owen, London 1993.

——: *The Silent Duchess* (*La lunga vita di Marianna Ucría*), transl. Dick Kitto and Elspeth Spottiswood. Peter Owen, London 1993.

——: *Bagheria* (*Bagheria*), transl. Dick Kitto and Elspeth Spottiswood. Peter Owen, London 1994.

Marcone, Maria: *A Woman and Her Family* (*Una donna e la sua famiglia*), transl. E. Addey. The Women's Press, London 1987.

Mazzetti, Lorenza: *Rage: A Novel* (*Rabbia: un romanzo*), transl. Isabel Quigly. Bodley Head, London 1965.

Milani, Milena: *A Girl Called Jules* (*Ragazza di nome Giulio*), transl. Graham Snell. Hutchinson, London 1966.

——: *The Story of Anna Drei* (*Storia di Anna Drei*), transl. Graham Snell. Hutchinson, London 1970.

Morante, Elsa: *The House of Lies* (*Menzogna e sortilegio*), transl. Adrienne Foulke. Harcourt Brace, New York 1951.

——: *Arturo's Island* (*L'isola di Arturo*), transl. Isabel Quigly. Collins, London 1959.

——: *History: A Novel* (*La storia*), transl. William Weaver. Knopf, New York 1977.

——: *Aracoeli* (*Aracoeli*), transl. William Weaver. Random House, New York 1984.

Morazzoni, Marta: *Girl in a Turban (Ragazza col turbante)*, transl. Patrick Creagh. Collins Harvill, London 1987.

Negri, Ada: *Morning Star (Stella mattutina)*, transl. Anne Day. Macmillan, London 1930.

Ortese, Anna Maria: *The Bay is not Naples (Il mare non bagna Napoli)*, transl. Frances Frenaye. Collins, London 1955.

———: *The Iguana (L'iguana*, 1965), transl. Henry Martin. Minerva, London 1990.

Petrignani, Sandra: *The Toy Catalogue (Il catalogo dei giocattoli)*, transl. Roy Lombardo. Boulevard Press, London 1990.

Rame, Franca and Dario Fo: *A Woman Alone and Other Plays (Tutta casa, letto e chiesa)*, transl. Gillian Hanna, Ed Emery and Christopher Cairns. Methuen, London 1991.

Ramondino, Fabrizia: *Althénopis (Althénopis)*, transl. Michael Sullivan. Carcanet, Manchester 1988.

Tamaro, Susanna, *Follow Your Heart (Va dove ti porta il cuore)*, transl. Avril Bardoni. Secker & Warburg, London 1995.

———: *For Solo Voice (Per voce sola*, 1990), transl. Sharon Wood. Carcanet, Manchester 1995.

Volpini, Flora: *The Woman of Florence (La donna di Firenze)*, transl. David Moore. Redman, London 1955.

———: *Yes, Madam (Sí, signora)*, transl. Arthur Oliver. Redman, London 1955.

Index